No Place of Rest

THE MIDDLE AGES SERIES

Ruth Mazo Karras, SERIES EDITOR

Edward Peters, FOUNDING EDITOR

A complete list of books in the series is available from
the publisher.

No Place of Rest

Jewish Literature, Expulsion, and the Memory of Medieval France

Susan L. Einbinder

PENN

UNIVERSITY OF PENNSYLVANIA PRESS

PHILADELPHIA

Published by
University of Pennsylvania Press
Philadelphia, Pennsylvania 19104-4112

10   9   8   7   6   5   4   3   2   1

Library of Congress Cataloging-in-Publication Data

Einbinder, Susan L., 1954–
  No Place of Rest : Jewish lierature, expulsion, and
the memory of medieval France / Susan L. Einbinder.
      p. cm. — (The Middle Ages series)
    Includes bibliographical references and index.
    ISBN 978-0-8122-4115-0 (alk. paper)
    1.   Hebrew poetry, Medieval—France—His-
tory and criticism.   2.   Jewish religious poetry,
French—History—To 1500.   3.   Jews—Persecutions—France—History—To 1500.   4.   Jews—
France—History—To 1500.   5.   Judaism—
France—History—To 1500.   6.   France—Ethnic
relations.   I. Title.
PJ5023.E463 2008
892.4′120944—dc22

                                    2008012681

In memory of Herbert C. Zafren z"l,
who showed me a new way to read

CONTENTS

Introduction

*Then he sent forth a dove from him, to see if the waters had subsided
from the ground; but the dove found no place to set her foot, and she
returned to him in the ark.*
   —Gen. 9:8–9

Your inheritance languishes,
Your dove goes from devastation to devastation.
The dove does not find
A place of rest.
   —Reuben b. Isaac, "Adonai, roʻed veḥared"

THE EXPULSION OF the Jews from France in 1306 was neither the first nor
the last time a Christian ruler ordered the departure of Jews from his land.
As far back as the twelfth century, the kings of France—to be sure, a much
smaller France than now—had experimented with expulsion. Toward the end
of the thirteenth century, however, expulsion signaled the failure of policies
that had achieved ever greater isolation of the Jews within Christian society,
not the conversion that was ostensibly their aim. In hindsight, a series of
small expulsions from territories west of the royal kingdom were an ominous harbinger of things to come: Gascony (1287), Anjou (1289), and Maine
(1289) all expelled their Jews early.[1] The small Jewish communities of these
territories disappeared over neighboring borders with barely a trace, and they
are unremembered today. In 1290, Edward I expelled the Jews of England,
and a Jewish population of approximately 2,000 departed, in a more or less
orderly fashion, from English ports for the Normandy of their ancestors, some
moving on to Paris and other parts of royal France.[2] Those who lived another
sixteen years would take the roads into exile again, a small minority among

the 100,000 men, women, and children who fled following a surprise mass arrest on a Sabbath morning in August 1306.

The expulsion of 1306 by Philip IV of France and its traces in later Jewish literature are the subject of this book. Nonetheless, this is not a straightforward retelling of the great expulsion of French Jews as they experienced and then remembered it; sadly, the extant Jewish sources do not permit such a reconstruction. Two literary sources cited frequently are, unsurprisingly, prose passages whose reference to expulsion is clear. One is by the Provençal writer Qalonymos b. Qalonymos and appears in the eclectic work known as the *Even Bohan*. Some scholars believe that it actually refers to the expulsion of 1322, a problem characteristic of Hebrew expulsion texts and one that we shall encounter throughout this study. The other passage is found in Yedaiah Bedersi's *Behinat 'Olam*, which I discuss in Chapter 2.

Yet these two sources really do not tell us much that we would like to know. The mechanics of expulsion have been excavated and retold from other documents and descriptions: what Jewish literature lacks in this regard has been found, with work, in other sources. Most recently, the historian William C. Jordan has meticulously investigated the expulsion of 1306 and the political, administrative, and logistical decisions surrounding its execution.[3] Like all stories of catastrophes we have nearly forgotten, this one is moving in its details and sobering for its efficiency as much as for its administrative shortcomings. Chief among the latter was the lack of an organized plan for evacuating those affected by the expulsion decree or for protecting them on the roads; the terse mentions of this incident in royal chronicles note that many of those sent into exile died of hunger and thirst along the way. This must have been the fate of a majority of French Jews from the northern and central parts of the kingdom, for whom the distance to safety was long.

In 1306, however, the majority of French Jews lived in the southern part of the kingdom, in the area known as Languedoc on the border of Provence, which was not yet part of France. Provence offered haven to many exiles from the north, and it was particularly convenient to Jews fleeing from Languedoc, so it is not surprising that this region, like Catalonia, preserves most of this expulsion's traces. Accordingly, all the writers treated in this book are men of the Midi—some originally from the north or the descendants of northern Jews, and some southerners for generations but witnesses, in one form or another, to the influx of French Jewish refugees and their struggles to adapt to new surroundings.

The story of expulsion is unlike the story of other catastrophes, which may be terminal for their victims but unfold among communities that remain relatively intact. Medieval incidents of judicial execution, for instance, commemorated as tales of martyrdom, involved a discrete event affecting a discrete subgroup of one or more victims known to a community and posthumously commemorated.[4] In contrast, expulsion casts its collective victims, each with his or her own memories of home and experiences of dislocation, into a multiplicity of new settings. Moreover, in the case of French Jews, expulsion was also a trauma experienced repeatedly. The great expulsion of 1306 was not ten years old when Louis X, Philip IV's son, rescinded his father's decree. True, only a small number of exiled French Jews heeded the invitation to return. Of that number, those who survived the bleak years of famine and violence that followed found themselves all too quickly reliving history when they were expelled again in 1322, many returning to Aragon and Provence.

Twenty-six years later, those lands, too, proved fragile reeds against the violence that accompanied the devastation of the Black Death (1348). Ironically, there is a bounty of Hebrew literature commemorating the persecution of Jews (who were often blamed for the outbreak of plague) during the Black Death, much of it from Ashkenaz and much of it in the traditional forms of commemorative poetry.[5] But anti-Jewish violence was not the worst blow dealt by the pandemic: the plague, estimated to have killed one-third to one-half of the population of Europe, struck down Jews as well. It also uprooted communities and age-old ways of life, rendering even more tenuous the anchors of communal memory and the ways that earlier traumas would be remembered and retold. The papal lands of the Comtat Venaissin were unique in offering protection to Jews fleeing plague-related violence elsewhere, and the influx of new refugees fragmented even further a coherent sense of the past.

In 1359, France again admitted Jews into its borders, mainly from Switzerland and in very small numbers. The royal incentive was financial—the king's desire to reap the profits of Jewish business (lending) in order to finance a disastrous war.[6] As revealed by the story of the physician Jacob b. Solomon, treated in this book, other Jews must have quietly returned to France during the 1360s and 1370s as well. This chapter, too, had an end, in 1394, when the Jews of France were expelled once again, not to return for centuries. Ironically, France's annexation of Provence in 1484 restored French identity to the descendants of exiled Jews, while bestowing it equally upon Jews who had never thought of themselves as French at all. Both groups almost instantly learned the price of that identity, exacted in anti-Jewish violence, emigration, and high—astonishingly high—rates of conversion to Christianity.

In other words, the story of 1306—and how it was remembered by French Jews—is far from a single story, even among those exiles and their descendants who continued to live nearby in Aragon, Provence, or the Comtat. The fragmentary, indeed kaleidoscopic, picture of the Jewish fourteenth century becomes even more variegated when we find its shards among communities farther away—for instance, over the Alps in northern Italy or over the Mediterranean in the Maghrebi kingdoms of northern Africa. Here, too, as we shall see, Jewish memory of a French past persisted through the lens of later experience. In Italy and Africa, that meant the indelible trauma of the Spanish expulsion of 1492, which poured frightened and destitute refugees into their communities. Some of them, of course, had French ancestry themselves, but in many cases, particularly in Africa, the memory of former "Frenchness" would rapidly be subsumed under the tidal wave of "Spanish" loss and commemoration.

Over the process of research and writing, this book gradually evolved from a search for the core experience of 1306 as it was commemorated by survivors to embrace the wider sweep of the century and its cycles of expulsion and trauma. The following chapters trace the arc of a century of dislocation and hence of collective memory in a near-continuous process of reconstitution or collapse. I begin with a Gascon poet whose fate anticipates many of the themes and concerns raised in subsequent chapters, and I end with a small group of poets in the Piedmont whose presence in northern Italy dates from the expulsion of 1394. In between, I treat texts produced in Majorca, Catalonia, the Comtat Venaissin, Algiers, and Salonika, which refer variously to dislocations from 1306 to the century's end. Indeed, each of these journeys takes us beyond the terminus point of 1394 to explore the fate of these fourteenth-century texts and the past that they sought to preserve or suppress in later times.

The attempt to recuperate this piece of the Jewish past has taught me many lessons, as much about forgetting as remembering, but certainly about the strategic ends of both. The last decades have seen the appearance of a multitude of important books on the construction of collective memory and identity, the strategic uses of the past, and the ways that both processes contribute to the formation of group or national identity. So, too, the material history of texts, the literature they transmit, and the role of both in constructing group memory have received worthy attention. From writers like Benedict Anderson to Dipesh Chakrabarti, from Hayden White and Stephen Greenblatt to scholars like Thomas Burman, Gabrielle Spiegel, Steven Justice,

Andrew Taylor, Ross Brann, and William Granara, recent scholarship has demonstrated increasing cunning in negotiating the distance between texts (what a small group of people wrote about) and context (what happened while they did), between history and the past.[7] Another relatively new, interdisciplinary field, diasporic studies has also scrutinized productively the dynamics and dialectics of relationships between populations at home and displaced. Some of its insights have been helpful to me in conceptualizing the ways in which communities of French Jews in exile modified, reified, and sometimes fabricated the yearning construct of France and home.[8]

Despite its significance, this scholarly activity has made few inroads into the study of medieval Jewish history and texts. On the contrary, medieval Jewish texts, especially Hebrew texts, continue for the most part to be read flatly, as windows, unwarped and transparent, onto a uniform experience of the past. Scholars of modern Jewish history and literature have been quicker to realize the significance of these new tools than have those who work in earlier periods. As a result, they have been able to ask new questions about the Enlightenment's construct of an Andalusian Golden Age; pre-Statehood European intellectuals and Zionist settlement in Palestine; collective memory and Israeli history; or, for instance, the reframing of Iraqi Jewish experience to conform to Zionist narrative expectations.[9] So, too, the theoretical concept of "post-memory" has yielded rich results when applied to post-Holocaust memory and writing.[10] Jewish medieval studies stand to benefit from these methodological insights and approaches.

Moreover, just because they are contemporary and written in Hebrew by Jews, texts do not necessarily represent the same past at all. We know this intuitively, if only from the discordant images of the present that we are asked to filter and interpret day to day. Put simply, different people have different notions of what happened, and this is true whether or not they are from the same nation or city; the same political, class, gender or confessional background; or writing in the same language. Even in medieval Provence, where the class of Jewish writers was homogeneous—elite, educated, male—it is possible to discern the fault lines of difference. Indeed, one of these fault lines has been amply treated by historians: the bitter, at times tumultuous, controversy that erupted among southern Jews over the value of secular ("Greek") learning. Yet it has rarely been asked how strongly held convictions opposing or favoring the study of "Greek science" translated into choices made in daily life. How, moreover, might they have permeated the outlook and writing of the authors when they wrote grammars or biblical commentaries, liturgical or philosophical poetry, medical texts or romances? Even more pertinent to this study, how did one's faith and convictions, whether a commitment to traditional religious values or to rationalist inquiry, influence the way that one understood recent history and its cataclysmic reach into personal life?

In this regard, it becomes striking how little French Jewish writing about expulsion survives in traditional, commemorative genres, particularly liturgical poetry. One reason may have been the intellectual temperament of those who wrote and their disinclination for traditional attitudes and practices. Yet how many Jews were represented by this elite? For the majority, traditional approaches to catastrophe presumably retained their meaning and value. The writers who represent this majority are nonetheless hard to find, and only two of the following chapters are dedicated to liturgical verse. The absence of more exemplars of this genre reminds us, for one thing, that although a large population in France, Jewish exiles rarely resettled in groups large enough to warrant commemorative works for communal (i.e., synagogal) use. At the same time, the surviving texts confirm that when refugees did cluster in a particular location, this type of commemorative writing was an option still valued and exercised. Chapter 3 treats the penitential hymns of Reuben b. Isaac, expelled from Montpellier in 1306. Reuben's hymns are simple, lyrical pieces that rely evocatively on familiar biblical tropes of dispossession and loss; their generic imagery is undoubtedly one reason that they remained popular among later users in the Comtat and in Algiers. The northern Italian poets discussed in Chapter 6 all use the name Trévoux, identifying them as exiles from that town on the Savoyard border, whence their ancestors had arrived from Lyons in 1306. Unlike Reuben's hymns, many of the laments written by the Trévoux poets are insistently threaded with local referents, which may have doomed these poems to historical oblivion. They do not seem to have been used beyond this immediate community and its itinerant descendants in Provence and the Piedmont.

In both cases, the ability of later users to link early and later experience through a careful manipulation of tropes and sequencing illustrates the great strength of liturgical writing—namely, its ability to read all subsequent tragedies as echoes of earlier prototypes. Thus, its listeners might be assured that whatever the catastrophe, they, like their righteous ancestors, lay safely within the framework of a divinely ordained plan. The durability of this message is evident also in the material biography of the manuscripts that preserve these poems, which testify to generations of use and the accretion of traumas nearer to the reader's present than the expulsion of 1306.

The competition between local detail and generic topoi, analyzed brilliantly by Dan Pagis in late fourteenth-century Hebrew laments from Spain, is implicit in much of this literature, too.[11] It was not always the generic topoi that triumphed, although over time the gradual erasure of local referents contributed to the misreading or abandonment of once-popular works. As Ann Carmichael has noted of early modern plague literature, the embrace of local detail and personal narrative were also stylistic choices that might serve the end of wider, more universal, appeal. The poignant essay treated in Chapter 5 is a good illustration of this claim. The work of the physician Jacob b. Solomon, describing his daughter's death from the plague in 1382, it aims for a much wider audience than those who might decipher its polemical attacks.

Like Jacob's essay, however, much of the literature discussed in *No Place of Rest* is generically eccentric, representing literary forms unfamiliar to students of Jewish literature of this period and sometimes of later periods as well. Elsewhere I have referred to the tendency of 1306 writers to invest in "highly perishable forms of commemoration."[12] This is, I think, not an accident, but a by-product of the elite, highly literate, and acculturated tastes of its authors. Jacob b. Solomon was a determined traditionalist, a man shaped by a northern French past he barely knew, but he is unusual among this group. His literary corpus is equally distinctive and represents the collision of many worlds, north and south, traditionalist and rationalist, even the medical instruction at the University of Paris versus that at the University of Montpellier. In contrast, authors like Yedaiah Bedersi, Joseph b. Sheshet Latimi, or Crescas Caslari were rationalists shaped by intellectual training and outlook. Sometimes philosophers and often physicians, they were less inclined to see the world around them as God's stage for collective punishment or redemption; indeed, a concern with expulsion as an allegory of spiritual alienation, or with personal salvation through enlightenment rings through the highly abstruse and formalistic elegies by Yedaiah and Joseph, treated in Chapter 2. The two Esther romances of Crescas Caslari, a successful physician whom expulsion landed in Avignon, are treated in Chapter 4. They reveal an educated physician's perspective on problems of recent history and politics, providing in the process a glimpse of the witty, cultured world of luxury and ideas accessible to a privileged Jewish elite.

Was the prominence of physicians among those who penned the texts of expulsion partly responsible for their later misappropriation or oblivion? Certainly, physicians were a subgroup among the exiles who were more equipped to adapt and even thrive in new surroundings. The fourteenth century was, in many respects, a golden age for medicine in Spain and Provence, and Jewish physicians, too, had access to wealth and unprecedented prestige. Their intellectual interests, which of necessity included a broad exposure to Christian learning, made it easier for them to separate themselves from the conditions and struggle of fellow exiles. Danièle Iancu has documented their high rate of conversion at the end of the fifteenth century, and it seems likely that, as a professional subgroup, their conversion rates in the late fourteenth century were high as well.[13] In brief, these were not men inclined to think of the "destiny of the nation" and their personal destiny as identical problems; nor was catastrophe likely to inspire their reflection in the plaintive language of biblical lament. Cultured and acculturated, their views of themselves and the world around them often had more in common with the perspective of Christian physicians than with that of traditional Jews (again, Jacob b. Solomon will prove an exception). One literary consequence was that they were less than likely to respond to communal catastrophe in traditional genres of commemorative writing or with traditional Jewish tropes of exile and return.

Yet for both traditionalists and rationalists, a past defined by expulsion could, and often did, become a construct for survival, either in a community forged in exile or among a small elite group of Jews disdainful of new neighbors and ways of life.[14] Certainly, the laments of Reuben b. Isaac, recited in Algiers with those of Simon b. Zemaḥ Duran (a late fourteenth-century descendant of exiles from Provence and probably France before that), or those of the various Trévoux poets aggressively cohere a community in exile around the signposts of a shared history. That history is also shaped implicitly and explicitly by the genre in which it is rendered. A liturgical hymn can, by virtue of recognized conventions, assert certain kinds of historical connection and causation: suffering is inflicted by God as a means of chastising a wayward people; politics is merely God's way of imposing His will; expulsion and degradation in exile will someday conclude in restoration and privilege. Likewise, a Neoplatonic elegy subtly modulates from external chaos to an interior landscape; chaos and strife in the social world become allegorical representations of the unenlightened soul. Narrative prose, in contrast, excels in nuanced, sometimes ironic, depictions of human beings in dialogue and interaction, permitting an emphasis on complex psychological states, motives, and passions. These distinctions become clear in those cases where the authors represented in this book wrote in more than one genre—for instance, Yedaiah Bedersi, Crescas Caslari, Jacob b. Solomon, and some of the Trévoux authors. The sensitivity of these men to the requirements and limitations of a given medium asks us to acknowledge that their own views are not necessarily defined by their words—or, at least that what is expressed by their words must be filtered through the conventions of the genre in which they write them. The attention to genre in decoding these texts has been underemphasized by previous scholarship, but I think that it is of major significance.

A combination of genre and social constraints also implies that inevitably, texts suppress evidence of parallel narratives of expulsion, struggle, homesickness, suffering, and faith. Indeed, all the texts here that "remember" expulsion do so by privileging some memories at the expense of others whose memories are expunged. Sometimes those others may be their own wives, sisters, or daughters, or the nameless "ordinary" Jews arriving, destitute and desperate, to depend upon the generosity of Jewish communal resources and goodwill in foreign lands. They might be Muslim refugees fleeing to Maghrebi towns and cities in the late fourteenth to fifteenth century, or indigenous Algerian or Italian Jews deemed culturally inferior by the émigrés. These figures may be invisible in the literature cited in this book, but there are sometimes clues to their presence outside of the space limned by texts.

The material history of the manuscripts preserving these poems also contributes mightily to the story told in these pages. Like the poems of Reuben b. Isaac and the Piedmontese Trévoux, many of the texts discussed in this book have never been published. With a combination of old scholarship and new catalogs and databases, I have found them in manuscripts scattered among libraries far and wide. The world of Hebrew manuscripts is a very special world, one that brings together scholars with a variety of interests, backgrounds, and skills—often in the chilly microfilm reading room of the Institute for Microfilmed Hebrew Manuscripts (IMHM) in Jerusalem, without which this book could not have been written. Paleographers are particularly stern about reminding the bleary-eyed denizens of the microfilm library that Hebrew manuscripts, fragmentary witnesses to a perilous journey, are not just the purveyors of disembodied "texts" to be copied, annotated and corrected, and naively read; they are physical objects, and the clues to their fabrication and transmission reinsert them into a moving historical narrative whose scenery changes over time. To the extent that this is possible, we must try to see them in that landscape, not only to enrich our reading of their contents but also to comprehend some of the scope of the world that they were either incapable of representing or chose not to represent.[15]

By now, it may seem that this book is not unlike one of those salvage operations whose commander, regarded dubiously by outsiders and sometimes by herself, stubbornly persists in dredging the depths for treasures she is not entirely sure exist. Thankfully, they do exist. And if this particular hunt was launched by a question, it was a question that bore some answers. How could a great Jewish community—great in size and in cultural achievement—disappear without leaving some record of its journey into exile? Reformulated, that question became the following: How did fourteenth-century Jews remember their own past, and what happened to their story later? In this form, the hunt truly began to yield riches.

Treasure hunters need maps, and mine, at least initially, appeared in volumes 27 and 31 of *L'histoire littéraire de la France*, authored by J. Ernst Renan and Adolphe Neubauer in the late nineteenth century. These works, to which I have become fiercely attached, are unmatched by any modern scholarship.[16] Their exhaustive résumés of authors and titles were supplemented by any number of regional studies of French and Provençal Jewry, many also nineteenth-century works. Any quest of this sort would be incomplete without the invaluable catalogs of manuscripts—some old, some new—the IMHM database and microfilm library, and the actual manuscript collections at Columbia University and the Jewish Theological Seminary in New York, the Brotherton Library at the University of Leeds, the JNUL in Jerusalem, and my own beloved Klau Library in Cincinnati. And the librarians, oh, the librarians, to whom I owe thanks.

All these resources pointed the way to the manuscripts and authors discussed in this book. Significantly, very few of my authors referred explicitly to the fact of expulsion, presumably sometimes because they did not want to and sometimes because the rules of the genre in which they wrote precluded explicit statements of the kinds modern historians prefer. As a result, many of the texts treated here would have yielded little to a critical lens posed frontally but spoke eloquently when viewed from other angles. This turn to sidewise reading, with a combination of imagination and literary tools, was ultimately rooted in my conviction that no work of literature is immune to the forces that shape the world of its creators. The author and his scribes, the users and transmitters of a poem or romance or scientific work, are all part of the world. They suffer in its wars, famines, and plagues, or uneasily exult in their safety; they compare themselves with some and distance themselves from others; they write, by day or night, or they read, by day or night, while other things are happening, and those "things" unexpectedly but inevitably mark the creation of a text.

For this reason, it is important, in reading what these men wrote and in reading what I have written about them, to remain sensitive to the marginal role of these texts in most people's lives. One reason is that the men who wrote literature about expulsion were the rare few who managed to regain sufficient stability, income, and repose to sit at a desk with a pen. That cannot have been the fate of most men and women cast rudely from home into exile. Moreover, there is no evidence that most of those unmoored men and women heard or read the majority of the literary compositions discussed in these pages. Only the simple, haunting lyrics of Reuben b. Isaac were works designed and destined for popular use, and we know that they were cherished in the Comtat and Algiers for centuries. Perhaps, if we take him at his word, Crescas Caslari's vernacular Esther romance also entertained "women and children, grandchildren and great-grandchildren." But did they know what it meant?

And if he had heard them, how would a French Jew, brutalized on the roads to Catalonia or Castile, have felt about the stylized verses of Yedaiah Bedersi or his epigones, converting the upheavals and sufferings of expulsion into the mental torments of the unenlightened soul? Would he not have felt disdain—or despair? Amazingly, scholars have continued to project a world of lived experience from the words of small groups of educated, privileged men. Even if the texts we had at our disposal reasonably reflected the literary output of medieval French Jews and their descendants, they would at best reflect the perspectives of a privileged minority. As these things go, however, the attitudes and experience of privileged men with pens say little about the attitudes and experience of most men and women. In this context, what is truly striking about Yedaiah's eccentric experiments in commemorative verse is not that they were popular but that we, today, who also sit and write safely in perilous times, share his weakness for thinking that our enlightenment matters. And does it? Probably not—but as for all these writers, from Isaac HaGorni to Yedaiah Bedersi, Joseph Latimi, Reuben b. Isaac, Crescas Caslari, Jacob b. Solomon, Simon b. Zemaḥ, and Peretz Trabot (Trévoux) and his kin, we are the record that will exist.

That said, it is significant that these texts, and many of their authors also, have been largely forgotten over time. This is partly because Jewish history swept onward, cruelly, to the upheavals of the fifteenth century and the final wave of European expulsions of the Jews from Spain (1492), Portugal (1497), Provence (1500), and Orange (1505). The Spanish expulsion in particular swiftly reconfigured the shape of the past. Indeed, to this day, it is the expulsion most likely known to students, scholars, and laymen beyond our university walls. In its wake, the Jewish past, and its recorded history, were dramatically reformulated as the parallel narratives of two super-communities, Ashkenaz (the Jews of Germany, France, England, and later, Central and Eastern Europe) and Sepharad (those communities descending from Iberian Jews, namely in the Maghreb, the Balkans, the Ottoman Empire). The Jews of the Middle East and eastern Arab world, Iraq, Iran, and Yemen, were sidelined until the twentieth century.[17] For the study of the European Jewish past, which is my concern here, what matters is that a multiplicity of communities distributed about the European and North African Mediterranean disappeared also because of the tenacious appeal of the Ashkenaz versus Sepharad binary.[18] As these poets and their writings make evident, other identity options were once available, and it is time to bring them back to light.

Regretfully, most of the texts excerpted or cited here will not be easy for readers to find in full. A few have been published in old and uncommon journals, where those lucky enough to live near great Judaica libraries will find them. Many others, as I have noted, are still in manuscript. Over the next few years, some will make their way to light: my own translation of Yedaiah's "Elef Alafin" (Supplication of 1,000 *alefs*) has appeared in a Festschrift in honor of Professor Raymond Scheindlin of the Jewish Theological Seminary, edited by Jonathan Decter and Michael Rand.[19] Two students of Professor Tova Rosen of Ben-Gurion University, Uriah Kfir and Margalit Schallman, are working, respectively, on critical Hebrew editions of the poems of Isaac HaGorni and the "Supplication of 2,000 *Mems*" by Shem Tov Ardutiel. Professor Benjamin Bar-Tikva of Bar-Ilan University has for some years been working on an anthology of critical Hebrew editions for all known Hebrew poetry from medieval Provence. I hope to produce editions and translations of some works in this study myself, perhaps to appear in a separate anthology.

Let me conclude this introduction with a turn to my simplest and perhaps most lyrical poet, Reuben b. Isaac of Montpellier. Reuben b. Isaac, lamenting the fate of his fellow Jews and himself, turned repeatedly to the image of God the Shepherd responsible for His flock. Straining to harmonize the cruel hand of history with the mercy and vigilance of an all-knowing God, Reuben evokes biblical echoes of wandering sheep, sometimes abandoned by their shepherd, sometimes straying in the hills, and once, frighteningly, forgotten altogether. God, too, it seems, has a memory, and sometimes it lapses, erasing wicked and innocent alike. So this book is not only about human memory and forgetting but also about human faith in the apparent face of divine disaffection. So, too, it is a story of literature in a time of expulsion, impoverishment, dispossession—and indifference, sometimes recorded and sometimes implicitly voiced between the lines. It is also about the rich and creative, even movingly optimistic, ways in which individuals try to cope and live fully in times of uncertainty and upheaval. We who write from safety, but well within reach of the news, will find it unsurprising that a God faced with humanity might be tempted at times to forget. From a mortal perspective, remembering is only part of a greater human challenge. Those of us who write attempt our small acts of salvage. Other gestures undoubtedly make a greater difference, and it puts us in our place to know it. The point, I suppose, is not to abandon our desire to understand the past but to struggle in the present to do a bit more.

CHAPTER ONE

Isaac b. Abraham HaGorni:
The Myth, the Man, and the Manuscript

THE EXPULSION OF the Jews of Gascony in 1287 was not a major event. Nonetheless, it was the first of a series of smaller expulsions that culminated directly in the larger dislocations of English and French Jews before and after the turn of the fourteenth century. A minor expulsion, moreover, is hardly minor for the man or woman it affects. The poet discussed in the following pages, Isaac b. Abraham of Aire, was a Gascon Jew who spent at least a period of his life adrift in Provence, where his place of origin aroused little sympathy and much disdain. What we know of Isaac's life and poetry thus presents us with a rich opportunity to ask questions about the paths taken by dispossessed Jews, how they fared in new surroundings, and how history chose to remember them. The fate of Isaac HaGorni and his poetry is in an important way a consequence of fourteenth-century upheavals, beginning with the 1306 expulsion; it is also a precocious illustration of the types of issues that will surface in my treatment of later writers and their work.

Two realities of late thirteenth- and early fourteenth-century Jewish life paint the backdrop to this chapter. Both were muted in the 1280s but reached crisis and climax in the next two decades. The first is the steady progression toward expulsion traceable in changing anti-Jewish policies and sentiment in England and royal France. Both mounting antipathy to Jewish minorities and the failure of royal and ecclesiastical efforts to bring about Jewish conversion led inexorably to expulsion as a political option. Several small expulsions from Gascony (1287), Anjou (1289), and Maine (1289) pushed Jewish refugees into surrounding territories under French, Aragonese, and Provençal rule. Edward I expelled the approximately 2,000 Jews of England in 1290. In France, Philip IV's mass arrest and expulsion of royal Jews, an estimated 100,000 men and women, followed in August 1306 and included those Jews who had earlier sought refuge in French lands. All these dislocations were characterized by great upheaval and a notable dearth of literary commemoration.

Isaac b. Abraham's story also marks time with the early stage of a great historical controversy, the heated curricular debate that animated the Provençal Jewish elite of the late thirteenth and early fourteenth centuries. This moment in Jewish intellectual history has been much studied by modern scholars, who have emphasized the feverish intellectual activity among the Jews of late thirteenth-century Provence, particularly in science and philosophy. This intellectual activity flourished in the fertile soil of a parallel Christian intellectual renaissance and as a partial result of the interaction of Jewish and Christian scholars. This is evident in the collaborative work of Jewish and Christian physicians in the orbit of the University of Montpellier, and the wide diffusion of their translations and ideas; Jacob b. Makhir and Armengaud Blaise come quickly to mind, as does the relationship between the works of Crescas Caslari and Arnau of Vilanova, or Jacob b. Solomon and Jean de Tournemire, discussed in later chapters. It is evident in stories like that of Samuel b. Judah ("Miles Bongudos") of Marseilles, who sought out copies of Aristotelian works among Christian scholars. And it is evident in the astronomical and astrological writings of great Jewish scholars like Levi ben Gerson in Orange and in the phenomenon of Jewish court astrologers serving Christian aristocrats and clergy.[1]

However, beyond the ranks of seriously trained scholars, there are signs that "new" philosophical and scientific ideas held appeal for a less sophisticated audience of readers as well. These readers, who have been described as a target audience for some of Levi ben Gerson's writings, did not necessarily study their subject matter thoroughly or in order. They testify, however, to a general enthusiasm for scientific and rationalist learning, perhaps even a requisite familiarity with its terms among the social elite.[2] Some of this enthusiasm would hit a famous wall in the bitter controversy that erupted in 1304, between the Jewish promoters of "Greek science" and the more traditionalist rabbis who worried about the damage that philosophical study might inflict on young minds. This chapter of the Maimunist controversy (so called because Maimonides' writings featured centrally in the debate) was neither the first nor the last curricular battle of its sort to roil Jewish communities in premodern Europe. It escalated rapidly into a serious crisis, one that was temporarily disrupted by the general expulsion of French Jews in the late summer of 1306.

Recently, there have been signs of interest in the spillover of the 1304 controversy beyond the small and elite world of rabbinic leaders and scholars.[3] As a result, some of the "second tier" of that controversy emerges, figures whose names and writings are largely forgotten, men who may have been mediocre philosophers and scientists or who lacked the training to be philosophers or scientists at all. Nonetheless, these men endorsed the diluted or popularized versions of philosophical and scientific ideas. More importantly, perhaps, along with those ideas they endorsed an entire worldview, one that prided itself on its sophistication and rationalism. They tell us that thinking and talking about philosophy, astronomy, and medicine were not just the activities of an elite and scholarly class. In some form, these were ideas whose life and import extended beyond the elite, shaping the values and self-image of a much wider circle of Jews.

Isaac of Aire, I believe, offers new evidence of this wider world. A poet's life is, almost by definition, part myth, part mystery, part the work of detractors and friends. On the one hand, Isaac's story offers particular interest for the ways in which his image was constructed and contested in his own lifetime and then effortlessly distorted in later years. On the other hand, the "myth" of Isaac HaGorni, the Hebrew troubadour of Provence, has also obstructed a fuller view of a cultural moment in which lively partisan debate about scientific topics and knowledge was widely admired and assayed. Thus, Isaac's story raises both historical and historiographical questions, which intertwine with each other and with more traditional concerns in the scholarship of this period.

Two approving mentions of Isaac from fifteenth-century sources are also important in reconstructing a more accurate picture of who this poet was. One fifteenth-century admirer, Jacob Provençali, was a Provençal Jew forced to flee to Italy; he is known as an ardent supporter of the controversial knowledge endorsed by Isaac's rationalist peers. Another fifteenth-century admirer was the copyist of HaGorni's poems. He, too, albeit unwittingly, betrays his commitment to the same views. We do not know if this unnamed copyist was in Provence or in Italy, or even whether he may have converted to Christianity, like so many of his Provençal Jewish compatriots, in the waning years of the fifteenth century. Nonetheless, the composite record of his interests leaves us some important clues.

Curiously, modern scholars have ignored the significance of the fact that Isaac's poetry survived among writers of this particular type and these interests. Unanimously, they have assumed that the "unintellectual" topics of HaGorni's surviving poetry remove him from this field of concern. Indeed, for the most part, the nonscientific literature of Provençal Jews has been treated as if it served an altogether different community from that represented by the audience for moral, philosophical, and scientific writing. Thus, Hebrew belles lettres of this period has been situated, almost indifferently, in the penumbra of Spanish Jewish writing and culture. Hebrew liturgical poetry, too, has been treated as a derivative of Sephardic composition, and this despite its innovative exploration of new forms, stylistic diction, and motifs.[4] Similarly, the rhymed prose narratives of Judah al-Harizi or Qalonymos b. Qalonymos have been treated as "Sephardic," and the remnants of Hebrew poetry that are more "secular" in tone, like Crescas Caslari's Esther romance or Isaac HaGorni's lyrics, or the philosophical poetry of Abraham and Yedaiah Bedersi, have likewise been gathered under this umbrella rather than treated as the specific products of a Provençal Jewish milieu. A lopsided picture results, in which medieval Jewish intellectuals in Provence excelled in scientific writing and pursuits while producing epigonic writing in other genres.

Isaac HaGorni suggests that, minimally, the worlds of science and poetry were not so distinct. Yet scholars interested in HaGorni have for the most part chased after him in other directions. Ernst Renan, writing in 1878, noted that little could be deduced about HaGorni beyond his endless wanderings and his "venal" character.[5] Eighty years later, the great Hebrew medievalist Haim Schirmann tentatively suggested that HaGorni was a troubadour, a Hebrew counterpart to the poets of love and valor who moved among the Occitan courts.[6] Schirmann's language was overtly romantic: "He was truly a 'wandering mortal who spanned the earth,' as Abraham Bedersi termed him, afflicted on the way by hunger and cold, a lack of funds, and the contempt of hardhearted men of means. In his manner of life, HaGorni recalls more than any other Hebrew poet the Provençal troubadours or jongleurs overwhelmed by fate."[7]

Notably, a 1949 essay in French was more muted in its claims. And by 1979, with the publication of what was essentially a restatement of that essay in Hebrew, Schirmann retreated from claims of identity to claims of influence and inspiration: HaGorni was in the right place at the right time and surrounded by the right vernacular, so he must have been *influenced* by troubadour life and "lyricism." Medieval Jewish culture in Provence *assimilaient toujours d'avantage la culture profane*, and literature was no exception.[8] Strikingly, Schirmann offered no real example from HaGorni's poetry to substantiate such a linkage. The poet's exchanges with Devash and Bedersi were not quite in the spirit of the Occitan *tenson*, and certainly not formally similar; HaGorni's epigrammatic codas are "variations" on the Provençal *tornades* or *envois*.[9] Indeed, of HaGorni's surviving poems, none is strophic, and none includes any indication of a refrain. Not only are these standard features of the Occitan repertoire; they are standard features of songs altogether.

Nonetheless, in a late, unfinished essay on HaGorni, Schirmann returned to the image of the cold and hungry wanderer who "recalls . . . the Christian [court] jokers of the Middle Ages or the troubadours of lower class origins."[10] Given his harsh wanderings, it was not surprising "that the poet sought now and then to distract himself from his disappointments by means of lovemaking and drink."[11] Significantly, this avenue of thinking required an entire section subtitled "the unfortunate delinquent and his persecutors," a direct evolution of the French essay's allusions to HaGorni the *débauché* and *pauvre pécheur*.[12] Ezra Fleischer, who edited and "completed" Schirmann's unpublished writings, concluded the essay on HaGorni with the following assessment: "HaGorni sought to support himself by writing poetry in a Jewish environment that did not respect this sort of profession. His poetry aspired to 'courtliness' in a place that knew no such concept. In the eyes of his fellows he was not practicing a legitimate profession, however eccentrically, but begging. Moreover, the man was an insolent bohemian, and apparently a drunkard and skirt-chaser, and because of this he was 'naturally' despised by those around him."[13] That the professional activity of the troubadour did not tolerate much lowbrow delinquency was irrelevant. A Hebrew troubadour was born.

The myth of Isaac HaGorni, the medieval Hebrew troubadour, succeeded in part because these readers misread their clues. Indeed, HaGorni's poems echo in a double context, his own and that of his fifteenth-century scribe. In removing HaGorni's extant poems from their unique manuscript setting, scholars have given free rein to a number of familiar stereotypes. In all cases, scholarly imaginations were titillated and distracted by a construct of "the artist" as a man on the edge. Their assumptions were variously Victorian, Romantic, and religious; without exception, they rigidified an anachronistic topos of the "popular" poet (bohemian, libertine, and "low-class") opposed by traditional rabbinic culture and its intellectual elite (respectable, pious, and eerily bourgeois).

I should like to dissolve that opposition, by rereading and resituating the poems in historical and material context. HaGorni emerges as a gifted and exuberant poet. He must also have been a vocal, if not terribly effective, participant in the elite philosophical debates of his time, as well as a dabbler in astronomy, if not astrology, both of which feature centrally in the controversy of 1304–6. Thus, the intellectual rifts of the early fourteenth century had been growing for some time, and the figures who would play a major role in the 1304–6 controversy had long been whetting their weapons.

First, let me put HaGorni and his poetry in sharper historical focus, and then look at the manuscript that preserves his poems.

Isaac ben Abraham HaGorni was born in Gascony, in what is now southwestern France, in the latter half of the thirteenth century. Etymologically, the name Aire, the town of his birth, refers to a threshing ground, in Hebrew *goren*, hence "Gorni," meaning "of Aire." Beyond the fact of HaGorni's origins, we know nothing of the medieval Jews of Aire, and little of the Jewish communities of Gascony.[14] Thirteenth-century Gascony was agricultural and wine country (it includes Bordeaux), with a strong, fractious local aristocracy.[15] It was an English colony, ruled by Edward I from 1254 as a young prince and from 1273 on as king, up to and beyond his decision to expel its Jews in 1287—a point beyond which we do not need to speculate about HaGorni's presence there.

In fact, it has never been recognized that HaGorni was, directly or indirectly, a product of expulsion and something of a stranger in all the places he wrote. Indeed, Schirmann assumed that HaGorni's peculiar defects of personality made it difficult for him to earn a living and forced him out upon the road.[16] This is unlikely. HaGorni seems to have left Gascony prior to 1287, perhaps in the wake of the heavy tallages of 1275 or 1281–82.[17] The 1287 decree, anticipating the expulsion of English Jews by three years, spilled destitute refugees into Catalonia, Poitou, and Provence.[18] A small song that HaGorni dedicated to the Aire community does not refer to exile.[19] The lyrics recall Aire fondly, both for its "lords who stand in the breach in her times of distress" and for its Jewish scholars and benefactors. HaGorni's sense of his own importance, an aspect of his persona that irritated contemporaries and astonished modern scholars, is already evident. Comparing Aire to Jerusalem, he observes that if only the Messiah knew that Aire was his (HaGorni's) birthplace, he would choose to be born there, too. The tone of this poem suggests that it predates the expulsion. In contrast, two other poems refer suggestively to *golat Ariel*—literally, the exile of Ariel, a biblical term for Jerusalem, but I think intentionally echoing the name of the medieval town, i.e., *golat Aire-iel*, the exile from Aire.[20]

Likewise, HaGorni's small song for the Jews of Manosque praises its French émigrés and the "Frenchness" of the community. Francophilia was hardly a dominant motif in Midi poetry, Jewish or Christian. Yet in addition to reflecting the peculiar demographics of this community, which did count many Jews of French origin, HaGorni's comments may also reflect familiar Gascon sentiments.[21] The Treaty of Paris in 1259 required the English king as duke of Aquitaine to pay homage to the king of France, and Gascony was appended to the English holdings in Aquitaine. As duke of Gascony from 1253 on, Edward was, as far as that territory was concerned, the vassal of the French king (Louis IX until 1270). Offered a new outlet for challenging the abuses of English policies in the colony, Gascon lords lost no time in appealing English justice to the French courts.[22] Thus, southern hostility toward the French (echoed in the disdain of Provençal Jews for their northern coreligionists) is not a ubiquitous Gascon trope.

HaGorni was a wanderer, and we can identify some of his stopping points from songs he dedicated to the Jewish communities of Aix, Apt, Arles, Carpentras, Draguignan, and Manosque. His exasperated rivals refer to him also in Narbonne, Perpignan, Luz, and Lucq.[23] In Perpignan, he tangled memorably with the famous rhetorician Abraham Bedersi. Bedersi's record of this encounter, which survives, helped seal HaGorni's "image." Confronted with his road life, ebullient persona, and the denunciations of rivals like Bedersi, modern scholars moved easily from judgments of problematic genius to embrace the notion of HaGorni as troubadour. No longer a court poet, the term "troubadour" was relocated to depict an itinerant and hedonist, a poet whose verse suggested an uneasy familiarity with Christian life and who was thus of necessity situated on the margins of "high" Jewish culture.

There is some evidence of vernacular Jewish troubadour activity in northern and southern France.[24] In the north, from near the Flemish border, about ten songs by Mahieu de Gand (Ghent) survive; however, he tells us that he had converted to Christianity before he wrote them. From Narbonne, one of HaGorni's stopping points, we have a curious *tenson* (debate poem) involving the celebrated troubadour Giraut Riquier and an otherwise unknown Jew called Bonfils. Whether Bonfils was a real person and participant in a poetic duel, or simply Riquier's construct, no one knows. One scholar has even suggested that the true identity of the Jewish singer is Abraham Bedersi—the main evidence being Bedersi's "combative personality" and the sturdy arguments presented by the Jew in Riquier's poem. This identification seems unlikely. Bedersi was fond of polemical troubadour poetry and lists his favorite vernacular poets—Peire Cardenal and Folquet—in a well-known composition.[25] His voluminous writings display no humor or playfulness, and his writing style is manneristic and dense; it is hard to believe that he would have improved in another language. It is also hard to believe that he would have endorsed this kind of interconfessional, poetic "game."

The huge problem posed by the representation of Isaac of Aire as a Hebrew troubadour is one of audience: medieval Hebrew is not a spoken language, and it had no popular use. Schirmann acknowledged this point in his 1949 essay, but it was gradually buried under the mounting enthusiasm for the romantic image of the tavern poet and lover.[26] Nonetheless, HaGorni's Hebrew, as we shall see, is erudite and wittily allusive. Formally, he never deviates from the traditional monorhyme (qaṣīda) verse forms of Spanish Jewish poetry—curiously, his surviving poems do not even include any strophic compositions, such as the popular Hebrew muwashshaḥ ("girdle poem"), zajal, or standard troubadour genres. Thematically, however, he is an innovator, and not because he uses common or "low-class" motifs. In several songs, for instance, he claims that he writes to save Hebrew, or Poetry, from oblivion, hardly a tavern house theme:

אל תתנני. יה. ביד מתקוממי!   למה ביום אבדי מליצה אבדה?
כי היא בעודי חי ואתי אחרי   בשאול ובחשך יצועה רפדה.

(O God, do not give me into the hands of my foes!
Why should the art of Poetry be destroyed along with me?
For as long as I live, it does. Then it will follow me
Into Sheol and cover itself with darkness.)[27]

In other poems, HaGorni alludes to musical settings and practices—lutes and drums, dancing women, perhaps professional guilds. Thus,

על משפחות המושלים עברתי   אתמול לארץ נוגנים שחרתי
כנור לנגן טפחה ידי. ועל   ימין יתרי בכלי קשרתי
ואננה—אולי ביום אתעדנה   ירוח למרי לב—ובשיר שרתי.

(I passed by the clans of storytellers the other day; I sought out the
land of musicians.

I learned to play the lute, I strung my instrument with my right hand,
And I played. Perhaps as I take pleasure, it will ease the bitter of
heart—so I sang a song.)[28]

Or the following:

או עם בתוף אשא לקולי—יצאו / לחול בנות עמי ושיר תשורנה
אף אחרי מיום ליום תלכנה / לספוד לקברי אהבה תזכורנה

(If I lift my voice to [the sound of] my drum, the young women will
come out dancing and sing along,

They will follow after me every day to lament over my tomb, recalling
[my] love.)[29]

Such processions were indeed a part of local life, as we learn from an almost-
contemporary source, the incriminating testimony of a witness describing
the extravagant welcome given by the archbishop of Aix to a friend: "au son
des trompettes et d'autres instruments de musique et . . . precédé de dan-
seurs."[30] Similarly, the impressive feast sponsored by the French king Philip
III in 1271 to mark his entry into Arras, or again in 1275 to honor the new
queen, Marie de Brabant, included "dancing women in the streets" as part
of the welcoming procession.[31] The reference to "clans of storytellers," perhaps "guilds of musicians," has long puzzled scholars, who have wondered if
HaGorni referred somehow to his own apprenticeship or instruction among
professionals. However, I think it is worth noting that HaGorni does not say
that he was a member of this guild or "clan" but that he "passed by" it. The
allusion may well be to the regular gatherings of jongleurs in guild "schools,"
generally during Lent.[32]

   In some of HaGorni's poems, he brazenly compares himself to Moses
or to the Messiah. The prose coda to a furious exchange with one rival,
Isaiah ibn Devash, is a noteworthy example; it concludes with the following
words:

כי שירי מעון כל חי נסתר ואדם לא ראהו כי שיר מלאך ה' צבאות
הוא. אני אני הוא נשיא נשיאך אשר במליצה נשא ונשגב אבי כל תופש
כנור ועוגב. יצחק הגרנו אבן אברם היושבי לוק

(For my song is the wellspring of all life and mystery, which no man
has seen, because it is the song of the Angel of the Lord of Hosts! I,
I am he, the prince, your prince who is exalted and borne aloft in
speech, the father of all who hold lute and lyre, Isaac HaGorni ibn
Abram who dwells in Lucq!)[33]

Other passages document a noteworthy familiarity with the Christian cult
of relics, to which he evidently received some exposure in Gascony and during his travels. The images may play gently with pharmaceutical concepts
also, as a number of them rely on the preparation of salves or "drugs" to cure
some ailment.

These poems have no parallel in Hebrew poetry of the Middle Ages:

וממרחק לכל רוכל יביאון / עפר קברי לתמרוקי עדינות
ומקרשי ארוני לעקרות / אזי תלדנה בנים ובנות
ורמתי לעלג ירקחונה / ואלם להגות שבעים לשונות
ושערותי יתדים על כלי שיר / וייטיבו באין נוגן גנינות
ואבנטי למחגרת מנאף / למען יחדל לנאף לזנות
וכל כלי כלי קדש ישימון / ושלמותי למשמרת צפונות
ומי ידק לעפר את עצמי / בטרם יעשון אותן תמונות?

(And from afar they will bring the dust of my tomb to be peddled as
    cosmetics to beautiful girls,
And the planks of my coffin shall go to barren women, to give birth to
    sons and daughters.
They shall grind up my lice for stutterers and mutes, that they may
    speak in seventy tongues,
And my hair shall turn into instruments' strings, to please those who
    can't play tunes.
My sash shall become an adulterer's girdle, that he may cease whoring
    and adultery,
And all my instruments shall become sacred relics, and my clothes
    guarded like treasure!
Oh, who shall pulverize my bones before they make them into
    icons?)[34]

Other poems embed historical tidbits—his cheap hosts in Carpentras and
Draguignan, the tax collectors who harass him, a French Jewish physician and

patron in Manosque.[35] In several poems, an aggrieved HaGorni complains
that he has been falsely accused of attempting to seduce local women:

אותי בחדריהם יחפשון / אורב ישימוני לפנתם
או לקדשים לילה אפנה / תרתי לבבי באמונתם
יאמרו כנואף אשמרה נשף / חסד אני זוכר ליונתם
ואני לקצוי הנדוד אברח / אם בחלום אפגש עדינתם!

(They seek me in their chambers; they think I lurk in corners
Or that I turn to whores at night and have strayed from their faith.
They said that like an adulterer, I wait for the night, that I show favor to
    Their darling girls—
But I would flee to the ends of the earth if I've even met their dainty
    one in dreams!)[36]

Interestingly, this last accusation does not survive in the poems of his accusers.
Isaiah ibn Devash and Abraham Bedersi charge HaGorni with drunkenness
and dishonesty, lowly birth, rudeness, writing poetry for money and writing it
badly, but not with seduction.[37] Nonetheless, Schirmann's French essay—and
curiously, only his French essay—assumes that HaGorni's troubles, and particularly his appeal to the *roshe-qehillot* (a regional council of Jewish community leaders) were directly a result of his womanizing. The women in question,
he deduces, were probably not Jewish but "slaves and prostitutes whom a man
finds to satisfy his lust."[38] While, of course, this is not impossible, it is hard to
imagine that consorting with prostitutes would generate such consternation.
Nor would HaGorni defend himself ("If I've even met their dainty one") in
the terms he uses. Sadly, about the actual lives of the Jewish women he might
have encountered, the wives and daughters of his hosts and critics, we can say
very little. They are not the same women as the singers and dancers whom
he fancies leading him into town or lamenting over his u,nknown grave. If
HaGorni's transgressions were real, they were exceedingly brazen for a stranger
whose well-being depended upon the courtesy and protection of his hosts.

   Bedersi, however, makes no reference to such moral peccadilloes. On
the contrary, he refers to the wanderer who shows no self-restraint (ואין מעצר
לרוחו) and who has left uprightness and morals behind him: "look at this
man so stained by his sin that soap and lye cannot clean him."[39] But it is
HaGorni's insatiable hunger for attention that particularly annoyed the pe-
dantic Bedersi, who threatened to squash HaGorni's songs in his gullet:

בטן רשעים מאז תחסר / גרני ובטן שמך נד וסר /
יום רנך אמעך במאסר
נפחך תמול כמרוח אשכך / סר שירך לא זרת ארכך....
רשתי פרושה אל תברח כסיל / תרד בשאול תעלה על רוך כסיל /
עטי כמקדח לך או כסיל
כחשות בערש חלכיו חלכך / תחשב וכגנב בחרכך
שובב כמואב בוש באבוד כמוש / קח מחרשתך שדך חרוש /
קרדומך תלטוש כנור תטוש
בחוץ כדוה תתמוך פלכך / בדד כזב שב החזק פלכך

(The wicked man's belly is never full, Gorni, and the belly of your
      reputation is a stinking jug, when I crush your singing inside it
Your inflated speech of yesterday is like your swollen testicles; your
      poem has left and you are not as long as a finger....[40]
My net is spread—don't flee, you fool! You can go down to Sheol or as
      high as Orion. My pen [will cut] like an awl or an ax.
You are sickly as a bedridden invalid; you behave like the thief you
      seem.
Rebellious as Moab, shamed by the destruction of Kemosh! Take your
      plow and plow your fields! Polish your ax and give up your lute!
Quarantined like a menstruating woman, hold on to your spindle;
      ostracized like a man with a flux, seize your crutch!)[41]

Interestingly, the unusual meter of Bedersi's poem, written in the popular
muwashshah style, is illustrated also in a liturgical poem by the Sephardic
poet Solomon Dapiera (b. ca. 1340–50). That poem, "Yeter se'et" (The boon
of endurance), whose refrain rhyme also repeats the rhyme of Bedersi's opening stanza, describes the speaker's ability to endure the suffering and uncertainty of his times without reliance on false "signs."[42] Both poems were
probably contrafacted to a common model, now lost, which may also have
thematically treated the distinction between true and false faith. If so, it may
be that Bedersi's crude attack on HaGorni embeds a critique of philosophical
outlook as well as style.

    Isaiah ibn Devash, a less-known figure than Bedersi, also exchanged
several vituperative poems with HaGorni. In fact, the copyist of MS Munich
128 seems to have been, at least in part, relying on a record of this exchange
sympathetic to Devash, as HaGorni's responses are headed by the phrase

"and the enemy [i.e., HaGorni] answered, saying. . . ." Some of the same criticisms, in better verse, reverberate through Devash's two surviving attacks. Referring to HaGorni as a "Canaanite slave" who should not be confused with a "free man," he asks, "And who are you to come and curse / your king and put my land to shame?" Moreover, what should he (Devash) find frightening in a "poem as dry as a meager loaf"?[43] In full:

ומה יפחיד ומה ירגיז לבבי / בשיר יבש כמו פת הצנומה ?
ומי יפחד ארי מן השפנים / ומשרץ ורומש באדמה
שמע עצה ברח לך חיש ורוצה! / אמת אין לך לעומתי תקומה
שתו יין ואיך דבר תדבר / ותחשוב שים כבודי לכלימה!

(How shall he frighten or enrage my heart with a song as dry as a
    meager loaf?
And who is a lion to be frightened of rabbits, or of insects and crawlers
    on the ground?
Hear some advice: flee and hurry up out of here! You have no hope
    against me.
Drunk with wine, how can you even speak—and [yet] you think to
    put my honor to shame?!)[44]

As already noted, Gascony, HaGorni's birthplace, was wine country; its inhabitants were tagged as drunkards and rustics as early as the eleventh century and as late as Montaigne or even Dumas.[45] Thus to some extent, Bedersi and Devash were plying cultural stereotypes, which modern scholarship has taken literally. They are also staging their dislike in a very public way. Like HaGorni's ripostes, the poetic slander of his foes situates the public activity of poetry in a world in which the ritual performance of rivalries and affections was a familiar part of social life. Historians of emotions have focused largely on the courtroom, or on extra-judicial feuding, as their source material for this language of affect. Nonetheless, literature clearly preserves its traces. Moreover, Jewish literature reminds us that medieval Jews shared many of the tastes and attitudes of their Christian neighbors. Fama, or reputation, mattered.[46] The dozens of letters that document the vicious attacks on philosophy and secular learning, as well as the counterattacks of their defenders, illustrate the same verbal willingness to go for the jugular. The friends of one contemporary rationalist, the encyclopedist and allegorist Levi b. Abraham, found themselves frantically defending not his views but his morals.[47] Levi was also poor and itinerant and may offer a fruitful comparison to HaGorni.

HaGorni's image, in his own words and in those of his attackers, is undeniably hyperbolic.[48] But beyond the withering accusations and exuberant self-praise, what can we really say about him?

Here the manuscript offers some clues. HaGorni's poems—what we have of them—survive in a single copy now in the Bayerische Staatsbibliothek in Munich, Cod. Heb. 128, a late fifteenth-century manuscript written in a cursive Sephardi script. The manuscript is copied rapidly in one hand, which occasionally slips into a near-scrawl.[49] The copy counts numerous spelling and transcription errors, some phonetic and attesting to the multilingual milieu of the copyist, some arguably obscuring passages that needed no additional obscuring.[50] The first twenty-eight folios contain Maimonides' commentary on the ethical tractate known as *Pirqe Avot* (Sayings of the Fathers), in Samuel ibn Tibbon's Hebrew translation from the original Arabic. Samuel, from an illustrious family of Provençal scholars and translators, was Maimonides' contemporary and "official" translator. Munich 128 also includes two astronomical texts, the "Six Wings" of Immanuel b. Jacob Bonfils (d. 1377); and calculations from the tables of Jacob (Bonjorn) Poel. From Immanuel's tables for eclipses and lunar and solar positions, the copyist has selected those that cover the period 1428–46. Similarly, he has elided Jacob Poel's tables, composed in 1361, to begin in 1392. Poel's tables are combined with sections of Jacob b. Makhir's almanac for 1379–1465—Jacob b. Makhir, the grandson of Samuel ibn Tibbon and a courageous defender of the study of "Greek science" in the controversy of 1304–6.[51] These astronomical works represent the essence of the controversial Greek science endorsed by Jewish rationalists and condemned by their foes. They remained popular for centuries; Immanuel's were particularly favored because they were arranged for the Jewish calendar.[52] Immanuel's calculations are made from Tarascon and Jacob's from Perpignan, making it tempting to conclude that our copyist came from the region of Catalonia-Provence. The script from this region is more or less the same.[53]

HaGorni's eighteen poems and epigrams are copied, partly crammed, onto twelve blank sheets among the astronomical texts. Schirmann understandably concluded that the copyist was eager to fill a few blank folios, which otherwise bore no relationship to the texts around them.[54] This is not quite true. Seven of HaGorni's poems, and one of the two attributed to his rival, Isaiah ibn Devash, use astronomical metaphors or images. Some are merely idiomatic expressions: "The stars of my glory will shine forth for them" and "If all the stars of heaven trumpeted for him, they would not tell all his glory."[55] One poem, however, significantly differs.

The poem "Ḥardu bene adam" (Tremble, O People) is difficult and has been mostly ignored. Blending braggadocio with distress, HaGorni proclaims that his songs sprinkle water like dew, act like eyes for the blind, and legs for the lame. Yet he is powerless as he sees some men unscathed by a catastrophe that has befallen their brethren. These men, who hound him mercilessly, include "the rhetoricians" of his day (מליצי הדור) (v. 36) who pander their "trade" for money and "devalue the genius of poetry." In the end, he cries, he will triumph and poetry will abide. The poem opens with an extended astronomical image:

חרדו בני אדם ואל תרגעו / יום מכנף ארץ זמיר תשמעו
מרום לקולי יחרצו סובבים / על חוג וישורו ויתרועעו
לו ככבי בקר ברעי שחחו / נגדי כסיל כימה ועש יכרעו
גם ככבי לכת בלכתי ילכו / שמש וירח בנועי נעו

(Tremble, O people, and do not be calmed, on the day you hear song
    from the end of the earth.
At the sound of my voice, the rotating [fixed stars on the] highest orb
    will be stirred; they will look and be shaken.
If the stars of morning [twilight] would bow down when I sang, then
    Orion, the Pleiades, and the Bear would kneel before me.
The planets would proceed when I proceeded, the sun and moon
    would move when I moved.)[56]

Medieval astronomers assumed the location of the fixed stars on a single sphere, equidistant from the earth, and beyond the concentric spheres of the planets.[57] As E. S. Kennedy has noted, medieval discussions of planetary theory were "in some sense philosophical, rather than an attempt to improve the bases of practical astronomy."[58] Here, HaGorni emphasizes his cosmic centrality, perhaps even depicting himself as the (divine!) force that sets the planets and stars in motion. He reiterates this motif later in the poem by declaring that poetry's birth and life span should be calculated by his skies (v. 29). In addition, a string of cryptic animal images may have cosmological or astrological significance beyond their literal meaning:

אלו שאגותי לתנין נהפכו / גברו ומטה אהרן בלעו
או על פני שחק יגוני יפרשו / עדפו יריעותיו והשתרעו
אם נחשלים אזרו חייל כפיר / שואג כשסע הגדי שסעו
חימות לבבי לו שפתי עברו / ירדן כמטה אל וים כרעו

> (If my roars have turned into a serpent and grown stronger until they
>   have swallowed Aaron's staff,[59]
> Or if my sighs have spread over the heavens, overflowed its curtains
>   and extended,[60]
> If the weak have gathered a roaring lion's strength, they have rent as
>   [the lion] rends the kid.[61]
> If the anger in my heart were to pass my lips, it would subdue the
>   Jordan and the sea like the staff of God.)[62]

Altogether, the astronomical—perhaps astrological—metaphors of this poem
suggest that Isaac of Aire was more than a rhyming barfly.[63] On the contrary,
beyond a solid grounding in traditional Jewish texts, which echo through
his verse, he demonstrates a serious (not necessarily systematic) exposure to
the rational sciences and learning whose acquisition in the south was either
coveted or despised, but hardly a thing of accident.

In this light, the tastes of the copyist appear more coherent. It behooves
us to focus on him as well: clearly, Munich 128 was copied for personal use
and constitutes a sort of notebook or commonplace book containing texts
useful to its owner. Rather than assume, as scholars have always done, that
the copyist's inclusion of HaGorni's poems was a whim unrelated to his interest in the other texts in his copybook, why not ask what mental universe
makes all his choices consistent? Does the rest of the manuscript offer any
indications of what kind of person the copyist was and why he copied what
he copied? I think it does.

For one thing, some years ago, Munich 128's text of Maimonides' commentary briefly attracted the attention of art historians Therèse and Mendel
Metzger. *Pirqe Avot* 5.3 lists the miracles preordained at Creation, one of
which, the parting of the Red Sea, was occasionally represented to show the
Israelites crossing the sea in (six or twelve) semicircular paths, tribe by tribe.[64]
Accordingly, folio 22a reads: "and the fifth [miracle] was that it [the sea] was
split into paths according to the number of tribes, like a rounded arc, as in
this picture"—and a blank space below.[65] Curiously, the Metzgers associated
this iconography of concentric arcs with Italian, not Sephardic, manuscripts

(prayer books and Haggadot as well as the Maimonidean text). They cite
fifteen Italian copies of the Maimonidean commentary, ranging from the
thirteenth to the seventeenth century, that include this image, and another
five fifteenth-century Italian manuscripts that include space for the picture
but no picture. One fifteenth-century Sephardic copy of the commentary exists with the picture, and one—our Munich 128—contains a space for it.[66]

Unlike the case of Latin or Greek, Hebrew script itself cannot deter-
mine a manuscript's provenance. Relatively speaking, very few Hebrew medieval manuscripts survive—40,000 is Colette Sirat's estimate—and even
worse, like the works themselves, the writers were extremely mobile.[67] In
other words, a Jew who learned to write in Catalonia or Provence but who
was forced to move, say, to Italy, did not acquire a new handwriting in the
process. Could our Provençal scribe be in Italy? For now, I note only that his
notebook reflects the intellectual interests or curriculum of a late fifteenth-
century rationalist Jew and testifies to an exegetical and iconographical tradition shared by his Italian Jewish counterparts.

I can reinforce that connection by noting the copyist's appreciation for
the literary culture of his own time, illustrated by the charming epigram
penned at the manuscript's conclusion. This epigram, which he may have
composed, has to date escaped the notice of the catalogers:

עת אש-אלה עמל מה ב-עדנים לו יבחר להושיב ראש שבו יחליף כח
מהר כעבד צל ישאף נפשו השיבני ויאמ[ר]ני מנוח

(When I asked Toil what pleasure he would choose first to restore
    strength,
Quick as a servant who longs for the shade, he answered me, [saying?],
    "Rest!")[68]

In addition to the unusual dashes in the first hemistich, indicating the writer's
attempt to count out his meter in a fixed pattern of long and short syllables,
the failure of the verses to conform to any recognizable metrical pattern
suggests that his colophon may have been one more bit of writing that this
copyist never finished. The allegorical personification in the epigram is not
medieval but is common in Jewish literature of early modern and baroque
Italy.[69] Of course, a passion for allegory was also associated with the medieval
Provençal Jewish rationalists, some of whose descendants found their way
to Italy.[70] The formal absorption of Provence into royal France in 1481 and

the subsequent anti-Jewish violence confronted Provençal Jews with hard choices. Danièle Iancu-Agou has estimated that half of Provençal Jewry, or approximately one thousand Jews, converted to Christianity during this difficult time. Others fled into the papal territories of the Comtat Venaissin, into Spain, North Africa, or Italy. Some would later make their way farther east to the Holy Land. This "voluntary" migration was a presage to the exodus to follow the official expulsions of 1492 from Spain and 1500–1501 from Provence.[71]

Given the precarious standing of the Provençal and Spanish Jewish communities in the late fifteenth century, confiscations and burnings of Jewish books in the Comtat and in Italy in the sixteenth century, and the willingness of Jewish zealots to burn books themselves from time to time, Munich 128 might not have lasted very long if it had remained in circulation. It found perhaps another generation of use: someone has doodled heavily over the section and table headings of some of the astronomical charts, and a child has exploited some blank folios to trace an alphabet and the beginning of a benediction from the daily morning liturgy.[72] How important it might have been for this child's father to impart some of his love for knowledge and "wisdom" may be inferred from the fact that the unsteady hand of the child has (incorrectly) inscribed the benediction that praises God for creating humans with (or by means of) Wisdom.[73] A later reader has tested a pen on the flyleaf, inscribing his name. As the first page of Maimonides' text testifies, however, by the first half of the sixteenth century, the manuscript had come into the possession of the great European Orientalist Johann Albrecht Widmanstetter (1506–57), known as the author of the first Syriac dictionary in Europe. Widmanstetter's travels brought him frequently to Rome, where he may have come upon this manuscript.

Alternatively, it is possible that he acquired it in Provence, especially if the copyist of Munich 128 was counted among the approximately 50 percent of Provençal Jews who converted between 1484 and 1500. In that case, the marks of Italian tastes and influence are really extensions of cultural interests whose origins lie among the Jews of Provence. In this scenario, the awkward tracings of the child inscribe a last attempt to pass on Jewish learning in the home, a domestic world that embraced a father, a child, and a book. It is a gesture toward continuity that is abruptly truncated by conversion, the erasure of a Jewish past and the construction of a new, Christian, identity.[74] Curiously, we know that the neophyte Christians, as Iancu terms them, retained a vestigial attachment to their Hebrew books for at least a generation. A rare inventory of a neophyte's library is one clue to this, but more numerous are the last wills and testaments that carefully delineate the fate of specific possessions, including books.[75] Thus our copyist, if he remained in Provence as a Christian, most likely held on to his personal library while he lived, and may even have bequeathed it to his child or children. Their generation, however, would have found Hebrew learning harder to come by, and Hebrew books less a doorway to knowledge than artifacts of a past that could have been viewed only with ambivalence. Indeed, only a generation from the copyist had to pass before Widmanstetter's acquisition of the book, perhaps from the grownup whose first childhood reach for wisdom still falters across two folios.

Sympathetically, we can hope that this copyist lived—indeed, lived as a Jew—and moved, either into the Comtat Venaissin or directly to Italy. But perhaps he did not, or both father and child were baptized in those fateful years, and the material legacy of a Jewish past was discarded. Either way, the trail was not long until Munich 128 fell into Widmanstetter's hands. Upon his death, it passed to the royal library in Munich, now the Bayerische Staatsbibliothek. There it remains.[76]

Scholars interested in HaGorni have had two outside sources to help them situate his work in a larger context. Yet the conscious or unconscious desire to corroborate claims for HaGorni's "low-class" and romantic marginality has encouraged a misreading of these sources as well as of the poems themselves. In fact, these sources reinforce my reading of HaGorni as a temperamental but mainstream member of an intellectual elite. One, the collected works of Abraham Bedersi, contains several long and unpublished poems by Bedersi attacking his rival.[77] These poems detail their meeting in Perpignan, which an infuriated Bedersi describes as a ruse by HaGorni to extract money from him. Wearied by pestering, Bedersi says, he agreed to meet with HaGorni, whose rhymes were so tattered that "no needle could sew them."[78] The men stayed up talking about poetry, and at dawn they parted as friends. HaGorni dutifully acknowledged Bedersi's superior talents and pocketed a donation. No sooner did he reach Narbonne, however, than he proclaimed, "Gorni is the prince of the princes of poetry, and Bedersi knows it!"[79] True, HaGorni is not exactly a model of humility. Yet no one has ever asked: Would Bedersi, the epitome of Jewish high culture in the Midi, have really spent the night talking poetry with a dissolute singer?

Our second source comes from the fifteenth-century Talmudist Jacob Provençali, who declared HaGorni one of the finest Jewish poets of Provence.

Schirmann and, later, Fleischer repeat the reference without further ado. But inadvertently, they have distorted its meaning. The context for Provençali's remark is his lengthy response to a query about the legitimacy of secular study, particularly philosophy and astronomy. In that context, Provençali observes:

> [T]here are wise men who are not eloquent and eloquent men who are not wise, and happy is the man who is both, for each is an attribute in itself. For it has been said that the philosophers like Homer the poet, Solon the eloquent, and Parmenides the mathematician were purer and more pleasing in [their] language than Aristotle and Plato, who were greater in wisdom.... [S]o, too, among our sages, may their memory be a blessing. For R. Judah HaLevi and R. Solomon ibn Gabirol and ben Falaquera, and also among our own in Provence HaGorni, HaHarizi and HaSulami were better with language and poetry . . . than Maimonides or Naḥmanides, may they rest in peace, who were wiser.[80]

The first group of Spanish and Provençal writers mentioned in this passage were poets and philosophers, albeit mediocre philosophers in the writer's eyes when compared to Maimonides and Naḥmanides, who were inferior poets. Amazingly, Fleischer concluded Schirmann's essay on HaGorni by disparagingly commenting, "if [HaGorni] had been a learned poet, he might have written poems in the style of reproach and frustration of Solomon ibn Gabirol or Moses ibn Ezra."[81] Clearly, from Provençali's perspective, the status of these poets (at least Ibn Gabirol and HaGorni) is comparable. Judah al-Ḥarizi is well-known, especially for his translation and original composition of the entertaining rhymed narratives called *maqāmāt*; he also translated Maimonides' works. The other writer, Samuel Sulami (also known as "la Escala"), was perhaps originally from the Dauphiné, but made his home later in Narbonne and Perpignan. With the exception of a fragment from a letter, his writings have been entirely lost, and today he is chiefly remembered as the man who gave shelter to the allegorist Levi b. Abraham (also known as Levi b. Ḥayyim). According to the letters describing the vicious controversy of 1304–6, he initially refused to evict Levi from his home, despite the insistence of R. Solomon b. Adret in Barcelona and the traditionalist camp that he do so. However, the unexpected death of Sulami's daughter convinced the grief-stricken father that the child's death was a divine punishment for his refusal to eject the condemned rationalist. The unfortunate Levi b. Abraham was sent on his way soon after.[82]

In other words, both al-Ḥarizi and Sulami, in addition to their reputations as poets, were staunch rationalists who played vigorous roles in the thirteenth-century debates over the legitimacy of the sciences. Jacob Provençali himself spent most of his life in Marseilles, the home of the Tibbonides. After the French absorption of Provence in 1481, Marseilles was the scene of severe anti-Jewish riots. With other survivors, Provençali, not a young man, departed—for Naples, where he studied astronomy.[83] In 1492, while he was there, Naples saw the first published edition of Maimonides' commentary on the Mishnah, in Ibn Tibbon's translation; the commentary on Avot had already appeared separately, in 1486, off the Soncino press.

Thus, the copyist of Munich 128 had coherent literary tastes after all. Perhaps, like many of his contemporaries, including Jacob Provençali, he ended his days in Italy. I do not know if this is true. However, I can say with some firmness that the poet whose work he saw fit to cram into his "notebook" was one he admired as a member of the intellectual milieu with which he himself, two centuries later, still identified. Was Isaac HaGorni a Hebrew troubadour? Probably not, no more and no less than the unfortunate Levi b. Abraham, whom no one has ever confused with such an identity. Was he a serious astronomer or philosopher? Again, probably not, but he may illustrate the appreciation for such study among a less sophisticated but literate group of men. Was he a rogue, a lover of wine, women, and praise? So it seems, but so was Samuel HaNagid, the eleventh-century Spanish Golden Age poet, Talmudist, and *wazir* of Granada as well—which may be the point. Like Levi b. Abraham, HaGorni had talent without wealth or power. He was also to some extent a foreigner, a man without a home, a man of strong opinions, and a man who used his poetry to redeem his own reputation as much as to participate, very publicly, in the tempestuous intellectual climate of his times.

"Beware of the poet," Abraham Bedersi's son Yedaiah would write, "for he can stay at home and take revenge on his enemies overseas."[84] Yes, but if he did not have a home, this apparently was not so easy. Late fifteenth-century readers, the Jewish intellectuals and their epigones in Italy and Provence, still saw HaGorni's wide career. They also saw the wandering poet and his interests much as they saw themselves, also intellectual men who had landed far from the home of their youth. Moreover, they recognized HaGorni as a legitimate participant in the elite debates over "Greek" science and its place in Jewish intellectual life. It is possible, of course, that Isaac b. Abraham composed other, lost, songs, perhaps even in Occitan, and these may have popularized some of his astrological or scientific views in ways that outraged some Jews. His critics were not traditionalists, but stalwarts of the rationalist camp, and whatever in HaGorni's combination of doctrine and megalomania inspired their wrath, it was not his ignorance. As Schirmann long ago noted, the disappearance of HaGorni's poems may not be entirely due to accident, and certainly the enlightened Jewish philosophers of his company were capable of "erasing" a foe.[85] The copyist of Munich 128, like Jacob Provençali, admired HaGorni's poetry, but that they acknowledged it at all seems to have been due to their ability to link him to the world of rational learning in which they lived as well as read. By the nineteenth century, much of what was needed to interpret the space around his poems—literally and figuratively—was lost or invisible to scholars determined to see something else.

This chapter has thus caught up the threads of two related narratives, one of a thirteenth-century poet and the other of later readers. As the discussion of HaGorni's feuds with his rivals, Abraham Bedersi and Isaiah ibn Devash, demonstrates, the Jewish intellectuals of Provence were capable of lively argument with one another in "same-time" also. Moreover, the kinds of curricular issues that engaged them in such heated debate have their origins in real issues and events that disturbed and challenged long-held views of who they were and what history, and their Christian hosts, might have in store for them. In many ways, HaGorni, his poems, and his fate offer a test case for the more complicated disruptions to follow the great expulsion of French Jews two decades after the expulsion from Gascony. Accordingly, the next chapter looks at a curious set of poems that have never been read as rooted in historical events (if they have been read at all), in particular the expulsion of 1306. The bizarre poetics of these poems also demands that we ask how these writers—one of them Abraham Bedersi's son, Yedaiah—understood the expulsion of French Jewry and their responsibility to the refugees who turned their world and sense of history upside down in the autumn of 1306 and 1307.

CHAPTER TWO

Form and History:
Hebrew Pantograms and the Expulsion of 1306

Ce que le texte propose, c'est, plus qu'une suite exemplaire d'épisodes,
un mode particulier de penser l'événement.[1]

IF THE MINOR EXPULSIONS of the late thirteenth century were an ominous prelude, the mass expulsion of the Jews from France in 1306 was a great Jewish catastrophe in its time. Nonetheless, unlike the incidents of persecution that marked the lives of northern French Jews in the two centuries preceding this expulsion, few literary texts preserve traces of this expulsion. Moreover, of the literature that survives—anecdotal asides, or late and distorted chronicle accounts—very little is poetry. Of that poetry, very little corresponds to the affective forms of traditional commemorative Hebrew verse. The moving hymns of the Montpellier poet Reuben b. Isaac are one exception and are treated in Chapter 3. Reuben's hymns tap images of suffering and ancient tropes of exile, delicately alternating despair and consolation. In many ways, they are the kind of poetic response that we should expect to follow a great, communal Jewish trauma: liturgical, simple, and biblically resonant.

Certainly, we might anticipate that poems about catastrophe would be emotional poems. Yet the dominant intellectual forces in Provence, where most of the refugees surfaced, would not have agreed. These men were philosophers, scholars, and physicians, nurtured on rationalist "Greek" learning. They rejected the poetry of emotion in favor of complex rhetorical forms of verse. In so doing, they created poems whose readers were asked to perform the journey to enlightenment through mental effort that the writers fervently endorsed. Tragedy not only could be packaged in these forms, but from the philosophers' perspective, these were the forms it deserved.

This chapter looks at one way Jewish rationalists experimented with the commemoration of catastrophe, in a small sample of alliterative poems that modern scholars have found especially precious. Nonetheless, I believe that at least initially, the poems of Yedaiah Bedersi and Joseph ben Sheshet Latimi constituted an attempt to respond to the historical catastrophe of 1306, and that they embody a philosopher's view of history that was shaken by events. Both men witnessed the 1306 expulsion not as its victims but from cities that attracted large numbers of refugees. Their alliterative elegies dazzled later readers more for their form than for their content, and their historical impulse was quickly obscured. Yet they remained surprisingly popular. An even earlier alliterative poem by Bedersi, the "Supplication in *Mem*," also gained renown and was frequently appended to his ethical treatise, the *Beḥinat 'Olam*. The *Beḥinat 'Olam* also refers to the events of 1306, and with the "Supplication in *Mem*" offers a useful counterpoint to the alliterative poems that treat the expulsion, as does the earliest known imitation of these poems, another "Supplication in *Mem*," by the Castilian poet Shem Tov Ardutiel.

Partly in reaction to its manneristic excesses, nineteenth- and early twentieth-century scholars of medieval Hebrew poetry in Provence and Spain referred often to the poets of the late thirteenth and early fourteenth centuries as inferior writers, inexplicable enthusiasts for the bad taste of their times. It is worth asking why such bad poetry, if it was such bad poetry, had meaning to the men who wrote it and, moreover, continued to be admired and read. Indeed, Bedersi's and Latimi's poems inspired a host of later imitations, beginning in Castile, then moving to Italy, the Ottoman Empire, and ultimately, to the scholars of the European Enlightenment whose affection for *melitzah* and for a nostalgic "Andalusian" past is attested in the generous number of eighteenth- and nineteenth-century copies of the earlier poems and in their own experiments in the genre. As I hope to show, later enthusiasm for this writing offers a way of gauging how it was read and to what kind of past later readers thought it belonged. Over time, that past became increasingly detached from the historical context that interests me here. If Bedersi's and Latimi's alliterative poems represent a serious attempt to meet historical upheaval with philosophical conviction, the choice of this form as a vehicle for commenting upon social disorder and catastrophe raises questions worth pursuing. How well suited was the philosopher's quest for pure Form to a representation of history, and whose history did it represent?

Bedersi's and Latimi's poems illustrate a type of hyper-alliterative poetry in which every word of a poem either begins with the same letter or contains that letter. This device is associated today with the works of the sixteenth-century French poets known as the *grands rhétoriqueurs*; the scholar Paul Zumthor coined the term "pantogram" for the French poems, and I have imported it for the earlier Hebrew exemplars.[2] With a variety of other eccentric genres in Hebrew, these poems were described (not by the term "pantogram") in a 1918 essay by Israel Davidson titled "Frivolities of Hebrew Poetry." Davidson gathered a number of poems he characterized as "emphasizing specific letters"; the Hebrew category also includes poems in which each word contains the designated letter (not necessarily at its head).[3] The latter category generates an obvious counter-type of verse that avoids a particular letter, Davidson's "missing letter" poems.[4] (The remarkable French novel of Georges Perec, *La disparition*, is a modern prose example.)

Hebrew poetry has a long history of playing alphabetic games, typically in the form of acrostics, but pantograms were initially rare.[5] A short hymn by the eleventh-century Andalusian poet Ibn Gabirol, "A'amir a'adir" (Let me declare and magnify), begins the words of each line of verse with the same letter, switching lead letters with each new line.[6] From twelfth-century Provence, chapter 19 of Judah al-Ḥarizi's masterpiece of rhymed prose, the *Taḥkemoni*, features a rhetorician who first produces a poem whose every word contains the letter *resh* (*r*), and then a poem none of whose words contains a resh. The poems by Yedaiah Bedersi and his Catalonian contemporary Joseph Latimi signal a new interest in this type of exercise, which they transmitted to later readers. Only a few decades later, in Castile, we find the 2,000-*mem Yam Qohelet* (Sea of Ecclesiastes), of Shem Tov Ardutiel (Santob de Carrión) and a now-lost poem in *nun* by Isaac al-Aḥdav. From there, the list continues into the early modern and modern periods in Italy, Turkey, Holland, Germany, Brazil, and Eastern Europe. I am aware of approximately two dozen pantograms, in *alef, bet, gimel, heh, lamed, mem, nun,* and *shin* (*a, b, g, h, l, m, n, sh*). The last is a sonnet in *mem*, composed in Paris in 1860 by Schneur Sachs for one of the pioneers of modern Hebrew literature, Abraham Mapu.[7]

The three poems that discuss the expulsion of 1306 were composed close to the event, between 1306 and 1308, in the cities of Perpignan and Lerida. Perpignan, geographically in Provence, was under Majorcan sovereignty; since the king of Majorca was a vassal to the king of Aragon (first his brother, then his nephew), it was technically Aragonese. Lerida, to the west of Barcelona, was Catalan, also part of the kingdom of Aragon. Neither city expelled its own Jews in 1306. Rather, both (especially Perpignan) found themselves the destination of Jewish refugees from Languedoc and Montpellier. In these strange poems, their authors managed to capture some of the moral and social turbulence that followed the expulsion and its impact on local bystanders.

At least one of these poet-bystanders, Yedaiah HaPenini (Bedersi), is a familiar name. Bedersi was active in the curriculum controversy of 1304–6, which spilled from Montpellier to Perpignan and Barcelona, and his *Iggeret haHitnatzlut* offered a vigorous defense of philosophy and secular studies. He also composed a small treatise on poetics, called the *Sefer haPardes*; a polemical defense of women; a commentary on Avicenna's Canon; a number of astronomical and philosophical essays; and a popular work of moral philosophy, the *Beḥinat 'Olam* (Examination of the World).[8] Whether or not he was a practicing physician is debated, but as with many of the intellectual Jewish elite, medical texts and theory constituted part of his intellectual training.[9] In contrast, we know nothing of Joseph b. Sheshet Latimi other than what may be deduced from his *alef* poem and a collection of forty-six *qinot* for men and women whose identities are today unknown.[10] Nonetheless, I would guess that he, too, belonged to the rationalist side of the 1304–6 controversy, and several medical turns of phrase in his pantogram may indicate his medical training or interests. Likewise, Shem Tov Ardutiel, Bedersi's and Latimi's first imitator, displays an affinity for medical metaphors and language in his *Yam Qohelet*. He may have encountered Yedaiah's "Supplication in *Mem*" by reading it with the *Beḥinat 'Olam*. Or he may have known it independently: a generation earlier, the Castilian courtier-rabbi Todros b. Joseph HaLevi Abulafia accompanied King Alfonso X and his queen to Perpignan, where he met Yedaiah's father, Abraham. Abraham, whose rhetorical excesses we have seen illustrated in vituperative attacks on Isaac HaGorni, continued to correspond with "Don Todros" after his return to Castile.[11]

Yedaiah's affinity for the pantogram was precocious. Among his youthful compositions was the *Baqashat haMemin*, a "supplication" of 1,000 words each commencing with the letter *mem*. Reportedly composed when Yedaiah was fourteen, the poem earned considerable and contemporary acclaim, enough so that some years later, either Yedaiah or his father, Abraham, a well-known *melitz*, returned to this formal constraint. Like the "Supplication in *Mem*" the resulting *Elef Alafin* consisted of 1,000 words, this time beginning with *alef.*[12] It was soon followed by the *Baqashat haLamedin* or *Beit-El*, which has 412 words (the numerical equivalent of בית אל), each of which contains a *lamed* and no letter of which occurs past *lamed* in the *alef-bet*. (*Lamed* is at the halfway point in the Hebrew alphabet).[13] The fame of this poem reached the crown of Aragon, where James II supposedly referred to the author as "the man who speaks in half the alphabet."[14] Bedersi's work impressed Jewish intellectuals as well as kings: in nearby Lerida, Joseph b. Sheshet quickly produced a new *Elef Alafin*, with meter and rhyme and laced with multiple acrostics.[15]

Both Bedersi's *alef* and *lamed* poems must have been written soon after the 1306 expulsion, because Latimi's "Supplication in *Alef*" responds to Bedersi's and is dated 1308. In 1306, Yedaiah Bedersi was in Perpignan, a natural destination for French Jews fleeing Languedoc southward.[16] Latimi's poem alludes to the expulsion also, and well it might: refugees from Perpignan who had flooded Barcelona within weeks of the July expulsion were in Lerida by the spring of 1307, where the relatively small Jewish community paid 1,000 sous for each refugee's right to settle in the city.[17]

The echoes of historical trauma in these poems argue against dismissing their rhetorical oddity as a form of verbal game. As Paul Zumthor and more recent scholars on the *grands rhétoriqueurs* have argued, the fantastic rhetorical exercises of these poets are also a studied assault on the accepted ways that language "means." Yet the French studies fall short of explaining the Hebrew phenomenon. For Zumthor, the essence of the rhetoricians' activity was the search for *un niveau imprévu de langage*, a reduction of language to pure sound and asemantical relationships.[18] But the Hebrew letter *alef* has no sound, for instance, and it is favored among pantogram writers of a range of ideological views. For all of them, the choice was not only about the relative abundance of words that could begin with this letter. *Alef* is the first letter of the *alef-bet*, the icon for the numeral "1" and a theological signifier of divine unity. It is also the first letter of the Hebrew word for "I" (אני) and the prefix for first-person-singular imperfect verbal forms. Consequently, the first *alef* poems operate antithetically to Zumthor's model: not pure materiality but pure Form, they give form to the philosopher's preferred retreat into himself, while dramatizing the collision of the speaker's "I" with collective destiny. This is not just playfulness; it is a privileged elite's reflection on history in a time of upheaval.

Less obviously, these poems are not mystical exercises, either.[19] Certainly, contemporary kabbalists displayed an active interest in the symbolic power of the alphabet. Several centuries later, that interest informs several pantograms, such as the *alef* poem by the seventeenth-century poet Israel Najara.[20] Medieval Jewish readers were familiar with midrashic treatments of the alphabet as personified or symbolic, including works like the *Midrash haOtiyyot*. An educated reader like Bedersi or Latimi also knew the mystical treatment of the alphabet in the popular *Sefer Yetzirah*. The *Midrash haHokhmah*, the mid-thirteenth-century encyclopedia of Judah b. Solomon of Toledo, dedicated a section to the meaning of the letters of the alphabet; according to Judah, each letter attached to the intellect governing one of the celestial spheres.[21] Likewise, the kabbalist Abraham Abulafia devoted considerable attention to the alphabet, comparing the relationship of letter to vowel, for instance, to that of body to soul, and claiming that the entire alphabet was generated from the Tetragrammaton.[22]

Medieval Jewish poets also incorporated mystical motifs into religious verse. Perhaps the most famous example, the great Spanish Jewish exegete Moses b. Nahman (the "Ramban," or Nahmanides; d. 1270), also adapted the familiar conventions of Andalusian Hebrew poetry to include kabbalistic elements. As Adena Tanenbaum has shown, one of the Ramban's great liturgical poems, preserved in the Sephardic festival liturgy, reshaped the conventions of philosophical poems that describe the journey of the soul by incorporating mystical language.[23] Yet the Ramban's poem was a liturgical composition, destined for and remaining in communal use; neither the Ramban nor the kabbalistically inclined poets (with the exception of Najara) experimented with poetic form in the hyper-alliterative style discussed here. The poems I consider below belong to the general category of "soul" poetry, but their manuscript history demonstrates that they were not primarily intended for public recitation.

Nonetheless, as it figures in the writings of rationalists or kabbalists, an interest in the iconic status of the letter took different forms. As we shall see, the themes of the early Hebrew pantograms remain rigorously consistent with those of the Neoplatonic rationalists and do not promote mystical readings at all. In their philosophical endeavors, these writers (including Bedersi) struggled to reconcile a received corpus of texts articulating an Aristotelian rationalism with other, Neoplatonic writings, some of which they knew in the guise of Aristotelian compositions.[24] In particular, Maimonides' emphasis on a cosmic, Active Intellect accessed by the philosopher by dint of rigorous learning and self-knowledge is a theme that surfaces in all the poems discussed below—a process that, memorably, the difficulty of the poems requires the reader to enact.

The poems treated below do show affinities for Neoplatonism—for instance, in their portrayal of the Soul in exile from its divine source and imprisoned in the Body, or in their allusions to the union of mortal with Divine Intellect, achieved through philosophical enlightenment, as the means of restoring the Soul to purity and immortality.[25] These poems show no signs of interest in mediated emanations of that intellect (such as the ten *sefirot*) or in a notion of the ongoing recycling of life-forms (reincarnation), which are central features of kabbalistic thought.

A preoccupation with the alphabet was related to other developments as well.[26] One was a new awareness of the power of the alphabet as a tool, attested in the university and clerical circles whose trends Jewish intellectuals followed closely. As a new search and research device, alphabetical order had a notable success in specific areas of professional knowledge. As universities developed standardized curricula, and as students had to master them, the corresponding need to find things in books without necessarily reading them end to end became critical.[27] Alphabetical indexes offered one solution to this need, and they appeared with increasing frequency in the thirteenth century in lists of biblical distinctions, florilegia, exempla, concordances, and medical works. The last included herbals, pharmaceutical catalogs, and recipes—not theoretical but practical works that might be searched by the physician on the job. For the same reason, alphabetized indexes circulated among the mendicant orders, whose members found immense practical value not only in new concordances but in alphabetized collections of sermon exempla and proverbs. The alphabet made its way into yet a third category of text as well: accounting, such as the alphabetical registers found in thirteenth-century France.[28]

Did Jews like Yedaiah and Joseph know about this new research technology? It seems more than likely, although a lingering preference for memorization hindered the rise of alphabetization in Jewish texts. Alphabetized school texts were popular chiefly in Paris and Oxford; traffic between the University of Paris and the papal court in Avignon was heavy.[29] We can only speculate about exposure to alphabetical concordances or catalogs used first by the mendicants. Jews engaged in polemical exchanges with the friars and were involuntary audiences for their sermons; some interest in their preparation methods seems reasonable.[30] In contrast, there is little chance that Jewish lenders might have noted the form of Christian accounts, particularly in the north, at this time.

Jewish familiarity with some of the alphabetical medical works is beyond doubt. The popular *Antidotarium Nicolai*, which listed hundreds of pharmaceutical recipes by letter, was translated into Hebrew about this time, and the anonymous translator went to the trouble of reordering the entries to correspond to the Hebrew alphabet.[31] Another alphabetical book of simples, Platearius's *Circa instans*, was translated into Hebrew by a Provençal Jew, Solomon b. Moses of Melgueil, in the second half of the thirteenth century.[32] One of Lerida's main attractions in the early fourteenth century was its new university, founded by James II in part to generate local physicians. Among indications that the new *studium* got off to a faltering start was the request from its first medical professor, Guillaume de Béziers, that the king impound precious medical texts from local Jews.[33] By 1308, however, the young university was up and running again, and, like its predecessors in Montpellier and Avignon (and pre-expulsion Paris), it must have been a magnet for refugees with medical training and interests. Interestingly, Latimi's *alef* poem occasionally presents a medical turn of phrase, such as his plea that God release "droplets of medicine" (אנלי-ארוכה) for the suffering people; the expressions suggest, if not medical training, at least the educated interest in medical thinking among early fourteenth-century Jews documented in the work of McVaugh and García Ballester.[34]

Medieval alphabetization—a tool found in ancient Greece and Rome, and known to the Arab world—did not rise without trouble. As the Rouses note, alphabetical ordering posed a direct challenge to a scheme of knowledge that hewed to natural order, that is, to the order of things as God Himself had made them.[35] Counterintuitive though it may sound, alphabetical order struck many medieval readers as inherently, even dangerously, illogical. Yet by the second half of the thirteenth century, if it had not conquered, its place was assured.

The distance from an alphabetical list of remedies or rocks to poetry and metaphysics is not so great if we understand these various phenomena as diverse manifestations of a concern shared by Jewish and Christian elites. Likewise, the Neoplatonic attitudes toward language and linguistic signs found among Jewish philosophers and kabbalists were part of a larger context in which, in Brian Stock's words, "the ideas represented by signs were eternal, while the spoken utterances by which we know them were bound by time."[36] Isaac b. Solomon al-Aḥdav, author of the lost poem in *nun*, described the words of his poem as "souls without bodies" (*neshamot bev'li guf*).[37] Shem Tov Ardutiel, al-Aḥdav's contemporary, also used this expression to describe another eccentric writing form he apparently attempted by cutting words out of paper with scissors.[38] Their interest in writing as pure form hews closely to the Platonic understanding of "outer experience" as an illusory veil over "an inner reality of forms."[39] For Ardutiel, al-Aḥdav, and arguably their panto-gram-writing friends, true meaning was an ideal, inner Form, whose shadow might be glimpsed in the signs or outer forms of language. From this perspec-tive, the monotonic language of the pantogram, which Zumthor has called a "quasi-absurd reduction to unity," represents an attempt to purify the poem of its dross, presumably including the instability of emotional affect.[40] Ye-daiah says as much in the *Beit-El* (v. 5):

ובהלל אנדלך בנודל / בדולחי ואבדיל בדילי.

(Through praise, I shall exalt You, increasing the crystal and removing the tin.)

Accordingly, Bedersi's pantograms reject the affective, musical, and rhythmic dimensions of verse in favor of unrhymed, unmetered, nonstrophic, purely alliterative language—a stark contrast to the descriptions of poetry in his own poetic treatise, the *Sefer haPardes*. The *Sefer haPardes* describes poetry that uses imagery, sound, and rhythm to praise one's friends and damn one's enemies, poetry that operates by means of suasion, seduction, and falsehood. In contrast, the pantograms suppress these elements in favor of what Bedersi may have felt was Truth, at least as close as language could get.

But what of the content of these poems, especially those that purportedly refer to the terrible expulsion of 1306? Both Bedersi's and Latimi's *alef* poems are dialogues between a speaker and God. Their overall narrative is simple, a journey of sin and redemption plotted along familiar lines of exile and return. Through all the rhetorical excess, we hear the voice of a speaker who comes to praise God and seek His forgiveness, who realizes he has strayed from God's truth, who confesses and vows to repent, and who hopes God will hear him. In these aspects of the poems, we find a predictable philosopher's universe, in which the search for truth enables personal awareness and a freedom from the destiny of blinder men.[41]

In other respects, the content of the two Supplications in *Alef* and the *Beit-El* is unusual. In all three poems, first-person-singular speech dominates

(this is predictable because of the grammatical uses of the *alef*). The speaker's
sin and salvation are private and not communal: the personal intersects uneasily with allusions to social distress. This tension between personal quest
and communal responsibility fissures both Bedersi's and Latimi's *alef* poems.
Midway through Bedersi's elegy, the speaker describes his grief upon witness-
ing the "annihilation of [the] people of faith":

איככה אוכל אראה אבדן אנשי אמונה? איכה ארעה, איכה ארביץ
אדמה אשר אררה אדני? אקוה אליך איחל אור, אמשש אישון אפלה.
אשתוללו, אנו אבלו אביוני אדם! אוספו אנשי אסופות! אוספו אספסוף
אגודה אחת! אראה אובד אמון. אמרו, אים? איה אלהיהם?

(How can I see the annihilation of people of faith? How can I pasture,
how can I water a land that has been accursed by my Lord? I shall hope
in You, I shall await the light as I grope about in absolute darkness. I
shall bewail: the most miserable of mankind mourns and laments! The
men of the assemblies—annihilated! The masses—annihilated in one
fell swoop! I see the obliteration of those who cultivated faith. They
said: Where are they? Where are their gods? [ll. 46–50])

Then he stops and utters the only words in the poem to use the first-person plural: אבל אשמים אנחנו, ארחות אנשי און אלפנו (but *we are guilty*; we
have learned the ways of wicked men—ll. 55–56). Amazingly, Latimi's poem
echoes this passage explicitly:

אצנו אל אורח און ארחנו / אבל אשמים אנחנו
אנחנו אלה אמצנו אלהי אמן / אטים אומנים.

(We hastened to walk down a wicked path; truly *we are guilty*.
We strengthened these gods [which are the work] of craftsmen [vv.
60–61])

The expression "we are guilty" cites Gen. 42:21, where Joseph's brothers confess having sold him into slavery. The words thus strike a chord whose tones
sound repeatedly in these texts, that of the failure of Jews to care for other
Jews, that of the fate of sojourners who turn to their brothers in foreign lands.
It was a timely point, as we shall see.

In other ways, the two *alef* supplications are distinct. The speaker in Bedersi's *Elef Alafin* begins by declaring his intention to give praise to God and simultaneously to express his misery, reminding God of His promise to love Israel and restore her to her marriage canopy. He cites the enemy's plans to destroy the Jews and their fine homes, to "swallow the land," and to scatter the people far and wide. The speaker's sense of horror at what he has witnessed leads him to list his transgressions, God declares His intention to redeem the people, and the speaker prays that this comes to pass.

Latimi did not slavishly reproduce the model he found in Bedersi's poem. Formally, at least, he saw it as a challenge to be exceeded, which he did by adding meter and rhyme. He has also employed *shirshur*, a poetic device familiar in Sephardic poetry: each new verse (here, couplet) begins with the last word of the preceding one. In addition, there are three acrostics, one running through the second letter of the first word of each odd-numbered line (an alphabet forward and backward plus the poet's name), one through the second letter of the first word of each even-numbered line (a rhymed couplet), and one through the second letter of the first word of the second hemistich of every second verse (backward alphabetical).[42]

The general track of Latimi's elegy, also in dialogue form, is also his own. The poem alternates speeches by the speaker and God, moving to a rapid stichomythia for most of the second half of the text. God's unity is a recurring theme. As in Bedersi's poems, speech is a major concern, whether as praise, confession, sin, or expression of true and false beliefs. Although Latimi's narrative is less linear, the general outline is clear. The speaker tells God his misery and hopes atonement will earn mercy. God promises to redeem the "captives" and take vengeance on Israel's enemies. The speaker promises to do what God wishes, to exert self-control (a philosopher's value), and to offer help to the "captives," whom God then assures him He shall shepherd safely home. The speaker again vows to seek God's "dwelling" and declare his love, and God again assures him that He shall punish the wicked and bestow wisdom upon those who love Him (v. 55). The speaker acknowledges his sins, and his despair before the enemy who challenges his faith, and God (again) says that He will punish those enemies and restore the "captives," who are mortally sick:

ארומם אולי אסירי אליהם / אכסוף אסוף אאסוף
אאסוף אסורי אנושים / את ארמנות אויביהם אשים.
אבל אנלי ארוכה אנשים / אליכם אישים!

(I shall raise up the first of my captives; I shall yearn for them and
    surely gather them in.
I shall gather up the mortally sick captives; I shall destroy the palaces
    of their enemies.
But I shall rain down droplets of medicine for you, O noble men!
    [vv. 86–88])

The dialogue form in the two *alef* poems invokes a long tradition anchored in
the reading of the Song of Songs as an allegorical dialogue between God and
Israel. This subtext sheds light on the half-ness of Bedersi's *Beit-El*, which is
constructed entirely as a monologue. Thus, not only is the "Supplication in
Lamed" a form of half-language, rendered in half the alphabet, but its missing half is its missing partner in dialogue—namely, God. The *Beit-El* also
raises familiar themes. The speaker wishes to exalt God in speech but knows
speech's inadequacy; he is ashamed of his "sickness," "filth," and "rags" but
admits he has caused destruction to himself. He is eager to atone, to offer
prayer and sacrifice, and he describes passionately the fate of his fellow Jews,
despoiled of land and wealth, moving into exile with their homes in ruins:

כלי גולה ולא כליל ונילה / לדל הגלה בגלולי גלילי
טלה חלב יבלוהו לבאיו / ולבו אל גליל טלה ובדלי

(The trappings of exile [replace] diadems and joy, for the wretch
    expelled by idols [?] and wealth;[43]
The lions wear out the milk-lamb, while his heart turns to Aries and
    Aquarius. [vv. 34–35])

The exiles, stripped of material wealth, hope only for redemption. Aries is a
bleak sign in medieval Jewish writing; associated with the planet Mars, it por-
tends disaster. It is also the sign of the ancient biblical kingdoms that included
Israel, Philistine, Babylonia, and Persia. Aquarius is associated with Saturn, a
negative sign linked by medieval writers to historical misfortune but also the
sign of the Jews.[44] Thus the victims yearn for an end to exile and for return
to a home that is simultaneously mythic and real. Accordingly, the *Beit-El*
concludes with an image of Ohalah and Ohalibah in birth pangs, symbols of
the exiled people anticipating the Messiah.

In all three poems, two types of sin disturb the speakers. One has to do with speech and is personal: the speaker makes false oaths, tempts and leads weaker men astray, is drawn to false doctrine, and espouses false beliefs. Repenting, he can confess, speak of God's truth and love, plead for God's intercession, and exalt God's Name. Intellectual effort, in turn, is the catalyst to intercession—in this context, the awakening that moves the speaker to enlightenment.[45] Bedersi and his rationalist colleagues repudiated the notion of God's direct intervention on behalf of individuals just as they did the notion of immutable destiny. The woes of their people in some sense reflected the degree to which the Jews had forfeited divine protection and their own agency through willful rejection of God's truth. Hand in hand with this forfeiture came their sense of fatalism. As Bedersi comments in the *Behinat 'Olam*, in the wake of catastrophe, despair is the comfort of fools; it is the easy recourse of men to whom determinism is preferable to mental and spiritual effort.[46] How such an analysis would have struck the stunned exiles is not hard to imagine, and none of the compositions designated for a communal commemorative repertoire ever dares to suggest such a theme.[47]

Yet the seeker of enlightenment can ignore neither the world around him nor the group whose collective destiny embraces his own. A second category of sin is featured in these poems: sins of dereliction. The speaker witnesses and sometimes participates in the abuse of the helpless, the "captives," the homeless and impoverished victims whose presence pierces all three poems. To read in this language a conventional response to exilic life would miss the mark. Certainly, these are typological images of guilt and transgression, presented in biblical language that was readily identifiable to later readers. But this is a typology notably lacking in Bedersi's other writings, including the *Behinat 'Olam* and the "Supplication in *Mem*," and it is absent as well in Ardutiel's composition. This set of allusions was therefore used selectively.

Yedaiah Bedersi's youthful "Supplication in *Mem*" offers a comparatively tepid typology of sin when compared with the later *alef* and *lamed* poems. It also survived much better; its glossy language and generalities, like those of the *Behinat 'Olam* (to which it was often appended), may have contributed to its long-lived popularity. In the "Supplication in *Mem*," sins of despair are a dominant theme; in keeping with contemporary attitudes toward melancholy, Bedersi refers to persistent sadness as a "sickness" that drives man away from God. But of social transgression he speaks in vague generalities: two striking mentions of contempt for teachers and their learning—a sin noticeably absent in the later *alef* and *lamed* poems—may reflect the immediate environment of a (very) young author.[48] Yet despite a fleeting reference to "companions who steal wealth and are learned in war" (מריעיו מגנבי ממון מלומדי מלחמה), the reverberations of acute social distress are not evident in this poem.

It is useful to look carefully at the description of the victims in these poems. In Bedersi's *Elef Alafin*, they are poor and they are widows, mourners, and brothers and sisters; they are men of rank as well as men of the masses, and they are repeatedly described as people of faith. Their treasuries have been devastated, and their homes destroyed or taken over, they are pursued and terrorized, taxed, and scattered. They are captives, and they cannot depend upon fellow Jews, such as the speaker, to help them out. The same images recur in the *Beit-El*, where the victims have lost their property and wealth, they are imprisoned and robbed, they desperately indulge in false hopes (Aries and Aquarius), they are "milked" by their overlords, and exiled.

From Lerida, Latimi describes a similar scene. There, in fact, we know that in addition to the entry fee that the Jewish community paid on behalf of the refugees, there was soon trouble with local Christians.[49] Not far away, in Barcelona, which absorbed at least a hundred families in the early weeks following the expulsion, there are also records of internal strife among established Jewish families and the destitute refugees.[50] Latimi describes the "mortal sickness" of the exiles, who are captives, uprooted from their mansions, devoured by their enemies, accursed, and debased. Latimi's hymn concludes with God's promise to restore the children to their mother's dwelling (v. 97), tapping the image of Mother Rachel crying for her children in exile (Jeremiah 31) but also, perhaps, tapping memories more recent and real—desperate mothers and children whose support had vanished, women separated from families and stigmatized by exposure to the roads, privation, and possible violence.

I do not think these are simply metaphorical or allegorical abstractions. Many of the same images are echoed vividly in the liturgical hymns of Reuben b. Isaac, expelled from Montpellier. Reuben also alludes to wandering and destitution, to "captives" and indentured men and women, to vulnerability and despair. If the resources of Hebrew literature for making visible this dimension of refugee experience were poor, the poems nonetheless suggest its presence to a class of readers who were used to reading between the lines.

The presence of these images—human, social, suffering—in these poems suggests also that the equilibrium of the philosophers was not immune to external reality. Reading the virtuosic acrobatics of the French *rhétoriqueurs*, Paul Zumthor saw men peculiarly addicted to order, whom fate had settled in instable times.[51] Certainly, the speakers in the Hebrew poems are introspective and self-doubting, repelled by disorder and the suffering of others. Their authors were also scholars, and the craving for order and tranquillity is a familiar academic lament. Other kinds of post-expulsion documents allude to the extent to which the loss of these things devastated medieval scholars—Estori HaParḥi in the prologue to his translation of Armengaud of Blaise's *Tabula Antidotarium*, Samuel b. Judah of Marseille reworking his translation of the *Nicomachean Ethics*, Simon b. Joseph writing after his expulsion from Montpellier.[52] In the *alef* and *lamed* poems, we hear the tones of moral paralysis as well. As Richard Emery showed long ago, many of the wealthier Perpignan Jews, and especially their physicians, were moneylenders, men of means and influence both within their communities and as liaisons to Christian councils and courts. They were surely involved in facilitating the resettlement of the refugees.[53] Notably, refugees like the famed antirationalist Abba Mari, also complained bitterly that their rationalist foes in Perpignan tried to bar them from the city.[54] It is hard to imagine that Bedersi was absent from these controversies.

Bedersi's preoccupation with the events of 1306 also found expression in chapter 9 of the *Beḥinat 'Olam*, which contains an extended passage on the expulsion. Bedersi's elegant if facile meditation on the illusions of worldly gain, the discomforts and temptations faced by the soul imprisoned in flesh, and the easing of these distresses in a blend of wisdom and religious duty achieved instant acclaim. It is cleverly crafted, and the prose is a dazzling weave of biblical and postbiblical phrases, juxtaposed to create startling puns and imagery. On the surface a repudiation of worldly temptations, chapter 9 is framed by allusions to prophetic and "historical" narratives, a striking choice given the work's overarching ethical and philosophical themes. It begins and ends with a careful brace of citations from Isaiah 36–37 (= 2 Kings 18–19). Bedersi's subtext is thus the story of King Hezekiah's panic before the Assyrian onslaught that has driven the neighboring kingdom of Israel into captivity, and of God's assertion that the Assyrian king, God's instrument of justice, shall be stopped before Judah, too, is utterly destroyed.

In seeking pleasure over virtue, Bedersi declares in this passage, the sinner leans "on a broken reed" (2 Kings 18:21 = Isa. 36:6)—but the "broken reed" of 2 Kings and Isaiah is not the arrogance of youth but the might of a dubious political ally. Likewise, if for the illusions of worldly gain, the speaker has been willing to "cast out [his] soul along with its body," God remains aware of his foolish pride: "Did you not know that your deeds are remembered, and overhead there is an eye that sees, an ear that hears all your arrogance and

rage! And now, on whom have you relied to break through the fences built by
the chiefs of the herds?" Here, again, the moral rebuke is caught in the threads
of biblical narratives, returning both to Hezekiah and God's assurance that
Assyrian arrogance has its limits, and to the story of Doeg, King Saul's chief
herdsman, glimpsing David and his men on the run. But Doeg is also an
Edomite, and "Edom" is medieval shorthand for the Christian nation; once
again, the political subtext to the struggles of the soul implies some sort of
maneuvering by neighboring Jews, the frailty of Christian promises and the
might of Christian empire—a might that, Bedersi's text reminds his readers,
must ultimately prove fallible, too.

Thus the frame of chapter 9 is carefully politicized. In contrast, the core
of the chapter, which deals explicitly with expulsion, largely avoids historical
prooftexts, again suggesting a desire to elevate social chaos to its truer, spiritual, meaning. Almost musically, the chapter modulates to a minor key, here
the dense (often obscure) poetic language of Job. Bedersi's speaker (a kind of
superego) tries to rouse the soul to see how she has been deceived:

מה לך נרדם! למה רמוך לתתך יורש עשר ארצות כאלה כל ימי
עולם ואתה שאול בירכתי ביתך מדת הימים. ארורים הם. כי גרשוך
מהסתפח בנחלת קדושים מצורם חצבת, מהתערב בסוד חיות החיוך.
ומעונות אריות היו לך למעון. ואם על אוצרות מפז וסגולות מדינות
אשר כנסת הוספת גאוה לגוה בהשפילך לפניה רוח נדיבה ראה
הוכת בשבט סכלות ונגעי עורון! העל אוצרות חושך צררת שנאת
צרורה בצרור החיים?⁵⁵

(What is it, you sleeper!⁵⁶ Why have they deceived you to sit in the
bowels of your house for the measure of your days, when you might
have inherited ten kingdoms for eternity? Let them be cursed, for they
have expelled you from your share in the heritage of the sanctified ones⁵⁷
in whose image you were hewn, from taking part in the mystery of
the [divine] Creatures that have animated you, so that lions' dens have
become your dwelling. And if you took pride in storehouses of gold and
the privileges of governments you amassed, as the wind of prosperity⁵⁸
abased you before it,⁵⁹ see, you have been struck by the rod of stupid-
ity and the wounds of blindness! For storehouses of darkness⁶⁰ did you
gather hatred for her who is bound in the source of Life [i.e., Torah]?)

The chapter modulates again, pivoting on an apocalyptic note in Daniel to a series of alliterative puns that concludes by reiterating the futility of longevity bereft by misfortune and the puniness of mortal glory. "How shall the fields of Sodom and the sheaves of Gomorrah (*shedemot sedom ve'amire-'amorah*) flourish?" Bedersi's pun on the "fields of Sodom" enlists the biblical word *shedemot*, found in Isa. 37:27 and 2 Kings 23:4, thus returning the passage full circle to the political echoes with which it opened.

The distinct formulations of Bedersi's ethical treatise and the poems in *alef* and *lamed* counterpoint each other instructively. The *Behinat 'Olam* elegantly allegorizes the psychological and moral conflict of the speaker, an educated man tempted by wealth and privilege that threaten to corrupt his soul. Why incorporate into this reflection the debris of real events? One reason was perhaps that those real events led to real situations that provoked the author's concern with sudden gain and temptation in the "real world" around him. Second, however, is the fact that for Bedersi and his friends, "real events" were not so real: history *was* allegory, upheaval and suffering two of its signifiers. The task of the philosopher was to read the world as the cipher of Truth it contained.

Yedaiah knew from experience the frightening capacity of fortune to turn men and women on their heads. If the *Behinat 'Olam* dates from the early fourteenth century, he had already watched his father gain, lose, and regain considerable wealth. He had lost two siblings and seen his family uprooted from Perpignan to Narbonne during the French-Aragonese conflict of the mid-1280s.[61] As he himself says in the pantogram acrostic that concludes some versions of the "Supplication in *Mem*," "the splendor [of my youth] departed, disturbances befell me, many incidents that exhausted and struck me down;/ Changing circumstances changed me, upheaval repudiated me; I believed that I had now become nothing."[62]

Shem Tov Ardutiel, author of the *Yam Qohelet*, also alludes to the vagaries of fortune that beset the author from youth. Shem Tov (or Santob) is known today primarily for his vernacular work, the *Proverbios Morales*; a confessional hymn preserved in the Sephardic festival liturgy; and the whimsical Hebrew allegory known as "The Debate of the Pen and Scissors."[63] The *Yam Qohelet* constitutes a clear attempt to "one-up" Bedersi's youthful composition in *mem*; the "Sea" contains 2,000 words, each beginning with *mem*, and alludes richly to both the "Supplication in *Mem*" and the *Behinat 'Olam*.[64] Schirmann noted with distaste Shem Tov's penchant for the verbal baroque, a proclivity reflecting "the degraded taste of his times . . . marred by excessive length, superfluous rhetoric, and wordplay."[65] For Schirmann, the *Yam Qohelet* was the supreme expression of these defects.

The motif of childhood spent in upheaval and isolation is developed in
an extended passage:

מעוז מלך משפט מאהב. מעט[66] ממך מצוקותי מנעורי מבחורותי
מעודי מושג מהומות מורדף מכלמות מתנודד מתבודד מובדל מרעים
מוזר מאחים מגורש ממשכנות[67] מבטחים מעליות מרווחים מנוחתי
מסובה [?] מחרדה מבטחי מזון מרוגז[68]. מנגינתי מיוסדת מדאגה[69]
מאכלי מצות מרורים משקי מהול מתרעלה משיחי מודלף[70] מטני מלב
מפחתי[71] מחצת מציק מעיק מעגלה מליאה מעמיר[72]. מהריון מלידה
מצאתי מבטן מהעתקי משדי מולדת. מהגמלי מחלב מינקת מעולם
מוסכתי מרוש. מעולמי מגודל מעמל מחוסר[73] מרגעה מחונך מתלאה
מורגל מאין מדה מצרה מלא משורה. מגור מסביב מתיירא ממקדים [?][74]
מוכעס [?] מתמורות מתנחם מתמולי מתעצב מיומי מתייאש ממחרתי.
משושי מצוא מערת מכפלה מבחרי. מחק מחיים. מות מעצמותי מוטב[75]
מהיותי ממורט מתועלת ממושל מתוחלת.

(O Stronghold, King who loves justice! Lessen my troubles. From my
boyhood, from my youth, as long as I have lived, I have been in the
grasp of unrest, pursued by shame, wandering,[76] isolated, set apart from
companions, made strange to brothers, expelled from secure dwelling
places[77] and spacious upper rooms.[78] My rest has been surrounded[?]
by fear, my security mixed in anger,[79] my song composed in anxiety.[80]
My food is bread with bitters, my drink is mixed with poison. My bed
is stained with tears[81] from the heart[?!], from fear of the wrath of the
tormenter,[82] of the oppressor who presses like a cart full of sheaves.[83]
Since [my mother's] pregnancy, from birth, since leaving the womb,
from when I was torn from the breasts of my homeland, weaned from
the milk of the nursemaid, I have always been anointed with bitterness,[84] raised in toil, lacking tranquillity,[85] educated by adversity,[86]
accustomed to immeasurable sorrow full to overflowing, surrounded by
fear,[87] afraid of what shall come[?], angered by changing circumstances.
I console myself for yesterday, feel sorrow for today, despair of tomorrow. My joy [would lie] in finding the cave of Machpelah, my chosen
one. Strangled by life, physical death would be preferable to [living]
bereft of purpose and in suspended hope.[88])

Whether this motif represents autobiographical detail or literary trope
is not easy to know. To at least some degree, it is a trope whose origins may

be traced back at least to the works of Moses Ibn Ezra.[89] Amazingly, one line of Shem Tov's description "translates" a line from the *Beḥinat 'Olam* (into *mems*!): Bedersi's מתעצב לעבר. נבהל להווה ירא לעתיד (feeling sadness for yesterday, panic for the present and fear for the future) becomes מתנחם מתמולי מיומי מתיאש ממחרתי מתעצב (console myself for yesterday, feel sadness for today, despair for tomorrow).[90] Still, it is a trope that has been omitted from the three pantograms that refer to the 1306 expulsion, where the upheavals of fortune detailed are those of others, not of the authors themselves. Once again, this suggests that Bedersi and Latimi engaged the startling formal constraints of the pantogram in the interests of a particular historical vision.

Unsurprisingly, it was the banal platitudes of the *Beḥinat 'Olam* that earned their author fame, and a combination of factors towed the "Supplication in *Mem*" in the wake of the ethical work's popularity. A cultural (perhaps human) preference to think of sin in terms of crimes against the self instead of crimes committed against others may have been one of them, and both the poem in *mem* and the *Beḥinat 'Olam* endorsed this focus in ways that the poems in *alef* and *lamed* do not. Bedersi's poem in *mem* refocused the reader of the *Beḥinat 'Olam* on this theme, which also preoccupied Ardutiel in the *Yam Qohelet*. Lacking Bedersi's elegant mastery, Shem Tov's poem is diffuse and often obscure. Nonetheless, its gravitation to familiar themes and its focus on the self is clear. Like Bedersi's meditation in *mem*, it considers the fate of the soul condemned to exile in the body and imperiled by its appetites and desires.[91] The temptations of the soul are located in the body, organ by organ and limb by limb:

מכל מאלה מבכה מסלדה מחילה מחלחלת מחבליה. ממבכירה
מאשה מצרדה. מתעלמת מבשרה מתרעמת מגוויתה מורבצת מתחת
משאה מאבריה מכל משרתיה. מלקחיה מחתותיה. מֵידִים ממשׁשׁות
מגע מטמא מֵעֵינַים מביטות מתיפות מנאפות מאזנים מקשיבות מזממי
מהתלות. מאַפִּים מריחות מבאיש מביע. מֵחִיךְ מטעים מפתבג מנואל.
מרגלים ממהרות מהלך מעוקל מַלֵב מתקנא מתאוה מתכבד מקלון.
מֵקוֹל מחצצים מבין משאבי מעינות. מת ...?... ת מדמעות מגרות מֵתְנַים
משוטטות מאין מבוא מעוזה מצולה מבין מתקיף ממנה מושיע מיגון.[92]

(From all these she weeps, is disgusted,[93] in great pain, she trembles in pain, [like?] a woman giving birth to her first child in her torment,[94] she hides herself from her own flesh,[95] is disturbed by her body groveling[96] under the burden of her limbs and all its 'helpers,' its snuffers and trays:[97] HANDS groping for contact with impurity; EYES gazing upon adulteresses making themselves beautiful; EARS listening to those plotting to mock;[98] NOSES smelling stinking odors;[99] a PALATE tasting rotten bread;[100] LEGS hastening to go on a crooked path; a HEART envious and lustful, weighed down by shame. From the SOUND[101] of archers among the watering places . . . flowing tears;[102] LOINS wandering without coming upon her Stronghold, [the one] who will save her from her attacker and rescue her from suffering.)

It is too easy to blame this kind of rhetorical excess for its fate. Yet unlike Bedersi's pantograms, Ardutiel's did not have a long life. All three extant copies of the poem were probably produced in the fifteenth century. One indicates that, at least briefly, the poem was known in Byzantine communities, perhaps brought to Greece or Salonika by later Spanish exiles. But the poem was never published, and even in modern times, no one has had the interest (or fortitude) to produce a critical edition.[103]

The "Supplication in *Mem*," content-wise by far the most superficial of the early examples, found itself appended to the *Beḥinat 'Olam* in many manuscript copies and later print editions. And many there were: Schirmann observed that the *Beḥinat 'Olam* was more widely read than any other Hebrew poetic composition of the Middle Ages, and the number of extant manuscripts (more than seventy) is equaled by the number of times the work was published.[104] It was one of the first Hebrew works ever published, between 1476 and 1480 in Mantua, on the press of Abraham and Estellina Conat. The edition may have been the work of Estellina, whose name appears in the colophon and whose labors and reading interests mark the success of this genre of literature in early modern Italian Jewish circles (even among learned women).[105]

What precisely those labors and reading interests entailed may be glimpsed in a snappish aside that prefaces a manuscript commentary to the *Beḥinat 'Olam*. The work of an otherwise unknown writer, Isaac Monteson or Monzon, the commentary is dated 1508.[106] The manuscript itself was acquired in the late nineteenth century by Abraham (Eliyahu) Harkavy, collector and bibliographer of the imperial library in Saint Petersburg, and a victim of the postrevolutionary violence following the First World War that brought the Soviet Union into being. In a twist of irony, the manuscript, after years in Saint Petersburg at the Society for the Promotion for Jewish Culture, apparently disappeared in transit to the Vernadsky Library in Kiev, following the dissolution of the Soviet Union.[107] At the end of the nineteenth century, Renan could still cite it, and the citation is illuminating:

אמר יצחק בן אברהם המכונה מונטישון ספרדי היושב פה העירה
סרקוסה אי איסקלייא למה שראתי הבחורים המתענגנים בהלצה זו עד
שיודעים אותה על פה בפיהם ובשפתותיהם כבדוה ולבם רחק ממנה
והיתה ידיעתה אצלם מצות אנשים מלומדה ותהי להם כדברי הספר
החתום לכל ישימו לב על פנימיותיה ואל צורתה אשר היא תכליתה
ונשארה כחומר בלי צורה מה שאין הפה יכולה לדבר . . . . . ואני
הצעיר בבית אבי חמלתי עליה לבלתי הכסות ולהראות צורתה אשר
היא כוונת מחברה ואבארנה מאמר מאמר עד השלים הכוונה בה

(Isaac b. Abraham, known as Monteson, a Sephardic Jew dwelling here in the city of Syracuse in Sicily, said: I saw the young men taking pleasure in this rhetorical work until they knew it by heart and they honored it with their lips while their hearts were far from it. They considered learning it mandatory, but it was like an esoteric book to them all. They would pay attention to its inner meaning and not to its form, which is its essence, and it was left like matter with no form, that which was unutterable. . . . [S]o I, a youth in my father's house, had pity on her uncovered state and so that her form would be visible, as was the author's intention, I have clarified it phrase by phrase until that intention was fulfilled.)[108]

Later editions of the *Beḥinat 'Olam* also mark tantalizing intersections with history, such as the early seventeenth-century work of Philippe d'Aquin, produced with a French translation and dedicated to Cardinal Bérulle in 1629.[109] D'Aquin, originally Mordecai Crescas, was born in Carpentras about 1578. With his conversion near the turn of the century, he embarked upon a lifelong career of polemical battle with the Jews, as well as a prolific career translating Hebrew works into Latin. The year his translation of the *Beḥinat 'Olam* appeared also marked the appearance of his Hebrew and Aramaic dictionary, the *Ma'arikh haMa'arekhet*.[110] The "Supplication in *Mem*," for its part, was admired by Christian humanists as well as by Jews; it, too, was often printed with commentaries or broken down into thematic sections with explanatory headings. Translations into Latin, German, and French appeared early and were reproduced well into the nineteenth century.

The majority of the three dozen manuscripts that include the Bedersi and Latimi *alef* and *lamed* poems include more than one of them; they are usually anthologies of didactic, philosophical, and polemical texts. One striking exception is a fifteenth-century Italian copy among the holdings of the Jewish Theological Seminary, a beautiful little prayer book with ornamental capitals and borders, clearly a luxury production for a wealthy and learned man.[111] In this manuscript, as in a few others, Bedersi's *alef* and *mem* elegies are broken into visual units and marked as separate *baqashot*, arguably a concession to the limits of concentration of more ordinary readers. Many of the copies, however, fall at the other extreme; they are hastily scrawled, most likely for personal use.

The easy conclusion is that these remained elitist texts and that their elitist readers pondered them silently and privately, in direct antithesis to the hymns of public prayer. Yet that judgment would be hasty. Certainly, these are texts to be read and not heard; it would be impossible from oral recitation to catch and decode internal acrostics such as Latimi's. But it is also the nature of this poetry that one does not keep it entirely to oneself. These texts construct an elite textual community, but it is still a community of more than one. The nineteenth-century scholar Samuel del la Volta, who first published Bedersi's *Elef Alafin*, confessed in his introduction to the poem that he was initially delighted upon discovering the poem. However, his gleeful anticipation of springing it upon the "sages of Jeshurun—even [those] in Vienna," gave way to dismay when he could not understand it and nearly abandoned the project. Fortunately, he enlisted the aid of a friend in Padua, Mordecai Morteira, who read the elegy with him and provided the text with vowels.[112]

In sum, far from representing eccentric literary tastes that were doomed to oblivion, the precious poetic exercises of Bedersi and his followers were popular among Hebrew (and non-Hebrew) readers and admired for precisely the hyperbolic mannerism that offends the sensibilities of modern readers.[113] The Supplications in *Alef*, *Lamed*, and *Mem* were copied and recopied, and apparently (like the *Beḥinat 'Olam*) memorized and declaimed with fervor if not comprehension. Their success came at the expense of their meaning. The early authors' need to embed history in allegory and allegory in pure form contributed rapidly to the erasure of any commemorative impulse, perhaps to the erasure of history itself. What remained was truly a testimony to pure form, and in that capacity these poems shimmered through centuries and spaces, their gleam dimming only in recent times. The changing light that dimmed their luster also signified changing assumptions about the space of poetry, for whom it was written, and what kind of expertise it required. So, too, modern disdain for these poems marked some length of the disciplinary barrier between "history" and "poetry" and the animadversion of historians to "history" packaged in anything but prose. These poems, strange though they now seem, communicate a different conviction. That is partly why, in the longer trajectory of the history that they saw differently, their way of seeing was lost.

Many of the characteristics that Paul Zumthor observed in poetry of the *rhétoriqueurs* are also visible in the Hebrew examples: the use of allegory and citation, dramatic dialogue and first-person speeches, multivalent readings, and a fondness for strange layouts or otherwise visual elements that elude oral performance. Like the *grands rhétoriqueurs*, many early Hebrew pantogram poets functioned in a court or patronage system, where spectacle and ritualized forms of expression prevailed. For Zumthor, the pantogram aesthetic reflected the high premium that court life placed on artificial forms of behavior and speech. In his reading, anxiety over station, like the fear of wider social upheaval, lurked closely behind the texts.

Given what we know of the Hebrew texts, this view requires revision. Hebrew pantograms span from Late Antiquity to Golden Age al-Andalus, fourteenth-century Provence and Catalonia, fifteenth-century Spain and Italy, sixteenth-century Salonika and the Balkans, seventeenth-century Amsterdam and Brazil, up to eighteenth- and nineteenth-century Europe and Russia. That is a lot of anxiety and upheaval, even for the most unrepentant believer in lachrymose Jewish history. The writers of Hebrew pantograms represent an identifiable and small group of men. Elite and academic, yes. Courtly, sometimes. Insecure, agreed. At least some of them seem to have been consciously striving to be historically resistant, in the name of a transcendent truth. If they did not entirely succeed in this endeavor, they came close: I have suggested that their novel way of "thinking the event," in Zumthor's words, doomed that event to near oblivion.

Nonetheless, wonderfully, each generation of pantogramists knew at least some of the work of his predecessors, identified with it as a poetic mode, and saw it as a challenge. Certainly, a delight in wordplay dominated production in some places and times. For others, a mystical dimension accrued to the pantogram form. Somewhere between, highly literate and verbal men found in the formal difficulty and monotony of the pantogram a meditative tool, a linguistic challenge, and a path to enlightenment. Possibly the scariest example is a liturgy by Zeev (Wolf) Buchner, first published in the late eighteenth century and republished several times thereafter.[114] Buchner's *Shire Tehillah* opens with a hymn entirely crafted of two-letter words, followed by a hymn of three-letter words, leading to a series of pantograms—in *alef* for Sunday, *bet* for Monday, *gimel* for Tuesday, and so on. These are followed by pantograms for each Hebrew month in which each word begins with the first letter of the name of the month, and then by compositions that use only the letters *alef* to *lamed* or *lamed* to *taf* (that is, the first or second half of the Hebrew alphabet).[115] Who used Buchner's work? We do not know.

Yedaiah Bedersi, his father, Abraham, and Joseph b. Sheshet in Lerida believed that with their learning they might master destiny in a way that eluded the unenlightened. It is all the more chilling, then, that both *alef* poems depict the dislocation and communal dissension that followed the 1306 expulsion with a veneer of conviction that is splintered by a note of collective guilt. After all, the image of Joseph's brothers in Egypt not only strikes the chord of Jews failing to help their "brothers." It also depicts refugees, once mighty and secure, now at the mercy of a powerful brother in a foreign land. Yedaiah's and Latimi's verses suggest that the Jewish elite who bore responsibility for absorbing the French exiles struggled to reconcile their intellectual convictions with the chaos around them. Whether those convictions were sustainable in the long aftermath of 1306 is a question that concerns all the studies that this book comprises. Whether they were comforting in the short run is a question raised by these poems.

The poetic choices of men like Bedersi, Latimi, and Ardutiel were resolutely linked to their way of thinking about the world. If, in the end, their elitism and their fascination with "high" language and with intricate wordplay contributed to the loss of the event they commemorated, would a more traditional set of choices have had a different fate? The next chapter looks at the sole surviving examples of literary commemorations of the 1306 expulsion in a traditional liturgical genre, the petitionary laments of the Montpellier poet Reuben b. Isaac, in the context of two very different paths of exile, one to northern Africa and the other into the papal territories of the Comtat Venaissin.

CHAPTER THREE

God's Forgotten Sheep:
Liturgical Memory and Expulsion

God, Your people tremble in fear like a woman in childbirth; they bleat
Like sheep who have no shepherd
And who have found no pasture.
So they move on, depleted of strength.

Our land is in enemy hands,
Desolate as if overturned by strangers
Thorns have grown over its strongholds,
Nettles and briars.

The looters have come
And plundered the tents.
They despoiled weary, toiling people,
And spread themselves out.

Your inheritance languishes,
Your dove goes from devastation to devastation.
The dove does not find
A place of rest.

Only the heart—for God's deeds are strange!
Prays that God will accept him.

Let him return to God, for the Lord our God
Will have mercy upon him. He is most forgiving.[1]

THIS CHAPTER LOOKS at a collection of liturgical poems referring to the 1306 expulsion of Jews from French lands and how they were transmitted to later generations. Among communities that mixed the survivors and descendants of many exiles and emigrations, liturgical poems commemorated a compound experience of exile constructed out of the fragmentary memories of multiple events. The hymns of Reuben b. Isaac, an otherwise unknown poet from Montpellier, are the only extant liturgical compositions referring directly to the great expulsion of 1306 written by one of its victims. The following pages trace Reuben's poetic corpus on two expulsion paths, first into the papal states of the Comtat Venaissin and then into Algiers. Not only do the poems acquire different meaning in their respective environments; that meaning continues to change in part because its liturgical framework, unlike the other forms of writing treated in this book, proved extraordinarily flexible. By attempting to reinsert these texts back into environments rich with the iconography of "home"—from food and ritual to architecture and clothing—we can gain some sense of how that flexibility worked.

In contrast to some of his philosophically inclined contemporaries, men like Yedaiah Bedersi, Estori HaParḥi, and David Caslari, Reuben's life is a mystery. He is mentioned perhaps once in the legal literature and seems not to have been a scholar of any note.[2] Modern scholars have barely noticed him, although Simon Schwarzfuchs has argued that a curious rabbinic query concerning ascetic practices was authored by Reuben's son.[3] Nonetheless, Reuben's hymns were known and remained popular in southern France and northern Africa for many years.[4] One poem concludes a mid-fifteenth-century prayer book owned by a Jewish merchant in Carpentras.[5] Another, perhaps by Reuben, perhaps by his grandson, appears in a fast-day liturgy in the Carpentras rite copied in 1389 in neighboring Orange.[6] Nearly four dozen *teḥinot*, or penitential hymns, survive in the *Seder haTamid*, a 1767 liturgy from Avignon; a similar collection appears in a liturgy from Algiers copied about 1600 by a scribe named Aaron Azubib.[7] Now in the Staats- und Universitätsbibliothek in Hamburg, MS Cod. Heb. 134 alternates Reuben's hymns with those of a later author, Simon b. Zemaḥ Duran, one of several hundred Majorcan Jews who fled the terrible pogroms of 1391 to North Africa.

In liturgical collections like Hamburg MS Cod. Heb. 134 or the later *Seder Tamid*, the historical memories of discrete communities and events are fused into a shared and seamless past.[8] Certainly, that is one of liturgy's functions. The result, even for treatments of historical incidents, is a warping of "linear" history to comport with a mythical, cyclical time.[9] The liturgical poems discussed in this chapter, like the secular and philosophical poetry we have already explored, still enlist the past in order to make sense of a present characterized by instability, loss, and dislocation. But, unlike the philosophers' poetic commemorations, they do so for a diverse community. Their goal is not to guide individual readers to enlightenment or refined analysis, but to reinforce the affective bonds that keep a community intact. Consequently, the "memory" captured in liturgical verse must be dynamic, even as it invokes an idealized and nostalgic past.

Comtadin Jews, who received a final pre-emancipation shuffling with the partial expulsions of the late sixteenth century, had developed a distinctive liturgy.[10] The Jewish communities in these cities were small enough that print liturgies were economically impractical for a long time; the *Seder haTamid* represented a first attempt to produce a local liturgy from an Avignon printing house. The timing is poignant. A little more than twenty years later, when the French Revolution marked the end of papal rule in the Comtat Venaissin, many of its Jews dispersed into wider France and their unique traditions gradually dwindled and disappeared. Even at that late date, however, a residual sense of historical continuity was cultivated by several families whose roots lay in the medieval past, and shaped by a unique Jewish dialect, liturgy, and musical traditions. That blend of elements fused and sustained a regional Jewish identity.[11]

Likewise, the experience and memory of expulsion represented by MS Hamburg 134 turns us to a rich cultural setting, one little explored by scholars for whom the shores of Africa all too often mark the final chapter of their European stories. On the contrary, in keeping with recent studies that emphasize regional affinities and cultural exchange around the Mediterranean, I am suggesting here that the story of Provençal Jews, through their descendants in Catalonian lands, belongs to the same greater context as that of later fourteenth- and fifteenth-century exiles from Catalonia to the Maghreb. In this context, Maghrebi Jews, particularly the "Sephardi" and "Provenzali" exiles, defiantly clung to—and, in a sense, created—a European identity and past.[12]

The contrast between the two expulsion paths traced by Reuben b. Isaac's

hymns, first into the Comtat Venaissin and then into Africa, thus testifies to
the ways in which local historical conditions shaped the transmission of past
experience and the contours that it would acquire in public memory. At the
same time, some of the distinctive features of the rich poetic traditions of
Maghrebi Jews derive from Provençal conventions and preserve this trajectory
of emigration. Their common heritage is illustrated even in the arrangement
of the petitionary hymns that, including Reuben's, form the corpus discussed
here. All the hymns in MS Hamburg 134 and in the *Seder haTamid*, which
are relatively short, were chanted, or sung, in petitionary liturgies recited on
(most) Mondays and Thursdays. They are arranged to accompany the scriptural reading (parashah) for each week. Some years ago, Ephraim Hazan
noted this unusual method of arrangement, which he concluded must be an
original innovation of North African Jewish writers.[13] However, the same arrangement characterizes the poems in the Comtat liturgy, suggesting that the
format originates in Provence.[14]

Most likely, Elie Crémieu, the eighteenth-century editor of the *Seder
haTamid*, knew nothing of the Rashbatz's *tehinot*, and if he did, he did not
think of them as part of a Provençal Jewish repertoire. He mingled Reuben's
tehinot with compositions of earlier and venerated Provençal and Spanish
Jewish poets like Levi al-Tabban and Zechariah HaLevi.[15] Like the many sev-
enteenth- and eighteenth-century manuscript liturgies upon which he drew,
Crémieu's liturgy also incorporates the works of later local poets who commemorated more recent events. In some cases, the pre-1306 poems shed light
on the way Reuben himself could recycle images and phrases from the repertoire that he had inherited. In others, the *Seder haTamid*'s use of Reuben's
poems can be fruitfully compared with the alternative arrangement in the
Algerian liturgy. An example will illustrate the point.

The last of Reuben's poems contained in Hamburg MS 134 is a prayer
for rain. This is a familiar topic in penitential liturgies, and the composition
here launches a series of hymns for relief from drought and plague.[16] "Adonai rokhev shamayim" (O God Who rides the heavens) describes starving
animals and the ruin of crops, vineyards and pastures, a time when "the
poor and needy / seek water and plead" (v. 7ab). These conditions assuredly
affected Provence as well as the Maghreb from time to time, but the *Seder
haTamid* does not preserve this poem, which disappeared from Provençal
Jewish memory. The reason may lie in the exceptional weather conditions
that assailed parts of Europe in the early years of the fourteenth century. We
know, for instance, that the decree of expulsion issued in 1306 was revoked,

briefly, in 1315 and that a few thousand exiled Jews decided to risk a return to French lands. It was a gamble they lost, in part because of the difficulties that awaited them at "home," culminating in a new expulsion in 1322.[17] The first three years of their tenuous return were, moreover, years of unrelenting rain from the Pyrenees north and east. The terrible rains and ruined harvests associated with the "great famine" of northern European affected the region around Montpellier as well.[18] Even if Languedocian Jews did bring Reuben's rain hymn back with them, they would have had no need for it.[19] In this case, the weather, and the proportions of tragedy it soon assumed, may have guaranteed the "forgetting" of Reuben's poem.

Yet other clues and allusions, literary as well as historical, create a web of linkages among the poems preserved, recited, and sometimes forgotten by Jews in the Comtat and Algerian communities. Some are half-buried and others may be lost to us for now or forever. But these divergent traditions also clarify what is singular or common between them, and hence some of the complex roles they played in the construction and preservation of communal memories. So it behooves us to untangle their stories. First, what can we reconstruct of the expulsion of Montpellier's Jews in 1306 and the life of exiles in the papal states of the Comtat Venaissin? Second, how is that experience preserved among those of their descendants who fled the violence of 1391 for Algiers and northern Africa? Finally, what do the respective liturgical traditions received by Algerian and Comtat Jews tell us about the reconstitution of expulsion memories for later use?

In 1306, the great concentration of the Jewish population under French rule was in the south. In general, Jews fleeing from the northern and central regions of the royal domain faced terrible journeys to safety. Small groups reached the Franche-Comté or Flanders, the Rhineland, Lorraine, and present-day Switzerland, often continuing on their way eastward.[20] As noted in Chapter 2, the journey to safety for southern Jews was far easier. Refugees from the eastern stretches of Languedoc headed into Provence, the Savoy, the Dauphiné, or Orange and the papal Comtat Venaissin. Those in the southwest turned to Provence and to the Spanish kingdoms of Aragon (including Catalonia and Majorca), and Navarre. As far as we can tell, their Jewish hosts were at least initially eager to offer help and to pay the entry fees demanded by their kings and municipalities for taking in the refugees. In many cases, after a period of dependence on their hosts, French Jews moved out into small neighboring towns and villages, establishing tiny communities where, prior to 1306–7, none had been attested.[21]

The situation of the Jews in Montpellier was unique. Like Perpignan, Montpellier was ruled by James II of Majorca, the uncle of King James II of Aragon. But the lord of Montpellier was also a vassal to Philip IV of France and could not ultimately halt the implementation of Philip's decree in that city. Negotiations between James and Philip delayed the expulsion of Montpellier Jews an additional three months, until October 1306.[22] While some Montpellier Jews turned east toward the Comtat Venaissin, many more headed south and west to Majorcan lands (including Perpignan) and Catalonia. Although, relatively speaking, the city lay near lands of potential refuge, the routes to reach those lands were not necessarily direct. The city lacked a real port and the Capetians had been gradually pushing sea traffic toward the nearby French city of Aigues-Mortes.[23] A Catalonian boycott of Majorcan ports was launched in the summer of 1306 and blocked water routes from Montpellier to Catalonia.[24] Moreover, by the time Montpellier Jews began their journey, refugees from cities under direct Capetian rule would have preceded them, and their arrival added to the burdens of Jewish communities already struggling with the consequences of their hospitality.

The poet Reuben ben Isaac was among the Montpellier exiles. For contemporary and later readers, his poems drew haunting images of a community in exile and pursued relentlessly by foes. Biblical phrases blend evocatively into depictions of medieval experience. Here, finally, are the affective echoes of dislocation and trauma. Israel (i.e., the Jewish people) is dispossessed and plundered, stripped of her property and lands, her mansions and sanctuaries. She is destitute, staggering, weak and despondent, and she is always wandering, in cold and frost, wandering to and fro in a land not hers:

אהים ואֵרֵד בשיחי / כי נגרשתי מבית מנוחי / ואלֵךְ מדחי אל דחי /
ירדוף אויב נפשי.

ואבקש מנוס ואין / ועל ההרים אשא עין / עזרי יבא מאין /
להחיות את נפשי?

(I am distraught and cry out
For I have been expelled from my place of rest
And I fall lower and lower.
The enemy pursues my life. [Ps. 143:3]

I seek shelter but there is none

I lift my eyes to the hills
From where shall my help come
To save my life? [Gen. 19:19])[25]

Tormented and helpless, the Jews are targeted by bullies, and onlookers delight in their misery. Israel is a dove who finds no place to rest her feet, or a
partridge chased from its nest.[26] More frequently, she is like sheep with no
shepherd or pasture, sheep that are lost, or worse, forsaken:

ה׳ רועה נאמן / עדרך נפוץ בצפון ותימן.

תועה כשה לא בקשת / על מי נטשת / מעט הצאן?

(God, O Faithful Shepherd
    Your flock is scattered north and south
Like a lost lamb You did not look for.
    To whom have You abandoned these few sheep?)[27]

One poem alludes specifically to Philip IV, whose anti-Jewish policies were
extended to southern Jews in the two decades preceding the expulsion:

ה׳ רוחי חובלה / בעלות צרי מעלה מעלה

ומלכותו בכל משלה / ואין עוזר לישראל.

(God, my spirit was broken
    When my foe rose higher and higher
And his kingdom ruled over all
    And there was none to help Israel.)[28]

Other poems refer to the financial dependence of the refugees on their hosts,
perhaps to forms of debt slavery. In the Algerian rite, "Adonai, refe' sheva-
reiha" (God, heal her fractures) is assigned to parashat Emor (Lev. 21:1–24:23);
in the Comtat cycle, it appears for parashat Mattot (Num. 30:2–32:42). The
Jewish liturgical calendar begins with Rosh Hashanah in the autumn, and
the scriptural cycle recommences with Genesis 1 a few weeks later. Leviticus
and Numbers are not read until spring or early summer. Tagged by its biblical citations to these readings, Reuben's poem could not have been recited
before the late spring or summer of 1307, when the despair—and debt—of
the refugees must have been acute. The poem's protagonist is a woman who

has sinned and whose "father" turns a deaf ear to her pleas for help. Reuben weaves together images of Israel as a woman who has failed to fulfill a vow with images of a woman who has been raped and who cried in vain for help (Deuteronomy 22, but a theme evoked also in the reading from parashat Mattot). The poem echoes with allusions to financial debt and to grieving and broken families:

ה' רפא שבריה כי מטה / עדתך ירדה מטה / ומיום גלותה לא שקטה
ראוה צרים / השיגוה בין המצרים / קולה כמבכירה תרים /
והחריש לה אביה.

אסירת שבי מבית כלאה / אליך עין נושאה / ולרחמיך קוראה
צעקה ואין מושיע לה / אהליבה ואהלה / להשיבה תוך אהלה /
מאן ימאן אביה.

(O God, heal her fractures, for Your community
Totters and goes down. [Ps. 60:4 = RSV 60:2]
From the day she was exiled, she has not known peace.

Foes pursue her
And overtake her in the midst of her pangs.
She raises her voice like a woman in labor
But her father is silent. [Num. 30:5]

Bound in captivity, from her prison,
She raises her eyes to You
And calls for Your mercy.

She cries out, but no one saves her [Deut. 22:24, 27]
Ohalibah and Ohalah![29]
Her father refuses [Exod. 22:16]
To restore her to her dwelling.[30])

Reuben's vignettes of exile were cherished by southern French Jews, perhaps many originally from Montpellier, who settled in the papal lands of the Comtat Venaissin. There, too, the Jews would know trouble and occasionally dislocation, but to a far lesser degree than that experienced in nearby lands. Only the Shepherds' Crusade, in the early 1320s, unleashed significant anti-

Jewish violence; it was followed by a partial expulsion in 1322.[31] Not until the French annexation of Provence in 1484 do conditions seriously worsen. But even the general expulsion of the Jews from Provence in 1500 and from Orange in 1505 did not affect Comtadin Jews, who retained their rights to residence until the expulsions of 1569 and 1593.[32] Those expulsions, the first of which exempted Avignon, sent the exiles into nearby Marseilles and Orange, and there are signs of their straggling return in the following decades.[33] With a brief interlude of French rule in the early eighteenth century, the Comtat remained under papal control until the French Revolution; at that time, the Jewish quarter (*carrière*) of Carpentras, the largest of the Comtat communities, numbered approximately a thousand Jewish inhabitants, many of whom, like their counterparts in Avignon, L'isle, and Cavaillon, willingly departed the lands they had called home.[34]

The oldest copy of any of Reuben's poems is preserved in a prayer book made for Haim de Cavaillon, a wealthy Carpentras Jewish merchant, sometime between 1447 and 1455.[35] The poem, "Adonai, rabbu mi-se'arot roshi" (God, I have more troubles than hairs on my head), must have been an early favorite—it holds a place of honor following the traditional Jewish martyrology, "Eleh ezkerah," found in Sephardic liturgies for the Ninth of Av. This is the only one of Reuben's poems to survive in three copies. "Adonai rabbu mi-se'arot roshi" is designated for the Fast of Gedaliah, commemorated on the third of Tishri in approximately September. It also alludes to familiar themes, the plunder of houses of worship, a swift and angry foe, harsh labor and suffering, and the desire for vengeance. Biblical allusions sound a richer story. The opening verse, for instance, cites Ps. 69:5, which reads in full "those who hate me for no reason are more than the hairs on my head" (רבו משערות ראשי שונאי-חינם). Rashi's gloss comments, "they hate me because I won't accept their faith" and remarks upon the need to bribe harassing authorities. A later allusion to Jezebel's plot to steal Nabath's vineyard for the king might have evoked equally strong, and recent, memories for listeners in Reuben's lifetime, who could recall the loss of their own lands and vineyards.

The story of Cincinnati's HUC MS 396 intersects sharply with a rare moment of violence in the later history of Carpentras Jews, an uprising in 1460 instigated by a disgruntled notary who exploited the hostility and resentment of peasants and citizens indebted to Jewish lenders. As I have described elsewhere, this uprising led to the sack of the Jewish quarter and assaults on Jewish property and homes outside the quarter as well, notably the home of Haim de Cavaillon. Haim, however, was not there, but in Rome seeking the repeal of new anti-Jewish legislation; his prayer book must have accompanied him, or it would most likely not have survived.[36]

Despite their claims to continuity, the Comtadin Jewish communities were a blend of Jews from different regions, customs, and languages, mingled over the centuries by forced and voluntary emigrations. Expulsions and anti-Jewish violence brought them northern French and Languedocian Jews expelled in 1306, 1322, and 1394, Catalonian Jews fleeing the pogroms of 1391 and Spanish Jews expelled in 1492, Jews expelled from Provence in 1485 and 1498, from Lunel in 1500 and Orange in 1505. In the Comtat itself, the Jews were expelled from Carpentras in 1269 and 1322, and from the wider region in 1569 and 1593.[37]

For these successive audiences, liturgical songs offered a coherent past and a meaningful present, in which their own difficulties marked one length of the long road to redemption. Reuben's biblical allusions also made his hymns powerful vehicles for the shaping of communal memory; when performed, their rhythmic and melodic traditions undoubtedly did as well.[38] Again, this was memory in which the past was intentionally unmoored from specificity.

Reuben's wistful typology served generations of Comtadin Jews. It took a second route as well, when the descendants of some of those Jews in Catalonia and Majorca fled the violence of 1391 for Algiers. There, Reuben's poems were refit to new settings quickly, as the format of MS Hamburg 134 attests. Let us look now at this second path into exile.

Of the hundred hymns in MS Hamburg 134, forty-nine are Reuben's, thirty-four are by Simon b. Zemaḥ Duran, and the rest by a scattering of authors. Simon b. Zemaḥ, or the "Rashbatz," has long been considered the towering authority of Majorcan and Spanish Jews in exile. He was descended from Provençal Jews, some of whom migrated to Majorca early in the century, where Simon was born in 1361. Simon's father, Zemaḥ, or Astruc, had inherited considerable wealth from his maternal grandfather, Judah Desfils (known also as Bongue de Mora); Astruc's mother was related to one of the most famous scholarly families of Jewish Provence, that of the Ralbag (Gersonides). Simon studied in Majorca and in Aragon, eventually marrying the daughter of his teacher in Teruel, Jonah de Maistre, a grandson of Gerondi and the Ramban (Naḥmanides).[39] A scholar and rabbi, Simon practiced some form of medicine, perhaps surgery, in Palma de Majorca.[40] The frenzy of anti-Jewish violence that swept Aragon and Majorca in 1391 left almost a third of Majorca's eight hundred Jews dead, and those, like the Rashbatz, who had the money to flee, spent most of what they had to do so.[41]

Like most of those who fled, Simon chose Algiers as his destination. Commercial ties and kinship with the small Jewish community in Algiers made this port city an obvious choice for Majorcan exiles. In 1391, its Jewish community was not the largest in North Africa; Geniza records from the previous century suggest a greater Jewish presence in Morocco, under Merinid rule.[42] Yet in 1391, Algiers and nearby Tlemcen received the lion's share of Majorcan Jews, while others (from Majorca and Aragon) spread along the coastal cities under Merinid and Zayanid control (roughly corresponding to modern Morocco and Algeria).[43] The third great Maghrebi kingdom, known as Ifriqiyya, with its capital in Tunis, was under Hafsid control. Unlike the Merinid and Zayanid rulers, which courted commercial relationships with Aragon and Castile, the Hafsid rulers had turned their backs on the Iberian kingdoms to develop trading ties with Italy.[44] They do not seem to have taken in many 1391 Jews. In contrast, from the thirteenth to the early sixteenth century, Tunis absorbed large numbers of Spanish Muslims and Moriscos as refugees. In those areas where Muslim Andalusian émigrés thrived, their presence may have inhibited the absorption of Jewish refugees with similar skills.[45]

Sweeping generalizations are, of course, unwise. The movement of Muslims and Jews between the Iberian Peninsula and northern Africa cannot be tidily captured in a simple narrative. Muslim emigration from the Iberian Peninsula into other Islamic lands began as early as the eleventh century and continued through the period we are bracketing here. It is helpful to remember, too, that for many years Muslims fleeing areas reconquered by Christian kings could find refuge right on the peninsula, in lands still under Muslim rule. Over the fourteenth and fifteenth centuries, in a curious analogy to the role played by Provence for French Jews, these shrinking zones welcomed the exiles of different principalities and traumas. At the same time, throughout all this period, the level of cultural exchange between Andalusian and Maghrebi cities was high.[46] Even when it was illegal, emigration increasingly turned Andalusian Muslims to Maghrebi lands.[47]

Ironically, the same Spanish rulers who ejected their Jews continued to tolerate Jewish commercial activity along the Maghrebi coast, and eventually even deeper down into the sub-Sahara. A small Jewish courtier class, always composed of the descendants of "Andalusi" exiles, found privilege and wealth in trade and diplomatic service to Muslim and Christian kings on either side of the Mediterranean.[48] Over the same years, Iberian armies struggled to gain control of important coastal cities of the Maghrebi kingdoms, and their periodic successes, such as in Oran and Bougie, inevitably spelled disaster for their Jewish inhabitants.[49] Thus, Jewish life, particularly along the coasts and Saharan trade routes, remained precarious, and local episodes of Muslim violence (rooted in economic resentment more than religious intolerance) also destabilized and terrorized individual communities.

In the immediate aftermath of 1391, however, the Jewish exiles in Algiers were able to settle and adapt. Like Iberian Muslim émigrés to the Maghreb, Jewish newcomers encountered some hostility from their new coreligionists.[50] The rabbinic correspondence documents a variety of conflicts over *shehita* (ritual slaughter), raisin versus grape wine, barefoot prayer in the synagogue, and polygamy. New ordinances issued in 1394 (redacted by the Rashbatz himself) sought to resolve discrepancies in inheritance and marital laws, but the signs of integration are hard to find.[51] Indeed, parallel liturgical traditions emerged quickly, along with separate synagogues and often separate neighborhoods for the *megorashim* (exiles) and *toshavim* (residents). European and Muslim travelers and writers through the early modern and modern periods also noted the distinctive clothing of the *megorashim*, whose beret or chaperon emphasized a "Spanish" or "Andalusi" mode of dress, in contrast to the local turban of the *toshav*.[52] Similarly, the elaborate wedding dress of the brides among the *megorashim* continued to attract comment for centuries.[53]

MS Hamburg 134 testifies to the incorporation of 1306 memory into a web of later traumas, and Simon b. Zemah's poems carry Reuben's forward into a new world in more ways than one.[54] Their language is more "modern"—in this case, denser and more opaque—in keeping with the grandiose style of late Spanish Jewish writers. Against this baroque language, the lyricism of Reuben's hymns stands in elegant simplicity; his striking purity of tone, evoking an earlier Andalusian style, surely sounded archaic to late fourteenth-century ears. Reuben's simple, affective imagery also confronts a new reality in MS Hamburg 134, where his scattered sheep and partridges face Simon's lions and wild beasts, allusions to famine, sickness, and human treachery.[55]

As befitting a scholar-rabbi, Simon emphasized his role as a religious authority. His penitential theology and setting are abundantly in evidence, and his hymns frequently stress ritual observance, piety, and prayer. Thus, in the hymn for parashat Vayera (Gen. 18:1–22:24), the speaker of the poem assures himself (and his audience, for whom he speaks) that forgiveness always awaits those who sincerely repent:

על חסיד ונבר / חסד אל גבר / עתיד ועבר
ואם רשעתי / ולפניו פשעתי / גם אנכי ידעתי / כי אם ה' חסד.

(For the pious and pure / God's love is great / future and past.
And if I have done wickedly before Him / I also surely know / that with
God there is love.)[56]

Even the biblical Abraham (the "righteous one") is praised, not just for his
willingness to sacrifice his son, but for his synagogue attendance:

צדיק באמונתו שקד / על דלתות נפקד / ובנו יחידו עקד

(In his faith, the Righteous One watched/ waited at the doors / and
bound his son.)[57]

Therefore, of course, his descendants should do no less, as for example in the
hymn "Adonai, shafakhti ṣiḥa" (God, I have poured forth speech):

נא עמך תשמרנו / מן הדור זו [!] תצרנו / תברך צדיק תעטרנו /
כצנה רצון.

בבית תפלתך בוחר / בא יבא לא יאחר / יום יום טוב שוחר /
יבקש רצון.

(God, please guard us, Your people. / Protect us from this generation, /
bless the righteous, / and cover us with favor like a shield.[58]
He chooses Your house of prayer, / he surely attends and does not tarry.
/ Daily he seeks what is good / and requests [Your] favor.)[59]

This poem, which entreats God to "extend Your favor to father and son" (v. 9),
was designated for recitation on Monday of parashat Emor (Lev. 21:1–24:3).
For Thursday of that same week, we find Reuben's hymn, "Adonai, refe' she-
vareiha" (God, heal her fractures), discussed earlier. Where Reuben's poem
had developed the image of Israel as a spurned daughter, this metaphor for
the community is now complemented by Simon's image of male continuity.
Simon's supplications also reflect his long exposure (direct or diluted) to the
philosophical currents of his time. "Adonai, atah yada'ta yitzri" (God, You

know that my inclination), designated for parashat ḥaye-Sarah (Gen. 23:1–
25:18), concentrates entirely on the contrast between the man who gives in to
his "evil inclination" (*yetzer haraʿ*, here truncated simply as the *yetzer*) and the
wise man who, with God's help, resists the will to do evil:

ה' אתה ידעת יצרי / כי הוא מלאך אכזרי. עומד על ימיני לשברי /
גבור כארי / לא ישוב מפני כל.

(God, You know that my inclination / is a cruel guide. / It stands to my
right to destroy me. / Strong as a lion / it will not back down for
anything.)[60]

Here we see language that we might expect from a student of philosophy:

עמל הכסיל תיגענו / עינו פקח ואיננו / מקומו עוד לא יכירנו. . . .
ואשרי הגבר / יצרו שובר / ושכלו גובר.

(The fool's labor will wear him out / he blinks and it is gone / his world
will forget him. . . .
But happy is the man / who breaks his inclination / and whose intellect
triumphs.)[61]

Considering his experience, it is not surprising that Simon b. Zemaḥ's hymns
refer bitterly to Christian foes, even directly to Christian attempts to convert
the Jews. Ephraim Hazan has treated some of this material, with special attention to the supplication "Adonai, sh'vor zeroʿa rasha'" (God, break the arm
of the wicked) and its description of conversionary pressure:[62]

מוכים עבדים / ונוגשים ורודים / בוזזים ושודדים
ופסו אמונינו / ומרוב עונינו / כלינו שנינו / קוה לשלום.
עתק מפיו מוצא / הבל פידהו פצה / עושה אשר ירצה
אויב כמוץ ידפם / יהדפם / ירדפם / יעבור שלום.
והוא מתעקש / להיות לי למוקש / למדיחנו מבקש
אומר לי לך עבוד אל זר / ויקם לך אמר תגזר / ובו תהיה נעזר /
וישם לך שלום.

(The servants are beaten, / and attackers and tyrants / plunder and
despoil.

Our faithful ones have vanished, / and because of our many sins / our
    Years come to an end: / We looked for peace—[63]
[The foe] speaks haughtily / he utters nonsense / he does what he wants.
Like chaff, the enemy drives [the Jews] away / repels them / pursues
    them / And passes on safely.[64]
Moreover, he persists / in making me stumble. / He wants to cast us off.
He tells me: "Worship the alien god! / If you decide on the matter, it
    will be established for you. / You will be helped by this / and it will
    go well with you.")[65]

A number of other poems enlist similarly harsh and polemical language. In
"Adonai, naḥalatkha kemo harah" (God, Your inheritance is like a pregnant
woman), the oppressor is a "nation of warriors," haughty, untruthful, and
idolatrous. To this foe, Simon declares, "You have cast Truth to the earth /
and it disappears like one dead. / Then you destroy all who once knew it"
(v. 8). Nor is Algiers, the new land of refuge, described generously; the Jews
have been "sold to the Ishmaelites" and debased:

שכנתי עם אהלי קדר / לא פאר ולא הדר / הכביד נחשתי בעדי נדר.

(I dwelled among the tents of Kedar
Without splendor or glory
He has put heavy chains upon me, and walled me about.)[66]

Thus, the supplications in MS Hamburg 134 suspend their users between two
moments: the expulsion of 1306 and the terrors of 1391, or, alternatively, the
flight from Christian lands to uneasy refuge in the lands of Islam. Together,
these two poles of experience create a third kind of time, cyclic and redemp-
tive, whose clock ticks steadily toward the messianic end of history. In the
cradle of that construct, the assurance of these Jews in their cultural superiority returns more or less intact. When the next large wave of exiles joins
the descendants of these Arago-Majorcan émigrés, that sense of superiority
triumphs: not only do the 1492 exiles cling fiercely to their "Spanish" identity
in the Maghreb, but in addition to the distinctive markers of clothing, liturgy, residence, and food, many refuse to intermarry with local families or to
speak their language. Notably, the same response characterized Muslim and
Morisco émigrés to the Maghreb.
    What are the consequences of this conflation of histories and texts?

First, the successive dislocations that were the catalyst for emigration into the Maghreb contributed to a major reconfiguration of Jewish identity. The effects of this reconfiguration were felt both among the direct victims of dispossession and among the local communities that received, resisted, and ultimately succumbed to their cultural, economic, and religious hegemony. Second, this process of Jewish "identity reorganization" was not a finite response to catastrophe, but ongoing and fluid. It was also dynamically related to the parallel process—equally ongoing and fluid—of psychological and physical regrouping that characterized the integration of Muslim and Morisco exiles from the Iberian Peninsula in the Maghreb.

Even though the secondary sources do not treat Jewish and Muslim expulsion together, they nonetheless inscribe a double narrative of exile and adaptation that in many ways is really one. Both versions retain traces of local resistance to an immigrant population that, Muslim and Jewish, was aware of its technological and cultural sophistication in areas of interest to the Merinid and Zayanid sultans. In the case of the Muslims (and later, Moriscos), it may be that their early saturation of coveted positions in fiscal administration and medicine served as a barrier to Jewish specialists in these fields.[67] If the Rashbatz did not work as a physician (or surgeon) in Algiers, it was not because Algiers possessed no physicians or interest in medical knowledge, although Algiers was certainly not a cosmopolitan consumer of such knowledge in the way that Palma, the major Catalan cities, or even Tlemcen, were. More probably, Jewish professionals such as Simon b. Zemaḥ Duran had no access to the more limited venues in which this knowledge was purveyed. Moreover, the educational system under Merinid rule, as it increasingly relied on a network of *medersas* and not on the centralized model of the European university, prevented by its very nature Jewish acquisition of the little science that was taught.[68]

Similarly, in the "culture wars" internal to Jewish life in the years following the 1391 expulsion, the signs of tension between the *megorashim* and the *toshavim* reflect both economic competition between a relatively stable but technologically backward local population and a desperately driven immigrant population with a marked edge in terms of technical knowledge and financial and commercial expertise. The exiles' cultural ideal ultimately dominates both Jewish groups, and indeed it has been suggested that the lines between the two were rarely clear.[69] By the mid-sixteenth century, a past "Andalusian-ness" dominated Jewish Maghrebi identity, much as the cultural ideal of "Andalus" had permeated Muslim Maghrebi culture, from architecture to food to clothing to music and poetry.[70] As late as the twentieth century, the performance of classic Andalusian music was still associated with Jewish musicians in the Maghreb, and it is a ubiquitous musical taste among Moroccan Jewish emigrants to Israel.[71]

What is fascinating is that two parallel exile experiences should follow the same wishful trajectory in reconstituting themselves in the image of the world that had rejected them. The irreducible "difference" of Iberian Jews and Muslims had demanded their expulsion. Nonetheless, it was "Andalusian-ness" or "Spanishness" that the exiles of both communities marshaled as the primary element of their identity in North African exile. The case of clothing is instructive. Although Muslim practice (*ghiyār*) imposed a distinctive garb on subject non-Muslims, it was unevenly enforced and relied largely upon the use of color (yellow) for Jews, and for Christians occasionally turbans, large sleeves, or a distinctive belt.[72] In contrast, the "Andalusian" dress of the exiles—the red berets and bridal gowns of the *megorashim*, the vivid blues and aristocratic robes of former Moriscos—was not part of this code but adopted voluntarily to distinguish its wearers from local coreligionists.

In fact, the public display of "Andalusi" fashion did not reconstitute lost reality. Jews did not appear publicly in Christian Spain without some mark or garment distinguishing them as Jews.[73] Usually, this referred to over-wear, a hooded capelet or tunic with the "Jewish badge," a yellow patch or circle of yellow, attached. For Muslims, the confused state of the scholarship regarding the distinguishing badges or marks in the lands of the Reconquista has its origins partly in the language of the Fourth Lateran Council, and later the *Siete Partidas*, which do not specify the use of emblems for Muslim residents.[74] Nonetheless, Ferrer i Mallol convincingly documents the use of a Muslim jacket and haircut throughout this period. As she repeatedly observes, the rigor of both policies and enforcement varied greatly during the fourteenth century in Aragon.[75] The imposition of a distinctive Muslim (male) haircut, called the *garseta*, is mentioned as early as the 1293 decree of James II and as late as the mid-fifteenth century. Although the term is ambiguous, it seems to refer to a cut that is cropped short in the back and long in the front, perhaps with bangs, alternatively with a part down the middle.[76]

It is hard to imagine that Muslim émigrés to the Maghreb imported these elements of their Andalusian past. Likewise, Jewish arrivals to North Africa were unlikely to flaunt a Jewish badge. The display of "Andalusi" or "Spanish" origins in the clothing of Maghrebi exiles therefore broadcast an (outer) identity that they had not lived while actually in Aragon, Castile, or ultimately, Spain. Even their clothing proclaims an idealized memory of "home."

The association of "Andalusian" style with the Iberian exiles to the Maghreb lingered into modern times. In some cases, the garb in question may actually have had a secondary derivation through Turkish (Ottoman) conduits. Yet the semiotic assignment of "Andalusi" value to Jewish and Muslim groups identified with Spanish origins—by themselves as well as by the Turks—is fascinating.[77] Marçais describes the ubiquitous wearing of the turban among Algerian Muslims in the fourteenth century and after, except for those "Musulmans d'Andalousie" who refused to wear it.[78] Likewise, the beret (or *qalansawa*, or *chéchia*) was not only associated with Algerians of Andalusian descent but was coded by color to indicate whether the wearer was a Muslim (red or green) or Jew (yellow).[79] Women's robes also marked their wearers confessionally by color (yellow for Jewish women, blue for Christian), according to Islamic practice, but the style of the garments even in modern (nineteenth-century) times was still derivable from "Spanish" precedents.[80] In other words, Jews and Muslims from Andalusia and their descendants *wanted* to distinguish themselves from their Maghrebi-born neighbors. The desire to do so survived into the Ottoman period, where it was also expressed in the adoption of Turkish, or even European, clothing elements (an affinity for the tie among Jewish men) as an additional sign of distinction.[81]

Because of the appreciation of Maghrebi sultans for the "finer" aesthetics of a lost Muslim Spain, the physical landscape of the exiles was reconfigured in the image of home as well. The taste for Andalusian architecture and architectural motifs in the North African kingdoms dates to the ninth century, but flourished throughout the fourteenth. In Tlemcen, the sultan 'Abd al-Wadid imported architects and craftsmen from Granada to design palaces, houses, and gardens in the Andalusian style (ironically, Christian prisoners provided the labor). Among the Merinid sultans in Morocco, the "sumptuous art of Granada" was considered the height of style.[82] The Hafsid rulers in Tunis also encouraged the physical transformation of their landscape, to which over the next few centuries "the Andalusians" restored long-vanquished olive groves, importing fruit and almond trees, viticulture, and Spanish-style irrigation.[83]

But this is not all. Ibn Khaldun describes the dazzling influence of Andalusian émigrés in Tunis, many originating in Seville (retaken by the Christians in 1248), cultivated by the Hafsid ruler Abu Zakariyya and his son. During the reigns of both men and long into the next century, Andalusian exiles rose to coveted positions of financial and political administration—again, perhaps a reason these routes were largely blocked to Jews.[84] In contrast, Jewish courtiers appeared under the Merinid sultans from the fourteenth to the sixteenth century, some amassing astonishing wealth and power. However, their grip on power was notably tenuous, rarely lasting more than a few years, and almost all of them died violently.[85]

The North African journey taken by Reuben's poems illustrates vividly the capacity of liturgical imagination to "remember" a history prior to exile, a history that was simultaneously characterized by comfort and insecurity. Certainly, the wishful recapitulation of the past is not surprising. What is moving is that the imagined past of the exiles (Jewish and Muslim) was one that they had never lived in quite the way they "remembered" doing. On the contrary, a Spanishness from which they were excluded, and the Spain from which they were expelled, became the core of exilic identity in a new world.[86]

The limits of this reconstituted European identity fluctuated among different local communities, and over time and space. Its porous borders may be located also in MS Hamburg 134's shifting views of history. In one, the fragmentary residue of a historical past was blended into a mythic narrative of exile and return.[87] That residue had already been compounded of discrete historical events. Aaron Azubib, the copyist of MS Hamburg 134, preserved a tradition that had already blended the two traumas of 1306 and 1391, and later users of MS Hamburg 134 inherited a polyphonic series of echoes in the hymns preserved in his hand. These poems sounded biblical chords of dispossession, suffering, and the yearning for return, but they also dictated the overtones of subsequent events so that later tribulations harked back to their originary notes.[88] Whether "home" was Jerusalem, Montpellier, Barcelona, or Palma de Majorca was not the point so much as the capacity of the narrative to enfold all subsequent history in a way that made sense of the world and its upheavals. As we have seen, this mythic vision received considerable reinforcement from its pervasiveness among Muslim émigrés as well, and the reification of "Andalusia" in their physical surroundings.

The historical trajectory of MS Hamburg 134 flies forward at the manuscript's end, where a series of hymns for times of drought and plague give way to a special Purim liturgy commemorating the defeat of Charles V at the gates to Algiers in 1540.[89] Other hymns are by survivors of the expulsion of Spanish Jews in 1492, such as Judah Uziel and Naḥman Sanbel.[90] Uziel, who settled in Fez and became one of its two chief rabbis, hosted the messianic pretender, David Reubeni, on his fateful visit to the Maghreb, and Sanbel was among Reubeni's intimates on that journey.[91] Indeed, the story told by MS Hamburg 134 is not so much one of the fragility of exilic identity as it is a record of the attempt to configure that fragility for greater flexibility and use.

The horrifying events of 1306 and 1391 framed a difficult Jewish century in the Comtadin liturgical tradition as well. Between those two great markers lay the years of the Great Famine (1315–22); the Shepherds' Crusade (1320) and expulsion of 1322; the Black Death (1348); and the trend to physical segregation of Jewish communities in Catalonia and the Comtat. The violence that might erupt against vulnerable Jewish communities, even those with a sturdy sense of their entitlement to papal protection, also frames the story of Cincinnati's MS 396, whose owner evaded the terrible attack on the Carpentras *carrière* in the summer of 1460 (Figure 1).

Like the Algerian liturgy, the *Seder haTamid* shifts easily from recyclable tropes of exile and return to a shifting present, sometimes reinforced by romance melodies or texts.[92] The many and late manuscript copies of the Comtat rite found in library collections on both sides of the Atlantic attest to the ongoing incorporation of new poets and commemorative landmarks into Provençal Jewish memory. These later poets, like Gad of Revel or Mordecai Astruc, are largely unknown today. So, too, the poetic commemorations of forgotten crises, from an otherwise unknown attack on the Carpentras *carrière* in 1682 to a famine in 1709, or prayers for the well-being of popes, kings, and princesses, weave an astonishing tale of local meaning.[93] Reuben's poems, chanted by generations of Comtadin Jews, thus traversed worlds in which multiple ways of seeing and remembering jostled each other constantly. Even Haim de Cavaillon's worn prayer book preserves the spirit of a man who could contemplate Reuben's anguished lament, "God, I have more sorrows than hairs on my head," with all its Jobian echoes, and still scribble the details of a commercial transaction beneath the text.

The printed Comtadin liturgy, including the *Seder haTamid*, appeared in the latter half of the eighteenth century, when the Comtadin Jewish communities were in what has been described as a state of cultural decline. Technically, this is beyond the terminus point of this study, but it is illuminating to follow the trajectory of Reuben's poems forward for a moment. The eighteenth-century communities were a curious mix of lively and stubborn personalities representing old and new elites, and provincial and Enlightenment sensibilities. The importation of rabbis from the lands of Ashkenaz implies not only a loss of local learning but a rupture in learned continuity with the local past.[94] In Carpentras, for instance, the eighteenth-century *carrière* was at its most populous, a teetering architectural hodgepodge and (as frequently noted by visitors) plumbing nightmare. In mid-century, the gated Jewish street contained eight hundred souls. This is a strain on housing but hardly a publisher's

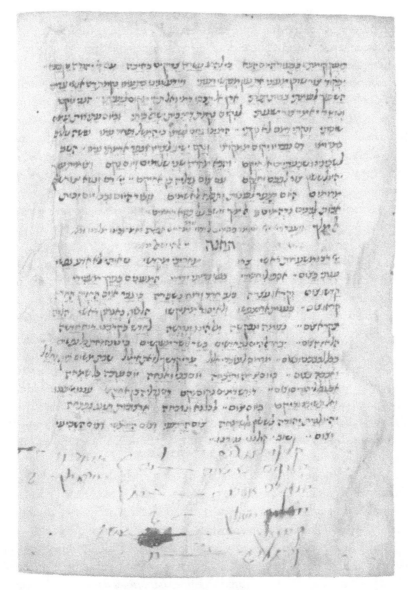

Figure 1. Cincinnati MS HUC 396, Seder kol-haShanah, was copied between 1447 and 1455. The last folio contains the earliest known copy of a liturgical hymn by Reuben b. Isaac. The owner, Haim de Cavaillon, scrawled the details of a business transaction, listing items of clothing and their quantities or costs, across the bottom of the page. Klau Library, Cincinnati; Hebrew Union College–Jewish Institute of Religion.

coveted market, and indeed, as Simon Schwarzfuchs has richly detailed, the attempt to produce a print liturgy was nearly a publishing disaster.[95]

Nonetheless, an initial series of print liturgies did appear, in 1737–62 and representing the liturgical traditions of Carpentras Jews. This series was the labor of Abraham Monteil (or Monteux), of a distinguished local family, who initially undertook the project as a young man and pursued it for decades. After failing to interest publishers in Leghorn and Florence, Monteil found an ally in Hirsh Levi haRofe' in Amsterdam, who not only printed four volumes but authored frequent letters to Monteil's weak-willed backers in Carpentras, taking them to task for depriving him of funds for the job and for subsistence.[96]

Monteil also took an interest (and was enlisted) in the efforts to publish the Avignon rite. With his assistance, Hirsch Levi's Amsterdam press produced the 1763 *Seder haAshmorot* of the Avignon rite, and the 1765 rite for the New Year. In a significant new undertaking, Isaiah Vidal and Mordecai Ventura then printed several works in Avignon, namely, the collection of occasional prayers known as the *Seder haKonteres* (1765) and the daily and Sabbath liturgies with additional local hymns and prayers, the *Seder haTamid* (1767).[97] The latter volume, which contains Reuben's hymns, was edited by the local Carpentras rabbi and teacher, Elie Crémieu—the same Elie Crémieu whose young son, Semé, had been forcibly baptized by a Jewish convert to Christianity in 1762 and taken into clerical custody. The baptism and kidnapping precipitated a series of frantic negotiations with the papal authorities in Rome for Semé's release, which failed to secure the child's return. It can only be imagined with what stern dedication to his task the heartbroken father applied himself to the *Seder haTamid*.[98]

As was true for their North African counterparts, the public, Jewish, identity of Comtadin Jews was also performed, and it was shaped deeply by the physical geography of the *carrière* and the Christian laws that marked them as Jews. Clothing again provides a striking motif, illustrated by the shifting fortunes of the *chapeau jaune* of papal Jews.[99] The yellow badge or circular patch featured in bulls of 1326, 1337, 1459, and 1525 had been emended in 1525 by Paul IV, who substituted a yellow *chapeau ou bonnet* for the (more easily concealed) patch. Over the years, the hat came and went, sometimes metamorphosing into a black hat with a yellow patch, sometimes disappearing nearly entirely, at other times reinstated and vigorously policed.

Whether there is a connection between the *chapeau jaune* of the Comtadin Jews and the yellow and red berets of the Catalonian Jews and Muslims is tempting to consider. It may be more prudent to note the limitation of texts when it comes to suggesting the vivid and sensory world in which people and their poems existed, a world characterized by colors and smells, landscapes and buildings, foods and images, sounds, music, dialects, marketplaces, and cemeteries, the richly symbolic ceremonies that marked births, marriages, and deaths. In that world, liturgy created a special space, in which the seamless fluctuation of mythic and historical time and events could mediate some of the stresses of a world that was learning to oppose secular and sacred in harsher ways.

Thus, the experience of expulsion and resettlement was in the short and long term recuperated by different Jewish communities in distinctive ways. These are reflected in the two textual traditions that I have followed in this chapter, each of which incorporates the poetic memory of 1306 according to its own needs and later experiences. In the next chapter, I turn to another instance of a text that survived among Jews in a Muslim context (in this case, Ottoman) as well as remaining among Comtat Jews. The Esther "romance" of Crescas Caslari also harbors memories of recent expulsion (1306, 1322) and expresses them in both vernacular and Hebrew narratives. Each in its own way illustrates a worldview that testifies to the deep assimilation of scientific and rational values among medically trained Jews. As we saw with Yedaiah's and Joseph Latimi's pantograms, Crescas's romance, the work of another literary physician, obscures history in ways that contrast profoundly with the typological, cyclic, and mythic vision of liturgists like Reuben b. Isaac or Simon b. Zemah Duran.

CHAPTER FOUR

A Proper Diet:
Medicine and History in Crescas Caslari's *Esther*

> *Persisting in his wickedness, he said, [this is] a wretched,*
>   *itinerant people.*
> *Look how they are scattered and separate in every region.*
> *Like strangers in the land, they go from city to city:*
> *Such is this people.*
>   —Crescas Caslari, "Mi kamokha"[1]

THIS CHAPTER TREATS a pair of early fourteenth-century texts by a Jewish physician in Provence. Their author, Crescas (or Israel) Caslari, was probably from the Narbonne region and expelled in 1306.[2] Composed around 1327 in Avignon, Crescas Caslari's two verse narratives recount the biblical story of Esther. One version, in rhymed couplets, is in the vernacular used by Provençal Jews, and the other version is in Hebrew.[3] The Romance version survives in two incomplete fragments, enough to demonstrate a lively adaptation of romance narrative conventions and a sure literary hand. Except as a curiosity, it very quickly faded from sight. The Hebrew version, albeit complete, has had only a slightly more secure footing in history. One manuscript version, dated 1402, survives in an anthology of Purim parodies and hymns copied in a Provençal hand; another appears in the same Cincinnati manuscript, HUC MS 396, that contains the earliest copy of a poem by Reuben b. Isaac, discussed in the preceding chapter. As noted there, HUC MS 396 is dated between 1447 and 1455. (Amazingly, I discovered Crescas's text only by accident while making the final changes to this book.) A third manuscript copy is preserved in an eighteenth-century festival prayer book of the Avignon rite. In the spring of 2005, I discovered a fourth copy, dated 1701 and clearly drawing on the same source as the Avignon liturgy; this copy is also in a Provençal liturgy, now owned by Columbia University in New York. A printed version containing some striking variants appeared in Salonika, on the press of Isaac Jehun, in 1853.[4]

Crescas used the plot of the biblical book of Esther to comment on a number of contemporary concerns, putting into the mouths of familiar characters Christian sentiments (or what Jews believed to be Christian sentiments) on the Jewish minority in their midst, and giving rein to a fantasy of reversal and revenge in lively narrative form.[5] It says something about subsequent history that so many of the specific allusions in this double tale are no longer comprehensible. Indeed, it is not just the fate of isolated details but the fate of Crescas's romance itself that illustrates a recurring theme of this book: the complexity of Jewish identity and memory, built on scaffolding assembled and reassembled over years of dislocation.

Crescas's Purim "romances" testify to the rich and venerable tradition of learned Purim literature from medieval Provence. The surviving illustrations of this literature mark a distinctive adaptation of the liturgical genres found in neighboring Spanish communities. The Hebrew narrative is a variation on a genre of liturgical poetry that flourished among medieval Spanish Jews. The "Mi kamokha" (Who is like you) compositions, generally terse quatrains concluding on a repeating drone word, were inserted into the morning liturgy as part of the *yotzer* cycle.[6] However, in Provence, the form evolved beyond its Andalusian precedents to quasi-autonomous status. The incipit to the Salonika edition indicates that Crescas's text was chanted to the melody of an early exemplar of this type written by the beloved twelfth-century poet Judah HaLevi. Interestingly, HaLevi's "Mi kamokha 'amuqot golah" (Who is like you, deep in Exile) was also a verse narrative of the Purim story. As Fleischer notes, HaLevi's poem relatively long verse length was unusual; this feature made it an attractive model for a narrative poem like Crescas's.[7]

The Salonikan edition, on the other hand, testifies to the displacement of Languedocian and Provençal Jews into the papal territories of the Comtat Venaissin and into Aragon, and later from the Comtat into Spain and from Spain into Ottoman lands.[8] Companion to a number of Ladino Esther "romances," at least one struck the same year by the same printer, Crescas's Hebrew story found a small new audience in modern times.[9] Salonikan Jews, many of them descendants of Provençal, Spanish, and Italian Jews, were also great aficionados of Purim pageantry and form.[10] If this audience could not entirely understand Crescas's allusions to local history and events, they may be excused: as I have already noted, the meaning of those allusions remains largely obscured today as well. Nonetheless, it was Salonikan Jewry that kept this text alive (a fate ultimately eluding its guardians), and it may have played some role in local Purim traditions.

Another set of allusions in these stories is more easily recuperated and sheds a great deal of light on the complex and interlocking worlds of the author and his peers. It was in part the loss of this interlocking existence that made aspects of these texts inscrutable to later readers. The upheavals of the fourteenth century were directly responsible for this loss, culminating in migrations into lands less hospitable to rational inquiry and the opportunities that rationalist affinity had offered a Jewish learned elite. Ultimately, by the late fifteenth century, much of what remained of that elite in the Midi would convert. Nonetheless, it is possible to recover some of the intellectual and cultural concerns that preoccupied Crescas in these texts, and these shed light on the way a rationalist physician might apply his scientific training and methods to historical questions. As we have already seen in the case of Yedaiah Bedersi, the embrace of biblical allegory is one tool beloved of the rationalists. However, the vernacular and Hebrew versions of Crescas's Esther story also cleverly engage a number of contemporary medical theories. The romances thus demonstrate the dissemination of these theories, popular among Christian physicians and their wealthy clients, among a wider community that included Jewish physicians and, presumably, their educated peers.

In the following pages, I treat two medical aspects of Crescas's poems. The first concerns Crescas's "diagnosis" of King Ahashverus as a melancholic whose condition is exacerbated by a volatile temper and abuse of alcohol. A second concern of the story is food, specifically in relation to contemporary notions of therapeutic diet. Among the "six nonnaturals," environmental or behavioral factors widely believed to influence humoral "complexion" (what we might call temperament, or constitution), food and drink achieved special significance in medical theory. Both Crescas's Hebrew and Romance Purim tales reveal the author's commitment to the latest theories of therapeutic diet circulating in his time. The stories also raise concerns about some of the social changes that accompanied the rise of the medieval physician, and the influence of medical models and language on other aspects of daily life. The use of the Esther story as a frame for voicing these concerns is, in fact, consistent with the controversial interest of rationalist Jews in allegory and analogy, and confirms Crescas's membership in a small and elite minority.[11]

As a belletrist, Israel b. Joseph Caslari, or Crescas Caslari, is barely remembered in the annals of Hebrew (or Romance) literature.[12] He is well-known, however, to historians of medicine, who have devoted considerable attention to his translation of an important work on medieval diet, the *Regimen sanitatis* composed for Jaime II of Aragon by Arnau of Vilanova (d. 1311).[13] Arnau, a leading exponent of the "new Galenism" (the integration of classical Greek and Arabic medical texts into medieval Christian theory and practice), was a towering presence on the medical faculty at the University of Montpellier. An extraordinary figure whose clients included popes and kings, Arnau's interests extended beyond medicine to an active (at times, controversial) engagement with the political and theological issues of his day. His theological and political critiques notwithstanding, his medical works commanded the highest respect throughout the century.[14]

It is thus not surprising that Crescas should have been acquainted with Arnau's work. As scholars have shown, Jewish physicians of the early fourteenth century in Spain and Provence were keenly interested in developments in medical theory and practice.[15] Although barred from universities, Jewish physicians benefited from what Luis García Ballester and others have called the "open" system of medical education that operated in parallel to that of the university: by studying privately in groups or alone, Jews (or Muslims, or women) who successfully passed an oral exam were licensed to practice.[16] And, as García Ballester, Lola Ferre, and Luis Feliu have argued in an important essay, Jewish physicians at the turn of the fourteenth century were not merely transmitters of medical knowledge but also purveyors of medical ways of thinking about health and infirmity and how these were produced. As such, they played a vital role in the so-called medicalization of fourteenth-century society, with its reverence for the technical and professional status of the physician, and a willingness to think about questions of public and private well-being in medical terms.[17] For Crescas, those medical terms were those of the intellectual community in the orbit of the famous medical school in Montpellier. Nonetheless, as we will see in the next chapter, Jewish physicians were not invariably committed to the medical positions associated with the scholasticism of their Christian counterparts; the divide between rationalists and traditionalists influenced medical thinking as well as theology.

Unlike his Jewish counterpart, the medieval Christian physician was the product of a university education and training that began with immersion in logic, rhetoric, and natural philosophy before passing to medicine.[18] In contrast, the Jewish physician was the product of two curricular models, one involving the mastery of traditional Jewish learning and texts, and the other following, as much as possible, the university curriculum and its sequence of studies. To some degree, these two models of learning were destined to collide, and so, in fact, they periodically did in Jewish communities of the south, sometimes violently. Nonetheless, the prestige of medicine was high enough in these communities that some form of medical training was always exempted from the traditionalists' bans on "Greek science."[19]

Even if we had no other information about Crescas Caslari, we could assume that his learning included traditional Jewish studies and texts. The world of the Jewish rationalist physicians permitted a rare synthesis of rab-binic and rhetorical expertise, sometimes indulged lightly, sometimes with heavy pedantry, in their literary efforts. Notably, the other known examples of Purim parodies roughly contemporary to Crescas's were also written by or to physicians. The rhetorician Abraham Bedersi wrote a Purim epistle to the physician Abraham b. Caslari in Narbonne; although the epistle is now lost, the introductory letter that accompanied it survives and gives some inkling of the work's parameters.[20] The well-known author, translator, and physi-cian Qalonymos b. Qalonymos also composed a Purim parody while in Italy around 1330; a copy of this work, which concludes with a series of drinking proverbs in Judeo-Provençal, immediately precedes one manuscript version of Crescas's Hebrew romance.[21] The Provençal philosopher and exegete, Levi b. Gerson (Gersonides), produced two Talmudic Purim parodies, the *Megillat Setarim* (Scroll of Secrets) and *Sefer Ḥabaqbuq haNavi'* (The Book of Habak-buk the Prophet).[22] And, a few decades later, the physician Shlomo HaLevi would write another Purim epistle while sitting in prison in London; this rue-ful complaint was addressed to another famed physician, Meir Alguadez.[23]

Medical poetry, at least in Hebrew, was not new, and Crescas surely knew some examples. The satirical portrait of the medical profession penned by Qalonymos b. Qalonymos in his *Even Boḥan* (Touchstone) had its own echoes in the spoofs of doctors and therapeutic diet in the lively rhymed prose nar-ratives of Judah al-Ḥarizi and Joseph ibn Zabara (both men also physicians). At least two well-known poets also composed Hebrew poems that surveyed Galenic theories of humors and diet.[24] Abraham ibn Ezra's "Shim'u na el divre harofe'" (Hearken to the words of the physician) and Shem Tov ibn Falaquera's "Bate Hanhagat haGuf haBari'" (A Verse Regimen for a Healthy Body) and "Bate Hanhagat haNefesh" (A Verse Regimen for the Soul) all attempted to encapsulate Galenic doctrines of humors and diet in elegant verse.[25] As Falaquera noted, perhaps with some exasperation, Hebrew posed a serious challenge to communicating such doctrine in necessary detail.[26] His frustration would be echoed, more prosaically, by any number of Hebrew translators of Latin or Arabic medical works.[27]

Nonetheless, Crescas's Purim "epistles" are unique in exploiting a biblical "romance" for the elaboration of medical motifs and debates. Crescas himself obscured this dimension of his texts by claiming early in the Hebrew tale that the Judeo-Provençal version targeted "children, women, grandchildren, and great-grandchildren" (טף ונשים נין ונכד). Later scholars, including me, easily misread the word *nekhed* (נכד), literally "grandchild," as *nekher* (נכר), or "gentile." We were abetted in this misreading by a desire to see the vernacular embrace this kind of audience, although careful perusal of the manuscripts unanimously confirms the former reading.[28] Thus, Crescas did not compose his vernacular Esther for a mixed audience of Christians and Jews; however, he does say explicitly that the vernacular could reach (Jewish) women and children. Certainly, this is the customary distinction drawn between those medieval Jewish texts written in Hebrew and those written in vernacular Old French, such as Jacob b. Judah's Old French lament for the martyrs of Troyes burned in 1288.[29] The rare survival of macaronic lyrics in Hebrew/Old French and Hebrew/Judeo-Provençal, many of them written for quasi-liturgical events such as circumcisions and weddings, also lends itself to such an interpretation. So, too, vernacular prayer books designed specifically for women reinforce the notion that the use of the vernacular was intended for greater accessibility, across gender, age, educational, and even confessional divides.[30]

Nonetheless, the association of the vernacular with scientific vocabulary also implies the reverse of this argument, so that in some ways the Romance text is also the better suited for a display of specialized and technical knowledge. Crescas's vernacular text may indeed have enjoyed a more diverse audience than its Hebrew analogue, but it does not at all follow that it was uniformly "simpler." Indeed, as we shall see, the comparatively rich resources of the vernacular for describing foods, fabrics, and table manners, as well as legal and courtly *realia*, meant that the vernacular romance would have appealed to medically sophisticated male listeners as well as to women and children.

The *Regimen sanitatis* translated by Crescas was one of Arnau of Vilanova's most popular works; it represented a genre that was both a medieval invention and one widely read in the thirteenth and fourteenth centuries.[31] The classic regimens, such as that of Aldebrandin of Siena for Beatrice of Provence or, in the Islamic world, the regimen composed by Maimonides for the sultan al-Afdal, were custom-tailored by their authors for their prominent clients; other exemplars, sometimes called "universal" regimens, were concerned with general advice.[32] As recent scholarship has shown, the burst of popularity enjoyed by these works in their heyday parallels what has been called the "medicalization" of medieval society: the desire of wealthy merchants, for instance, for dietary regimens is a sign of their diffusion among a greater public, just as the fundamental principles upon which the regimen rested became the basis for early discussions of public health and policy.[33] Although a variety of organizing principles governed the various regimens, the most common arrangement was that of the "six nonnaturals," a concept central to the medieval curriculum.[34]

The six nonnaturals were factors that influenced human health or sickness and that were subject to manipulation and change. They included air (air quality, also climate, or environment), exercise, sleep, food and drink, evacuations (including bodily eliminations and sexual activity as well as medically induced purging, phlebotomies, and so on), and mood (emotions).[35] Technically, the therapeutic regimen covered all these factors; in reality, food and drink tended to occupy the lion's share of the works. Inasmuch as each human being was composed of a delicate balance of humors—hot, cold, moist, and dry—the nonnaturals were understood in relationship to their impact on humoral balance. From this perspective, maintaining "health" was a dynamic process that required attention to climate and season as well as to a patient's age, gender, and humoral complexion. Moreover, when the patient in question was a monarch or pope, his physical and emotional health were of more than personal interest.

The biblical story of King Ahashverus and his Jewish queen, Esther, is read annually for the Jewish Purim festival, celebrated on 14 Adar, roughly in March of the Christian calendar. The story begins when the Persian king foolishly commands Queen Vashti to come before his feasting companions, and she refuses. Vashti is banished, and an empire-wide beauty contest brings her successor, a Jewish orphan named Esther, to the court. Mordecai, who has raised his orphaned niece, earns the enmity of Ahashverus's chief adviser, Haman, who plots the destruction of the Jews. With Mordecai's guidance,

Esther approaches the king, reveals Haman's plot, and achieves the salvation of her people.

The biblical story is set in the ancient Persian capital of Shushan. The *realia* of Crescas's royal court, however, evoke Provence and not an unknown East. Indeed, in any number of ways, both versions of Crescas's story allude to local customs, institutions, and particular personalities and events. The historical allusions are frustrating, as their referents are largely lost. The recommendation of Ahashverus's counselors to burn Vashti at the stake, for instance, represents a striking deviation from the biblical text, and from rabbinic and medieval exegetical traditions. It must have been a local topos, as it appears also in Abraham Bedersi's Purim letter to David Caslari.[36] Yet in Crescas's case, the motif uneasily echoes contemporary events such as the burning of beguines in nearby Narbonne.[37]

Similarly, Crescas's depiction of King Ahashverus presents a striking portrait of mental instability exacerbated by alcoholic excess, and a tendency to alternate angry (often drunken) outbursts with despondency. The Judeo-Provençal text notes ominously the effects of his drinking and rage, which lead directly to at least two executions: Vashti's and Haman's. In both versions, the king's rages collapse into melancholy and amnesia.[38] In the Judeo-Provençal text, the king's first response to Vashti is furious:

Lo rei fon plen de malenconi.
Dis: "Que farem d'aquest demoni?"
E am sa gran felonia,
Dis a tota sa baronia,
"Sapias, barons, per ma corona,
Que ieu non atrobiei mais persona
Que tant me fezes airat."

(The king was filled with melancholy.
He said: "What shall we do with this devil?"
And in his great wrath,
He said to all his barons,
"Know ye, barons, by my crown,
That I have never met anyone
Who made me so angry." [vv. 242–49])[39]

After Vashti's execution, the king

fauzet son vin, tenc se per fol
e de Vasti lo cor lhi dol.
Non sabia con l'avia perduda.

(put away his wine, thought himself crazy
and his heart grieved for Vashti.
He did not know how he had lost her. [vv. 356–58])

The Hebrew offers a reasonably parallel depiction. The king's drinking disorders his mind and inspires his foolish demand.[40] Vashti's response infuriates, then depresses, him:

חמת המלך בערה בקרבו / ותתפעם רוחו ויתעצב אל לבו.

(The king's wrath burned inside him,
his spirit was disturbed and he grew sad.)[41]

In both versions, the king's counselors fear to advise him, recognizing that once he has sobered up, he will regret his outburst and blame them for its consequences. In contrast to the amnesia he experiences in the Judeo-Provençal text, however, the Hebrew realizes their fears:

אחר כל זאת זכר את ושתי מר ממות מצא / וינחם כי נבלה עשה
ויאמר אל ממוכן אתה את עונה תשא / תחת אשר עשית את הדבר הזה.

(Afterward, he recalled Vashti, [whom] he found bitter as death.
He regretted having done a foolish thing
And said to Memucan, you shall bear her sin
For having done such a thing.)[42]

Certainly, the papal court at Avignon was slurred for its allegedly drunken popes and lavish excess, and Crescas may be joining a local literary trend in social critique.[43] But the pope had no wife, neither a Vashti nor an Esther, and the allusion cannot evoke the papal court exclusively. The king's temper and melancholy are aggravated by abuse of alcohol, which in moderation might alleviate melancholy.[44] So, too, his desire for a new queen is described in the vernacular romance as advisable for his health:

Lo tems non vuelh que vos denemre:
Ela fon preza en dezembre,
Al tems que cas la neu e.l glas
E a tot om lo solas plas.
Car am conpanh[a] pot jazer
L'un cors am l'autre pren plazer. (vv. 420–25)

(I don't want you to forget the season:
She was taken in December,
At the time when snow and ice fall
And every man likes company.
For with a lady companion he can lie
One body taking pleasure in the other.)

The Hebrew, less explicit, also recasts the effects of the winter season; the cold augments the king's desire to replace his missing wife:

כתר מלכות שם על ראשה ונזר / בחדש טבת אשר כפור כאפר יפזר
טוב לגבר על אבדתו תהי מחזר / החדש הזה.

(A royal crown and diadem he put on her head,
In the month of Tevet when the frost is scattered like dust.
It is good for a man to return for what he has lost
During this month.)[45]

Crescas's description, on its surface a delicate evocation of the human craving for warmth and company in the bleak winter months, triggers a notable set of associations for an educated Jew. The expression "return for what he has lost" is rabbinic, found in a discussion of why a man seeks a woman in marriage and not the reverse.[46] Once again, Crescas is counting on his audience to identify the context of his source; the Talmudic passage asserts male authority. Moreover, its continuation directly associates alcohol abuse with "gonorrhea." The connection between alcoholic excess and sexual disease (and disgrace) made explicitly by the Talmudic text is thus incorporated implicitly into the romance narrative.[47]

Like any "modern" fourteenth-century king, King Ahashverus believed in multiple medical opinions, and at least at the story's beginning, Mordecai and Haman are in positions to offer such advice. In both versions of the story, they are jointly in charge of the menu and wines for the king's first feast, which is described in great detail and to which I shall return below. As Haman rises in the king's favor and Mordecai is marginalized, the king—with Haman's prompting—makes a series of regrettable decisions, including his authorization of Haman to dispose of the Jews. The link between poor medical advice and poor political advice—or, alternatively, between the king's poor judgment in choosing physicians and statesmen—is subtly emphasized in the story.

Haman, it is true, is the story's villain, and Crescas had no reason to paint him generously. Even so, it is striking that Mordecai accuses him of a lack of professional credentials. Haman, as we recall, is ordered by the king to honor Mordecai, who had uncovered a plot against the king's life but was not rewarded. The omission comes to light because of the king's insomnia—another symptom associated with melancholy.[48] In a beautiful vignette, which embellishes the rabbinic sources, Haman arrives at Mordecai's home to find him studying (Talmud!). When Mordecai hears his purpose in coming, he first sends for a barber and then forces Haman to shave him instead. The Judeo-Provençal fragment does not reach this part of the story, but the Hebrew is dramatic:

. להמן הביא ספל ומספרים / ויגלחו ועינו יורדה מים
ויאמר מרדכי מה היום מיומים? / חרה לך על הדבר הזה?
הלא זה בו היו חיי אבותיך / ובקורייינוס עשרים ושתים משנותיך.
חדל לך מפרשות כי נכריה עבודתיך / טוב אשר תאחוז בזה!

(He brought Haman a basin and scissors
and [Haman] shaved [Mordecai] while crying.
Mordecai said, why should today be different from any other?
Are you angry about this?
This is how your fathers made their living,
And you for twenty-two years in Corinnus.
Cease your hypocrisy, for you are [merely] a laborer—
It's good for you to stick to this!)[49]

After he is newly shaved and dressed in royal robes, Mordecai is promenaded through the streets on the king's best horse, guided by the downcast Haman (whose daughter unwittingly empties a chamber pot on his head).[50] Significantly, Mordecai, too, appears as a physician, garbed in the rich colored silk of the physician's robes.[51]

Mordecai is honored at a moment when the future looks bleak for his fellow Jews. At his urging, Esther has sought an audience with the king to plead on their behalf. In a deliberate contrast to the behavior of her predecessor, whose refusal to come to the king was interpreted as a defiance of the law (legs/*dat*), Esther's reluctance to go to the king is rooted in modesty and *fear* of the law, which forbade anyone to approach the king unsummoned, on pain of death. Piously, she fasts for three days before entering the royal chamber, where her life is spared.[52] As in the biblical story, she then invites the king and Haman to a feast, which Crescas describes as replete with wine (notice Haman's promotion):

ויקם המלך מכסאו / ויאמר אל המן שר צבאו.
ולבית היין כרצון אסתר הביאו[53] / וצוה אותו על הדבר הזה.
ויאכלו וישתו עמה.

(The king arose from his throne
And spoke to Haman, the lord of his army.
He brought him to the wine house as Esther wished
And commanded him about this matter.
Then they ate and drank with her.)[54]

The second feast, too, is characterized by drunkenness. Esther reveals her identity and proclaims that her fate will be that of her people. The king is astounded to learn that his queen's people have been "sold for a destruction unwritten in the Torah" and rashly proclaims that whoever is responsible will pay with his life. Esther then identifies "the oppressor, the foe, this evil Haman!" In a rage, the king goes out into the garden to cool his temper but discovers instead that workmen are uprooting his trees. When he learns that they are obeying Haman's orders, he is further enraged.[55] In the meantime, Haman has thrown himself on Esther's mercy—literally, on the couch on which she reclines. The king reenters the "wine house" and concludes the worst. In the Oxford Bodleian manuscript, his hasty judgment even leads him to question Esther's motives:

עבדי המן הגן בתה / ואסתר עם המן ברית כרתה?
המערת פריצים היה הבית הזה?

(Haman's servants have stripped the garden [cf. Isa. 7:19]

While Esther has conspired with Haman?
Is this house a den of thieves?[56] [Jer. 7:11])

In due order, Haman and his sons are hanged, the king issues new writs
denouncing Haman's perfidy and permitting the Jews to defend themselves,
Mordecai is elevated to Haman's post, and the ancient tale of Jewish triumph
and revenge concludes with a detailed description of medieval Purim observance. There are dietary specifications plus admonitions to dress in festive
clothing, give gifts to the poor, and to drink and rejoice—recommendations
that would have earned no physician's scorn, as they echo many of the pre-
scriptions designed to deter melancholy in the regimens.

To summarize our findings thus far, Crescas's reworking of a familiar
biblical story, which had acquired equally familiar rabbinic and medieval
accretions, created a series of subtle new emphases that highlighted the problematic behavior of the king in medical terms. I have underscored the king's
weakness for alcohol, as it reinforced a tendency to anger and melancholy.
Medieval medicine sought to explain temperament, as well as emotions, in a
variety of ways; for the most part, theorists agreed that while the state of the
soul was not a doctor's business, the emotional balance or imbalance experienced by a patient was at least partially a question of humoral equilibrium
and subject to a physician's manipulation. Arnau of Vilanova, whose work
Crescas esteemed, explained "sadness" as a direct result of a loss of vital heat
to the heart, a detriment that causes thickening of the blood and a diminu-
tion of nutriments to other organs. Sadness, then, was a condition characterized by an excess of cold and dry humors.[57] The physicians attempted to
refine this category by distinguishing between an inherent, constitutional
sadness (*tristitia*), and an affective anxiety or grief (*angustia*), very much
evocative of the modern distinction between clinical and situational depression. *Tristitia* was a fixed and essential part of a human "personality," while
angustia was subject to treatment and change. *Angustia*, however, was a complicated emotional state that was caused by a double movement of heat both
away from and into the heart. The experts disagreed on the exact etiology
of this condition, but significantly, it was Arnau who theorized a fusion of
depression (melancholy) and rage as the cause.[58] This is a position with which
Crescas apparently agreed, depicting a melancholic in action, as it were, and
the potential consequences of his illness.

Foods also play an important role in this story, illustrating both lavish
extravagance and scientific precision, as well as the necessity of tailoring a

diet to the particular complexion of the eater. Whether the mixed audience of the vernacular text, or the more elite male audience of the Hebrew, all of Crescas's listeners knew that the Purim story began with a royal feast. In the Judeo-Provençal version, the cuisine is exquisitely detailed. On the one hand, this kind of attention to culinary detail and etiquette might be expected to appeal to a mixed audience, especially if then, as now, women were assumed to be interested in these matters. On the other hand, as already noted, the vernacular lent itself to specificity in a way that Hebrew could not; this specificity permits us to recognize the technical, medical, interest of the menus. Ahashverus initially orders his *bailes* to prepare for a huge crowd and to tell the cook to keep the cauldrons burning all day:

> E que tenga tot entorn
> Asts de capons e de galinas
> E de totas autras salvezinas.
> A tot om lhi sie donat
> Bolia, raust o cozinat. (vv. 98–102)

> (and that he have all about
> skewers of capons and chickens
> and all sorts of wild game.
> Let everyone receive
> A boiled, roast, or cooked dish.)

The corresponding passage in Hebrew simply reads:

פנים בפנים צוה המלצר / ראה צוויתיך ידך אל תקצר.
וטבוח טבח והכן לי בשר / לתת לכל העם הזה.

> (He directly commanded the steward:
> See, I have commanded you not to be stingy.
> Slaughter and prepare me meat
> To give to all these people.)[59]

The menu is elaborated soon after. In the vernacular text, the city is overflowing with "ducs, marques e vescomtes" and "senhors" (vv. 126–27), who seat themselves to be served "a la novella maniera," apparently in serial courses.[60] The detail is extraordinary:

Ministreren morteirols
Aquels vengron a plens pairols
Bueu e mouton venc am pebrada
Amb eruga e am mostarda
Deron cabrit en gratonia
Mujols e lops en gelaria
Simple broet det am galina
Am bona salsa camelina.
Aucas venon totas farsidas
E pueis vengron perditz rostidas
Grases capons lor det en ast
Que avian lonc tems estat a past
Cabrols, brufols, cervis salvages
Det am jurvert e am borages.
De gals feizans fes entremes
Anc non fon fag per nengun res.
Mangeron tartas per fizica
Aisi con medicina poblica.
En redier det ris am sumac
Per confortar lor estomac,
Piement e neulas ben calfadas
Que semblavan encanonadas.
Per frucha det codons e peras
Aprop manjar matins e seras.
Lo vin que begron fon aital
Con cascun beu en son ostal,
Que non lor montet al cervel.
Mais aiso mes vin novel.

(They served stews
that came in filled cauldrons,
beef and mutton came with pepper sauce,
with arugula and mustard.
They served kid in pâté[61]
Mullets and sea bass in jellied sauce.
He gave [them] plain broth with chicken
And good cameline sauce.
The geese came all stuffed

And then came roast partridges.
He gave them fattened capons on the spit
Which had been fed a long while,
Roebuck, buffalo, wild deer
He served with parsley and borage.
He made a dish of pheasants
That had never been made before.
They ate tarts for their health
Just as medicine prescribes.
Finally, he gave them rice with sumac
To calm their stomachs,
A spicy wine and hot wafers
That were well rolled.
For fruit, he served quince and pears
After eating morning and evening.
The wine they drank was such
As each one would have drunk in his home,
that did not go to their heads.
He also put out new [light] wine. [vv. 133–60])[62]

Here we immediately see the language problem confronting Hebrew writers.
The entire preceding passage shrinks dramatically in Hebrew:

כרצון איש ואיש היו היינות. / מרדכי והמן הכינו המנות.
גם ושתי המלכה עשתה משתה בנות / העיר כמשפט הזה.
איל וצבי ויחמור שור שה כבשים / עגלי מרבק וברבורים אבוסים
לכולם נתן ובדם ענב מתבוססים / אלה מזה ואלה מזה.

(The wines were to each man's taste.
Mordecai and Haman prepared the dishes.
Queen Vashti also made a feast for the women
Of the city, according to the law.

Ram and deer and roebuck and sheep
Fatted calves and stuffed swans[63]
He gave to all, [served] steeped in wine
This side and that. [Josh. 8:22])[64]

Amazingly enough (unless you are an Atkins fan, in which case you will feel vindicated), this was a very healthy meal by the standards of the regimens Crescas knew and admired. Arnau de Vilanova's *Regimen sanitatis,* which Crescas had just translated, is brought to life in some of these dishes, as is the contemporary regimen of Maino de Maineri (d. ca. 1364), whose book of sauces was composed somewhat later but is essentially an expanded section of his regimen.[65]

Since the operative principle behind the therapeutic diet was the regulation of the humoral qualities (ranked by degree) of various foods, the foods best suited to a balanced ("temperate") constitution were those that reinforced the eater's ideal humoral balance. For those whose constitution lacked equilibrium, the qualities of various foods had the potential to adjust or aggravate his condition; therefore, the physician considered his individual patient carefully in prescribing a diet.[66] A crowd, of course, is not a patient. The royal feast described in Crescas's romance is overall a deliberately conceived arrangement of dishes, prepared to enhance their moderately moist and warming properties for winter consumption. It is designed for people of balanced temperaments, who, moreover, have the sense to moderate their consumption based on their own needs. In this context, Crescas's depiction of the guests drinking as they would "at home" offers a novel reading of the biblical verse, "and the drinking was according to the law, no one was compelled" (Esther 1:8), a verse richly glossed by generations of commentators. In Crescas's reading, the biblical phrase refers to the unique climatic factors that govern local complexion. The guests drank wisely, in deference to physiological tendencies influenced by their native geography and climate. Indeed, Crescas emphasizes that the discretion of the guests, who came from far and near, must be honored:

חמר חדת ועתיק לבן אדמדם / על כל רב ביתו מצותו קדם.
כי אינך יודע רוח האדם / זה יכשר הזה או זה.

(Wine new and old, white and reddish
Each head of household's demand should take precedence.
For you do not know a man's temperament:
Some will do well with this one or that. [Eccles. 11:6])[67]

As several scholars have noted, the nature of the clientele for a regimen—initially royalty, high-ranking nobility, or clergy, and later a larger, still-wealthy, urban bourgeoisie—encouraged preciousness. Generally, the most highly endorsed foodstuffs were the most expensive, ranging from meats and fish to flour and spices.[68] It is also possible to detect a corollary attention to labor-intensive preparation in the cooking methods and condiments. The prevalence of roast game and sauces among the main courses is another indication that the feast took place in winter. Almost all meats were considered cold and dry, properties one would not wish to accentuate in frigid weather. Roasting would add heat, although, of all forms of cooking (boiling, baking, roasting), it was most given to add dryness as well. Meat roasted on a spit was considered particularly drying and conducive to choler.[69] However, these defects might also be balanced by selecting meats that were hotter than others, such as wild game, or moister than others, as in particular fowl, both categories amply represented here. Also recommended was the use of sauces, which were valued as correctives as much as for decorative or gustatory enhancements.[70]

Specifically, we can see that beef and mutton, the first course and the least healthy of the meats, also the coldest and driest, are served "in cauldrons" with a *morteirol* (ragout); the boiling or stewing of the meat in a sauce counteracted its injurious properties. *Pebrada* (pepper sauce) was ubiquitous in medieval cooking; the pepper added heat but was adjusted by the addition of vinegar in winter so that its chief effect was moderate.[71] Cameline sauce, cinnamon-based, was often recommended for small fowl (also rabbits and fish); it, too, added moisture and mild warmth, with the cinnamon moderated by counteracting ingredients.[72] The mustard and arugula sauce of verse 136 tended to heat, and hence was recommended for winter use; Arnau suggested tempering its strength with honey or sugar, or alternatively, with a combination of cinnamon, almond milk, and ginger.[73] Fattened fowl appear in a number of regimens, and partridges, pheasants, and paon or grouse were also considered warm and moist and ubiquitously approved.[74] Likewise, the jellied fish, described as a "galantine" by Maino de Maineri and in the early fourteenth-century Latin *Liber de coquina*, was constructed both as a means of tempering the "meaty" (cold, dry) qualities of the fish as well as a means of preserving it; as Laurioux notes, the latter benefit would have been particularly desirable for *des maîtres d'hôtel des grandes maisons princières*, whose menus Crescas surely evokes here.[75]

As Pansier noted long ago, the dessert menu—in particular, the pears and quince—also indicates a winter setting for the feast.[76] This tells us that the king's second betrothal and remarriage (to Esther) in successive Decembers marked the anniversary of an earlier winter banquet. Although fresh fruit was regarded suspiciously by most medieval physicians, quinces and pears were favored for their astringent qualities and considered good digestives. Sumac was also a familiar digestive aid.[77]

In sum, King Ahashverus, whatever his defects, was a very "modern" king, calling upon the assistance of medical professionals (Haman and, by implication, Mordecai) to craft a state-of-the-art banquet that was impressive not merely in terms of luxury and cost but also as an exemplary, scientifically approved menu for his guests. Surely, Crescas's vernacular audience would have heard this section of the romance in different ways. "Women and children" could have enjoyed the description simply for its representation of stupendous bounty and wealth. Physicians, on the other hand, or even merchants or scholars aware of medical trends, would have appreciated the author's virtuosity on another level as well.

Was Crescas merely showing off for this elite group of listeners? Or was he also illustrating a medical problem we know preoccupied him as a professional—namely, that the entire theory of therapeutic diet required that a regimen be tailored to an individual man or woman? As Crescas noted in the introduction to his translation of Arnau's regimen, "it could almost be said that every man needs a text written for himself."[78] Mordecai and Haman designed a banquet that aimed for a dietetic version of the Golden Mean; the foodstuffs and methods of preparation were best suited to men of temperate complexion. Nonetheless, we know that the king was not such a man, but of a melancholic disposition; repeatedly, the various regimens warn against many of the very foods served at the banquet for an individual subject to melancholy.[79] Crescas may have been illustrating another kind of medical problem here—namely, the complications arising from the misappropriation of a regimen designed for one type of person by another. Alternatively, the diet's impeccable equilibrium may clear the meal of blame for the king's behavior, which is then attributable to his excessive drinking and melancholia. Either way, Crescas sets up a clear contrast between the exquisitely planned courses and the king's inebriated disruption of events.

The Hebrew romance, despite its lexical limitations, also pays acute attention to the consumption of food and alcohol. As it is also a full version of the Purim tale, we see that it includes two feasts: the royal banquet that leads to Vashti's death; and the celebratory feast of the Jews at the end. Indeed, this latter feast, which is prescribed for Crescas's contemporary audience, is also quite interesting. In the version found in the Oxford Bodleian manuscript, we read:

ואחר כל חזון ונבואות נחתמים / מגלת אסתר אינה בטלה לעולמים.
במשתה ובשמחה קבעו חכמים / זכור את היום הזה.
לעשות כדת היום מנהגים ידועים / לזכור מאכל אסתר ושלשת השועים
יאכל בני ישראל מן הזרועים / בלילה הזה.
ביום שלשה עשר באדר קבעו להתענות / ולקרות את המגלה
ביום ובלילה לשנות
ומתנות לאביונים ומשלוח מנות / היום הזה.
לזכר פורים כי עשתה יפת העין / משתה המלך לזכרהו על היין!
לכל נשים חובת היום לאפס ולאין / לא אשתה מים במקום הזה.
האיש אשר במרום הרים כרמו / לכו דודים שתו ושכרו עמו
ואם יאכל עם תרנגלת שמנה לחמו / גדול יהיה כבוד הבית הזה.
למאחרים על היין האוכלים למעדנים / להציל ממות נפשם נכונים [....] 80
לשד השמן לאכול היום אם תבחר / השמר פן יחל גרונך ונחר
שום תשים עליה ואל תאחר / מעט הדבש הזה.

(After all the vision and prophecies were sealed,
The Scroll of Esther is eternally valid.
The sages decreed that in feasting and joy
We should remember this day,
[and] follow the known customs as they should [even] today.
In remembrance of Esther's diet and the three nobles
Let the children of Israel eat chickpeas
On this night.

On the thirteenth of Adar, they decreed that we fast
And read the Scroll by day and study at night
Give gifts to the poor and exchanges
On this day.

In remembrance of Purim, for the beautiful one
Made a banquet for the king—remember it with wine!—
The obligations of women are naught this day:
"I won't drink water in this place!"

Come, O Friends, let's drink and get drunk
With the one on high [who] raised up his vineyard [Noah?]
And if he eats plump chicken with his bread
This household will be greatly honored.

Those who tarry over [their] wine and eat delicacies
Are prepared to save themselves from death.
[I shall make faithful witnesses testify for me
and they shall wish to][81]
If you choose to eat marrow this day
Be careful lest it stick to your throat!
Put garlic on it and don't delay
[with] a little of this honey.])[82]

MS HUC 396 replicates this text, with minor variations (mainly of word order). Columbia X893 CJ55 v. 31 and British Library Addendum MS Heb. 19663 also repeat essentially the same text, with the exception of the second quatrain, where the reference to legumes has been mangled. Instead of "Esther's diet" (מאכל אסתר), both copyists have written "Esther's dictate" (מאמר אסתר) and correspondingly truncated the next phrase to read only "the children of Israel shall eat / on this night" (יאכלו בני ישראל / בלילה הזה) (Col. fol. 83a; BL fols. 31b–32a). Since Esther's "words" are not really at issue in this point of the story, the corruption appears to be an attempt to make sense of an otherwise misunderstood reference to her diet. The Salonikan edition differs even more strikingly:

ואחר כל חזון ונבואות נחתמים / מגילת אסתר לא תכרת לעולמים.
במשתה נעשית ובשמחה קבעוה חכמים / זכור את היום הזה.
על כן לא יאכלו בני ישראל מן הזרעונים / לזכר מאכל אסתר כי
בו שבת מחרונים.
ואיש ישראל נגש להגדיל הששונים / הוא הלילה הזה.
ועשו אותו יום משתה שמנים / ובדברים אבוסים ואווזים ופסיונים.
ועל שולחן הזהב יפרסו האבלים למעדנים / בעצם היום הזה.
ישמחו כל חוזה אנשי חיל מתולעים / ותצאן כל הנשים כי מקשטן
מקלעת פקיעים
כי רמה קרנם בשליטת השועים / הנה אלהינו זה!

(After all the vision and prophecies were sealed,
the Scroll of Esther will not ever be cut off.
It [the holiday?] is celebrated with drinking and joy; the sages have
    decreed
That we remember this day.

Therefore the children of Israel shall eat no chickpeas
In remembrance of Esther's diet, on which his wrath abated.
Let every Jew approach to make joy
On this night.

Let them make it a day of drinking [and] rich foods,
Stuffed swans and geese and pheasants.
And on a table of gold, let them serve delicacies to the mourners[83]
In the midst of this day.

And let all the men of vision and might rejoice in crimson
Let the women go forth in flowered brocade
For their horn has been exalted with the noble ones' dominion:
Behold, this is our God! [Salonika, 12b])

Like the dishes offered in the royal banquet, the combination of marrow with honey and garlic sauce (a culinary custom that thankfully did not survive) makes sense in medieval medical terms. Marrow is a temperate meat product, moderately cold and moist, and honey and garlic offset each other's acuter properties to create a moderately warm, moist sauce recommended by Maino de Maineri in the *Opusculum de Saporibus*.[84] The Salonika edition also includes an injunction to the Jews to drink spiced wine and pomegranate juice (12b); pomegranates regularly received high ratings in the regimens and often found their way into sauces or desserts.[85] The carnival aspects of the story demand drunkenness, but the food, though rich, demonstrates a high degree of class and control. From a literary perspective, too, the celebratory feast of the Jews echoes the opening description of the king's banquet in the Hebrew texts, emphasizing the turn of fortune that is the story's theme and moral.[86] The interest of the Salonikan version in festive clothing, a detail unmentioned in the 1402 manuscript, may reflect another manuscript tradition; it minimally reflects the role played by Salonikan Jews in the production of and commerce in high-end textiles. Tellingly, a surviving illustration of an early twentieth-century Purim pageant from Salonika features a young Jewish boy dressed as the Persian king and draped in luxurious brocade robes.[87]

The chickpeas pose a fascinating problem, which, fittingly, leads us back to our larger themes of expulsion, memory, and the journey of texts in exile. Which version of Crescas's text is accurate, and why did he insist on the inclusion or exclusion of this legume? The Hebrew words *zera'im* and its cognate *zer'onim* are generic terms derived from the singular form, *zera'*, commonly translated as "seed." The plural form is used throughout rabbinic literature to refer to a variety of garden seeds, legumes, or pulse. We can be fairly sure that Crescas used this word to mean "chickpea," however, by consulting the Latin and Catalan texts of Arnau's *Regimen sanitatis* and comparing it with Crescas's Hebrew translation.[88] In the section on legumes, the word translated by Crescas as *zer'onim* is the Latin *cicera*; in medieval Catalan, *ciurons*.[89]

Chickpeas, as it turns out, were not highly esteemed in medieval regimens, although their broth was considered healthy. This may in part reflect their lower-class status, although in season the chickpea was more expensive than the more common fava or lentil.[90] From a humoral perspective, the chickpea (or garbanzo) was on the hot and dry side, and generated an excess of humors that was manifested in swelling, flatulence, and overproduction of urine and semen or menstrual blood. On the other hand, with appropriate seasoning (ginger, saffron, sugar, and almond milk, or an alternative preparation with cinnamon, spikenard, and saffron), the legume could stimulate a lagging appetite.[91]

In Arnau's regimen, the chickpea, while producing the same general effects as those just described, is explicitly less pernicious than other legumes.[92] Arnau noted that the frequent consumption of legumes during Lent tended to aggravate their negative properties; he recommended a first course of chickpea broth as a digestive and counteragent to the constipating qualities of dry or fresh beans. The same enthusiasm for the digestive and laxative effects of chickpea broth appears in the Regimen of the Four Masters of Montpellier, whose full recipe combines the broth with parsley, hyssop, onions, garlic, white wine, and a little cinnamon and spikenard or cilantro.[93]

The Catalan translation retained the formulation of Arnau's Latin, as did any number of the Hebrew manuscripts that preserved Crescas's translation. I offer one example below:

> E, per ço con en la corema ha hom sovén usar les viands qui fan opilacions, axí con peys e manjars de cuylera, profitosa cosa sera a conservar sanitat que hom raeba al començament del menjar .i. poc de brou de ciurons ho de pèsols.[94]

ואמנם בימי העינוי אשר זמן מנהג הקטניות והקמחים או מן המאכלים

העושים סתומים הוא ארוך אז יועיל לשמור הבריאות לקחת קודם
המאכל פורייא הוא מי הזרעונים והאפונים.

(Yet during Lent [lit., the "days of affliction"], when the custom of
eating legumes and flours, or other constipating foods, is of long dura-
tion, then it is healthful to first partake of a purée, that is, the broth of
chickpeas and peas.)[95]

The Hebrew translation offers excellent testimony to the fact that Jewish physicians were interested in dietary regimens for treating their Christian patients as much as their Jewish ones. And we learn something else as well—that
chickpeas, like fish and flour dishes, were commonly eaten throughout the
Lenten period, with some concomitant gastrointestinal distress. The malaise,
however, is less interesting than the direct association of chickpeas with a period of Christian fasting. The association is confirmed by the overwhelming
appearance of chickpea soup on the menu of the papal court in Avignon for
the month of March.[96]

The Fast of Esther, commemorating the queen's three-day fast before
her appeal to the king, takes place on 13 Adar, roughly the same time as the
Lenten fast. Among observant Jews today, it is marked as a day of abstinence
from food, in accordance with the modern understanding of a fast. Apparently, neither Crescas nor his fellow Jews in the Midi understood "fasting" in
this way; rather, they observed something similar to a Christian "fast," which
referred primarily to abstinence from meat. The Esther text specifically associates the eating of chickpeas with a commemoration of Esther's fast.

Thus, on the day when fourteenth-century Comtat Jews were marking
their mythical triumph over their gentile foes, they were doing so in accordance with gentile custom. What is particularly striking is that Crescas wrote
this exhortation in the same year (1327) that a series of anti-Jewish statutes
sought to further segregate Comtat Jews from their Christian fellows. Some
of these statutes, such as the wearing of a Jewish badge, or the prohibition
against Christian patients using Jewish doctors, were at best laxly enforced
in the Comtat. The new regulations also called for the confinement of the
Jews to the Jewish quarter during Holy Week, the final week of the Lenten
period. At precisely the moment that Crescas's texts demonstrate the deeply
acculturated traditions and beliefs of local Jews, Christian law was struggling
to mark their difference.[97]

It is not surprising, then, that the endorsement of chickpeas was reversed in the nineteenth-century Salonika edition: in the Ottoman Empire, for Muslims and Jews, a fast meant total abstinence. Chickpeas, otherwise ubiquitous in a Mediterranean diet, were certainly forbidden. The British Library copy also reflects the confusion of the copyist on this issue. Like the Salonikan edition, it is an eighteenth-century version of the story, in a square hand found in other contemporary manuscripts made in the Comtat or in Italy for Provençal owners.[98] The Cincinnati manuscript, copied only a few decades after the Oxford Bodleian, still reflects familiarity with the relaxed definition of fasting among Comtadin Jews. The Columbia University copy dated in the summer of 1701 (i.e., 15 Iyar 5461) is also from the Comtat; it is the work of Immanuel b. Gad Milhaud (1663–1716), from a prolific family of scribes. But by the turn of the eighteenth century, any Jewish affinity for Lenten-style fasting was apparently forgotten. For these copyists and users, the notion of a chickpea "fast" would have been meaningless as well.

In conclusion, in addition to their other interests, Crescas's Purim tales embody in dramatic form a number of contemporary medical theories and debates. The popularity of dietary regimens and the competing, remunerative impulse to treat a client's complaints—particularly a wealthy client's complaints—with pharmaceutical compounds had serious socioeconomic reverberations in the medical community of Crescas's time.[99] Crescas's treatment of this issue tells us that he was a "modern" practitioner with an interest in theory and abreast of contemporary developments in his field. The little we know of his subsequent career reinforces a portrait of a successful physician in a part of the world where professional competition would have been stiff. In 1348, during the terrible year of the Black Death, we find him treating plague patients, one of whom returns to him in 1357.[100] In addition, a list of remedies attributed to "Israel Caslari," which survives in a roughly scrawled manuscript in Parma, suggests a medical reputation of some durability.[101] The ailments addressed range, in no discernible order, from jaundiced eyes to kidney stones, sore throats, ear- and toothaches, pregnancy problems, nail and arrow wounds, fevers and various intestinal woes, and cracked lips. Curiously, of the approximately three dozen recipes, four of the five eye-related remedies aim to "restore whiteness" to the eyes. How often, in the sumptuous setting of the Avignon court, did Crescas find himself treating jaundice, a symptom linked to liver disorders associated, among other things, with long-term alcohol abuse? Perhaps, here, too, we have another echo of the real-life figures behind the dissipated, melancholic Ahashverus of Crescas's romance.

Throughout Crescas's career, medical debates reverberated within a society newly appreciative of medical science and metaphor. The tumultuous controversies that Arnau himself provoked during the last decade of his life suggest the inroads that medical thinking could make into theological discussion, and vice versa, with terrible political consequence.[102] The argument that non-Christians threatened the purity of the Christian nation is one that had obvious ramifications for the Jews, and in fact Arnau had already exploited this argument in his attempts to curb Jewish physicians from practicing in Avignon and its environs. The importation of medical metaphor into theory of the body politic supported the image of the Muslim or Jewish presence as a festering wound, leprous impurity, or diseased organ or limb whose excision was necessary for the health of the corporate Christian body. In this context, Haman's denunciation of the Jews in Crescas's Hebrew romance musters an ominously contemporary set of concerns:

דתיהם כדתי המלך אינם / בנשך יתנו כספם והונם.
דבר שקר למדו לשונם / לכל אשר יאמר העם הזה.
יין משתיהם זבוב מת לא יבאישנו / ואם אדני המלך יגענו
על הארץ כמים ישפכנו / ויאמר הנה נגע זה!
והיה כי תקראנה [!] מלחמה / אל יצא איש ממקומו דברו בערמה
שבת היום פסח היום לא נוכל דבר מאומה / בעצם היום הזה.

(Their religion is not that of the king.
They lend their money and wealth at interest.
This people has taught their tongues to lie
In all they say.

The wine of their drinks is not dirtied by a dead fly
But if my lord the King should touch it,
They will spill it like water on the earth
And say it's contaminated!

And if there is a call to war
Not a man will set forth from his place. With cunning, they will say,
"Today is the Sabbath, today is Passover, we cannot do a thing
On this day.")[103]

Mordecai's depiction of the impact of Haman's decree likewise departs from the biblical story. The book of Esther describes Mordecai and his fellow

Jews in sackcloth and ashes, "fasting and weeping and lamenting" at the king's gate (Esther 4:1–4). Crescas also describes this scene but adds his own bit of detail, uneasily evocative of the scenes of expulsion embedded in the verses of Yedaiah Bedersi, Joseph Latimi, and Reuben b. Isaac:

ויאמר לה מספד כיענים וכסיסים / היהודים האומללים עושים.
ימה וקדמה עברים נסים / משני עברייהם מזה ומזה.

(He said to her, "The wretched Jews
Make lament like ostriches and swallows.
Eastward and westward, Jews are fleeing
From this side and that.")[104]

And here our texts come full circle, returning us with some frustration to the historical allusions that elude us in this story. Some of these are legal, some are biographical, and some defer to customs and controversies whose shadows move dimly behind the pointed language.[105] Some are also the shards of expulsion memories, embedded unexpectedly in a tale of near-tragedy reversed in triumph.

To a great extent, the Hebrew text survived only because its later readers forgot these layers of the story, and abridged, deleted, or reinterpreted them to contour an ancient story to later contexts and communities. Ironically, the revival of Salonikan Jewish learning, which had languished through much of the seventeenth and early eighteenth centuries, owed much to the benefaction of a wealthy Jewish physician from Livorno (Leghorn), Moses Allatini, who settled in Salonika and single-handedly brought the community's cultural and educational institutions to life.[106] The Livorno Jews had a long history of relationship to the Jews of Provence as well, and here again, the paths of multiple exiles and expulsions and communities converge.[107] What survived of that convergence was constructed of cultural debris, the remnants of colliding histories and memories and texts, some clutched tenaciously and some buoyed only by chance. A slender strand—Crescas's Hebrew Esther—remained part of the heritage of Comtadin Jews for centuries, even as they emended and misread it to make sense of what they no longer understood. Another slender strand of that same romance found its way into the life of Salonikan Jews. Other threads floated farther and deeper, tracing in their silent journeys the ebbing memory of exiles moving wearily from Provence into Italy and Spain and finally into the possession of collectors and nations who held and forgot them for the future.

Expulsion and exile, of course, were not the only traumas to threaten the memory of French fourteenth-century Jews. The middle of that century was rent by a natural disaster that devastated Europe and the Mediterranean alike. Beginning in late 1347, when plague was first reported in the Middle East, and landing on European shores in Italy and Marseilles in 1348, terror and death swept through Europe in a pandemic whose dimensions had been unheralded since the sixth century. The estimated loss of one-third to one-half of the population in Europe; the dislocation of survivors during and in the wake of the Black Death; the ongoing plague-related violence against Jewish communities, pushing terrified Jews from France and Provence into the relative haven of the Comtat Venaissin—all these factors make a consideration of the plague and Jewish memory important to this study. Our next chapter therefore turns to another Jewish physician in Avignon during the second half of the fourteenth century, Jacob b. Solomon the Frenchman. Most likely the child of French Jewish refugees in the Comtat, Jacob, writing to commemorate the death of a beloved daughter in the plague of 1382, has a great deal to say about the relationship of science to faith, as well as the memory of a Jew from France.

CHAPTER FIVE

Physicians and Their Daughters: Memory and Medicine during the Plague Years

*I tell everyone that because of this aforementioned plague, all my days
are pain. Even on Sabbaths and holidays, I sigh and weep out of grief,
and I write now in tears. Perhaps because of what has happened,
which I have related, the name of Jacob b. Solomon will be exalted and
made great.*
— *"The Great Mourning," Jacob b. Solomon of Avignon*

THE PLAGUE RETURNED to Avignon late in 1382. In the autumn, it took the
life of Jacob b. Solomon's son, Israel, and in February, his daughter Sarah.
A second daughter, Esther, died some weeks after, in March. All three were
beloved, but it was Esther, known as Trina, whose death found a place in literature, concluding a manuscript now in the Bibliothèque Nationale. Copied
in 1395, the Paris manuscript represents Jacob's attempt to collect his religious
writings, beginning with a three-part exegetical work, *Mishkenot Ya'aqov*, and
a proof for the creation of the world ex nihilo.[1] A separate, Oxford manuscript preserves his original treatise on vertigo, and the JNUL in Jerusalem
recently acquired the famed Wolf Haggadah, for which Jacob, a curious poly-
math, was the scribe.[2] Among art historians and liturgists, the Haggadah has
achieved some renown. In contrast, Jacob's scholarly essays have brought him
no fame, and if the name Jacob b. Solomon HaTzarfati ("the Frenchman") is
known today, it is not due to these literary efforts.[3]

Of Jacob's prose works, only the closing text of BN Heb. 733 has drawn some interest. The *Evel Rabbati* (Great Mourning), Jacob's moving description of Esther's illness and death, was published by David Kaufmann in 1895, and again by Ron Barkai in 2001.[4] For Kaufmann, Jacob's intimate family portrait was striking in a literary tradition that resolutely avoided sentimentality of this sort.[5] For Barkai, a historian of medicine who has written about plague tractates composed or translated by Jewish physicians, Jacob's essay illustrated the close relationship of father and daughter and, by extension, the strength of family ties unbroken even through a brutal epidemic.[6] Finally, Elliott Horowitz also treated this story in a more popular article on Jewish attitudes toward death published in 1995.[7]

This chapter argues that neither the *Evel Rabbati* nor Jacob's motives for writing it are so simple. Certainly, the *Evel Rabbati* commemorates Esther's idealized death and Jacob's personal suffering; the relationships depicted represent Jacob's subjective and strategic perspective. On this level, Jacob's memoir confirms Ann Carmichael's claim, made for later plague literature, that the most effective forms of plague "histories and testimonials" relied on "local and personal" memory.[8] But the *Evel Rabbati* is a polemical text as well as a commemorative one. Its framing sections explicitly attack Jewish rationalists who favor allegorical readings of Scripture, and its narrative core implicitly links those rationalists to Christian theories on the nature and transmission of pestilential disease. Thus, although this is certainly not its only message, the *Evel Rabbati* suggests an ongoing debate among Jewish physicians regarding the nature of the plague epidemics and the ways their communities might ideally respond to them.[9] The clash between rationalists and traditionalists over the allegorical interpretation of Scripture has been featured in several chapters of this book. For Jacob, the proud son of French Jews driven southward, the debate found a new point of application, which he engaged with a theological conservatism that was French to the core. Those scholars who abandoned the literal meaning of the Hebrew Bible were also those scholars who repudiated the notion of plague as divine punishment, interpreting it instead according to the laws of natural science. Jacob responds to these foes with a dramatic narrative commemorating his daughter's death as an act of God and his response to calamity as a trial of faith.

On the surface, the *Evel Rabbati* represents a genre of prose unknown to medieval Hebrew literature. How do we categorize this text and with what literary genres should we associate it? Certainly, the *Evel Rabbati* renders a literary portrait—however idealized—of a grief-stricken father and an astute, sensitive, and painfully mature daughter on the verge of death. Still, the *Evel Rabbati* is not an objective report but a story, and as a story it has been consciously crafted to represent its subject matter in specific ways.[10]

In fact, the *Evel Rabbati* draws on a variety of literary precedents, beginning with the book of Job, which lends its rudimentary structure and polemic to Jacob's narrative. Like Job, the work begins and ends with a polemical frame, in which Jacob discusses his motives for writing and his distress with fellow Jews, "would-be philosophers" (*mitpalsefim*) who undermine the religious authority of sacred texts by reading them allegorically. Sandwiched between these sections is an account of Esther's last hours, in fluid rhymed prose, detailing the last phase of her illness, her farewell to her loved ones and public confession, and the rituals attending her death. Jacob states flatly that the undeniable truth of his own experience, which can be attested by numerous witnesses, "proves" that Job's sufferings were also real.

The medieval Hebrew and vernacular narratives that dramatized the book of Esther may have also inspired the form of Jacob's work. These narratives were popular in Provence in the thirteenth and fourteenth centuries, and one—treated in the previous chapter—was even written by another physician in Avignon, Crescas (Israel) Caslari.[11] Emphasizing his daughter's Hebrew name, Jacob draws upon scenes in the biblical book of Esther to portray a pious "queen" summoned to meet her King.

A third, Christian, genre may have influenced Jacob's writing, too: the depositions describing medical cures found in the dossiers promoting the canonization of Christian saints. This truly was a new genre in Jacob's time. When they involved miraculous healings, these formal depositions were by definition dramatic faith narratives in which faith trumped science. From the late thirteenth century on, they increasingly featured physicians, both as men of science to be trumped, and as expert witnesses to medical recoveries from seemingly hopeless afflictions.[12]

One such deposition is particularly relevant for a study of the *Evel Rabbati*. This is the testimony by Jean de Tournemire, a physician to Pope Clement VII in Avignon, chancellor of the medical faculty at the University of Montpellier, and author of a plague tractate.[13] In 1387, Jean's eighteen-year-old daughter, Marguerite, developed a tumor in her breast that her father diagnosed as fatal. Miraculously, she was saved by prayers to the recently deceased Peter of Luxembourg, and by the medical adaptation of Peter's relics to therapeutic use. Marguerite's story, like her father's emotional and professional participation in her cure, offers a striking parallel to Jacob's text—despite their very different outcomes.[14]

Curiously, the lives of these father-narrators were closely intertwined. When Jean de Tournemire was in Avignon as physician to the pope, Jacob was physician to the pope's brother, Count Pierre of Geneva.[15] Esther died in the spring of 1383. Just three years later, the young cardinal Peter of Luxembourg arrived in Avignon, his health already gravely debilitated. At least one of the many physicians who treated him over the next year was Jewish; in 1387, Jean de Tournemire attended his deathbed. Marguerite, Jean's daughter, fell ill that autumn and was healed by November. Jean recorded his testimony in 1388, and canonization proceedings for Peter began in 1390. (He was never canonized, but many years later, in 1524, he was eventually beatified.)[16] As the colophon of BN Heb. 733 indicates, Jacob or his copyist collected his works in 1395, concluding his anthology with the *Evel Rabbati*.

The tight overlap of time and place strongly suggests that the paths of the two physicians crossed, or at least that in the elite and competitive circle of physicians attached to the papal court, Marguerite's story came to Jacob's ears. As the depositions in favor of Peter's canonization reveal, Jacob may even have treated another patient who was later healed by Peter's posthumous intervention.[17] Surely it must have irked the Jewish physician and father, whose daughter was lost, to hear an eminent Christian physician vouch for his daughter's healing. Yet Jacob may have equally argued that *his* was the tale of greater faith. In this context, too, the *Evel Rabbati* illuminates the space where medical theory intersected with practice, and where science intersected with faith.

Narrative movingly illuminates the fault line of both intersections. Great psychological insight is unnecessary to see why Jacob compares his suffering to Job's. Jacob asserts vehemently that Job's travails must be understood literally as a historical account; the true "diagnosis" of Job's condition unfolds with the narrative of his travails. As Jacob noted in the lively case history preserved in his tractate on vertigo, "a disease and its causes are unknown to the physician except by means of the sick person's narrative or what he undergoes, for these are the physician's proofs."[18] As we shall see, the *Evel Rabbati* enlists narrative in the cause of diagnosis—in this case, for an illness that human science is powerless to cure.

Jacob takes sides in a medieval Jewish polemic of reason and faith that is familiar to us by now. In the heart of Avignon, he remains true to his northern

French ancestors and stakes out his position firmly on the side of traditional faith. A leitmotif of earlier chapters, the collision between rationalism and traditionalism among the Jews of Languedoc and Provence had a surprisingly long life. Here it surfaces in another generation, still in the orbit of Montpellier and Avignon, but in a moment when the stakes were very high and when points of theory had grave implications in the world of lived experience. The enormity of the crisis before medieval physicians comes through in many contemporary plague writings.[19]

It was a crisis of memory as well. For this book's overarching exploration of the impact of the fourteenth-century expulsions on Jewish memory, this chapter has special significance. The great population loss and subsequent displacement of survivors that characterized the Black Death severely tested the ways that communities remembered and reconstructed their pre-1348 past. Unsurprisingly, Jacob's *Evel Rabbati* is threaded with memory claims. At one point, the author even blames gaps in human memory for allowing the allegorists to confuse the real and fictitious past:

כשנאמר מספור מה כתוב בספר לא היה ולא נברא אלא משל היה
לשלמים. וזה מאתם לסבת אורך הימים הראשונים הכל נשכח ואין
זכרון לאשר היה אז אל הבאים אחריהם קמים.

([They] say that a story written in a book never existed and never was but is a fable for the enlightened. The reason for this is that it is so long since the early days that all has been forgotten; there is no memory of what was for those who have come after them.)[20]

Jacob's explanation suggests a weary consciousness of the ways that time and suffering can erode memory, and it is not surprising that he links questions of personal loss to public memory and meaning.[21] For Jews, the violence that frequently accompanied the Black Death further tore the tapestry of communal memory and life: following the plague across Aragon, Provence, and Italy, pogroms and their legacy of terror and dislocation altered the shape of the past.[22] Avignon was especially noteworthy for its lack of anti-Jewish persecutions; Clement VI barred entry to the flagellants and issued two bulls of protection for "his" Jews.[23] As Clement VI noted in a denunciation of Christian attacks, plague killed indiscriminately, and Jews were also among its victims.[24]

More recent perspectives on the plague years have also emphasized persecution and violence at the expense of other experience and concerns. Simon

Bernfeld's anthology of Hebrew laments, a classic exemplar of "lachrymose" history, contains sixty-seven pages of poetry described as poetry of the Black Death. All the examples commemorate incidents of persecution and have nothing to do with the devastation wrought by the disease.[25] Not only has this approach distorted perceptions of the past; it has left ignored and unanswered the very important question of how Jews responded to the plague itself. Thus, an investigation of Jewish responses to the plague is desirable both for what it tells us about southern European Jewish communities and for a fuller picture of the impact of the plague on all the communities of this region. For the questions of expulsion and memory considered in these chapters, the upheavals of the plague years are also significant. The plague, particularly the Black Death of 1348, rent communities that had already felt the blows of expulsion or the impact of absorbing the exiles. The stress on these communities also strained their ability to sustain a continuous past.

Jacob does not record an incident from the first fourteenth-century outbreak, but one that took place some thirty-five years and several plague waves later.[26] Indeed, although most historians of the plague have focused their attention primarily on the great outbreak of 1348–49, later outbreaks came soon and frequently; as we have already observed of the victims of expulsions that cyclically uprooted Jewish communities throughout the fourteenth century, those revisited by plague instinctively relied on "memory" of former epidemics to interpret and respond to later ones.[27] Esther's short life spanned from 1363 to 1383, and thus she was born not long after a plague year (1361) in Avignon, the city where she died. Jacob, her father, must have been born not long before the first great pandemic, which may have forced his parents from northern France into the relative safety of the papal Comtat Venaissin.[28] Jacob returned to the north to study or practice medicine, but was back in Avignon by the early 1380s when the plague struck again. He was still alive in 1395, but probably died soon afterward.

One of the last projects of Jacob's life was to assemble his theological writings, including the *Evel Rabbati*. Another was to turn to the work for which he has garnered more acclaim in recent years. Sometime in the last decade of the fourteenth century and presumably near the end of his life, Jacob copied a Haggadah, the liturgy for the Jewish Passover festival meal. History is mute concerning its next few hundred years; the graceful illuminations and pen-and-ink drawings it bears seem to have been added in Italy.[29] The Milanese collector Carlo Morbio put the work up for public auction in 1892, and the purchaser, Albert Wolf, donated it in 1907 to the Berlin Jewish community.[30] There it remained until Kristallnacht of November 1938, when it was confiscated by the Nazis and sent to Poland. In 1948, the so-called Wolf Haggadah was transferred to the Jewish Historical Institute in Warsaw, whence it disappeared in 1984 following its removal for an exhibit in the United States. The Haggadah reappeared on the auction block in Geneva in 1989, and following a long trial, was returned to Poland and then granted in 1997 to the Jewish National and University Library in Jerusalem.

The Wolf Haggadah has garnered interest for several reasons beyond its dramatic wanderings. As noted, it includes a number of beautiful pen-and-ink drawings that were long attributed to Jacob. The Haggadah is also noteworthy for its liturgical peculiarities. Despite Jacob's Sephardic-Provençal script, the rite is northern French; where the liturgical text adheres to southern custom, a marginal notation often refers to the alternative French rite. Kaufmann argued that Jacob was preserving northern customs he knew even though he had grown up practicing in a southern milieu, where he also acquired his handwriting.[31] Shlomo Zucker notes an aside that Jacob makes in his treatise on vertigo, indicating that some, if not all, of his medical study involved a sojourn in Paris, another curious allusion to the continuing attraction of the north for émigrés.[32] Hence, in this regard, too, he is part of our larger story of French Jewish exile and illustrates, very much like the Piedmontese exiles of the next chapter, the tenacious clinging to "Frenchness" that characterized the children of the refugees.

Yet, as Zucker also notes, it is not a coincidence that the liturgical work Jacob was moved to produce was a Haggadah, commemorating the exodus of the biblical Israelites from bondage in Egypt. The second part of his exegetical treatise also treats a segment of the Exodus narrative, the significance of the Ten Plagues and the mnemonic acronym by which they are inscribed in the Haggadah.[33] As we shall see below, the biblical plagues also interested a number of plague theorists, who cited them as "proof" that the Black Death, too, was an act of God. And allusions to the Egyptian plagues have a place in the *Evel Rabbati*, where, as part of the intertextual backdrop to a tragic personal narrative, they subtly guide the reader to interpret that tragedy in a specific way.

Let us begin with Jacob's family as he represents them in the *Evel Rabbati*, and let them introduce us to some of the issues that concern us.

The figure who holds center stage in the *Evel Rabbati* is Jacob's daughter, Trina, known also as Esther. Although we can assume that Trina was her common name, Jacob chooses her formal, "Jewish" name for his narrative.

This permits him to emphasize her as a model of Jewish female piety and also to invoke the biblical heroine for whom she was named.[34] In fact, Jacob cites disproportionately from Esther 5, exploiting the description of the biblical queen's courageous decision to approach the king on behalf of her people in order to describe Trina preparing to face her heavenly king.

At the time of her illness and death, Esther was twenty and married to a first cousin, Nathan, all of whose siblings had already perished in the plague. Esther has lost two siblings, whose deaths are recorded with strange brevity in the beginning of the text (did Jacob love them less? We do not know). A young brother, Israel, or Monrilet, died shortly after Jacob's recovery from illness in Tishri 5143.[35] A sister, Sarah, sickened in the early spring. She died on Thursday, 5 Adar 5143, and was buried the next day, the first anniversary of her wedding. Esther fell ill soon afterward and died on Sunday, 26 Adar. Jacob and his wife were present at her death, as were Nathan, Nathan's parents (Moses and Douce), and a large press of friends, servants, and onlookers. We hear of a younger sister, Yentish, and at one point "children" in the plural, implying other siblings. We know from Jacob's marginal notation in another manuscript that at least one son survived to adulthood.[36]

From Jacob's perspective, Esther was learned, pious, and deeply attached to him, her uncle, and her husband, Nathan. She addresses these men with affectionate respect, deferring to their authority. Her mother and Aunt Douce are sketched with greater ambivalence. The mother in particular is marginalized: it is Jacob who flings himself across his daughter's bed sobbing, Jacob who twice coaxes her to sip some broth, Jacob who receives her passionate dying kiss. He weeps that he did not deserve the daughter "borne him by his wife" (80) but displays no sentiment toward the wife herself. The *Evel Rabbati* remains silent even with respect to the mother's grief, a topos of contemporary fiction. The ambivalence is arguably Jacob's and not Esther's. Esther's remarks to her mother, as reported by Jacob, may lack fervor, but they demonstrate compassion and respect. At one point, she requests that, if Nathan should remarry after her death and a daughter be born to him, the infant take her name:

לבעבור סבב לך אבא מרי הנאה פורתא [לרגליה]. ואולי אחרי אמי
תתנחם בה קצת העת על ברכים תשעשע אותה בין רגליה.

(So you, *abba mari*, will find a little pleasure. And after I am gone, my mother will be somewhat consoled when she dandles her on knees.)[37]

Indeed, Jacob contrasts Esther's warm affection for the men in her life (Jacob, Moses, Nathan) with distant formality toward her mother or strain toward her Aunt Douce. Is this depiction accurate or the author's projection?[38] Does Jacob's story preserve a genuinely special bond between father and daughter, or Jacob's wish to portray such a bond? The answer may be that both impulses are at work.

It is useful to compare Jean de Tournemire's family portrait to Jacob's. Jean had a "commuter marriage": his wife and daughter lived in Montpellier, where he served on the medical faculty of the university while commuting to Avignon, the home of his prestigious client, Pope Clement VII. There he encountered the ailing Peter of Luxembourg, who arrived in Avignon in 1386 and died there on July 2 of the following year.[39] Peter had been young for the ecclesiastical honors heaped upon him (he was a bishop by the age of fifteen and a cardinal at sixteen), and his precocity extended quickly beyond death. As Renate Blumenfeld-Kosinski recently noted, Peter was posthumously enlisted in support of Clement VII and the Avignon papacy, an endorsement the young cardinal would have perhaps resisted in life.[40] It was Jean who examined Peter's corpse and verified its miraculous resistance to decay. Peter was near the age of Jean's daughter, Marguerite, who had recently married Peter Suisse and was expecting a child.

Upon his visit to Montpellier in September 1387, Jean's daughter revealed a "hard and painful tumor" in her left breast. As an expert physician, Jean knew very well what a cancerous tumor looked like. But he did not wish to stun his daughter with the bad news—a merciful impulse that his wife tactlessly undermined. Here, too, an affective father-daughter bond is contrasted with matter-of-factness between husband and wife:

Ipse autem vidit ipsam praegnantem, sibique dixit, non dubites, quod est ratione Foetus: mater vero sua sibi respondit: quomodo est hoc, quod non sit idem in alia mamilla?

(He saw that she was pregnant and said to her, "Do not doubt that this is on account of the pregnancy." But her mother replied, "How can that be, since it is not the same in the other breast?" [232])[41]

But Jean was certain of his diagnosis:

I videns ipse loquens ipsam passionem esse cancrosam, & esse cancrum

absconditum, qui est morbus mortalis . . . imo veniens ad aperturam &
crepituram in mamilla, moriuntur infra annum, vel infra annum cum
dimidio, ex corrosione carnis, nam mamilla tota corroditur paulatim.

([He] saw that this pain was cancerous and that it was a hidden cancer,
which is a mortal illness. . . . Indeed, once it has ruptured and opened
on the breast, they die within a year or within a year and a half, from
the putrefaction of the flesh, for almost the whole breast is consumed
[in such cases]. [§232])

After seeing Marguerite's tumor, Jean told "the mother of his daughter"[42]
to have the daughter avoid certain foods and to pray with her to an image
of "that most glorious cardinal, Lord Peter of Luxembourg." Returning to
Avignon, the distraught father visited Peter's tomb and went to the bishop to
beseech a piece of Peter's robe. The bishop granted him a small piece of linen,
perhaps from Peter's shroud, and a thread from Peter's scourge. Jean sent these
items to Montpellier with instructions to his wife to rub Marguerite's abscess
daily with the linen and to insert the holy thread directly into the wound.
By November, Marguerite had worsened and miscarried. Hastening home,
Jean found her "very weak" but noted in surprise that the "hardness" on the
cancerous breast was surrounded by healthy flesh, "contrary to the nature of
this cancer." He declared:

quod est etiam contra naturam cancri, quibus visis & consideratis, hoc
reputat a Deo esse factum, & a dicto glorioso D. Cardinali. . . . & dixit
in foro conscientiae suae, quod quadraginta annis practicavit, & non
vidit aliquam, similem morbum patientem, curari.

(he considered this contrary to the nature of cancer, [but] achieved by
God, with the intercession of the lord cardinal. . . . And he said that he
had practiced [medicine] for forty years and that he had not seen any
woman suffering from such an illness to be healed.)[43]

Jean notes in his testimony that he had made a vow at Peter's tomb but
that no one was present when he swore this vow. In contrast to Jacob's narrative, with its multiple witnesses to Esther's pious death, the miraculous drama
of Jean's deposition unfolds in a stark setting, devoid of domestic detail.
Jacob's story echoes that of his beloved Job, whose tragedy is also set amid

family and friends. In contrast, Jean's actions dominate his account of events, as he rushes from Avignon to Montpellier and back, goes to Peter's tomb and to the bishop, sends his wife the relics, examines his daughter. Whatever mother, daughter, and the young husband felt during those fraught weeks, the deposition does not record.

As Laura Smoller recently described for the canonization proceedings for Vincent Ferrer, men and women often remembered identical "miracles" in distinct ways.[44] Smoller observed that male witnesses tended to focus on action, and on themselves taking action, while women tended to pay attention to domestic interiors and details. This model holds for Jean's testimony but not for Jacob's record of events, which shows a prodigious attention to domestic detail and people: relatives, neighbors, furniture, jewelry, and household and ritual items, are minutely observed. Even the broth he attempts to feed her is "in a silver bowl," and the taper in Don Meir of Narbonne's hand, as "he groaned and wept," was a havdalah candle, which Esther urged him to give to one of the servants "as my soul is not yet ready to be gathered to its people" (79).[45] Through Jacob's eyes, a vivid picture emerges of the intensity of his love for this daughter.

Jacob's perspective is, of course, subjective. The *Evel Rabbati* displays discretion in its portrait of Esther's husband, Nathan, for instance. Esther's openhearted affection for her uncle, Nathan's father, is contrasted with her obedience and devotion toward her husband. Indeed, in rapid succession, she offers three clues to her married life. First, she rejects her aunt's proposal that young Yentish become Nathan's next wife, saying that Yentish's youth makes her unsuitable for the "great and mighty" Nathan. She then begs a family friend to intervene in a soured business deal that has alienated Nathan from an old comrade. And she urges her father to reunite his and Nathan's households, "to eat bread at one table as it was in the beginning" (79, 79, 79). All three incidents suggest that Nathan was a temperamental, even angry, man—but it is Esther's anxious devotion and diplomacy that Jacob wishes to convey, not the difficulties of a match he had arranged. In contrast, Jean de Tournemire ignores Marguerite's husband, Peter Suisse, because he is inessential to the healing narrative.

Medical knowledge, however, is essential to the story told by Jean de Tournemire, and a blend of theory and clinical detail fills the space taken up in Jacob's narrative by dialogue and mourning. Jean's role in his deposition is both as physician and father; as an expert witness, his testimony is particularly persuasive and filled with attestations of professional knowledge. The dietary regimen he recommended to his daughter was scientific and reflected his professional knowledge of the humoral properties of foods and their potentially beneficial or deleterious properties.[46]

So, too, the application of the sacred relics to Marguerite's breast adapted standard medical procedure for the treatment of abscesses. From the Greeks, medieval physicians had inherited the belief that a wound must stay open to form pus, the body's way of eliminating putrid matter. Among Jewish physicians, the method known as fontanel, which involved inserting a pea—alternatively, "hair, cords, or threads"—into a wound in order to prevent healing and generate pus, was known from Late Antiquity. Christian physicians, including the Italian masters Teodorico and Lanfranco, adopted this practice as well. Lanfranco's surgical compendium was among the library holdings of at least one Jewish physician in Avignon. A student of Jean de Tournemire, Valesco de Taranto, noted also that Jean adopted Lanfranco's distinctive approach to hernia surgery.[47] Thus, what is unique about Jean's protocol for the breast tumor is not the idea of inserting a thread into her abscess but of substituting for a regular thread one taken from the cord used by Peter of Luxembourg for self-flagellation.

At no point does Jean cease medical treatment for his daughter, and at no point does he deviate from responsible medical protocol, even though he is convinced that the prognosis is dire. His behavior may reflect his Parisian teachers' attitudes toward disease. In their tractate on the 1348 plague, the Parisian masters considered the question of unnatural (i.e., divinely wrought) disease. Even if God were responsible for the plague, they concluded, medical treatment should continue. In contrast, the plague tractate of Jacme d'Agramont, believed to be the earliest plague treatise (composed in Lerida in 1348, while the plague still raged), posed the same hypothetical question, and concluded that if the epidemic was an act of God, "medical art" was futile.[48]

Jacob, who also revered his Parisian teachers, behaved in a strikingly different manner.[49] It may have been his professional assessment that no medical intervention could save Esther, but the *Evel Rabbati* spends no time on medical analysis. The only moment when Jacob displays any technical knowledge comes in an aside about the benefits of broth. Then as now, broth was recommended for the sick or weak, but its use hardly represents an advanced level of technical expertise.[50] Rather, the *Evel Rabbati* emphasizes that human science is useless before divinely ordained disaster.[51] His explicit focus on Job in the preface and conclusion to the text underlines his conviction that what he has experienced is not only "like" the trials undergone by Job, but that the trials of both men originate with God.

Let us look closely at the description of Esther's final moments. Esther begs permission to kiss her relatives good-bye, so that Jacob can bless her "before I die and fly away to my heavenly dwelling" (81). In grief, Jacob kisses his daughter:

ואני נשקתי מתקי על שפת הידועה בתי. והחזיקה בי ונשקה לי עד
כמעט דבקתני הרעה ומתי. ותנשק לכל אחיו קרוביו וקרובותיה
בנשיקות פיה מדבש מתוקה. ואחר כמעט פרחה רוחה ומתה בנשיקה.
והקול נשמע בבית אנשי קהלנו בצאת נפשה כי מתה ויחרדו ויצא לבם
בנערנו ובזקננו כי איננה. ותלקח אסתר בית המלך י"י צבאות.

(And I kissed my sweet one, my daughter, on the familiar lip. And she seized me and kissed me, until I feared that the disaster would overtake me and I would die.[52] Then she kissed his brothers and relatives[53] and her relatives, with kisses of the mouth that were sweeter than honey. Afterward, she lost her breath and nearly died with a kiss. When her soul departed, the word went out among our community that she had died, and people were aghast. Their heart went out to her, young and old, for she was no more: Esther was taken away to the house of the King, the Lord of Hosts. [81–82])

This passage sends up a number of flares for educated Hebrew readers. Esther's kiss is described with the language of Prov. 7:13, which refers to the wiles of the foreign prostitute, often conflated by Jacob's time with the false attractions of foreign learning. The text then cites Gen. 19:19: "lest the disaster overtake me and I die," quoting Lot's hesitation to flee Sodom before its destruction (and his incest with his daughters). The description of Esther kissing her relatives fuses an allusion to Canticles 1:2 ("the kisses of her mouth") with an evocation of Samson's first wife's betrayal ("sweeter than honey"—from Judg. 14:18). The text then echoes descriptions of the matriarch Rachel's death (Gen. 35:22) and Moses' demand that Pharaoh release "the young men and old" or suffer the plague of locusts (Exod. 10:9). The final moment of Esther's death evokes the biblical Esther, brought to the house of the king (Esther 2:8).

This passage (and it is just one example) illustrates how Jacob's allusions can enrich the plain meaning of the text. Beneath the surface flows a recurring set of associations to heartache triggered by the love of women, with echoes of divinely wrought plague. So, too, Jacob's current pain is due to his love for his daughter. The reference to the prostitute of Proverbs 7 may reveal Jacob's preoccupation with the rationalists, who have (as he later tells us) been led by "foreign knowledge" to deny the veracity of Torah, saying, "it is an allegory for the enlightened" (83). Moreover, this passage is one of many in the *Evel Rabbati* referring to biblical "plagues," whether the biblical plagues that befell the Egyptians in Exodus 9–13, the destruction of Sodom and Gomorrah, the sickness of Na'aman, or divine promises to annihilate Jerusalem or the people. The allusions, like Jacob's medical nonintervention, argue that God has unleashed this disaster as well.[54] The blow that has struck his household, killing three of his own children and nearly all his nephews and nieces, is divinely wrought. It must be endured, not resisted.[55]

Among Christian physicians, as noted, Jacme d'Agramont held this view. The passage in which he describes medical art as useless (*poch valen*) is followed immediately by these words:

> And to confirm this, a sentence of the Holy Scripture can be quoted
> . . . [from] Deuteronomy 28: *Percutiat te dominus ulcere egipti, et partem
> corporis per quam stercora egeruntur scabie quoque et prurrigine, ita ut
> curare nequeas.* Thus it is vulgarly said that when God wisheth not,
> Saints cannot. For there is none who can oppose the might and power
> of God. The supreme remedy in such a case is to acknowledge our sins
> and our failings by hearty repentance and oral confessions.[56]

Jacme refers elsewhere to the terrible pestilence promised by God in Deuteronomy 28 if the Israelites should abandon His law. Unsurprisingly, he cites the Ten Plagues unleashed upon Pharaoh's land and people in Exodus 7–13 to illustrate that plague may befall us from God "because we deserve it" (*per obra de Déu e per mérits nostres*).[57] So, too, his regimen includes references to the destruction of Sodom and Gomorrah in Genesis 19; the plague sent by God to the rebellious Israelites in the desert in Numbers 14; the plague with which God punished the Israelites under King David in 2 Samuel 24; and King Solomon's prayer in 1 Kings 8 that God hear Israel's prayers in times of pestilence, drought, and calamity. When he turns, in contrast, to his analysis of "moral pestilence," all his citations are from the Gospels.

Most of these passages appear in the writings of other Christian plague physicians. And with the exception of the New Testament citations, they appear in the *Evel Rabbati*, too.[58] God's vow to punish the Israelites, "the people who have seen My glory and My signs that I wrought in Egypt" (Num. 14:22), yet continued to disobey Him, echoes in Esther's poignant response to her father's weeping:

ואיך לא תנוד ולמה לא תבכה. כי כל <u>האנשים הרואים את כבודי</u>
והעדרי מרבים בכה ואבל.

(And why shouldn't you lament and why shouldn't you weep? For <u>all the people who see my glory</u> and my absence will cry and mourn greatly. [81])

Shortly afterward, the phrase becomes Jacob's:

<u>הרואים את כבודי</u> ואת מאמר אסתר כדבר איש האלים. . . . <u>כי כל</u>
<u>האנשים הרואים את</u> דברי אלה אשר שמעו דבר המלכה.

(And <u>those who see my glory</u> and hear Esther's speech like that of a messenger from God. . . . <u>For all the people who see</u> my words that they heard, the speech of a queen. [83])

Jacob implies that God acts through Esther's death, and by extension through those who acknowledge His hand in the great mortality that has engulfed them. Indeed, Jacob's depiction of Esther has her follow Jacme's recommendation precisely: she confesses her sins and accepts her fate, inspiring those about her to acknowledge God's active role in current events.

In all these plague writings, the use of biblical prooftexts is strategic. Another instructive example comes from the work of another Avignon physician, Moses b. Samuel of Roquemaure. Moses is better known as Juan de Aviñon, the name he assumed after his conversion to Christianity in Avignon in 1353. His post-conversion career was in Seville, where he died about 1383–84.[59] Prior to his move, he spent a period of time in the papal court at Avignon. García Ballester has emphasized Juan's admiration for scholastic medicine, evident not only in his original compositions but in the works he chose to translate into Hebrew.[60] The *Sevillana medicina*, Juan's original compendium, was written in Castilian and links questions of human health to social setting—specifically, to the ambit of a particular urban environment.[61]

The *Sevillana medicina* devotes several chapters to epidemics and pestilential fevers. Juan runs through the familiar list of distant (celestial) and proximate (terrestrial) causes. In keeping with contemporary theories of the action of the plague upon the human body, he explains that inhalation of corrupted air corrupts the humor around the heart, brain, or liver; the affected organ tries to send the excess spirit to its "emunctory" (corresponding roughly to the lymph system) in the armpit, neck, or groin:

> Y esta razón que yo digo de las landres, esso mismo digo de qualquier dolencia que acaece de mortandad, que son infinitas, ca dellas veemos por la Biblia, que acaecio de morir por afogamiento de agua o de flema, el diluuio, y bilis amarilla, y dellas de colera quemante o de quemamien de fuego saluaje, assi como acaecoi a los de Sodoma y Gomorra, segun dize el verso. . . . Assi como Abimelech, Rey de Egypto. . . . Y dellas de muerte subitaña, assi como la dezena deciplina de Egypto, que murieron todos los primogenitos; dellas de fiebres agudas y de culebras quemantes, assi como dize en la Biblia, en el Libro do los numeros. . . . Otrosi, en el tiempo de Samuel . . . y en tiempo del Rey Dauid fue tres dias mortandad de muerte subitaña, por manera de miraglos. Veemos, en nuestro tiempo, muchas mortandades, [que] acaecieron desde .xxix. años.[62]

José Mondéjar, who has recently edited this work, thought it was neither very "original" nor particularly "Christian" (it is undeniably anti-Jewish).[63] In fact, Juan's "proofs" from Hebrew Scriptures are testimony to his Jewish beginnings and offer additional information on how a Jewish physician in Avignon during the plague years might have approached the question of epidemic etiology.

Muslim authors on the plague also refer to the biblical plagues brought upon the Israelites and Egyptians.[64] Some Muslim tractates try to provide a chronology of earlier epidemics, incorporating plague into a universe whose every event is ordained by God. Unlike Jacme d'Agramont, however, or Alfonso de Cordoba, who also theorized the possibility of artificially (i.e., humanly) engendered epidemic, Arab authors generally refused to acknowledge that pestilential diseases could be transmitted by any vehicle other than God. With one exception, Muslim physicians who wrote about the plague accepted its divine origins as a bar to any discussion of what we would generally call contagion.

I accept Ann Carmichael's position that "when used to understand and combat the spread of bubonic plague, 'contagion' is not a very helpful term."[65]

In a rich study of the 1467 plague in Milan, Carmichael demonstrates that the word and concept of "contagion" had "different meanings for different diagnosticians."[66] For the purposes of this chapter, I use the word mainly as a counter-theory to the divine causation of epidemics. In this more generic, admittedly sloppy, sense, "contagion" may describe both what we now know as diseases transmitted person to person and diseases transmitted by a nonhuman carrier. By today's definitions, only the former is truly contagion, but the latter also presupposes an identifiable, non-divine, vehicle for the transmission of disease. If, as is commonly believed, the Black Death was bubonic plague, it was not transmissible from human to human but, as we know today, transmitted by rodent-borne fleas. Some early Christian tractates duly connect the outbreak of disease with recycled bedding or clothing, granaries, ships, or refuse heaps—all vehicles for fleas or rodents. The bubonic plague also developed pneumonic or septicemic strains that were highly contagious. Mortality from bubonic infection was high; for the other strains, fatality was an almost certain outcome, often within a matter of hours.[67]

Studies of the Black Death that refer to Muslim and Christian societies routinely characterize attitudes toward contagion as a defining difference between the two communities.[68] According to this perspective, Muslims (learned and lay) were forbidden to endorse contagion. Jurists relied on several oft-cited hadith, some attributed to the Prophet himself, declaring that epidemic was an act of God.[69] Like any other divinely wrought disaster, an epidemic was to be endured rather than met with resistance or flight. For the pious Muslim, death by plague was considered martyrdom. Pre-Islamic notions of plague delivered by the darts of the jinn, traces of which survived in later literature, permitted a theory of transmission that included randomness and pandemic.[70]

Islamic medical regimens dealing with the plague thus avoid the standard advice of Christian physicians, which is to flee areas infected with plague. They are notably devoid of any notion of the plague as a punishment for sinful acts committed by the religious polity. Even when Muslim physicians describe the contagious nature of the plague, as does the Andalusian physician Ibn Khatima, they do so indirectly.[71] The famous exception, Ibn al-Khatib, also Andalusian, courageously declared that "the existence of contagion has been proved by experience, deduction, the senses, observation, and by unanimous reports"; the author was later arrested, in part on charges of heresy, and assassinated.[72]

Significant as these distinctions may be for identifying scientific and theological positions, they also imply culturally distinct psychological and emotional frameworks in which the bereaved might locate the experience of grief and loss. Certainly, Muslim physicians also lost children to the plague, and some of them wrote to commemorate their deaths. The ways in which they did so illuminate the kind of cultural distinction relevant to this chapter. For instance, Muhammad al-Manbijī's *Fī akhbār aṭ-ṭā'ūn* (Report of the Plague) was composed in Syria at the end of the plague of 1362–64. Al-Manbijī was a Ḥanballite jurist, thus an adherent of the most conservative school of Islamic law.[73] His plague tractate condemns those who have responded to the pandemic with "innovative" legal and customary practices; these have no place in a world where all disease comes from God.

Al-Manbijī wrote a second plague-related work, in which he mentions his son's death. The *Tasliyat ahl al-maṣā'ib* (Consolation for Those in Distress) is dedicated, in Dols's words, to "the spiritual meaning of adversity for plague victims . . . [and] the proper conduct for their survivors."[74] Similarly, Jacqueline Sublet refers to the plague tractate of Ibn Haĝar, titled *Baḏl al-mā'ūn,* as possibly inspired by the deaths of two daughters in the plague of 1417. Once again, the subject of the work is not the children's lives or deaths but "the causes of the epidemics and especially how one should conduct oneself in case of plague."[75] Despite its narrative form, Jacob's *Evel Rabbati* serves much the same end as these tracts, and indeed, the author's conservative views align him with Muslim authors he most likely had never read.

Christian physicians, on the other hand, moved gradually to a theory of plague transmission that embraced what we would call contagion. (They also recommended flight from infected areas, as immortalized in the bucolic retreat sought in Boccaccio's *Decameron.*) In many cases, this position merely acknowledged that proximity to the sick, their belongings, homes, or even cities could sicken an otherwise healthy person. In extreme formulations, like those of Alfonso de Cordoba or Jacme d'Agramont, the idea that epidemics could be caused had dire consequences for the Jews, considered predisposed to such ingenuity.[76] More commonly, ships in ports, visitors from plague-infested areas, textile or grain shipments, bedding, and food were all identified as problematic. Interestingly, Christian authors found theology no obstacle to a notion of pestilential disease whose origins and movement obeyed the laws of natural science. By the last quarter of the century, public measures to contain plague outbreaks included the isolation of victims in rudimentary forms of quarantine.[77]

What was the position of Jewish physicians? Barkai claims that they unanimously rejected contagion, but the reality may be more complex. Abraham Caslari's tractate on pestilential fevers, written during or immediately after the plague of 1348–49, tries to differentiate among pestilential diseases, saying some "spread" and some do not. His position defers to the treatment of epidemic diseases by Avicenna; minimally, he acknowledges a form of disease transmission that is not exclusively engineered by God:

וראיתי להזכיר הסבה הזאת הנה מפני שהתפארו קצת המתחכמים
לאמר שהחליים דבריים מפני שחייבם הדבוק ואמנם שהם היו מן
החליים המתפשטים ואולם עזר בהולדם הדבוק אך לא כל חולי
מתפשט ואשר יחייבהו הדבוק או ממשלת כוכב דבריי וגם לא תתחייב
לפי משפטי הכוכבים שימשך לדבוק הזה תולדת איכות דבריי אמתי.

(I thought to mention this particular cause because some of our so-called sages think that pestilential diseases are caused by [astrological] conjunction. Even if they are among the transmissible diseases, conjunction may be a factor in their causation, but not in every case. In those cases caused by conjunction or by a pestilential array of stars, the laws of astronomy do not mandate that the severity of true pestilence will follow from this conjunction.)[78]

Even if the majority or all of the extant Jewish plague tracts reject contagion theory, *some* Jewish physicians must have endorsed the idea. Jacob's attack on the allegorists refers explicitly to foes "among our people," and if I am correct, he is linking the allegorists to a pro-contagion theory of disease. Ibn al-Khatib, the sole Muslim proponent of this view, also endorsed allegorical readings of the ḥadīth and sharīʿa in order to reconcile their statements with observable reality.[79] On the other hand, Jacob b. Solomon could not have been a proponent of contagion theory, and this is evident—perhaps deliberately evident—in his description of Esther's final hours. Like the Muslim writers who emphasize the divine origins of epidemic, Jacob is concerned with conduct in the face of catastrophe. Staunchly, the *Evel Rabbati* describes gestures of social and physical intimacy that by the 1380s were generally accompanied by dousings of vinegar or rose water, incense, and other counteragents to contaminated air; bedding and clothing were increasingly (though by far not ubiquitously) suspect.

A crowded roomful of relatives, friends, and servants watches Esther die. Their role as witnesses is to verify Jacob's account and internalize the lesson of a model death. Esther publicly distributes her financial assets to charity and bestows her clothing upon friends (78). In another indication that her husband's family could be difficult, she returns all but her wedding ring to her uncle:

ואתה דודי רבוני קבל מני טבעותי המונחים באצבעותי יוסרו יען יהיו
פלטים. ולא יסבו להיותך חושד בכשרים העת ילין בכי... האמנם
באצבע קטנה שלי הניחו את הטבעת שבו קדשני בעלי.

(And you, my uncle and master, receive these rings on my fingers from
me. Let them be removed and be remnants, so that there is no suspicion
[of theft] during the ablutions when weeping tarries . . . but leave me
the ring on my little finger with which my husband betrothed me. [80])

Finally, she kisses her beloved family good-bye. Jacob has deliberately included reference to contact with Esther's bedding, jewelry, clothing, and body. After Esther's death, likewise, her body is washed and attended by her female companions. The only people whose presence or touch Esther shuns are distanced for reasons of religious law: Nathan because she is menstruating; her Uncle Moses because he is a *kohen* and forbidden contact with the dead; the young student's wife for fear she might miscarry. The narrative explicitly rejects the notion that contact with the sick woman, her belongings, or her environment could pose a hazard.

Reinforcement for this reading appears in Jacob's exegetical writings, which precede the *Evel Rabbati* in the Paris manuscript possibly copied in his own hand. In one section of a tripartite theological essay, Jacob analyzes the ten biblical plagues in Egypt. Here, indeed, we find all the medical theory suppressed in the *Evel Rabbati*, particularly in his discussion of the tenth plague, which brought death to the Egyptians' firstborn sons. Plague theorists, trained to think in terms of the particular humoral affinities of their patients, were confounded by the notion of an epidemic that could strike collective populations regardless of the accidents of birth, climate, or temperament. The belief that personal complexion governed states of health or illness proved a difficult obstacle to a doctrine of contagion. As a result, medical theory sought to explain the phenomenon of epidemics in general, and the plague in particular, by hypothesizing a corruption in the air, which affected everyone. The catalyst for this corruption might be a climate change, whose origins were either celestial (planetary conjunctions) or terrestrial (putrefaction in bodies of water or crops, even unburied corpses).[80]

To a physician's eye, this is precisely the epidemiological problem posed by the tenth biblical plague. Jacob observed that the firstborn sons of the Egyptians, of a variety of ages, astrological signs, and complexions, all died despite that variety of attributes—ועם כל זה מתו. He added:

הנה אם כן לא נשאר מקום . . . לומ' שהיא . . . בסבת החשך שקדם לה. ולא בסבת אויר דברי או מעופש. ולא בסבת מערכת הכוכבים ומבטם בעת לידת האישים ההם כמו שביארנו. ואפשר שעל שלש אלה רמזו רבותינו ע"ה באמרם: ועברתי בארץ מצרים אני ולא מלאך והכתי כל בכור אני ולא שרף ובכל אלהי מצרים אעשה שפטים אני ה' ולא השליח.

(Thus, there is no room . . . to say that this . . . was due to the [plague of] darkness that preceded it. Nor was it due to pestilential or corrupt air, or the configuration or appearance of the stars at these people's birth, as we have explained. It is possibly to this that our rabbis, peace be upon them, alluded when they said [citing the Passover Hagga-dah and its exegesis of God's statement in Exod. 12:12]: "I shall pass through the land of Egypt—*I and not an angel*—and I shall strike every firstborn son—*I and not a seraph*—and I shall render judgment upon all the gods of Egypt—*I, God, and not an intermediary.*")[81]

In sum, the literary evidence argues convincingly that the *Evel Rabbati* was a polemical composition as much as a commemorative one. The author has enlisted literary, rhymed Hebrew prose to craft a narrative that corresponds indisputably to a real event and could in no way be confused by his audience with allegorical fiction. He has purposefully elided all technical, "scientific" information from that narrative, modeling it lightly on structural and moti-val elements taken from the biblical books of Job and Esther. He has, again deliberately, woven into his text biblical prooftexts critical to contemporary debates over the causes and nature of the plague. In so doing, the *Evel Rabbati* "testifies" to God's intervention in matters of sickness and health, offering a pointed rebuttal to those who sought to explain these phenomena with the tools of natural philosophy. Indeed, Jacob declares pointedly that Esther's death was not due to "natural" causes:

מיתה משונה היא זו מכל מיתות המתים שכבר מתו זה אלף מן השנים./ ומכל ההשכבות האמורות בתורה שבכתב ושבעל פה, אשר נשמעו

ונראו בספר פנים בפנים./ ומה רחוק מציור האמת מי שיחשוב שזה
לשון הענין על דרך משל ומליצה צחה!

(This is an unnatural death, more than all the deaths the dead have
already died these thousand years, and more than all the burials told in
the Written and Oral Law which have been heard and seen in a book
directly. How far from imagining the truth is anyone who should think
that the language of this matter is an allegory or pure rhetoric! [82])

My reading of this text holds whether or not Jacob personally saw Jean de
Tournemire's deposition or heard Jean relate some version of it. Nonetheless,
he was in a position to have at least heard his colleague's story. Among the
several hundred depositions collected in 1390, one contains the testimony of
a woman who had been paralyzed for four months, losing the ability to speak
or eat.[82] An appeal to Peter of Luxembourg brought about an immediate improvement in her condition, so that she could lift some gruel to her mouth;
three days later, she managed to travel to Peter's tomb. Prior to her desperate
appeal for Peter's intervention, however, she had been treated by two Jewish
physicians, Jacob and Abraham, who diagnosed her case as hopeless. Pansier
lists only two Jewish physicians named Jacob in Avignon in this period, and
one is Jacob b. Solomon.[83] So it is at least possible that Jacob had direct knowledge of the canonization hearings and the deposition process. In either event,
as far as their goals may be surmised, Jacob's and Jean's testimonies have
much in common. Jean de Tournemire also stressed that Marguerite's cure
was "contrary to nature" (*contra naturam*). Though not describing a plague
case, Jean sought to demonstrate that God could—and would—intercede in
a natural disease process. Jacob likewise emphasized that faith could triumph
over medicine—whether or not the patient died.

To argue that the *Evel Rabbati* is not "merely" about Esther's death does
not demean its commemorative power. Nor does it invalidate the author's
anguish over the death of a favorite daughter, the incident that inspired—
perhaps required—the father to write. A series of allusions throughout the
Evel Rabbati sheds some light on Jacob's struggle with the depth of his feel-
ings for Esther. If it seems strange when Jacob uses the language of Canticles for his daughters, the Hebrew Bible provided him with few options for
expressions of paternal love. Close reading of the text reveals how much a
motif of unseemly attachment to Esther is reinforced through Jacob's allusions. Echoes of Haman's drunken collapse upon Esther's bed (Esther 7:5–8),

the harlot's kiss of Prov. 7:13, Eve's temptation of Adam in Genesis 3, and Lot's hesitation in Genesis 10 all thread the text at moments of high emotional stress. Thus, for instance, when Jacob flings himself across his dying daughter's bed in sobs, he quotes Esther 7:8:

והמלך שב מגנת הביתן אל-בית משתה היין והמן נופל על המטה אשר אסתר עליה ויאמר המלך הגם לכבוש את-המלכה עמי בבית?

(And the king returned from the palace garden to the place where they were drinking wine, as Haman fell upon the couch were Esther was; and the king said, "will he even assault the queen in my presence, in my own house?" [Esther 7:5, RSV])

ובעוד היותי נופל על המטה אשר אסתר עליה ואשתומם על המחזה והדבור ועיני עיני יורדה מים.

(And even as I fell on the bed where Esther was, I was stunned by the scene and speech, and my eyes flowed with tears. [78])

So, too, Esther's deathbed kiss, excerpted above, has a disturbing quality, with its echoes of Prov. 7:13 and Gen. 19:19:

והחזיקה בו ונשקה לו העזה פניה ותאמר לו: זבחי שלמים עלי היום שלמתי נדרי : על כן יצאתי לקראתך.

([The harlot] seizes him and kisses him, and with impudent face she says to him: I had to offer sacrifices, and today I have paid my vows; so now I have come out to meet you. . . . [Prov. 7:13–15])

ואנוכי לא אוכל להמלט ההרה פן תדבקני הרעה ומתי.

[And Lot said to them, . . .] behold, your servant has found favor in your sight, and you have shown me great kindness in saving my life; but I cannot flee to the hills, lest the disaster overtake me and I die. . . . [Gen. 19:19]

והחזיקה בי ונשקה לי עד כמעט דבבקתני הרעה ומתי.

And she seized me and kissed me until disaster nearly overtook me and I died. [81])

All these passages, I think, bare a survivor's guilt, and imply that the father's unguarded love for his daughter has been punished by her death. Jacob's sin was not to have loved Esther more than he loved Israel or Sarah, for instance, but simply to have loved her that deeply at all.[84]

This leaves us with a problem thus far unnoticed by other readers. The "authenticity" of the *Evel Rabbati* announces itself with any number of prose techniques advancing the "realism" of the narrative. Times and dates, names, dialogue, dishware, furniture, clothing, jewelry, candles—details that describe the onlookers and knit them into a web of communal history and relationships—create a rich and interlocking web of realia to uphold the narrative description of Esther's death. From the opening of the text, Jacob situates a sequence of illnesses, concluding with Esther's, in time and place. (In fact, we have no idea whether the casualty list really stopped there, or if other members of the family died later.) He himself fell ill first, on Wednesday, 5 Tishri, and recovered after "many days." His son Israel sickened and died shortly afterward. Sarah died on Thursday, 5 Adar, the following spring, and was buried the next day, on Friday, 6 Adar. Esther died on Sunday, 26 Adar, and was buried, at her request, beside her sister.

The fifth of Adar, February 8 by the Julian calendar, did indeed fall on a Thursday in the spring of 1383, and 26 Adar, or March 1, did fall on a Sunday. But 5 Tishri, which corresponded to September 13 according to the Julian year of 1382, fell on a Saturday, not on a Wednesday; it fell on a Wednesday, September 10, 1383, the following year, after Jacob's three children had already died. Did Jacob fail to recall the sequence of dates so critical to the unfolding of his narrative? Is it possible that his own illness followed his children's instead of preceding it? Would that not undermine the guilt that runs through his account, guilt that I have gently attributed to his grief in bereavement, the guilt of loving a child too well? Does the narrative require Jacob to trigger the illness in his home, to suffer the cruel punishment of surviving to see his children suffer and perish?

What does it mean when a narrative constructed to make you believe that it happened embeds within it a factual impossibility?

To this puzzle I have no answer. But I know that Jacob did not like to make things simple, and perhaps it is better to let some mysteries be. Whatever he intended, Jacob's attempt to honor his daughter's memory while enlisting the tale of his suffering to respond to his foes has left us a rare and precious testimony to his faith. The *Evel Rabbati* also reveals a great deal about one Jewish physician's response to the devastation of the plague years and how that response was shaped ideologically. In the larger context of the studies that constitute this book, Jacob's ideological fixity has additional meaning. A child of French Jews, although raised in the south, his loyalties reflect the determination of his parents to ensure that the values of the north would endure in exile. Even the collection of essays containing the *Evel Rabbati* is inscribed with the author's full name: "Ya'akov ben Shlomo Tzarfati," Jacob ben Solomon the Frenchman, an identity that clearly gave him pride.

Indeed, as noted in the beginning of this chapter, the name Jacob b. Solomon of Avignon is today most likely to evoke the scribe of the so-called Wolf Haggadah, currently at the Jewish National and University Library in Israel. Dated to the century's end, the Wolf Haggadah has long intrigued scholars. Its elegant illuminations are now believed to have been added in Italy, pointing to yet another exilic journey. The marginal notations, like the Haggadah itself, are Jacob's, and as I have already indicated, they emphatically endorse the rites and rituals of his beloved France. On folio 4r, for instance, we read in the body of the text: "this is the opinion of the rabbis of France and that is how my teacher, R. Nathan, used to do it—and so do I." However, when we look at the illustration of this ritual in Jacob's Haggadah, we can see that it fell into the hands of a later, probably Italian, user. Despite the explicit practice described in the text, where Jacob rejects the non-French custom of removing the egg and shank bone from the seder plate, the illumination shows a lofted seder plate minus those two items.

At the end of a terrible Jewish century, what did being "French" mean to Jacob b. Solomon? Something worth preserving, at least in part because it provided fortitude and faith in a time of terrible tribulation. Ironically, it was not the medical opinions of his French masters that guided Jacob through the plague years that stripped love and family from him; it was the religious rigor of his French Jewish teachers, his parents, and R. Nathan, and the instruction they provided, that held him upright through that storm. In the process, he has left us two things. First, of course, is Esther, perhaps, to paraphrase Ben Jonson, Jacob b. Solomon's "best piece of poetry." Second, and equally moving, Jacob reminds us of the complex construction of human memories, and the myriad motives for which they are enlisted. In the next chapter, we will see how a small community of exiles, victims of the last French expulsion of the century in 1394, bequeathed to their descendants an equally tenacious grip on a past marked by "Frenchness." It is to the poets of Trévoux, originally from the Savoy region, we now turn.

CHAPTER SIX

Refrains in Exile:
French Jewish Poetry in Northern Italy

WHATEVER THEIR SURFACE concerns, the great expulsion of French Jews in 1306 echoes through the works treated in the previous chapters. In some cases, it sounds explicit or implicit motifs of dislocation in exile, a blend of yearning for what has been lost with a determined adaptation to the new. Lyric, philosophical poetry, romance, and medical literature all preserve in some fashion the traces of an uncertain century for European Jews. Over the fourteenth century, the seismic reverberations of 1306 shook Jewish communities with an ongoing ripple of general and local expulsions both in royal France and in neighboring principalities. The last of these expulsions was in 1394, when the remnants of French Jewry, whose parents and grandparents had been expelled and recalled several times over, fled once more. Many of them turned to the papal and imperial territories that flanked the southeastern border of France.[1]

What did French Jews remember of their fourteenth-century past, and how did their own experience continue to shape and reshape those memories? The preceding chapters have followed French Jewish exiles into Provence, Spain, the papal Comtat Venaissin, North Africa, the Savoy, Dauphiné, and Italy. My focus in this chapter is on a small group of Jews who settled in the Piedmontese region of northern Italy, where as late as the twentieth century Jewish liturgical traditions preserved elements of French Jewish practice that have survived nowhere else.[2] The poems these Jews left behind them testify to their efforts to sustain an identity rooted in "Frenchness" and linked to the experience of expulsion. So, too, the material remains of these poems, both secular and sacred, offer clues to the ways in which that identity was constructed and sustained, and for whom.

The following pages concentrate on a particular manuscript containing a collection of liturgical laments. By its very nature, liturgical poetry privileged the blurring of past and present over a documentary-style narration of facts. On the one hand, this explains why historians have not traditionally shown much enthusiasm for plumbing poetic texts. On the other, liturgical poetry and collections of poetry arrange historical memory in ways that illumine what was important to their users. In the case of the collection treated below, the individual laments, their arrangement in a liturgical sequence, and the subsequent alteration of that sequence illustrate changing approaches to the interpretation of expulsion in historical and sacred time. The liturgical approach was surely complemented by others, but it served well those users for whom it provided a means of understanding present difficulties as well as a sense of their own uniqueness as a community.

All the Jews I discuss here lived—or were the descendants of Jews who had lived—in the town of Trévoux, on the border between France and the Savoy. Their ancestors came to Trévoux from farther north, probably fleeing Lyon and nearby towns in the wake of the 1306 expulsion.[3] Over the fourteenth century, the Savoy continued to welcome Jewish refugees from France, a number of whom settled in Trévoux and eventually (particularly after 1394) moved on and over the Alps into Savoyard and Piedmontese communities. We know who they were because they were referred to by their place of origin, sometimes Trévoux, sometimes shortened to Trèves, or Italianized to Trabot or even Trabotto. The most famous of them is probably Yohanan Trèves, prior to 1394 the chief rabbi of France and known in part for his struggle to recapture that title in the Savoy.[4]

But many Trabots or Trévoux labored to keep aloft the banner of tradition and learning—perhaps better described as *their* tradition and learning, for whether or not they were actual kin, the Trabots made some effort to preserve a common voice. Many were authors of ethical, liturgical, or grammatical works; some were scribes as well. Intellectually, and despite their southern credentials, they reflect their northern origins and the strong stamp of Ashkenazic attitudes in lands under imperial control.

The Jews of Trévoux also brought to northern Italy a perspective on persecution and tragedy—again, *their* persecution and tragedy, from the experiences of the 1394 generation through the experiences of their children and grandchildren in Italy. This perspective was both inherited and dynamic: just as the past pressed hard on the interpretation of contemporary events, the present pressed hard on the past. This might be illustrated in a number of ways; I am going to use the case of poems, and focus on a late fifteenth-century manuscript found in the Parma Biblioteca Palatina, Heb. 1883, or De Rossi 485.

Parma 1883 is a fast-day liturgy made for personal (versus commissioned) use, first by one copyist, who penned the majority of its laments, and then by a second copyist, who added several more and attached the whole to his copy of the text of Lamentations and excerpts from the *Sefer Shorashim* of David Qimḥi (d. 1235), a dictionary of words from the book of Job. The selection and arrangement of laments has led scholars to identify this liturgy as an illustration of the Carpentras rite—not, as we shall see below, entirely true. Of the eighteen laments, some, including those added by the second copyist, represent cherished authors from Provence and Andalusia; several are by unknown poets.[5] Of the original laments, nine are by Trabots: at least three by Peretz Trabot, a survivor of the 1394 expulsion; two by Gabriel Trabot, who was active in the first half of the fifteenth century; two, possibly three, by Peretz Yeḥiel Trabot. One Peretz Yeḥiel is known to us from the mid-fifteenth century, and another—perhaps his grandson—from the latter part of the century.[6] A long concluding lament is signed Netanel, possibly the father of the earlier Peretz Yeḥiel.[7]

The Trabot compositions form the heart of the poetic section of Parma 1883. This is especially true if we discount for now the four interpolated laments by other poets, inscribed on paper and inserted by the second copyist.[8] Thus, Parma 1883 preserves for us a uniquely "Trabottian" view of Jewish history, at least that part of Jewish history that might be compressed into a penitential matrix and presented to inspire reflection on that theme. That is not a comprehensive view of history, of course, and the Trabot poets represented in Parma 1883 testify elsewhere to a range of literary and historical interests. Their writings chronicle teaching frustrations, professional achievements, poetic and personal rivalries, social practices, and discussions of religious law. They treat, in other words, life. And by "life," I mean contemporary events that surely weighed on their authors' minds even when their ostensible subject matter was the past.

The type of liturgy represented by Parma 1883, despite its Ashkenazi script, reflects the Sephardic tradition of reciting laments during the three-week period concluding with the Ninth of Av, the fast day associated with the destruction of the First and Second Temples.[9] The liturgy consists mainly of Lamentations and a selection of poetic laments that was fluid enough to incorporate local favorites. As Dan Pagis and Joseph Yahalom have shown for the case of Spain, manuscript collections of laments used by Spanish Jews frequently reflected on moments of historical crisis. This is especially true of the later medieval collections, some of which commemorate the two great traumas of Spanish Jewry roughly contemporary to the 1394 expulsion from France: the pogroms of 1391; and the violence and mass conversions following the Disputation of Tortosa in 1412–14. Among other things, such collections document the impulse to commemorate the experience of a specific community. Those who found solace and meaning in their reading of history also treasured a sense of commonality and even exclusiveness with respect to outsiders. The elision of these texts from later print editions reinforces our sense of how local they were.[10]

Dan Pagis noted forty years ago that the authors and transmitters of Spanish Hebrew laments commemorating the terrible violence of 1391 or the Disputation of Tortosa handled factual content in several ways. Sometimes the authors fused concrete details with typological motifs, perhaps to boost their impact, perhaps to throw censors off the track. Sometimes they, or later writers and copyists, added imagery to link a historical incident with the tragedies commemorated on fast days like the Seventeenth of Tammuz or the Ninth of Av. Alternatively, they could "neutralize" historically specific references by eliminating them altogether; or "realize" them by adding factual details from a later incident better known to a contemporary audience.[11]

The Trabots, we will see, were familiar with these techniques. Let me therefore begin with the world of Piedmont Jews, and the French refugees among them, before turning to their poems.[12] When read against the backdrop of historical events, I believe that we can see that although the poetic hymns of Parma 1883 exploit generic tropes, they do so in order to comment cunningly on local events.

The expulsion of 1394 is poorly documented in Jewish literature; among the stray references that we do find in Jewish texts, poetry is almost nonexistent. Curiously, one of the most explicit comments on this trauma survives in a popular dictionary of biblical Hebrew. That dictionary was written by Peretz Trabot the *Naqdan*, or "Punctuator," a grammarian who was hired to "point" the vowels into Hebrew manuscripts.[13] Scholars have long identified the Peretz of our laments with this Peretz, a victim of the 1394 expulsion.[14] Called the *Maqré Dardaqé* (That Which Makes Children Read), his lexicon of biblical Hebrew lists Hebrew roots alphabetically and glosses them in Occitan and Arabic with the relevant biblical citations. A later contributor added Italian glosses, and the trilingual version was first published in Naples in 1488.

Peretz begins the *Maqré Dardaqé* with a poem, plying the familiar topos of Israel's forfeited sovereignty and subjection to the descendants of slaves. While "the maidservant's son" (Christianity) basks in light, the son of noble birth (Israel) lies wounded in perpetual servitude.[15] The prose that follows turns bitterly to recent events: "[The enemy] rises like a lion from his lair, turning this way and that seeking prey, and suddenly he devours. So now, in 1394, most of the root has borne bitter and poisonous fruit. Israel's pride is evident, and [their punishment] is from God. [Thus] they were expelled from France.[16] Like aliens, they bent to put their yoke on their necks, [and] the wealthy were despoiled of their riches. They were forced to give up their grain, [but] they would not sin [i.e., convert] in exchange for bread."[17]

Peretz turns quickly from this account to the frustrations of teaching biblical Hebrew, a task whose urgency is linked to conversionary pressures. Far too many Jewish parents with money to spend on their sons' education prefer to speed them past biblical Hebrew on a fast track toward either Talmud or secular philosophy. As a result, proud fathers boast of prodigies who remain ignorant of Hebrew Scriptures, the primary Jewish text in the *Christian* arsenal. If, Peretz observed, the ignorant student does not know what to answer his challenger, the "heretics" will triumph and the student be led to apostasy.[18]

The situation in Spain and Italy suggests that this was not an idle concern. In fact, polemical exchanges with mendicant preachers, or compulsory attendance at mendicant sermons, were known not only in Provence and Spain but would become a feature of Savoyard Jewish life as well. Vincent Ferrer, the Dominican "Angel of the Apocalypse," preached throughout the Savoy and Piedmont in 1402–4 and again in 1417–18.[19] John of Capistran followed him several decades later.[20] In between and in their wake, a network of friars and Inquisitors increasingly intersected with the world of Piedmontese Jews. The friars and their preaching cast a growing shadow over the hymns of Parma 1883, too, and the past they interpret and construct. Allusions to expulsion and impoverishment in the hymns of Peretz the Punctuator give way to images of harassment, book burning, conversionary pressure, and seasonal violence, some in laments by Peretz and some by later Trabots.

Significantly, over this same period, Jewish life in the Piedmont was marked by expansion and prosperity. When Vincent Ferrer preached against usury in Lausanne in 1403–4, moving on to Fribourg and then the Savoyard city of Estavayer-le-lac, he was targeting *Christian* lenders. Indeed, the closing of Christian lending banks opened the doors for Jewish lenders to move into the region—which they did, and thrived.[21] The robust vitality of these Jewish communities is noteworthy. Their infrastructure was never so eroded by economic harassment, discriminatory social policies, or persecution that it could not respond in times of crisis.[22] Over time, those crises took predictable forms: a growing trend to physical segregation of Jewish residential and commercial activity; the enforcement of Jewish "badges" on outerwear; conflicts over meat and grain markets; festival violence; even ritual libels. To protect themselves, Jewish leaders played popes against Inquisitors or dukes; dukes against friars, Inquisitors, and town councils; even emperors against popes.[23]

In this world, Jews could be confident—even smug—as well as worried, and there are plenty of indications that they were both. Only a social setting that guaranteed Jews significant protection could produce a colorful figure like Sanson of Louent, a "magister" of Jewish law from nearby Bourg-en-Bresse. A vocal opponent of Yohanan Trèves's efforts to name himself chief rabbi of the Savoy, Sanson was tax-farming fellow Jews throughout the 1390s.[24] In 1404, he was accused of having announced to "many Christians" that "if the Christ [they] revered were to be resurrected today, he would crucify him again immediately."[25] Sanson purportedly characterized a curate as usurious for taking a florin for a mass that was not worth a gros. Sanson, alas, was also suspected of having carnal relations with (several) Christian women. And thirteen years later, after months of imprisonment and torture, Sanson was one of two prominent Savoyard Jews to confess publicly to the anti-Christian blasphemies of the Talmud. The books were burned; Sanson vanishes from the records.[26]

Mendicant preaching made inroads into the Savoy also. During the fifteenth century, bulls of protection for the Jews (the so-called *sicut judeis* bulls) came with stern warnings to the friars not to incite anti-Jewish violence in their sermons. Descriptions of Vincent Ferrer or John of Capistran (or later, Bernardine of Sienna) leave no doubt that this concern, too, was well-founded. Saint Vincent's hagiographers proudly credit him with the voluntary conversion of 25,000 Jews. Scholars continue to debate his actual role in the bloody pogroms of 1391 and in the mass conversions that followed the Disputation of Tortosa in 1412–13. While modern defenders of the saint have sometimes taken refuge behind the literal text of his sermons (which, they note, do not specifically call for violence), violence against the Jews quite often followed them.[27] If this was so in the case of an eloquent scholastic and master of homiletics, the aftermath of cruder preaching can only be imagined.

Trouble erupted especially in the years following the Disputation of Tortosa, a two-year "debate" between Spanish rabbis and Christian friars.[28] The debate was endorsed by antipope Benedict XIII, whose confessor was Vincent Ferrer, preaching in Aragon during this period. During the waning months of the public hearings and in their aftermath, thousands of Spanish Jews converted. Tortosa had a ripple effect in the Savoy, where by 1416 two former Jews were ensconced in the Franciscan monastery in Chambéry, inspecting Jewish books for heretical or blasphemous statements.[29] The physicians Pierre de Macon and Guillaume Saffon had converted in 1414, probably in response to Tortosa; they had quickly found employment as censors during an Inquisitorial investigation of Jewish books in the Dauphiné.[30] In Chambéry, their efforts, accompanied by the mass arrests and torture of prominent local Jews—remember Sanson—led to the condemnation of the "Talmud" and its consignment to the flames in January 1417.[31]

Over the next few decades, the influence of the friars grew. The Franciscan Inquisitor Pons Feugeyron expanded his jurisdiction beyond Christian heresies, which category included the practices of converted Jews, to investigate heretical or deviant practices *among* Jews. Although Pons's excesses earned him a number of rebukes from Pope Martin V and Eugene IV, he remained in his post as Inquisitor for Avignon and much of the Savoy into the 1440s.[32]

This historical trajectory is embedded in the arrangement of Parma 1883, where the memory of "France" is locked into place in a messianic chronology leading from the biblical past to an Italian present. With the exception of the closing hymn, the laments of Parma 1883 are not lengthy. Most range from a dozen to two dozen verses, each verse subdivided into four to six units of a few words apiece; a few poems contain indications for refrains. Although the metrical schemes are irregular and must have been disciplined by a now-lost musical setting or recitative format, the verses scan crudely according to Sephardic (quantitative) convention. In several cases, a syllabic, near-iambic, emphasis is also discernible.[33] Metrical inconsistency is not unusual for poetry beyond the borders of Andalusia and reminds us, in this case, that the vernacular of the poets was far from the Arabic that influenced the quantitative verse forms associated with Sephardic poetry.

Parma 1883's opening lament, the anonymous "Esh tuqad be-qirbi" (A fire burns inside me), was popular among the Jews of Provence, where this liturgical compendium spent some time. The placement of this lament tells us that its popularity traveled over the Alps as well. The Italian-based émigrés who dominate the remainder of the laments, along with the ways that their compositions reflect local experience, place the first copyist in the Piedmont but link him also to the traditions and late tastes of his past. For a long time, this poem was attributed to the beloved late twelfth-century poet of Provence Isaac HaSeniri, although recent scholarship has convincingly argued against this attribution.[34] "A fire burns inside me" is constructed in alternating expressions of hope and despair, each verse concluding "when I went out from Egypt" or "when I went out from Jerusalem." The hymn ends with a long series of verses that describe the cultic apparatus of the biblical Temple. By the late thirteenth century, as Eva Frojmovic has demonstrated, a Catalonian or Provençal Jewish audience easily read these images as intimations of a messianic era.[35]

Running down the inside margin of "A fire burns inside me" is another hymn that had a long life in liturgies for the Ninth of Av. Also of unknown authorship, this hymn begins "My beloved, I lift my eyes to you in my exile! Pursue [the enemy] in wrath and destroy them from under the heavens!"[36] Three stanzas describe Israel's ancient enemies (Caesar, Vespasian, Titus, Hadrian), her expulsion and wandering, and her prayers for restoration; the opening call for vengeance serves as a refrain. Visually, then, the first poem's dialectic of Egypt and Jerusalem, redemption and exile, is framed by the anonymous poem. On the facing page, two more hymns sweep around the trailing last stanzas of "A fire burns inside me"; they, too, emphasize images of biblical destruction and exile, with pleas to return to Zion.

Peretz Trabot is Parma 1883's first local contributor. Indeed, Peretz's hymn "Eikha ukhal" (How can I watch) opens with the same topos enlisted for his lexicon's introductory verses:

איכה אוכל / ואראה / צר מתגאה / על בן-מלך

עבד רוכב / עלי סוסו / הרים נסו / בכל פלך?

לאמר ילך / כדל הלך / מפחדתו / בשרו סמר

כלה קיץ / קציר עבר / את הדבר / אביו שמר.

(How can I watch the foe who boasts over the son of the king?
The servant who rides his [master's] horse, raising his banner in every
    region?
Saying, "Let him [the Jews] leave!"

Like wretches, they did leave, their flesh shivering in fear of him.
The summer is over, the harvest is passed.
Their Father observed what had come to pass.)[37]

Peretz's seasonal imagery may be read with a double meaning. The phrase
cites Jer. 8:20's "the summer is over, the harvest is passed"; the biblical verse
ends "and still we are not saved." In this form, it was also cited bitterly by Isaac
Abrabanel, an Iberian refugee in Italy at the end of the century; Abrabanel
remarks that the prophets who had promised Jewish redemption "were liars,
for the summer is over and the harvest is passed, and still we are not saved."[38]
But beyond an exhausted messianism, the phrase simultaneously supports a
reference to the autumn of 1394; Charles VI's order for expulsion was dated
September 17.[39]

Like most Jewish liturgical poets, Peretz does not narrate a clear chain of
events. Indeed, some of his allusions are to disturbing acts of violence that the
historical record has not preserved. "How can I watch" invokes dark images
of lost homes, arrest, and harassment; the desecration of synagogues and their
conversion into Christian chapels; the plowing of cemeteries and tyranny of
"lions." Midway through the poem, a single verse laments the execution by
fire of "the blue-eyed one, a perfect offering." Who this Jew was, described
in terms that evoke the biblical David, is a mystery; we do not even know
whether his death occurred in France or in his new home. We do know that
in 1394, the Jewish cemeteries in France were destroyed; in Roger Kohn's eloquent words, the dead were expelled with the living.[40] These faint historical
echoes suggest that the 1394 expulsion, if not the sole trauma commemorated
in this hymn, is one of its major referents.

Peretz's two other hymns in this collection also embed shards of historical experience into generic tropes of exile, disinheritance, and pleas for vengeance and restoration.[41] In the hymn "Ivḥat ḥarbi" (My glittering sword),
which follows "How can I watch," Peretz again refers to exile and expulsion;
a "house of God" used as a church; the looting of wealth; and the murder of
the innocent.[42] Peretz tersely remarks, אחרון הכביד / עם לא אלמון, referring to Isa. 8:23 [= RSV Isa. 9:1] and again transmitting two meanings at
once: God has lately "weighed down" a people but not forsaken them, or God
will ultimately bring glory to the people He has not forsaken. The medieval
glosses place Isaiah's words in the context of the multiple expulsions endured
by the Jews, and the "weightier" blow that befell those who thought they were

safe. Peretz's words thus embody a reproach to those Jews who saw the clouds gather and thought they would remain untouched. In a familiar theological move, expulsion has struck the overly complacent, those who have grown lax in their piety or strayed to the temptations of gentile learning and ways.

"My glittering sword" also strives for erudition, both in biblical citations and rabbinic locutions. This kind of allusive density marks the aesthetic distance of the Savoyard Trabots from the stylistic norms of Andalusian poetry and, to a lesser extent, Hebrew poetry in Provence. It says something also about Peretz's intended audience and its dexterity with the rabbinic literature treated indifferently by the rationalists and with growing concern by Inquisitors and popes. As a form of performance, this poetry constitutes a polemical challenge as much as a literary pastime. The "Talmud trial" of 1240 or the Disputation of Barcelona in 1263 would have been ancient history for Peretz and his children. But attacks on rabbinic literature were a vivid reality of their lifetimes, and in the wake of the Disputation of Tortosa they could be terrifying.

Read against the backdrop of historical events, the hymn "Azkirah tzoq ha'ittim" (Let me commemorate the distress of the times) appears to respond to this terror. The opening words prepare us to hear about something contemporary, but on the surface, at least, the poem does not comply. As a didactic composition, the poem refers to the rabbinic regulations governing the four traditional fasts commemorating the destruction of the biblical Temple, on the Tenth of Tevet, the Seventeenth of Tammuz, the Ninth of Av, and the Fast of Gedaliah following Rosh Hashanah.

Peretz's lament refers sequentially to these commemorative landmarks, beginning with the biblical siege of Jerusalem on the tenth month (Tevet— the first fast).[43] In the "fourth month," Tammuz, the enemy put an icon in the Temple and burned the "Torah" (the second fast):

להעמיד בהיכל צלם / בית מקדשי ושועי / ונשרפה התורה / בחדש הרביעי

(He put an icon in the Temple, the place of my sanctuary and supplication, and the Torah was burned in the fourth month.)[44]

Two verses later, the "tablets of the faith" are "broken like an unsealed pot cover" and the daily sacrifice abolished—still the Seventeenth of Tammuz, traditionally the day on which Moses broke the first Tablets of the Law, and the end of the sacrificial offerings in the Temple. Chaldeans, Ammonites, and Moabites invade the speaker's palace, and his mourning marks the month of Av (the third fast). The children of Zion are "chased from their homes," pursued by troubles, and humiliated by a "stupid and foolish people"; they are crushed in the "dust among the lions." The speaker recalls the slaying of Gedaliah (the fourth fast) and prays for consolation.

How could such a litany mark the "distress of the times"? Peretz refers to the burning of the "Torah" in Tammuz, or the height of summer. This detail is preserved in the Mishnah, Seder Mo'ed Ta'anit 4:6, which describes the "five things" that befell the Jews on the Seventeenth of Tammuz: Moses' breaking of the first Tablets of the Law; the end of the daily sacrifices; the breach of Jerusalem's walls; the tyrant Apostomos's burning of the Torah; and the installation of an icon in the Temple.[45]

Is this the "burning of the 'Torah'" to which Peretz refers? Or might he also be referring to the cascade of Inquisitorial confiscations and burnings of Jewish books ("Talmuds") that swept through the Dauphiné, Savoy, and Bresse in 1416–18? Remember, Pierre de Macon and Guillaume Saffon were examining impounded books in Chambéry as early as October 1416. Amadeus VIII had ordered the books confiscated months earlier.[46] In July, the duke permitted the restitution of prayer books, Bibles, and medical books that had been seized with the offending "Talmuds." In September, he let the Jews "borrow" their prayer books, presumably for festival use. The censors' investigation concluded with the condemnation of Talmudic blasphemies on January 26, 1417, the confessions of Rabbis Sanson and Aguin de Nantua, and an immediate order to burn the condemned books.

January 26, 1417, corresponds to 29 Tevet on the Jewish calendar. Jewish books were burned again later that summer in Bresse, on June 27, corresponding to 4 Tammuz. The poem hovers over these months of Tevet and Tammuz, January and June, as months when a Jewish community was under siege and the "Torah"—in its expanded meaning of Oral and Written Law—was burned. It would be burned again in May 1418 in the Savoyard city of Châtillon, and in 1426 in Chambéry.[47] In 1429, the Jewish books in Trévoux, the hometown of our writers, were confiscated and an order for their burning was issued later that year.[48] Thus, Peretz has apparently sought to compress recent events into the symbolically charged chronology of the ancient destruction of the Temple—the very strategy described by Pagis for the laments of 1391 and 1412–14. He asks us to make a direct connection between the threat to

Jewish worship posed by the destruction of the Temple cult and that posed by the destruction of Jewish books. Moreover, the listener now understands the preceding laments to narrate a sequence of woes. Because of our sins, we were expelled. Because of our sins, we continue to be punished. Because of our sins, God is angry—but the cycle also promises restoration and redemption, hope and consolation. For this end (literally, End), we wait.

Peretz, it must be said, was not a great poet. His style is choppy, his prosody at times uncertain, and identifying his allusions does not always clarify what he is trying to say. Indeed, almost all the poems discussed here revel in a highly elliptical, near-pointillist use of language that demands associative reading and a great deal of filler in translation. It may be that this kind of pointillism was admired by Piedmontese Hebrew poets, who seem to exemplify the hybridity associated with Provençal Hebrew writing, an aesthetic neither "Sephardic" nor "Ashkenazic." The corrupt form of some of the verses, where the rhyme and meter have been mangled, may also be indications of later tampering. But "Let me commemorate the distress of the times," like Peretz's other hymns, suggests the exiles' awareness of the commemorative strategies enlisted by the Spanish poets of this time. Embedding a historical incident in the mythic past, Peretz emphasizes its tragic core while shading delicately allusions to the present through a cautious selection of topoi. It may be that later copyists further obscured what were once more recognizable allusions to contemporary events.

Between Peretz's second and third hymns, the copyist has inserted a hymn by a later poet, Peretz Yeḥiel Trabot. This Peretz was the descendant of another 1394 exile, Levi Tzarfati ("the Frenchman"), who left France for the Savoy and Italy, and then Italy for the Holy Land.[49] Peretz Yeḥiel may be the mid-century poet whose lament "Shelaḥ yad el tzayyad" (Raise Your hand against the hunter) is found in MS Parma 2306, or a later fifteenth-century descendant.[50] His lament "Can a stone cry out from the wall" uses standard tropes for the Ninth of Av, interwoven with rabbinic motifs.[51]

A second poem by Peretz Yeḥiel hints more explicitly at contemporary realities. "Ani yashen ve-libbi 'er" (I sleep but my heart is awake) swings forcefully away from the mythical past. Opening with the familiar words of Canticles 5:2, "I sleep but my heart is awake," Peretz Yeḥiel twists them darkly:

אני ישן ולבי ער / בקול ילל כים סוער / עד מה חמת מלך בוער /
ומסוכתו היה לבער

(I sleep but my heart is awake, with a voice of wailing like a stormy sea
How long will the king's wrath keep burning, and his hedge be
devoured?)[52]

The poem continues, "The enemy gaped at me, saying, 'who is this and where
is he?' He and his camp hope [to destroy me]" (v. 2). The allusion is to Lam.
2:16, a verse often put into Christian mouths by Hebrew polemical poets:
"All your enemies rail against you; they hiss, they gnash their teeth, they
cry: We have destroyed her! This is the day we have hoped for, now we have
it, we see it!" The central verses of the poem detail the enemy's exploits—the
desecration of synagogues, their conversion into chapels, the loss of children
into "slavery." The latter may allude to the forced baptism of Jewish children,
documented in the midyears of the century:[53]

צר בהיכל העמיד חלאה / מי שמע זאת ומי ראה / תוכו הושיב סמל קנאה /
ובשפתו גאה גאה
יוצרי פסל הודי חללו / כי עוללי בשבי גלו / לפסיליהם בל יועילו /
המה כרעו ונפלו

(The foe has stood filth in the Temple. Who has heard or seen such a
    thing?
Inside he set the "image of jealousy" [the cross], and boasted:
The makers of idols have defiled my Glory, for they have sent my
    children into slavery.
To their useless idols they bowed and fell.)[54]

The expression *semel ha-qin'ah*, Peretz Yeḥiel's euphemism for the cross, appears also in a lament that originally commemorated 1391 violence but was
adapted to respond to the Disputation of Tortosa.[55] It may be that Italian Jews
encountered this lament in its reworked form.

These images climax in the following poem, "Eikha yashva qiryat dodi
ḥana" (How solitary sits the city where my beloved camped).[56] The acrostic
signature "Peretz" in this poem does not tell us which Peretz is the author (the
Punctuator or Peretz Yeḥiel). Its coded references to the incursions of "Chaldeans and Moabites," terms that run through these poems, do not by themselves
tether the poem to the early or late part of the century. However, the poem's
"Chaldeans and Moabites" write "bitter things" against the Jews, and they
operate in a very specific way, during festival seasons and with grim results:

חגים ינקופו / בתער הגלבים / את היכלי שרפו / צלעות והעבים
פרוש עלי מלון / ענן וערפל / מרום נתן קלון / ועשירים בשפל

(The holidays run their rounds with the *ta'ar ha-galabim* [barber's
razor]. They have burned my Temple, roof and wall.
Cloud and fog is spread over [our] homes. Shame came from on high,
and the wealthy [fell] low.)[57]

The phrase *ta'ar ha-galabim*, literally, barber's razor, is found in Ezek. 5:1. The
word *galabim* (singular: *galab*) appears in Hebrew Scriptures only in this passage, and it is glossed unanimously by the medieval rabbis as *galaḥim*, literally,
shaved or "tonsured ones," the common Hebrew term for the friars. What this
Peretz is saying, therefore, is that the holiday seasons (Lent?) bring the friars
and with them violence. As direct references to the friars in Hebrew poetry
are almost nonexistent, this is an extraordinary poem. Later in the poem,
"young men" mock the speaker and, by extension, the Jews collectively; they
cry, "See, your calculations [for messianic salvation] have not been vindicated!
To whom will you cry now? In whom shall you hope?"[58]

Thus the sequence of laments in Parma 1883 suggests a commemorative
and even polemical impulse whose lines are clearly drawn. The three following laments continue to press generic themes. Two are by Gabriel Trabot and
one is by the unknown Jacob Levi. In these concluding hymns, God has let
His people linger in bitter exile, where "traitors survive, while there is no cure
for the lost ones."[59] Amid images of expulsion, war, and plunder, the Jews are
shamed, hungry, and overwhelmed by death.[60] At the same time, in keeping
with the Trabots' didactic tastes, Gabriel's lament "Gever darko" (It is a man's
custom) encapsulates ritual instructions for observing the fast day.[61]

The final lament in Parma 1883, by Netanel, includes a long review of the
blows that befell Israel with the destruction of the ancient Temple. Again,
classical motifs unfold in an epic poem that runs over three and a half pages,
alluding opaquely to contemporary distress:

נבל משל / כחי כשל / עלי משל / משלו מושלים
המתחללים / המתהוללים / באומללים / שבט מושלים
זוללים שוללים / הם הפלילים / גם האלילים / כליל יחלוף
עברים גולים / בנחשתים / בעצלתים / בית ידלוף. . . .
תבעיר שעיר / צעיר רודם / הררי קדם / אודם פטדה. [62]
תוך המזרק [63] / ירוק ירק / עליו זורק / מי הנדה

אח לא פדה / עבד הנביר[64] / יושב כביר / אביר סלה.
על הכבודה / ידו הדה / שחל עדה / עדה צלה.[65]

(The depraved one ruled [while] my strength faltered. The storytellers
   made me a legend.
With the rulers' scepter [approval?], the jubilant riot against the
   wretched.
Looting and plundering, they are criminals. Their gods replace the
   sacrificial offering.
The Hebrews are expelled in chains; through neglect, the roof caves
   in. . . .
Seir [i.e., Edom = Christianity] sets them ablaze, a young tyrant presses
   them over the east mountains of ruby and topaz.
He spits into the ritual basin, casts pollution into it.[66]
[Esau] did not redeem his brother. The master's servant sits mighty and
   powerful forever.
He has raised his hand against the beloved one. The lion crossed over,
   [with] Ada and Zillah.)[67]

Netanel reverses the language of Job 28:8, which refers to the molten core
of the earth that no lion has passed over. Here, the lion (France?) has crossed
into foreign territory, pursuing the Jews while allying himself with "Ada and
Zillah," the biblical Lamech's wives and hence the clan of wicked Cain. Is
Netanel writing about biblical enemies, the Roman destruction, or his own
world and times? Did those who heard his hymn make a real distinction? Or
was only the End unique?

For the northern Italian users of Parma 1883, the trajectory mapped by
these hymns traces a macro-version of the structure that Pagis described for
individual laments: biblical padding on the outsides with "the event" embedded in the core.[68] At either end of the collection, we find the most generic
hymns; laments containing historical realia were at one point in the middle of
the sequence. The final, epic lament, with its own historicized center, repeats
the circular journey, perhaps evoking the most recent events. A later owner
in Carpentras, judging from the later title of the work, combined the laments
described so far with four hymns used by that community, which he inserted
into the center of the manuscript. The four inserted hymns are by Isaac HaSeniri (d. early thirteenth century), Solomon ibn Gabirol (d. 1053–58), and two
unknown authors. The addition of these works, long favorites of Provençal

Jews, restructures the trajectory of the original collection, undermining the chiastic structure I have described in favor of an ahistorical dialectic of sin and redemption. This arrangement and rearrangement suggest competing attitudes toward the place of the present in the past. That is not surprising if we think of a liturgy originating in the Piedmont making its way to the papal territories of the Comtat Venaissin—and, at some point, back again to end up in the Parma library. As we have seen in Chapter 3, the Jews of Carpentras, the largest of the Comtadin communities, were themselves constituted of many histories and emigrations. With one thirteenth-century exception, Carpentras did not expel its Jews; on the contrary, it received the victims of other expulsions and dislocations, and there were many over the years. Apparently, the generic conventions associated with a desire to commemorate, however obscurely, specificities of experience, were not cultivated by the second copyist, and perhaps they were unnecessary among his Carpentras peers.

In contrast, the main copyist (whom I locate in Italy) has either deliberately or intuitively repeated the chiastic structure of the individual laments in his overall arrangement (or replication of a received arrangement) of the group of laments. In this format, the recent and particular past is safely tucked into the distant, mythic, and collective history of the Jews. This arrangement has the psychological advantage of situating the specific traumas of the audience within the orbit of theological time; like the great calamities that befell the Jews of the past, the troubles of recent history are part of a cyclic movement of punishment and redemption that will culminate only with the messianic era.

The association of historical crises within recent memory with those of biblical and rabbinic times also elevates the experience of a particular group to a special place in the sacred history of the people. Notably, this reading of their experience validates the experience and standing of a cultural, social, and economic elite such as that represented by the Trévoux. Insofar as they are armed with this perception of themselves, the first-generation exiles and their descendants in the Piedmont replicate their hegemonic dominance of Jewish religious, cultural, and economic life. At the same time, they marshal a sense of historical destiny as a means of coping with the competing message of their debasement in Christian eyes. Indeed, we have seen a similar process unfold in Algiers among the exiles of Majorcan and Catalonian Jewish communities and their descendants.

Significantly, the relatively underdeveloped principalities and kingdoms that opened their doors to Jewish refugees fleeing France (and later, Majorca and Aragon) saw the acquisition of a skilled Jewish elite as a means of advancing their desire for institutional and administrative centralization. The near-total absence of documented Jewish communities in regions like the Savoy and Dauphiné prior to 1306 and in the Savoy prior to 1394 corresponds to a period of decentralized fiscal and administrative authority in those regions. Amadeus VIII never truly succeeded in his attempt to centralize administration of a transalpine duchy of Savoy, but the period of his rule provides ample evidence of his interest in doing so. The three sets of statutes he issued over the years as duke also testify to his growing interest in legislating social hierarchy and order, *un projet d'ordre* in Rinaldo Comba's words, that was ratified and readable in the details of clothing, address, privilege, and profession of the duchy's residents.[69] These conditions reinforce the strategic value implicit in the sense of exclusivity—an identity traced from its origins in common trauma to its projected common destiny—that may be discerned in Parma 1883 and its community of users.

The copyist who penned the text of Lamentations that opens Parma 1883 and the four interpolated poems that disrupt the longer sequence of laments had a somewhat different view. For that copyist, compiling a liturgy for use by Jews who followed the Carpentras rite, it was sufficient to emphasize the traumatic moments of the mythic past and their cycle toward messianic redemption. Whether he was consciously disrupting a sequence that sought to insert recent events into that cycle, or whether their local meaning had been so effaced as to make it invisible to him, we cannot know. His final rearrangement of the earlier liturgy thus reclaims it to constitute "French" (Comtadin) memory by erasing the Italian experience at its heart. Ironically, that Italian experience was also a construct of memory that had its own core in expulsion from France. Like Russian dolls, one world of memory encapsulates another, which is not eliminated so much as it is engulfed by later claims.

Overall, the local hymns of the Trabots, while hardly memorable works of literature, adhere to features they understood to be the rules of a commemorative poetic genre. The authors blur some details and sharpen others, while demonstrating a well-developed instinct for aligning the chronology of recent history with the mythical high watermarks of the biblical and rabbinic past. Messianism—an eye toward the far end of history—is a consistent motif. But France, too, as a place of origin from which expulsion propelled the Trabots into history, occupies a self-conscious place in the lineup of liturgical events: following the destruction of the Temple cult, the echoes of 1394 lead directly into a series of allusions to the crises and trials of life in exile, namely, Italy. As we have seen, those echoes are muted, coded, perhaps even semi-erased.

At the same time, the conflation of France with Jerusalem and Italy with the lands of expulsion comes replete with a set of judgments about the nations (lions, Moabites, Chaldeans) and the political and religious institutions that intersected with Jewish life.[70]

It would be too easy to say that poets like the Trabots did not "make the cut," as it were, to print liturgies because their poetry is not very good. In fact, it is not very good, by our standards or theirs, but that is not the issue. As Pagis noted, many of the more historically specific 1391 laments were poetically weaker than the generic laments of the classical Andalusian period *and* the martyrological laments of Ashkenaz.[71] It is not history that ruins them but perhaps the rules of the genre itself.

In striking contrast to those 1391 laments, the Trabots made no effort to thread the names of towns or communities into their poems. This is probably because, unlike the situation in 1391, none of the crises they foggily commemorate resulted in the actual destruction of a Jewish community. Even the expulsion left a remnant—notably, them. And the Trabots had a distinctive sense of themselves to convey, rooted in the memory of French origins and the relative superiority that those origins seemed to offer in the Jewish hinterlands of the Piedmont. These are men who insist on referring to themselves as Frenchmen when they were not even born in France. So, for instance, Peretz b. Netanel Elia Trabot, a late fifteenth-century scribe whom Green identified as the grandson of Peretz the Punctuator, signed off on a copy of Albo's *Sefer ha'Iqqarim* as "Peretz the son of R. Netanel Elia, may the righteous man's memory be a blessing!, the man of Trévoux, the Frenchman."[72] A colophon by Berachiel b. Hezekiah Raphael Trabot, another late fifteenth-century scribe, reads "the youngest of thousands and the humblest among the Frenchmen."[73] Likewise, among Trabot scribes, some point their names carefully to indicate French pronunciation—"Trévoux" rather than "Trabot."[74] And Yohanan Trèves, the exiled chief rabbi of France, clearly assumed that he had no local rival worthy of the name in the duchy of Savoy. Tellingly, one of Yohanan's surviving responsa deals with the right of "outsiders" to recite Kaddish, the traditional prayer for the dead, for kin who have died in or outside of "the city." The tiered categories of entitlement in the responsum describe a community characterized by degrees of "inside" and "outside" status, a striking reflection of the growing impulse to social regulation in Amadeus's statutes.[75]

For those who actually lived through it, the expulsion of 1394 was a real trauma, and the poems of Peretz Trabot the Punctuator, like his brief autobiographical comments in the *Maqré Dardaqé*, preserve some sense of the author's

Figure 2. Paris Bibliothèque Nationale MS Heb. 114, Psalter with Targum, copied in northern Italy, ca. 1470–80. Two copyists, one for text, one for vowels, signed off on this magnificent example of Hebrew micrography. On fol. 148, shown here, the main scribe, Levi Halfan, included his signature in the center of the page. Below, the punctuator, Netanel Trévoux (Trabot), added his name. Both men were among the exiles of the 1394 expulsion from France; the stunning fleur-de-lis may, as suggested by Michel Garel, evoke the emblem of the town of Trévoux, Netanel's place of origin. Courtesy of the Bibliothèque Nationale de France.

shock. Nor did Peretz's sense of dislocation evaporate quickly, even if today we must seek its traces in dim and forgotten poems. A manuscript preserved in the Oxford Bodleian library, for which Peretz provided vowels, presumably while safe in Italy, concludes: "Finished by the Frenchman, the Punctuator, Peretz Trevot: may he be saved from massacre, sword, and destruction."[76]

How his children and grandchildren experienced that cloud hanging over him we cannot know. But clearly, strategic as well as formative, honor as well as shame, the memory of expulsion left its mark among Piedmontese Jews. For those who hearkened, it was memory with a lesson: France had bequeathed them their fate. As we have seen throughout this book, it was also memory that was formative, permitting the reconstruction in exile of social institutions, hierarchies, and even rivalries rooted in a faraway home. With that reconstruction, personal fortunes rose and fell, and some memories—and the texts that asserted them—outlived others.

In retrospect, it is remarkable how the memory of "France" and the rude expulsion from a cherished homeland served the varied edifices of identity of small communities of exiles scattered about the Mediterranean and northern Italy. For the most part, historical specifics were not remembered with detail or clarity. Often, shards of factual, historical record were either transmitted without comprehension or misread for new contexts; over time, local detail was increasingly abandoned in favor of generic topoi of loss and yearning that might speak to communities of Jews representing multiple pasts and experiences of dislocation. By the end of the fifteenth century, such mixed demographics were the rule.

Soon, as we know, that rule also changed. Over the last two decades of the fifteenth century, approximately half of those Jews remaining in Provence would convert to Christianity, and many others would flee. Some of those Jews were indigenous, some were the descendants of early expulsions like that from Gascony in 1287 or of the great expulsion of 1306, and some were the children and grandchildren of Jews fleeing plague and violence in 1348. All too soon, their ranks would be swelled and overwhelmed by the waves of new refugees from Spain in 1492. This, too, contributed to the erasure of local memory, particularly French memory, in later records. Only in the Comtat and in the Piedmont did stubborn traces of French Jewish rite and custom persist; over time, these links to the past were increasingly severed from historical memory and increasingly embedded in historical myth.

While some of these chapters have relied on published texts, many of those publications were old and rare; every chapter has incorporated material from manuscripts that a general reader certainly would not have known about or had access to. This in itself testifies to the failure of French Jewish exiles, fragmented and dispersed, to sustain a distinct sense of the past. It testifies also, as I have tried to suggest, to the willingness of later readers and historians to collude in historical forgetting, often in service to a convenient binary of "Sephardic" versus "Ashkenazic" trajectories. And it warns us of the dangers of projecting a history exclusively from the arc traced by texts, whose survival is as capricious as the tastes of later generations. Nonetheless, the tethers that lead from the obscure poems and essays and tractates I have gathered to the Jewish men and women who could remember their beginnings in "France" are there to be seen for those who will see them. Frayed and sometimes splintered, they tell a story that should be told, a story of remembering and forgetting that implicates modern writers and readers as much as ancient ones. Some may say this book is chiefly an act of salvage, a quixotic search for the fate of the Jews from France. Some may say it is potentially our story, too, not just as we forget it, willingly or unwillingly, but as we may be forgotten by those who come after us. It is up to each reader to decide.

Epilogue

לזכור מה שאבד לנו מהם בפשיעתן כל אחד יתן אל לבו.

(In order to remember what we lost of them through their sin, let every one pay heed.)
— *Cincinnati HUC MS 2000, fol. 87v*

IN THE RARE book and manuscript collection of the Hebrew Union College library in Cincinnati, a small liturgical codex tells a story of wandering. It is a variation on the story told by all the manuscripts I have cited in this book. Most of HUC MS 2000 is written in a Provençal hand that has been dated to the fourteenth century, but a later writer has come along to fill in missing sections in a French-style script. The liturgy is replete with *piyyutim*, many of them favorites of Provençal Jews and a number, presumably local, unknown. Although the codex itself was lovingly produced and illuminated, the opening Haggadah contains a blistering curse that suggested, according to one paleographer, "a period of severe persecution."[1] From this end of history, we know how that period ended. Between then and now, this small codex journeyed. By the seventeenth century at the latest, HUC MS 2000 was in Islamic lands, perhaps far to the east; additional prayers with eastern vocalization and an owner's entry in Arabic conclude the volume. Far from its birthplace, the title page preceding the Haggadah still proclaims that it follows the rite of R. Amram and "the French gaonim."[2]

HUC MS 2000 is only one illustration of a neglected source on the medieval Jews of France and Provence. Another, Vat. Heb. MS 553, is found among the vast collection of Hebrew manuscripts in the Vatican library; this manuscript consists of two Provençal fast-day liturgies joined together to form a whole. The first section has been bound haphazardly so that some of the folios are upside down and out of order. The scribe, Simon b. Samuel, inserted his colophon on what is now folio 87v, indicating that he copied and finished his work in the imperial principality of Orange in 1389. That was two years before anti-Jewish violence would sweep across Aragon, killing thousands of Jews and leading to the conversion of thousands of others, and five years before the final expulsion from France, which would propel new exiles into Simon b. Samuel's city. Vat. Heb. 553 also preserves otherwise unknown hymns by Provençal Jewish poets, in addition to beloved favorites; its laments for the Ninth of Av begin with the same "Esh tuqad beqirbi" that launched the Trabot poets' collection of laments and has been associated with the rite of Carpentras Jews.

Among its liturgical poems, Vat. Heb. 553 counts several by Don Durand of Lunel, a writer otherwise known to us as Simon b. Joseph, the stalwart ally of Abba Mari in the vicious curricular controversies that spilled outward from Montpellier in the early fourteenth century. There are hymns by Abraham of Carpentras, David b. Jonathan of Marseille, and Don Bondia of Aix—poets whose names will appear in no textbook or survey of the literature or history of medieval European Jews. There is even a hymn by Reuben b. Isaac, identified by the scribe as a deceased kinsman whose father is still alive—problematic if this is the Reuben b. Isaac of Montpellier treated in Chapter 3 but perhaps a descendant of that poet. The second half of the manuscript, which includes prayers and divine names of a decidedly mystical bent, has also been dated to the fourteenth century.[3]

These are just two examples of forgotten clues to the life and literature of medieval Jews who traced their origins to France, and continued to cling to some notion of Frenchness—first in Provence and the Comtat Venaissin, and later in places like Orange, Italy, Spain, North Africa, and farther east. They cannot be unique; other manuscripts in these and other libraries undoubtedly have more to add to their tales. Cincinnati's Klau library alone contains approximately forty Provençal liturgies ranging from the fifteenth to the eighteenth century, and each one transmits a history, not always originating in northern France but eventually tumbled together with French Jewish history and traveling with it through the centuries. Had we been looking harder for this story, these traces would still be relatively few and far-flung, but we would have found them. For reasons that have to do as much with our own constructs of the Jewish past as they do with the damaged and fragmentary record, we were not looking very hard.

It would have been nice if respected Jewish poets, men who had honed their rhetorical skills in years of listening, imitating, and sometimes even innovating, responded to the expulsion of 1306—or 1322 or 1394—with an artful array of reflections on *gerush tzarfat* (the expulsion from France). Certainly, our view of the Jewish past would be altered if such poems had managed to nestle in Jewish prayer books or amid a secular canon, to find their way into modern anthologies or learned conferences and publications on the Jewish literature of catastrophe and what it means. In the preceding pages, I have tried to suggest some of the reasons that this did not happen. The survivors of the great expulsion from France in 1306, for one, did not often surface in the same communities in numbers that would support the use of traditional commemorative laments. For another, even where they did cluster in some strength, fragmentary communities of exiles were rapidly struck by new disasters and dislocations, ranging from famine, violence, and plague to new expulsions. If at the end of the century what remained of earlier commemorations tended to the generic, this is really no surprise.

Whether the direct victims of expulsion and terror wanted to record their experience in writing—or whether they found the stability and leisure to do so—is a factor to consider as well. It is no accident, I think, that two of the extant prose accounts of the 1306 expulsion were written by physicians; whatever their personal misfortunes, this group possessed unique skills and connections to start life anew and to regain the status, renown, and ease they had formerly known at home. From this vantage, writing comes considerably easier, and past terrors can be integrated into a longer narrative of misfortune nobly suffered until patience and virtue find their merited reward. Two notable examples, Qalonymos b. Qalonymos and Estori HaParhi, both included autobiographical reminiscences among secular writings dedicated to other themes entirely.[4]

In general, the intellectual elite French exiles encountered in the Midi preferred different ways of "remembering" from the conventional forms of liturgical verse. Yedaiah Bedersi in Perpignan, a physician, philosopher, and witness to the 1306 expulsion, chose to embed the traces of this event in an allegorical treatment of spiritual disorder and alienation from God. Twenty years later, Crescas Caslari refracted his historical judgments through the prism of romance narrative in Hebrew and Judeo-Provençal. Even Isaac HaGorni, a Gascon exile writing before the expulsion of 1306, conveys the pervasiveness of rationalist thinking and attitudes in his secular verse.

In contrast, other physicians, like Jacob b. Solomon of Avignon or Simon b. Zemaḥ Duran of Majorca and then Algiers, embraced more traditional

values, religiously and culturally. Notably, these were also the poets who demonstrated an affinity for traditional commemorative genres, writing hymns of
supplication, legal responsa, and theological exegesis. Even Jacob's interest in
copying his own Haggadah and indicating the divergence of local custom from
that of his ancestral France is the mark of a conservative theologian, for whom
traditionalism and science were not foes when they hailed from the north. In
this context, Jacob's idiosyncratic experiment in the *Evel Rabbati* confirms
traditional science and theology even as it breaks new ground formally.

For all these writers, though, expulsion is more often mentioned indirectly than directly. In a sense, it is memory repressed—recalled despite itself and unsummoned, peeking through walls built to bar it from conscious
recall. Genre is thus critical to unearthing the buried cries of the past, for it
is genre that determines the design and stuff of the walls and where they are
strong or weak. In other words, those who seek history in literature must first
learn to read it as literature, or they will miss its meaning and distort or dis-
miss its claims. Moreover, as the highly artificial poetic exercises of Yedaiah
and his followers illustrate, all the texts discussed in these pages remind us
also that the entire concept of literature and when it has beauty or value is
culturally determined and shifts over time.

In "modern" times, perhaps even as early as 1493, the story of French Jews
in exile was rapidly overshadowed by the catastrophe of the Spanish expulsion in 1492. From a historiographical perspective, Western scholars since the
Enlightenment have privileged a binaristic reading of the European Jewish
past, dividing its communities by sweeping them grandly under the umbrel-
las of "Sepharad" or "Ashkenaz."[5] This construct, too, clouded and eventually
eclipsed the wider variety of community identities around the Mediterranean
basin and particularly that of Provençal Jewry, which received so many of the
French exiles and integrated their stories into their own. Indeed, this book,
which also began as a search for "French" identity and memory, evolved to
focus primarily upon the communities of Provence and what befell them.
Yet, as I hope I have demonstrated, Provence provided a distinctive context
for Jewish life, thought, and creativity. It is important to recognize how formative that context was and where it extended, without subordinating its
characteristics to one or the other end of a binary that did not exist until
modern times.

When I first began this project, I innocently expected the literary remains
of the French expulsions to announce themselves obligingly from a conventional series of texts—less than popular texts, certainly, but straightforward

and identifiable once sought. As this book has made clear, I did not find what I was initially seeking. Indeed, there was a point, fruitlessly reading microfilms in Jerusalem in the summer of 2003, when I wondered whether such a project was feasible at all. On one particularly rough day, I remember confessing to Haym Soloveitchik over lunch that I did not know how I would solve the problem posed by a lack of texts explicitly linked to the 1306 expulsion of French Jews. More eloquently than I can rephrase him, Haym leaned over his plate and reassured me that somehow I would figure it out. I could not have imagined at that moment that the ensuing journey would take me through astronomical texts, theological texts, medical texts, and papal depositions. But I am convinced that any serious attempt to understand the world of the medieval rabbis and physicians encountered in this study demands trampling modern disciplinary boundaries. Beside the wide-ranging interests and profound intellectual curiosity of these men, our narrowness of knowledge is stunning; we distort who they were by diminishing them to our scale.

In sum, I have tried to convey in these pages that there is a way to read a series of forgotten texts and detect within them the echoes of expulsion's trauma. I hope also to have raised some questions about why these echoes were eventually silenced, to ask who is responsible for forgetting, how historical amnesia happens, and how we smooth over the gaps to restore a sense of continuous past. Surely there are threads that remain untied, and questions that remain unasked, which is a way of encouraging others to join in the task. In the words of the Preacher, "of making many books there is no end" (Eccles. 12:12). This is true, as well, when it comes to forgetting those that have been written. We can only hope that as we struggle to find the past, the future will someday look for us.

NOTES

INTRODUCTION

1. William C. Jordan, *The French Monarchy and the Jews* (Philadelphia: University of Pennsylvania Press, 1989).

2. Robin Mundill, *England's Jewish Solution: Experiment and Expulsion 1262–1290* (Cambridge: Cambridge University Press, 1998); Robert Stacey, "The Jews of England in the Thirteenth Century and the Problem of Expulsion" (in Hebrew), in David Katz and Joseph Kaplan, eds., *Gerush Aḥar Golah: Yehude-Anglia beḤilufe-haZemanim* (Jerusalem: Zalman Shazar Center for Jewish History, 1993), 9–26.

3. William C. Jordan, "Administering Expulsion in 1306," *Jewish Studies Quarterly*, forthcoming. See also Bernard Blumenkranz, "En 1306: Chemins d'un exil," *Evidences* 13 (1962): 17–23.

4. See Susan L. Einbinder, *Beautiful Death: Jewish Poetry and Martyrdom from Medieval France* (Princeton, N.J.: Princeton University Press, 2002).

5. Simon Bernfeld, *Sefer haDema'ot* (Berlin: Eshkol, 1924), 2:87–154.

6. Jordan, *The French Monarchy*, 248–49.

7. It is impossible to list all the works that have (sometimes slowly) made a difference in conceptualizing this book. A few authors and titles, with many more cited gratefully in the notes to individual chapters: Benedict Anderson, *Imagined Communities* (London and New York: Verso, 1983); Dipesh Chakrabarti, *Provincializing Europe: Postcolonial Thought and Historical Difference* (Princeton, N.J.: Princeton University Press, 2000); Prasenjit Duara, *Rescuing History from the Nation* (Chicago: University of Chicago Press, 1995); William Granara, "*Extensio Animae:* The Artful Ways of Remembering 'Al-Andalus,'" *Journal of Social Affairs* 19.75 (2002): 45–72; Stephen Greenblatt, ed., with Catherine Gallagher, *Practicing New Historicism* (Chicago: University of Chicago Press, 2000); Steven Justice, *Writing and Rebellion: England in 1381* (Berkeley: University of California Press, 1994); Gabrielle Spiegel, *Romancing the Past: The Rise of Vernacular Prose Historiography in Thirteenth-Century France* (Berkeley: University of California

Press, 1993); Andrew Taylor, *Textual Situations: Three Medieval Manuscripts and Their Readers* (Philadelphia: University of Pennsylvania Press, 2002); Hayden White, *Tropics of Discourse* (Baltimore: Johns Hopkins University Press, 1978).

8. I am especially grateful to Paulla Ebron of Stanford University, an anthropologist and my neighbor during a sabbatical year at the Institute for Advanced Study in 2004–5. Professor Ebron's own work in progress, "Making Tropical Africa in the Georgia Sea Islands," some of which I have heard or read, has been illuminating for me and helpful. See, too, her earlier work, *Performing Africa* (Princeton, N.J.: Princeton University Press, 2002). If it is tempting to measure the nostalgic construct of "France" embraced by the exiles as a form of proto-nationalist consciousness unknown, by contrast, to the average Frenchman of the time, Dr. Ebron's work clarifies that this leap is unnecessary. What is at stake is a construct of "home" as a place where one had possessions, property, status, and continuity, not a construct of national identity.

9. See, e.g., the collected studies in Ross Brann and Adam Sutcliffe, *Renewing the Past, Reconfiguring Jewish Culture: From al-Andalus to the Haskalah* (Philadelphia: University of Pennsylvania Press, 2003); David Myers, *Reinventing the Jewish Past: European Jewish Intellectuals and the Zionist Return to History* (New York: Oxford University Press, 1995), and idem, *The Jewish Past Revisited* (New Haven, Conn.: Yale University Press, 1998); Reuven Snir, *'Araviyyut, Yahadut, Tziyyonut: Ma'avaq Zehuiyot Beyetziratam shel Yehude-'Iraq* (Arabism, Jewishness, Zionism: Clashing identities in the writings of Iraqi Jews) (Jerusalem: Ben Zvi Institute, 2006); Yael Zerubavel, *Recovered Roots: Collective Memory and the Making of Israeli National Tradition* (Chicago: University of Chicago Press, 1995).

10. See, for instance, Marianne Hirsch, "Surviving Images: Holocaust Photographs in Work of Postmemory," *Yale Journal of Criticism* 14.1 (spring 2001): 5–37.

11. Dan Pagis, "Laments for the Persecutions of 1391 in Spain" (in Hebrew), *Tarbiz* 37 (1968): 355–73.

12. Susan L. Einbinder, "Recall from Exile: Literature, Memory and French Jews," *Jewish Studies Quarterly*, forthcoming. This essay originated as a plenary talk delivered at Princeton University in October 2006, at a small conference commemorating the seven-hundredth anniversary of the great expulsion of French Jewry.

13. Danièle Iancu-Agou, *Juifs et néophytes en Provence (1469–1525)* (Paris and Louvain: Peeters, 2001). Richard Emery, "Jewish Physicians in Medieval Perpignan," *Michael* 12 (1991): 113–34.

14. The enlistment of collective emotional states, from despair to a desire for revenge, alienation, contempt, hostility, and suspicion, is also noteworthy in some of the texts I gathered for use in this book. These are socially useful emotions whose expression is channeled toward the construction of exilic identity. See some of the recent work on history of emotions in medieval contexts, e.g., Paul Hyams, *Rancor and Reconciliation* (Ithaca, N.Y.: Cornell University Press, 2003); Barbara Rosenwein, ed., *Anger's Past: The Social Uses of an Emotion in the Middle Ages* (Ithaca, N.Y.: Cornell University Press, 1998).

15. See, most recently, Colette Sirat, "New Catalogues for Medieval Hebrew Manuscripts?," in Festschrift for Albert van der Heide (forthcoming). I thank Dr. Sirat for making an early copy available.

16. Ernst Renan and Adolphe Neubauer, *Histoire littéraire de la France*, vol. 27 (*Les rabbins français*) (Paris, 1877), 431–776, and vol. 31 (*Les écrivains juifs français du XIVe siècle*) (Paris, 1893).

17. In popular discourse, they were increasingly, because of their Islamic context, lumped with "Sephardic" communities. The Jews of Palestine and the Fertile Crescent had their own special status.

18. See the current and forthcoming work of Ross Brann on the rise of the category of "Sepharad." Professor Brann's talk "Andalusi Moorings: Al-Andalus and Sefarad as Tropes of Muslim and Jewish Culture," delivered at a conference in honor of María Rosa Menocal held at the University of Toronto in March 2007 and organized by Suzanne Akbari and Kate Mallette, should be published with the conference proceedings.

19. Susan Einbinder, "Yedaiah Bedersi's *Elef Alafin*," in Jonathan Decter and Michael Rand, eds., *Studies in Arabic and Hebrew Letters in Honor of Raymond P. Scheidlein* (Piscataway, N.J.: Gorgias Press, 2007), 37–46.

CHAPTER ONE

1. Bernard Goldstein, *The Astronomical Tables of Levi ben Gerson* (New Haven, Conn.: Connecticut Academy of Arts Sciences, 1974); idem, "Levi ben Gerson's Contributions to Astronomy," in Gad Freudenthal, ed., *Studies on Gersonides* (Leiden: Brill, 1992), 3–20; Jean-Claude Margolin, "Bonet de Lattes: Médecin, astrologue et astronome du pape," in G. Tarugi, ed., *L'umanesimo e l'ecumenismo della cultura—Atti del XIV Convegno internazionale del Centro di Studi Umanistici* (Florence: Olschki, 1981), 107–48; Colette Sirat et al., eds., *Les méthodes de travail de Gersonide et le maniement du savoir chez les scholastiques* (Paris: Librairie Philosophique J. Vrin, 2003); Joseph Shatzmiller, *Justice et injustice au début du XIVe siècle: L'enquête sur l'archevêque d'Aix et sa renunciation en 1318* (Paris: École française de Rome, 1999).

2. Menahem Kellner, *Perush leShir haShirim leRabbi Levi ben Gershon* (Ramat-Gan: Bar-Ilan University, 2001). Kellner focuses on the seeming paradox of a text addressed, on the one hand, to an intellectual elite and, on the other hand, to "beginners in philosophy" (24); the Ralbag's emphasis on studying subjects in order (25); and the suitability of the commentary for would-be sophisticates who study philosophy but do not have a deep understanding of it (לחובכתם מודעים שאינם פילוסופיה לחובבי, 37).

3. James Robinson, "Secondary Forms of Transmission: Teaching and Preaching Philosophy in Thirteenth-Century Provence" (unpublished paper). Thanks to Patricia Crone for alerting me to this work.

4. Hopefully, Benjamin Bar-Tikva's work will change this view. Bar-Tikva is currently gathering all the known Hebrew liturgical poetry from medieval Provence for

publication. See also Pierre Vidal, *Les juifs des anciens comtés de Roussillon et de Cerdagne* (Perpignan: Mare nostrum, 1992); as Eduard Feliu notes in his preface to this work, the Feliu culture of Catalan Jewry was also distinctive and neither "Sefardic" nor "French." For the traditional perspective: Schirmann's classic anthology mixes poetry from Spain and Provence indiscriminately, and overviews of the cultural activity in Provence routinely describe the literature as derivative. In a 1949 French essay on HaGorni, Schirmann's view was explicit: "La tradition espagnole, fortement enracinée, s'avéra tenace." See Haim (Jefim) Schirmann, "Isaac HaGorni, poète hébreu de Provence," *Lettres romanes* 3.3 (1949): 178. In pleasing contrast, see Benjamin Bar-Tikva, "Reciprocity between the Provençal School of Piyyutim and the Schools of Catalonia and Ashkenazi France," in G. Sed-Rajna, ed., *Rashi: 1040–1990: Hommage à Ephraïm Urbach* (Paris: Éditions du Cerf, 1993), 375–83; "Two Qedushta'ot for the Special Lections by R. Isaac b. Zerachia" (in Hebrew), *Qovetz 'al Yad*, n.s., 16 (2002): 143–85; and note my "Hebrew Poems for the 'Day of Shutting In': Problems and Methods," *REJ* 163.1–2 (2004): 111–35; idem, "A Proper Diet: Medicine and History in Crescas Caylar's *Esther*," *Speculum* 80.2 (2005): 437–63.

5. Ernst Renan, *Histoire littéraire de la France* (Paris: Imprimerie Nationale, 1878), 27:722–23.

6. Haim Schirmann, *HaShirah ha'Ivrit biSefarad uveProvans* (HPSP) (Jerusalem: Mossad Bialik; Tel Aviv: Dvir, 1960), 4:472. Schirmann's anthology included five of HaGorni's poems and one epigram, 475–84. Schirmann returned to the term "troubadour" with greater conviction in the Hebrew expansion of his 1949 French essay; see "Isaac HaGorni: A Hebrew Poet from Provence" (in Hebrew), in Schirmann, *LeToldot HaShirah vehaDrama ha'Ivrit* (Jerusalem: Mossad Bialik, 1979), 1:397–438. This Hebrew/French pair of essays offers the only real scholarly overview of HaGorni's work to date. A less than reliable transcription of most of the poems found in Munich MS Bayerische Staatsbibliotek Cod. Heb. 128 (henceforth cited as Munich 128) was published by H. Gross, "Zur Geschichte der Juden in Arles," *MGWJ* 31 (1882): 510–23; two additional poems were published by M. Steinschneider in an appendix to the collected works of Abraham Bedersi, *Ḥotem Tokhnit*, ed. Isaac Pollak (or Polk) (Amsterdam, 1865). There is no modern edition of the poems, although this is currently the dissertation goal of Uri Kfir of Tel Aviv University.

7. *HPSP*, 4:472. Interestingly, HaGorni never complains of being hungry or cold, although he does have plenty to say about the stinginess of some of his hosts.

8. Schirmann, "Isaac Gorni," 177.

9. Schirmann, *LeToldot haShirah vehaDrama ha'Ivrit*, 425. The French-language essay of 1949, cited in full above (n. 4), is essentially restated in the later Hebrew piece. See Schirmann, "Isaac Gorni," 175–200. The comparisons to the *tenson* and *tornade/envois* appear, respectively, on 185 and 187 of the French (1949) article.

10. Haim Schirmann, *Toldot haShirah ha'Ivrit biSefarad haNotzrit uveDrom Tzarfat*, ed. and completed by Ezra Fleischer (hereafter cited as Schirmann/Fleischer) (Jerusalem: Magnes, 1997), 485.

11. Ibid., 494. HaGorni is discussed on 484–98.

12. Ibid., 493; idem, "Isaac Gorni," 193.

13. Schirmann/Fleischer, 498.

14. Georges Passerat, "Les juifs en Tarn-et-Garonne au moyen âge," *Bulletin de la Société Archéologique de Tarn-et-Garonne* (1979): 84–96, is a light survey. Théophile Malvezin, *Histoire de Juifs à Bordeaux* (Bordeaux, Ch. Lefebvre, 1875); William C. Jordan, *The French Monarchy and the Jews* (Philadelphia: University of Pennsylvania Press, 1986), 182–83.

15. Mireille Mousnier, *La Gascogne toulousaine aux XIIe–XIIIe siècles* (Toulouse: Presses Universitaires du Mirail, 1997); Margaret Wade Labarge, *Gascony: England's First Colony 1204–1453* (London: Hamish Hamilton, 1980); J. P. Trabut-Cussac, *L'administration anglaise en gascogne sous Henry III et Edouard I* (Geneva: Librairie Droz, 1972).

16. Schirmann, "Isaac Gorni," 180: "Gorni . . . ne parvint jamais à se faire une situation. Aussi fut-il réduit à errer de ville en ville."

17. Trabut-Cussac, *L'administration anglaise*, 312–13; Robin Mundill, *England's Jewish Solution: Experiment and Expulsion 1262–90* (Cambridge: Cambridge University Press, 1990), 270, 276–82.

18. Gérard Nahon, "Les juifs dans les domains d'Alfonse de Poitiers, 1241–71," *REJ* 125 (1966): 167–211; Jordan, *The French Monarchy*, 182–83.

19. The poem was not included in Gross's 1882 transcription. It appeared later in an appendix to Pollak's edition of *Ḥotem Tokhnit*; see n. 6 above. It may also be found in MS Munich 128, fol. 56a.

20. Poem to Arles, v. 3 (ביום העיר אריאל נלכדה); poem "Tremble, O People," fol. 54a, v. 43 (נולת אריאל הנני נוגנך).

21. Joseph Shatzmiller, *Recherches sur la communauté juive de Manosque au moyen âge* (Paris: Mouton, 1973), 1–31.

22. Trabut-Cussac, *L'administration anglaise*; Labarge, *Gascony*, 32.

23. It is futile (and foolish) to speculate on the order of HaGorni's itinerary. The copyist has clearly inherited an arrangement of poems that links individual compositions by means of prose incipits purportedly describing the circumstances that gave rise to a particular poem. This method of arrangement bears some similarity to that of the biographical *vida* that introduces a troubadour's corpus; however, it is also familiar as the standard way of organizing an Andalusian Hebrew or Arabic *dīwān*. There is no reason, in short, to believe that the poems were composed in the order indicated by the "biography" or that, concomitantly, the poet's journeys followed the order of the songs. See Margarita Egan, *The Vidas of the Troubadours* (New York: Garland, 1984).

24. The poet Mahieu le juif from Ghent, by his own claims a convert to Christianity, wrote in Old French, and Rutebeuf refers to a "Charlot le juif" whom he calls a jongleur; *Histoire littéraire de la France* (Paris: 1892), 20:740–41; Hans Wolff, "Dichtungen von Matthäus dem Juden und Matthäus von Gent" (Berlin: Königlichen Universität, Greifswald, 1914). M. C. Viguier, "Un troubadour juif à Narbonne aux XIIIe siècle," in *Juifs et source juive en Occitanie* (Valdarias: Vent Terral, 1988), 81–92; Viguier

hypothesizes that "Bonfils" is the vernacular name of Abraham Bedersi (!), 83. See also Jean Regné, *Étude sur la condition des juifs de Narbonne* (Narbonne: F. Caillard, 1912, repr. Marseille: Laffitte, 1981), appendix 3 ("Un troubadour juif"), 217–20.

25. HSPS, 4:467.

26. Schirmann, "Isaac Gorni," 181.

27. Poem to Arles, *HSPS*, 4:479, or fol. 54a, vv. 23–26.

28. Poem to Apt, *HPSP*, 4:476–77, or fol. 55a, vv. 1–3.

29. "Esh halevavot," fol. 59b, vv. 7–8; compare the poem to the Jews of Carpentras, "Be-Karpentras radfuni," fol. 55a, v. 11, ‏אבני להם ואיל לא קדמוני / ואל יצאו במחול לי‎ ‏ותופם‎, which I translate as "They did not greet me with jewels and oxen, nor did they go forth with dancing and drums for me."

30. The archbishop, Robert de Mauvoisin, was also a Gascon, and the testimony was part of the inquest into his affairs in 1317–18. See Joseph Shatzmiller, *Justice et injustice au début du XIVe siècle: L'enquête sur l'archevêque d'Aix et sa renunciation en 1318* (Paris: École française de Rome, 1999), 108–9.

31. Nancy Regalado, "Chronique Métrique," in Margaret Bent and A. Wahey, eds., *Fauvel Studies: Allegory, Chronicle, Music and Image in Paris, Bibliothèque nationale, MS français 146* (Oxford: Clarendon, 1998), 478.

32. Nancy Regalado, *Poetic Patterns in Rutebeuf: A Study in Non-Courtly Poetic Modes of the Thirteenth Century* (New Haven, Conn.: Yale University Press, 1970), 196; according to Regalado, the jongleur guilds or schools met during Lent, "when feasts were forbidden and the singers out of work."

33. MS Munich Cod. Heb. 128, fol. 59b.

34. "Leḥishqi," *HPSP*, 4:483–84. Munich 128, fol. 59b. See also "Nogen s'ḥoq," the poem to Draguignan, fol. 55b, vv. 20–23:

‏כמה אני ירא ליום מותי / פן יעשון אותי תמונתם‎
‏מן אז לקטר יחדל לגד / ויקטרו עלי לבונתם‎
‏או לישישים ירקחו עטי / בו הייתה ענגה לזקנתם‎
‏מי יאסוף מילי ויחצבון / מצור ובלוח תבונתם‎

(How I fear the day of my death, lest they make me their icon! / Forsaking the burning of incense to Gad, they will burn incense to me!/ Or they will grind up my pen for old men, who will find pleasure in it in their old age./ Who will gather my words and engrave them in rock, and in the tablet of their intellect?)

35. Poem to Carpentras, fol. 55a; Poem to Draguignan, fol. 55b. The tax problems appear in "Le-mi anus," *HPSP*, 4:475–76, fol. 55b; and in the poem to Manosque, fol. 54b. On the Jewish community in Manosque, see Shatzmiller, *Recherches sur la communauté juive de Manosque*, 13–26; and idem, *Médecine et justice en Provence médiévale: Documents de Manosque 1262–1348* (Aix: L'université de Provence, 1989), docs. 3, 7, 12, 13, 15, and 16.

36. Poem to Draguignan, fol. 55b, vv. 10–13.

37. Indeed, if Rossiaud is correct, an outsider to the community would be one of the least likely men to risk such behavior and one of the least likely to escape retribution. See Jacques Rossiaud, "Prostitution, jeunesse et société dans les villes du sud-est au XVe siècle," *Annales* 31.1 (1976): 289–325.

38. "[D]es esclaves et des prostituées, qu'un homme trouvait à satisfaire sa lubricité"; Schirmann, "Isaac Gorni," 195.

39. ראו גבר מאד נכתם עונו / אשר נתר ובורית לא ידיחו, in "Adon 'olam shelaḥeni," London MS Brit. Lib. 930, fol. 15b; the wording is drawn from Jer. 2:22.

40. Or, "a span in length" (Isa. 40:12—ושמים בזרת תכן); the expression from Isa. 40:12 is echoed in Solomon ibn Gabirol's great cosmological poem, the *Keter Malkhut,* section 9: ותכן שחקים בזרת.

41. This goes on for eighteen verses in the same tasteless fashion. "Beṭen resha'im," London MS Brit. Mus. 930, fol. 20b. The language is not always clear, but I have tried to give it some coherence, and readers may consult the Hebrew for themselves.

42. *HPSP*, 4:579–80; no. 432.

43. ומי אתה אשר באת לקלל / במלכך ושים ארצי ל[ש]מה?. Munich 128, fol. 59a, vv. 12–13; and Gross, "Zur Geschichte der Juden in Arles," 519.

44. Ibid., vv. 17–19; Munich 128, fol. 59a.

45. For the eleventh century, see Fausta Garivini, "Je suis Gascon, et si...," in Joseph Michelet, *Poètes gascons du Gers depuis le XVIe à nos jours* (Geneva: Thomas Bouquet, 1972, repr. of 1904 ed.), 141; Margery Kirkbride James, "The Fluctuations of the Anglo-Gascon Wine Trade during the Fourteenth Century," in *Studies in the Medieval Wine Trade* (Oxford: Clarendon, 1971), 1–38; J.-Chr. Cassard, "Vins et marchands de vins Gascons au début du XIVe siècle," *Annales du Midi* 90 (1978): 121–40. I thank Devin Stewart for reminding me that Dumas's Dartagnan of *The Three Musketeers* was also a Gascon rustic.

46. This focus has emerged in several recent and illuminating studies. See Barbara Rosenwein, ed., *Anger's Past: The Social Uses of an Emotion* (Ithaca, N.Y.: Cornell University Press, 1998); Daniel Lord Smail, *The Consumption of Justice: Emotions, Publicity, and Legal Culture in Marseille 1264–1463* (Ithaca, N.Y.: Cornell University Press, 2003); Thelma Fenster and D. L. Smail, eds., *Fama: The Politics of Talk and Reputation in Medieval Europe* (Ithaca, N.Y.: Cornell University Press, 2003). As Shatzmiller's studies of criminal trials in medieval Manosque make clear, Jews shared the new Christian enthusiasm for seeking legal remedy for complaints, and as studies of violence against women in medieval Provence equally demonstrate, "outsiders" (like HaGorni) were only a small minority of the perpetrators. See Shatzmiller, *Médecine et justice en Provence médiévale*; and Leah Otis, "Prostitution and Repentance in Late Medieval Perpignan," in Julius Kirshner and S. Wemple, eds., *Women of the Medieval World: Essays in Honor of John H. Mundy* (London: Basil Blackwell, 1985), 137–60; and Rossiaud, "Prostitution, jeunesse et société."

47. Abraham S. Halkin, "Why Was Levi ben Hayyim Hounded?" *Proceedings of the American Academy of Jewish Research* 34 (1966): 65–76; Charles Touati, "La controverse de

1303–1306 autour des études philosophiques et scientifiques," *REJ* 127 (1968): 21–37. See also Colette Sirat, "La composition et l'édition des texts philosophiques juifs au moyen âge: Quelques examples," *Bulletin de Philosophie Médiévale* 30 (1988): 224–32, which treats the *Livyat Ḥen* of Levi b. Abraham.

48. HaGorni's "poetic persona" is the subject of the only recent piece written on his work. See Ann Brener, "Isaac HaGorni and the Troubadour Persona," *Zutot* 1 (2001): 84–91.

49. It was (re?)bound in the nineteenth century, incorrectly; I have therefore refrained from drawing any conclusions based on specific folio order. See Moritz Steinschneider, *Hartza'ot 'al Kitve-Yad 'Ivri'im* (Jerusalem: Mossad Harav Kook, 1965), 48. That the copyist was working for himself is clear; deluxe editions of his astronomical texts are exquisitely designed and executed. The Jewish Theological Seminary library in New York has three copies of the tables, NY MSS JTS 2610, 2614, and 2555. No. 2610 is an eighteenth-century Italian copy, and 2614 a sixteenth-century Italian copy, both in poor condition and visually uninteresting. MS 2555, dated 1520, is a luxury edition produced in Perpignan. The British Library, for that matter, preserves the magnificently illustrated copy of Jacob Poel's tables produced in Catalonia in 1361–62 and possibly the copy made at the author's request for Pedro IV of Aragon. This manuscript, MS Sasson 823, can be viewed in the online digital archive of the University of Pennsylvania's Schoenberg Collection of Electronic Texts, manuscript number ljs057 at http://dewey .library.upenn.edu/sceti.

50. See Raffaella Cribiore, *Writing, Teachers and Students in Graeco-Roman Egypt* (Atlanta: Scholars Press, 1996), 91–93.

51. Renan, *Histoire littéraire de la France*, 27:599–624.

52. Bernard Goldstein, *The Astronomical Tables of Levi ben Gerson* (Hamden, Conn.: Archon, 1974), 27.

53. See, e.g., Malachi Beit-Arié, "Hebrew Script in Spain: Development, Offshoots and Vicissitudes," in Haim Beinart, ed., *Moreshet Sefarad* (The Sephardi Legacy) (Jerusalem: Magnes, 1992), 1:282–317.

54. Schirmann, *LeToldot haShirah vehaDrama ha'Ivrit*, 421: אסופה קטנה של שירים עבריים. שאין לה כל נגיעה לשאר השקסטים. See also Schirmann, "Isaac Gorni," 175.

55. "'Ir Manosque," fol. 54b, v. 5; "Le-mi anus," fol. 56a, v. 9; "Shetaim zo be'shom'i" (to the poet in Manosque), fol. 57b, v. 6.

56. "Tremble, O People," fols. 57b–58a, vv. 1–4.

57. But the nature of the nested spheres, with the earth at their center and the fixed stars at the outer orb, was debated, in part by the thirteenth-century Levi b. Gerson (Gersonides) in Orange. Goldstein, *The Astronomical Tables*, 29; E. S. Kennedy, "Late Medieval Planetary Theory," *Isis* 57.3 (1966): 365–78. Renan refers to a treatise on the fixed stars by Abu Ishaq al-Zarqala, translated by Samuel b. Judah of Marseilles in the early fourteenth century; see Renan, *Histoire littéraire de la France*, 31:221 (BN 1036.3).

58. Kennedy, "Late Medieval Planetary Theory," 366.

59. HaGorni exploits the easy conflation of the Hebrew words for "jackal" and "serpent." See Mic. 1:8 (howling jackals); Exod. 7:12 (Aaron's staff turned serpent and swallowing the magicians' staffs). The "serpent's head" (ראש תנין) can also have the technical meaning in astronomical texts of "ascending node." See Bernard Goldstein, *Ibn al-Muthannā's Commentary on the Astronomical Tables of al-Khwārizmī: Two Hebrew Versions* (New Haven, Conn.: Yale University Press, 1967), 269. This passage in HaGorni's poem is obscure to me, but I cannot help feeling that it is more than a string of images of violent and irrepressible grief. As astronomical terms, the "serpent" can refer to the ascending or descending nodes, where the lunar path crosses that of the ecliptic, marked by a lunar eclipse; and the goat and lion are familiar zodiacal signs (Capricorn, Leo). Does HaGorni wish to suggest that his suffering has been decreed by a particular conjunction of planets? This would make sense of his later outrage that some men have been immune to fortune's blows (לא יקראו [יקרהו?] פגע ונגע, v. 19).

60. Exod. 26:12–13; Isa. 28:20.

61. Deut. 25:18; the expulsion context is noteworthy.

62. Isa. 10:26, perhaps also Joshua 4.

63. Ron Barkai, "L'astrologie juive médiévale: Aspects théoriques et pratiques," *Le moyen âge* 93.3–4 (1987): 323–48. On the status of astrology among fourteenth-century Provençal Jews, see also Shatzmiller, *Justice et injustice au début du XIVe siècle*, 129–49 (chap. 5).

64. Mendel Metzger, "Un maḥzor italien enluminé du XVe siècle," *Mitteilungen des Kunsthistorischen Institutes in Florenz* 20 (1976): 158–96 and esp. the appendix on 192–96. The illustration appears on 193.

65. MS Munich Cod. Heb. 128, fol. 22a.

66. Metzger, "Un maḥzor italien," 195.

67. Colette Sirat, *Hebrew Manuscripts of the Middle Ages*, trans. Nicholas de Lange (Cambridge: Cambridge University Press, 2002), 8–9.

68. I thank Raymond Scheindlin of the Jewish Theological Seminary for his help in trying to decode this couplet.

69. See Dan Pagis, *Hebrew Poetry in the Middle Ages and the Renaissance* (Berkeley: University of California Press, 1991); Dvora Bregman, *Shvil haZahav* (Jerusalem: Ben Tzvi Institute, 1995), now translated as *The Golden Way* (Tempe: Arizona Center for Medieval and Renaissance Studies, 2006).

70. They took their love of astronomy with them, too. See Bernard Goldstein, "The Hebrew Astronomical Tradition: New Sources," *Isis* 72 (1981): 237–51.

71. Béatrice Leroy, *Les édits d'expulsion des juifs* (Biarritz: Atlantica, 1998); Danièle Iancu, "Les parentés juives comtadines de quelques néophytes aixois (1490–1525), in G. Audisio et al., eds., *Identités juives et chrétiennes: France méridionale XIVe–XIXe siècle* (Aix-en-Provence, 2003), 72–85.

72. The child's handwriting appears on fols. 26a, 28a, 34a, 49b, and 53a.

73. Fol. 26a. The correct form of the blessing is: ברוך אתה ה'/ אלהינו מלך העולם אשר יצר את האדם בחכמה וברא בו נקבים נקבים חלולים חלולים. It is both sensible and,

in retrospect, touching, that a father interested in the natural sciences and a rationalist curriculum would begin instructing a child with this benediction.

74. Danièle Iancu-Agou, "Les juifs exilés de Provence (1486–1525)," in Friedhelm Burgard, A. Haverkamp, and G. Mentgen, eds., *Judenvertreibungen in Mittelalter und früher Neuzeit* (Hannover: Hahnsche, 1999), 119–33; and idem, *Juifs et néophytes en Provence (1469–1525)* (Paris and Louvain: Peeters, 2001).

75. Danièle Iancu-Agou, "Médecins juifs et néophytes en Provence (1460–1525)," *Vesalius: Acta Internationalia Historiae Medicinae* 4 (special number) (November 1988): 33; idem, "L'inventaire de la bibliothèque et du mobilier d'un médecin juif d'Aix-en-Provence au milieu du XVe siècle," *REJ* 134.1–2 (1975): 47–80.

76. See Benjamin Richler, *Guide to Hebrew Manuscript Collections* (Jerusalem: Israel Academy of Sciences and Humanities, 1994); Giorgio Levi della Vida, *Ricerche sulla formazione del più antico fondo dei manoscritti orientali della Biblioteca Vaticana* (Vatican City: Biblioteca apostolica vaticana, 1939), passim; and Hans Striedl, "Geschichte der Hebraica-Sammlung der Bayerischen Staatsbibliothek," in *Orientalisches aus Münchener Bibliotheken und Sammlungen* (Wiesbaden: F. Steiner, 1958), 1–37 and esp. 1–7.

77. In a little-read essay on Abraham Bedersi, Schirmann cautions against using the standard term *dīwān* for the collection. As he notes, the word appears nowhere on copies of the work. He decided that the term was inappropriate for this collection because "it contains no internal order as is customary in Arabic *dīwāns* (according to the content of the poems, their form or with respect to the alphabetical ordering of their rhymes)." See Haim Schirmann, "Observations on the Collected Poems and Rhetorical Exercises of Abraham Bedersi" (in Hebrew), in S. W. Baron et al., eds., *Sefer Yuval leYitzhaq Baer* (Yitzhak F. Baer jubilee volume) (Jerusalem: Jewish Historical Association, 1961), 154–74 and for the citation 154 n. 1.

78. BL 930, fol. 15b.

79. Ibid., fol. 17a. The story is cited in Schirmann, *LeToldot haShirah vehaDrama ha'Ivrit*, and in Schirmann/Fleischer, 489–90.

80. Jacob Provençali, "Responsum on the Matter of Studying the Sciences," in Eleazar Ashkenazi, ed., *Sefer Divre Ḥakhamim* (Metz: Imprimerie J. Mayer Samuel, 1849, repr. Jerusalem: n.p., 1969), 70.

81. Schirmann/Fleischer, 498.

82. Halkin, "Why Was Levi ben Hayyim Hounded?"; Renan, *Histoire littéraire*, 27:700–701; Touati, "La controverse," 28. See also Schirmann/Fleischer, 485 n. 65; and A. Zunz, *Zur Geschichte und Literatur* (Berlin, 1845), 475.

83. *Jewish Encyclopedia*, "Provençali"; Henri Gross, *Gallia Judaica* (Paris, 1897), 383–84. Italy is not the focus of Bernard Goldstein's study on the fifteenth-century continuators of the astronomical traditions of Provence, but what he does mention reinforces my claim; see Goldstein, "The Hebrew Astronomical Tradition."

84. Yedaiah (haPenini) Bedersi, *Sefer haPardes*, in Y. Luzzato and A. Lass, "Orot me-Ofel," *Otzar haSifrut* 3.1 (1890): 12.

85. Schirmann, "Isaac Gorni," 177.

CHAPTER TWO

1. Paul Zumthor, *Le masque et la lumière: La poétique des grands rhétoriqueurs* (Paris: Éditions du Seuil, 1978), 84.

2. See ibid. and idem, "From Hi(story) to Poem, or the Paths of Pun: The Grands Rhétoriqueurs of Fifteenth-Century France," *New Literary History* 10.2 (winter 1979): 231–63; "Les grands rhétoriqueurs et le Vers," *Langue française* 23 (1974): 88–98; "Le carrefour des rhétoriqueurs: Intertextualité et Rhétorique," *Poétique: Revue de théorie et d'analyse littéraires* 27 (1976): 317–37. A similar phenomenon is found in the alliterative English poems of the later fourteenth-century "alliterative revival," although nothing quite on the order seen in the Hebrew or French. See, e.g., Bernard Levy and Paul Szarmach, eds., *The Alliterative Tradition in the Fourteenth Century* (Kent, Ohio: Kent State University Press, 1981); Christine Chism, *Alliterative Revivals* (Philadelphia: University of Pennsylvania Press, 2002).

3. Literally, בעלי אותיות בולטות. See I. Davidson, פרפראות לשירה העברית in Simon Ginzburg, ed., *Luaḥ Aḥiʻever* (New York: Histadrut Aḥiʻever, 1918), 90–109.

4. בעלי אותיות נשמטות.

5. A few examples appear in classical *piyyut*—for instance, by Kallir—but whether Bedersi would have known this seems doubtful. Fleischer refers to Arabic examples from the east, by Nisi al-Nahrawani and Saadia Gaon; see Haim Schirmann's posthumously published work, edited and completed by Ezra Fleischer, *Toldot haShirah ha'Ivrit biSefarad haNotzrit uveDrom Tzarfat* (Jerusalem: Magnes, 1997), 475 (hereafter cited as Schirmann/Fleischer). The 1,000-word limit of some of the pantograms may originate in the same convention that produced the popular Arabic grammatical work known as the *Alafiyya*; see Muhammad ibn ʻAbd Allah Ibn Malik, *Alifiyya, ou la quintessence de la grammaire arabe* (Paris: Oriental Translation Society, 1833). There is also an example of a poem in Ibn Gabirol's model, hyper-alliterating by verse, among the poems of Solomon Simḥa of Troyes. The poem, which commemorates a 1288 martyrdom in Troyes, may have been written in the late thirteenth century, that is, close to but earlier than Bedersi's compositions. Solomon's work is altogether idiosyncratic and mystical; see the references in Ephraim Kanarfogel, *Peering through the Lattices: Mystical, Magical, and Pietistic Dimensions in the Tosafist Period* (Detroit: Wayne State University Press, 2000), and my "On the Borders of Exile: The Poetry of Solomon Simḥah of Troyes," in Teolinda Barolini, ed., *Medieval Constructions in Gender and Identity: Essays in Honor of Joan M. Ferrante* (Tempe: Arizona State University, 2005), 69–87.

6. אאמיר אאדיר אפודת אגודת אורתך, Maḥzor Aragon (Salonika, 1529), Musaf to Yom Kippur, 80–81.

7. מי מקים מעפר מאשפות מרים מליצה, published in the *Archives Israëlites* 1 (1860): 97. In addition to Davidson, cf. n. 1 above. There is a long list of these poems in Schirmann/Fleischer, 500–501 nn. 6–9. See also E. Carmoly, "Zikkaron leRishonim ve-gam le-Aḥronim," *HaKarmel* 6.11 (1866): 85; Samuel de la Volta, "Notes," *Kerem Ḥemed* 2 (1836): 115–17.

8. See Schirmann/Fleischer, 499–513; Halkin, "Yedaiah Bedersi's 'Apology,'" in Alexander Altmann, ed., *Jewish Medieval and Renaissance Studies* (Cambridge, Mass.: Harvard University Press, 1967), 165–85; E. Renan, *Les écrivains juifs du XIVe siècle* (vol. 31 of *L'histoire littéraire de la France*) (Paris: Imprimerie nationale, 1893), 359–403; Marc Saperstein, *Decoding the Rabbis: A Thirteenth-Century Commentary on the Aggadah* (Cambridge, Mass.: Harvard University Press, 1980). For a summary of Bedersi's philosophical work, see Colette Sirat, *A History of Jewish Philosophy in the Middle Ages* (Cambridge: Cambridge University Press; Paris: Éditions de la Maison des Sciences de l'Homme, 1985), 273–77.

9. See Michael McVaugh, *Medicine before the Plague: Practitioners and Their Patients in the Crown of Aragon, 1285–1345* (Cambridge: Cambridge University Press, 1993); Joseph Shatzmiller, *Jews, Medicine, and Medieval Society* (Berkeley: University of California Press, 1994); Nancy Siraisi, *Taddeo Alderotti and His Pupils: Two Generations of Italian Medical Learning* (Princeton, N.J.: Princeton University Press, 1981); and idem, *Medieval and Early Renaissance Medicine* (Chicago: University of Chicago Press, 1990). Shatzmiller calls Yedaiah one of the greatest physicians of his time, although the basis of this claim appears to be chiefly the evidence of the Avicenna commentary.

10. Dov Yarden, "The *Qinot* of R. Joseph ben Sheshet ibn Latimi" (in Hebrew), in Meir Benyahu, ed., *Sefer Zikkaron lehaRav Yitzhaq Nissim* (Jerusalem: Yad haRav Nissim, 1984), 5:185–236.

11. Isaac Baer, *A History of the Jews in Christian Spain* (1961; reprint, Philadelphia: Jewish Publication Society, 1991), 1:119. The trip is described in many sources. See, e.g., Abraham Kahane, "R. Abraham HaBedersi and the Nature of His Books" (in Hebrew), *'Otzar haSifrut* 5 (1896): 219–21; H. Schirmann, "Some Considerations on the Collected Poems and Rhetorical Exercises of Abraham Bedersi" (in Hebrew), in S. Ettinger et al., eds., *Sefer Yuval le-Yitzhaq Baer* (Jerusalem: Jewish Historical Association, 1961), 154–73; Schirmann/Fleischer, 471–72.

12. Published for the first time by S. de la Volta, in *Kerem Hemed* 4 (1839): 57–65. I also consulted the copies in MS JTS 4067 (fifteenth century). For the purposes of this paper, and in accordance with most of the manuscripts, I attribute the poem to Yedaiah and not to his father. Schirmann did also, although Fleischer mysteriously and arbitrarily elides his argument: במקור פרופ' שירמן מעלה כאן שוב את הסברה ש'בקשת האל"פין' trarily elides his argument: וכן 'בקשת הלמ"דין' נכתבו בידי ידעיה. השמטתי את הפיסקה הזאת.—Schirmann/Fleischer, 501 n. 10. The argument of this chapter is not much affected if Schirmann and I are wrong, as Bedersi *père* may be associated with many of the views of his son.

13. I have used the published text in the *Sefer 'Olelot haBohen* (Fürth, 1805), with Hebrew commentary and Judeo-German translation, 19b–28a; MS BL Add. 27168 = 930/1 (JNUL no. F 05833), fols. 1b–3a.; Esc G-IV-5 (= F 10074), fols. 29ff. The numerological puns illustrated in the "titles" of the Hebrew poems are apparent also in the preference for 1,000- or 2,000-word compositions. On this feature in the Middle English alliterative poems, see John V. Fleming, "The Centuple Structure of the *Pearl*," 81–98, in Levy and Szarmach, *The Alliterative Tradition*. Fleming also refers to modern scholars' disdain for this type of poetry; see 93.

14. Schirmann/Fleischer, 476; Abraham Gavison, '*Omer haShikhehah* (Livorno, 1748; repr. Paris, 1972), 126a.

15. I have used the text published originally in 1570 Constantinople by I. Akrish, and republished by Abraham Geiger, *Iggeret Ogeret* (Breslau, 1844), 3a–6a. MSS Esc G-IV-5 (F 10074), fols. 87a–89b, an early fourteenth-century copy; NY MS JTS 4067 (= F 24969), fols. 37b–44b, a fifteenth-century Sephardic copy; and MS Oxf. Bodl. Can. Or. 104 (= F 05833), fols. 107–14, an Italian fifteenth-century copy, were also consulted. The poem appears in a much larger number of manuscripts than might be expected, confirming its popularity.

16. Yom Tov Assis, "Juifs refugiés en Aragon (XIIIe–XIVe siècles)," *REJ* 142 (1983): 298.

17. Ibid., 302–3.

18. Paul Zumthor, *Anthologie des grands rhétoriqueurs* (Paris: Union générale d'éditions, 1978), 13. See also Dennis Hue, *La poésie palinodique à Rouen* (Paris: Champion, 2002); R. Lebegue, "Rabelais et les grands rhétoriqueurs," *Lettres romanes* 12 (1958): 5–18; Mario Maurin, "La poétique de Chastellain et la 'Grande Rhétorique,'" *PMLA* 74.4 (1959): 482–84.

19. As Colette Sirat has observed, the Neoplatonic assumptions of both philosophers and kabbalists meant that the avenues taken by their thinking were not always as distinct as their conclusions, especially in this period. Sirat, *A History of Jewish Philosophy in the Middle Ages*, 249. See also Adena Tanenbaum, *The Contemplative Soul: Hebrew Poetry and Philosophical Theory in Medieval Spain* (Leiden: Brill, 2002), 36–44, for a description of medieval Jewish exposure to Neoplatonic writings in al-Andalus, which are abundantly evident in the work of Ibn Gabirol.

20. אהיה אשר אהיה אלהים אל אמת, in Meir Aharon Saadia Iraqi haKohen, ed., *Sefer haPizmonim* (Calcutta, 1842), no. 107, p. 35.

21. Sirat, *A History of Jewish Philosophy in the Middle Ages*, 250–55; and idem, "La qabbale d'après Juda b. Salomon ha-Cohen," in Gerard Nahon and Charles Touati, eds., *Hommage à Georges Vajda* (Louvain: Editions Peeters, 1980), 191–202; Y. Tzvi Langermann, "Some Remarks on Judah ben Solomon ha-Cohen and His Encyclopedia, *Midrash haHokhmah*," in Steven Harvey, ed., *The Medieval Hebrew Encyclopedias of Science and Philosophy* (Dordrecht: Kluwer Academic Publishers, 2000), 371–90; Resianne Fontaine, "Judah ben Solomon ha-Cohen's *Midrash ha-Hokhmah*: Its Sources and Use of Sources," in Harvey, *The Medieval Hebrew Encyclopedias*, 191–211.

22. Sirat, *A History of Jewish Philosophy in the Middle Ages*, 262–66; Elliot Wolfson, *Abraham Abulafia: Kabbalist and Prophet* (Los Angeles: Cherub, 2000), 56–57, 68.

23. Tanenbaum, *The Contemplative Soul*, 222–23.

24. Lenn E. Goodman, ed., *Neoplatonism and Jewish Thought* (Albany: State University of New York Press, 1992). In this collection, see especially the essays of Alfred L. Ivry, "Maimonides and Neoplatonism: Challenge and Response," 137–57; Idit Dobbs-Weinstein, "Matter as Creature and Matter as the Source of Evil: Maimonides and Aquinas," 217–37; and Moshe Idel, "Jewish Kabbalah and Platonism in the Middle

Ages and Renaissance," 319–53. See also Samuel Miklos Stern, "Ibn Ḥasdāy's Neoplatonist: A Neoplatonic Treatise and Its Influence on Isaac Israeli and the Longer Version
of the Theology of Aristotle," reprinted from *Oriens* 13–14 (1961): 58–120 as essay 7 in
idem, *Medieval Arabic and Hebrew Thought*, ed. F. W. Zimmerman (London: Variorum,
1983).

25. The bibliography on this topic is abundant. In addition to the works cited
immediately above, see Fernand Brunner, *Métaphysique d'Ibn Gabirol et de la tradition platonicienne* (Burlington, Vt.: Ashgate Variorum, 1997), in particular essays 8 ("Le
conflit des tendances platoniciennes et aristotéliciennes au moyen âge") and 12 ("Le
néoplatonisme au moyen âge").

26. See, e.g., Brian Stock, *Listening for the Text: On the Uses of the Past* (Philadelphia: University of Pennsylvania Press, 1996), esp. chap. 2 ("Medieval Literacy, Linguistic Theory, and Social Organization"), 30–52.

27. The Rouse studies are many, and I cite only a few here: Richard Rouse, "La
diffusion en occident au XIIIe siècle des outils de travail facilitant l'accès aux texts
autoritatifs," in George Makdisi et al., eds., *Enseignement en Islam et en Occident au
moyen-âge* (Paris: Librairie Orientaliste P. Geuthner, 1977): 115–47; Mary Rouse and
Richard Rouse, "La naissance des index," in *Histoire de l'édition français* (vol. 1 of *Le
livre conquérant*) (1982), 77–86; idem, "Biblical Distinctions in the Thirteenth Century,"
Archives d'histoire doctrinale et littéraire du moyen âge 41 (1974): 27–37; idem, "Concordances et index," in Henri-Jean Martin and Jean Vezin, eds., *Mise en page et mise en
texte du livre manuscrit* (Paris: Promodis, 1990), 219–28; and "*Statim invenire*: Schools,
Preachers, and New Attitudes to the Page," in Rouse and Rouse, *Authentic Witnesses:
Approaches to Medieval Texts and Manuscripts* (Notre Dame, Ind.: University of Notre
Dame Press, 1991), 191–220. See also Louis-Jacques Bataillon, "Intermédiaires entre les
traités de morale pratique et les sermons: Les *Distinctiones* bibliques alphabétiques," in
Les genres littéraires dans les sources théologiques et philosophiques médiévales (Louvain-
la-Neuve: Institut d'Études Médiévales de l'Université Catholique de Louvain, 1982),
213–26; Lloyd Daly, *Contributions to a History of Alphabetization in Antiquity and the
Middle Ages* (Brussels: Latomus, 1967); Ana Mussons, "Estudio del *Recull de Exemples y
Miracles per Alfabeto*," *Literatura Medieval* 2 (1993): 105–9; Olga Weijers, *Le maniement
de savoir* (Turnhout: Brepols, 1996), esp. chap. 11 and 12. The following discussion
draws on all these works.

28. Daly, *Contributions to a History of Alphabetization*, 83. The registers are from
northern France, one a list of debts kept by Johannes Sarracenus, chamberlain to Louis
IX, and one the account book of Jehan d'Ays relating to costs of the Aragon expedition
of 1285. There is almost no chance that a Jew would have seen these registers.

29. Rouse and Rouse, 1990, "Concordances et index," 228; Robert Brun, *Avignon
au temps des papes* (Paris: Librairie Armand Colin), 1928, esp. 246ff.; M. de Maulde, *Les
juifs dans les états français du Saint-Siège* (Paris: H. Champion, 1886). It is interesting
to note that the *grands rhétoriqueurs*, in Zumthor's reading, were also affected by the
inflated court pomp and ritual in Avignon.

30. Note the appearance of the *Manipulus florum* in 1304 and the *Alphabetum narrationum* between 1297 and 1308, the latter work by a Dominican, Arnoldo de Lieja; see Rouse, "La diffusion en occident," 123; Mussons, "Estudio del *Recull*," 106.

31. L. C. MacKinney, "Medieval Medical Dictionaries and Glossaries," in *Medieval and Historiographical Essays in Honor of James Westfall Thompson* (Chicago: University of Chicago Press, 1928), 240–68, esp. 258; Moritz Steinschneider, *Die hebraeischen Uebersetzungen des Mittelalters* (Berlin, 1893), no. 508, pp. 811–16. For an early Old French translation, see P. Dorveaux, ed., *L'antidotaire Nicolas* (Paris: H. Welter, 1896). There is no published edition.

32. It was translated again into Hebrew by Solomon b. Elia in 1414. See George Sarton, *Introduction to the History of Science* 2, part 1 (Baltimore: Carnegie Institute of Washington, 1931), 241.

33. Michael McVaugh and Luis García Ballester, "The Medical Faculty at Early Fourteenth-Century Lerida," *History of Universities* 8 (1989): 1–25; McVaugh, *Medicine before the Plague*, 83–84.

34. Michael McVaugh and Luis García Ballester, "Jewish Appreciation of Fourteenth-Century Scholastic Medicine," *Osiris*, 2nd ser., 6 (1990): 85–118; McVaugh, *Medicine before the Plague*. See Chapter 4 below.

35. Rouse, "La diffusion," 134: "Dieu ayant créé un univers harmonieux, ses parties devaient avoir entre elles un rapport logique harmonieux. Un auteur utilisant un classement alphabétique semblait refuter ces rapports logiques, ou confesser qu'il était incapable de les discerner." See also Rouse and Rouse, *Authentic Witnesses*, 202–4; and Stock, *Listening for the Text*, 51: "[T]he world of the text was the world of nature, obedient to natural laws and part of the universe of sense experience by which nature was ultimately known."

36. Stock, *Listening for the Text*, 50.

37. Al-Aḥdav was born in the mid-fourteenth century and wrote into the fifteenth. He emigrated from Castile to Sicily, and his later writing is from Syracuse and Palermo. See *HPSP*, 4:582–85; and *Shire-Yitzḥaq ben Shlomo al-Aḥdav*, ed. Ora Ra'anan (Lod: Makhon Habermann, 1988), nos. 15 and 16, pp. 85–86. No. 15 begins: דני ים שירתי נשמות בבלי גוף / והשם בם מושאל ואין פורץ פרץ. See also Schirmann/Fleischer, 618; Carmoly, זכרון לראשונים וגם לאחרונים, in *HaKarmel* 6 (1866): 85. Carmoly apparently saw the manuscript of Al-Aḥdav's "Nun Elegy" while living in Brazil; see Ra'anan, 17. The seventeenth-century writer Isaac Aboab, who authored the *alef* pantogram / אהיה אשר אהיה אלי ארוממך, also sojourned in Brazil; see Meir Kaiserling, "R. Isaac Aboab the Third" (in Hebrew), *HaGoren* 3 (1902): 155–67. Thus, to be properly inclusive, a survey of Hebrew pantograms would have to explore its New World expressions also. Cross-Atlantic attestation of a Hebrew genre is extremely rare, and this reinforces my sense that, in the eyes of its earlier readers, the pantogram was not viewed derisively at all.

38. See Shem Tov's charming rhymed prose allegory, "The Debate of the Pen and Scissors," excerpted in *HPSP*, 4:529–40; the full text is found in Sanford Shepard, *Shem Tov: His World and His Words* (Miami: Ediciones Universal, 1978). See also Susan Einbinder, "Pen and Scissors: A Medieval Debate," *Hebrew Union College Annual* 65 (1994): 261–76.

39. Stock, *Listening for the Text*, 31 (describing Boethius's Platonism vs. Abelard).

40. Zumthor, *Anthologie des grands rhétoriqueurs*, 55, 249.

41. This is discussed ubiquitously in the philosophical works. See, e.g., Sirat on the Ralbag (Gersonides), *A History of Jewish Philosophy in the Middle Ages*, 296ff.

42. This kind of rhetorical overkill may be found among the works of the *rhétoriqueurs* also. See, e.g., the selections by Destre (fl. 1501) in Zumthor, *Anthologie des grands rhétoriqueurs*, 205–10; for an especially good example, the poem to Princess Margaret on 208, in which the princess's name is embedded in a vertical and horizontal acrostic in the verses.

43. Josh. 7:26; Esther 1:6.

44. See Abraham ibn Ezra, *The Beginning of Wisdom*, ed. Raphael Levy and Francisco Cantera (Baltimore and London, 1939); idem, *Sefer ha'Olam*, in *Sefer Mishpete-haKokhavim*, ed. Meir b. Isaac Bekal (Jerusalem, 1971), 51. Ron Barkai, "L'astrologie juive médiévale: Aspects théoriques et pratiques," *Le Moyen Âge* 93.3–4 (1987): 342–43, 347, citing the writings of Abraham ibn Ezra, Abraham bar Ḥiyya, and Yosef Tov Elem haSefaradi. My thanks to Tzvi Langermann for his suggestions and bibliography.

45. Brunner, essay 12.

46. ופקח עיניך כי רבים חללי היאוש ועצלות ירים אשר הפיל. מחללי הגזירה החרותה אשר היא נחמת הפתאים. . . . ואל ישיאך הרפיון והעצלה שיש לזמן גזירות רשומות. כל השתדלות עמהם שקר כי זאת עצת נפתלי לבב כל ידעו בנפשותם.
Ed. Naftali Mendel Schor (Lemberg, 1871), 28.

47. See the following chapter.

48. מקלה מוריו מתנאה מחבר מהתלות ממשל משלים ("belittles his teachers, boasts, composes riddles and fables"); and just below, משדד מכל מלמדיו מתחשב משכיל מיסריו משסף ("does violence to all his teachers, considers himself learned, splits open those who torment him"—classical and medieval education strongly advocated negative reinforcement, and the "tormenters" are most likely teachers). See Raffaella Cribiore, *Gymnastics of the Mind: Greek Education in Hellenistic and Roman Egypt* (Princeton, N.J.: Princeton University Press, 2001); Ephraim Kanarfogel, *Jewish Education and Society in the High Middle Ages* (Detroit: Wayne State University Press, 1993).

49. Yom Tov Assis, "Juifs refugiés en Aragon (XIIIe–XIVe siècles)," 285–322; "Les juifs de Montpellier sous la domination Aragonaise," *REJ* 148 (1989): 5–16; Bernhard Blumenkranz, "Chemins d'un Exil," *Évidences* 13 (1962): 17–23. Additional references appear in my lecture, "God's Forgotten Sheep: Jewish Poetry and the Expulsion from France," Shelby Cullom Davis Center, Princeton University, February 14, 2003; see n. 2 and passim.

50. A. Cardoner, "El 'hospital para judios pobres' de Barcelona," *Sefarad* 22 (1962): 373–75, refers to "las luchas entre los miembros de las principales familias judías y aún vino a sumarse el problema representado por la llegada de numerosos hebreos franceses expulsados de su país por su soberano Felipe IV" (375). See also Noël Coulet, "L'expulsion des juifs de France," *L'histoire* 139: 9–16; and Béatrice LeRoy, "Entre deux mondes politiques: Les juifs du Royaume de Navarre," *Archives Juives* 20 (1984): 35–39.

51. Citing earlier research in this vein, Christine Chism makes the same argument for the alliterative Middle English poems. See Chism, *Alliterative Revivals*, e.g., 32.

52. For the sources, see my "God's Forgotten Sheep," 30–31 and the notes there.

53. Richard Emery, "Jewish Physicians in Medieval Perpignan," *Michael* 12 (1991): 113–34, esp. 117.

54. Simon Schwarzfuchs, "La communauté juive de Montpellier au XIIIe et au début du XIVe siècle dans les sources hébraïques," in Carol Iancu, ed., *Les juifs à Montpellier et dans le Languedoc* (Montpellier: Université Paul Valéry, 1988), 108–11. J. Ernst Renan and Adolphe Neubauer, *Histoire littéraire de la France*, vol. 31 (*Les écrivains juifs français du XIVe siècle*) (Paris: Imprimerie nationale, 1893); Rami Bar-Shalom, "Communication and Propaganda Between Provence and Spain: The Controversy over Extreme Allegorization," in Sophia Menache, ed., *Communication in the Jewish Diaspora* (Leiden: Brill, 1996), 171–226.

55. Ed. Schor, 11.

56. Jon. 1:6.

57. 1 Sam. 26:19. The allusion may be intended to suggest that the French king was persuaded to expel the Jews by his advisors.

58. Job 30:15.

59. Job 22:29.

60. Isa. 59:10.

61. How much his repeated condemnations of fellow Jews who chase money and rank are a deflected critique of his father is tantalizing to consider but impossible to know. Certainly, Abraham Bedersi, Yedaiah's father, had great admiration for his son's precocious facility with manneristic composition. A number of manuscript copies of the youthful Yedaiah's "Supplication in *Mem*" are prefaced by Abraham's introductory verses:

בטורי מי זהב	בני חוצב להב
בהמנע כפרם	ראה ערכם ורהב
אזי באדומיך	ראה אם מימיך
ונתתי מכרם	היאמר עמך

(My son has blazed forth with columns of liquid gold:
See their value and take pride as they refuse all ransom.
See if from your waters and then from your wine
Your people will say: I have paid their price. [Num. 20:19])

Leopold Dukes, "Gedichte über die בקשת הממין des Jedaiah Penini," *Der Orient* 12 (1851): 24. The article includes a total of seven verse introductions, by various authors, to Yedaiah's poem.

62. הוסר הודם הלמוני המולות / המון המקרים הלאוני הלמוני // המירוני התמורות הניאוני הפכות / האמנתי היום היותי הבל

The poem, beginning אמרתי אשמרה אורח אמת, and spelling out in acrostic "I am Yedaiah haPenini the son of Abraham," was published by Rashi Fein, "By Yedaiah haPenini" (in Hebrew), *HaKarmel* 1 (1861): 337. It is appended to some, but not all, of the manuscript and print editions of the *Baqashat haMemin*.

63. See above, n. 38, and Clark Colahan, "Santob's Debate: Parody and Political Allegory," *Sefarad* 29.1: 87–107 and 39.2: 265–308. The *Proverbios Morales*, dedicated to Pedro I, has been edited by Theodore A. Perry: *Proverbios morales, Santob de Carrión* (Madison, Wisc.: Hispanic Seminary of Medieval Studies, 1986).

64. The *Yam Qohelet* has never been published and survives today in three manuscript copies: MS Cambridge Add. 1499.3, fols. 1r–4v (hereafter cited as C1), with the beginning supplied by Carmoly on an inserted page cataloged as Camb. Add. 1499.2; MS Cambridge Add. 1512.1, fols. 1r–6v (hereafter cited as C2); and Berlin Staatsbibliothek 825 Qu. Or, fols. 1a–5b (hereafter cited as B). Paris MS BN 970, fol. 74v, was until recently considered a fragmentary copy of the poem also; Benjamin Richler has just "reattached" it to Cambridge Add. 1499.3, which was until now missing its "head." Personal communication, Richler, January 2005. Margalit Schalmann, a student of Professor Tova Rosen's, is currently working on a critical edition of this poem.

65. *HPSP*, 4:529.

66. C1: מעט מעט.

67. C2: משכנות.

68. C2: מחם.

69. Here I have used the version of C2. C1: מיוסדת מגנה.

70. C2: [!] משיח מודלק.

71. C2: מפחד.

72. C2: מעמים.

73. C1: מחוסה. Here I have used the wording of C2.

74. C2: ממקום. The sense seems to be a fear of the future, although *qadim* is biblically an eastern wind. I am not sure what to do with this, and the indecipherable word following does not help.

75. C1: מרוב.

76. Isa. 24:20.

77. Isa. 32:18.

78. Jer. 22:14.

79. Cf. Ezek. 12:18.

80. Lam. 3:63.

81. משיחי מודלף מטתי מלב; and in C2: מטתי [!] משיח מודלק. My translation is based on Ps. 6:7, אשחה בכל לילה מטתי, but Ardutiel's phrasing is difficult, and it is not clear what the "heart" has to do with the rest of this "sentence."

82. Isa. 51:13, 2 Kings 22:3.

83. Amos 2:13.

84. Ps. 69:22—poison?

85. Isa. 28:12.

86. Lam. 3:5.

87. Jer. 6:25.

88. Perhaps again evoking Lamentations 3, here Lam. 3:18.

89. See Moses Ibn Ezra, "Nafshi ivvitikha ba-laylah" (With my soul I long for You in the night), discussed in Tanenbaum, *The Contemplative Soul*, 111–31, with the full text and translation on 111–17. In stanza 6, the poet refers to the foolish dissipation of his youth.

90. *Beḥinat 'Olam*, chap. 11.

91. This is a standard concern of the medieval Hebrew "poems on the Soul" from Spain, Provence, and Italy. See Tanenbaum, *The Contemplative Soul*.

92. The visual emphasis on the hands, eyes, legs, and so on, is found in MS C2, not in C1.

93. Job 6:10.

94. Jer. 4:31. MS C1 has inserted the missing מבכירה in the margin.

95. I think in the sense of hiding herself from kin; see Isa. 58:7. MS C1, fol. 2a, col. 2, line 182 (counting from the beginning of the poem) has מתעלצת instead of מתעלמת. I follow the reading in C2, which corresponds to the verse in Isaiah.

96. Like a beast (מורבצת).

97. Exod. 25:38, 37:23. I.e., the body and its appendages, often described in the medical literature as "servants" or "helpers."

98. Job 17:2.

99. Eccles. 10:1.

100. Dan. 1:5, 8.

101. *Qol*—which means both "voice" and "sound" in Hebrew. The reference is to Judg. 5:11. The RSV translated the verse as "the sound of musicians," but the glosses of Qimḥi and Gersonides derive the word מחצץ from חץ (arrow) and understand it to refer to archers.

102. Lam. 3:49. Unfortunately, the preceding word is unclear in both copies.

103. See n. 64 above.

104. Schirmann/Fleischer, 509. A check of the online catalog at the Jewish Theological Seminary in New York revealed more than seventy copies, approximately twenty with the "Supplication in *Mem*." Most of the latter are eighteenth- and nineteenth-century editions. Manuscript copies date back to the fifteenth century, and the earliest print copy listed is from 1520. The Library of Congress holdings include twenty-seven editions, seventeen with the "Supplication in *Mem*." The Hebrew Union College catalog, unfortunately not online, contains thirty-eight listings for print editions, the earliest the Soncino edition of 1485; thirteen contain the "Supplication in *Mem*." My thanks to HUC reference librarian Arnona Rudavsky for providing the count.

105. See "Abraham Conat," *Jewish Encyclopedia* (New York: Funk & Wagnalls, 1901), 4:203–4; Haim Friedberg, *HaDefus ha'Ivri be'Italia, Aspamia, Portugalia veTugremah*, 2nd ed. (Tel Aviv: Bar-Yuda, 1956), 10–11; Abraham Habermann, "The Hebrew

Printer Abraham Conat and His Letter Types" (in Hebrew), *'Alim* 2 (1935/36): 81–88; Shlomo Simonsohn, *Toldot haYehudim beDikusat Mantova* (History of the Jews in the Duchy of Mantua) (Jerusalem: Qiryat Sefer, 1964), 424, 498.

106. Cincinnati HUC MS Acq. 2007–12, a bibliographic miscellany, mentions a Joseph Monzin (the patronymic inserted in Latin characters) with the Hebrew comment יוסף הלוי מעיר מונסון בארגון [שבט יהודה], i.e., Joseph HaLevy from the city of Monzon in Aragon. Our Isaac Monzon is thus most likely a Spanish exile living in Italy.

107. Benjamin Richler, *A Guide to Hebrew Manuscript Collections* (Jerusalem: Israel Academy of Sciences and Humanities, 1994), 73, 98, and private communication. See also Tzvi Harkavy, "Abraham = Eliyahu Harkavy," in Samuel Mirsky, ed., *Ishim uDemuyot beHokhmat Yisrael beEuropa haMizrahit* (New York: Ogen, 1959), 116–37.

108. Renan, *Les écrivains juifs*, HL 31: 41–42. Strangely, the French translation elides the central part of the passage.

109. Fleischer's description of the work has the dedication to Cardinal Richelieu. The copy in Cincinnati's Hebrew Union College Klau library shows this to be in error.

110. Leon Kahn, *Les juifs à Paris depuis le VIe siècle* (Paris: M. Lipschutz, 1889).

111. Jewish Theological Seminary, MS 4067.

112. ותדע ובחנת כי אחרי שהעתקתיה מחדש מצאתי בה הרבה מלים עלומי הבנה. ובהרבה מקומות לשון משחת ועניין נרפש אין הבין. עד שכמעט אחור נסוגותי מאשר חשבתי עליה טובה. ואמרתי לטמנה בתוך אהלי.

De la Volta, *Kerem Hemed*, 4, 58. In my own case, I am grateful to my colleagues Stephen Kaufman and Ezra Spicehandler, who waded through some of these poems with me in Cincinnati and whose sheer love for Hebrew and its endless capacity to awe always outweighed the perplexities of the texts. David Aaron and Richard Sarason also spent time on segments of the Beit-El, to my great profit.

113. Derek Pearsall makes the same point about the ME alliterative poems. See Pearsall, "The Origins of the Alliterative Revival," in Levy and Szarmach, *The Alliterative Tradition*, 2.

114. Largely forgotten today, Buchner was a prolific author and stylist who produced imitations of Ibn Gabirol's *Keter Malkhut* and al-Harizi's *Tahkemoni* as well as collections of epistolary models and his own hefty correspondence with notable figures of his day. Tersely, the author of the entry in the *Jewish Encyclopedia* (3:414–15) comments, "He endeavored to imitate Gabirol, al-Harizi, and Bedersi, but he had not the depth of the first, the invention of the second, or the force of expression of the third."

115. Zeev Wolf Buchner, *Sefer Shire Tehillah* (Berlin: Jüdische Freischule, 1808).

CHAPTER THREE

1. Reuben b. Isaac, "Adonai, ro'ed ve-hared," Hamburg, Staats- und Universitätsbibliothek MS Cod. Heb. 134, fols. 4b–5a. All translations, unless otherwise indicated, are mine.

2. Parma, Biblioteca Palatina, MS Heb. 3175 (= De Rossi 166), a late fourteenth-century Provençal collectanea, includes a responsum from Benjamin b. Judah to a query from a Reuben b. Isaac on prohibited wines (fols. 26v–27v). Perhaps this is our Reuben. According to the Parma catalog, a complete copy of this collection of texts is preserved in MS Oxford, Bodleian Library, Opp. Add. 40,127, fols. 17–145. See Benjamin Richler and Malachi Beit-Arié, eds., *Hebrew Manuscripts in the Biblioteca Palatina in Parma* (Jerusalem: JNUL, 2001), catalog entry no. 1555.

3. Simon Schwarzfuchs, "La communauté juive de Montpellier au XIIIe et au début du XIVe siècles dans les sources hébraïques," in Carol Iancu, ed., *Les juifs à Montpellier et dans le Languedoc* (Montpellier: Université Paul Valéry—Centre de recherches et d'études juives et hébraïques, 1988), 104–5, treating a response to David b. Reuben from the Rashba.

4. The nineteenth-century author of a rare multivolume commentary on the liturgical traditions and poetry of Provençal Jewry still recalled Reuben's work with reverence (if not much detail):

וה"ר ראובן ב"ר יצחק. אשר חננו אל שחק. שכל טוב ממרחק. מה מתקו כל אמריו

("And R. Reuben bar Isaac, favored by the heavenly God with intelligence [bestowed] from afar, how sweet are all his words!")

Moses Crémieu, *Ho'il Moshe Be'er*, part 1, vol. 2 (*Al seder arba' parshiyot vetzom Esther*) (Aix: Pontier fils ainé, 1830), 2b. On this work, which was published originally in only twenty-five copies and is now exceedingly rare, see Naftali Ben-Menahem, "The Book *Ho'il Moshe Be'er* of Moses Carmi/Crémieu" (in Hebrew), in *BeSha'are Sefer* (Jerusalem: Mossad Harav Kook, 1967), 164–72. The French version of his introduction paraphrases this sentiment: "Quelle portée d'esprit, quelle mélodie dans les paroles du Rabin RUBEN, fils du Rabin ISAAC! Ses supplications divines attestent tout son mérite." Ibid., 6b.

5. Cincinnati, Hebrew Union College MS 396.

6. Vatican, Biblioteca Apostolica ebr. 553, fols. 51v–52r. The copyist, Simon bar Samuel, refers to a no-longer-living Reuben as his relative. His inscription of Reuben's name, however, indicates that Reuben's father is still alive, impossible if our Reuben is intended. See the epilogue to this book.

7. On the *tehinah*, see Ezra Fleischer, *Shirat haQodesh ha'Ivrit Biyeme haBeinayim* (Jerusalem: Keter, 1975), 409–11. On the Comtat Venaissin rite, see Cecil Roth, "The Liturgies of Avignon and the Comtat Venaissin," *Journal of Jewish Bibliography* 1–2 (1939): 99–105. For studies specifically related to the published rites, see Noé Gruss, "L'imprimerie hébraïque en France (XVIe–XIXe siècles)," *REJ* 125 (1966): 77–91; R. Moulinas, "Documents sur des livres en Hebreu imprimés à Avignon ou à l'usage des juifs d'Avignon et du Comtat au XVIIIe siècle," *Archives juives* 7.2 (1970–71): 23–25; Simon Schwarzfuchs, "On the Woes of Book Publishing: The Carpentras *Mahzor*" (in Hebrew), *'Ale-Sefer* 6–7 (spring 1979): 145–56. The *Seder haTamid* was reprinted in 1855.

8. The same point is central to the argument of Prasenjit Duara, *Rescuing History from the Nation* (Chicago: University of Chicago Press, 1995).

9. Jan Assmann's review of the history of the distinction between cyclical and linear time is concise and helpful. Liturgical time is "cyclical" because it is, among his categories, "mythic." Eliade's early ascription of linearity to Christian sacred (end-oriented) time versus the cyclic repetition of profane time is the reverse of the opposition I develop below, i.e., between a cyclic liturgical time that absorbs historical events into preexisting tropes and a linear historical time in which events unfold sequentially and causally. See Jan Assmann, *The Mind of Egypt: History and Meaning in the Time of the Pharaohs*, trans. Andrew Jenkins (New York: Metropolitan, 2002), 12–17.

10. Indeed, it varied among each of the four cities (Carpentras, Cavaillon, L'Isle sur Sorge and Avignon) that accounted for the majority of this population. Isidore Loeb, "Les juifs de Carpentras sous le government pontifical," *REJ* 12 (1886): 161.

11. Cecil Roth, "The Liturgies of Avignon and the Comtat Venaissin," *Journal of Jewish Bibliography* 1–2 (1939): 99–105; Schwarzfuchs, "On the Woes of Book Publishing"; Armand Lunel, "Lost Jewish Music of Provence," *Reconstructionist* 224.14 (1958): 25–28; Jules Salomon Crémieux and Mardochée Crémieux, *Chants hébraïques suivant le rite des communautés Israélites de l'ancien Comtat Venaissin* (Aix-en-Provence, 188–?).

12. As noted, I am primarily interested here in the poems of Reuben b. Isaac, which form the core of the expulsion memory retained in the collection, but of necessity I will shuttle between Reuben's poems and those of the Rashbatz. Certainly, most of the later poems in MS Hamburg 134, including those of the Rashbatz, are unknown and deserve their own attention, which hopefully they shall merit in their proper place. The Rashbatz's poems are for the most part unpublished. See Isaac Moraly, "*Tzafenat Fa'aneakh*: Remnants of the Poetry of the Ribish and the Rashbatz" (in Hebrew), *Qovetz 'al Yad* 7 (1896–97): 5–47; and Ephraim Hazan, "*Teḥinot* haRashbatz for Mondays and Thursdays" (in Hebrew), *Masoret haPiyyut* 2 (2000): 111–17. The poems contained in MS Hamburg 134 are not listed in Davidson.

13. Ephraim Hazan, *Piyyutim veQit'e Tefillah min haSiddur* (Jerusalem: Ministry of Education and Culture, 1979), 112, where Hazan comments that the use of *teḥinot* for Mondays and Thursdays for the entire year is a "surprise," in contrast to their usual introduction on fast days, the Ten Days of Repentance between Rosh Hashanah and Yom Kippur, and during the end of the month of Elul, 112. See also idem, "The Weekly Scriptural Reading in *Piyyut* and Poetry," in E. Hazan, ed., *Meḥqere Misgav Yerushalayim beSifruiyot 'Am Yisrael* (International Congress on Sephardic and Oriental Jewry) (Jerusalem: Institute for Study of the Legacy of Sephardic Jewry, 1987), 87–98; idem, "*Teḥinot* of the Rashbatz for Mondays and Thursdays," in E. Hazan and B. Bar-Tikva, eds., *Masoret haPiyyut* (Ramat-Gan: Bar Ilan University, 2000), 2:111–19. Hazan was not working with the Hamburg manuscript but with a late nineteenth-century copy that included selections from it. The copy was made by the renowned collector, L. Dukes, and is catalogued as Oxford, MS Mich.146 (old no. 846) = Cat. Neubauer no. 1180.

14. See Schwarzfuchs, "On the Woes of Book Publishing"; Susan Einbinder, "Hebrew Poems for the 'Day of Shutting In': Problems and Methods," *REJ* 163.1–2 (2004): 111–35; *Seder haTamid*, ed. Abraham Monteil (Avignon, 1767).

15. MS Hamburg 134 also contains a few poems by earlier poets, such as Zechariah, or Judah HaLevi, two poems with the acrostic signature Joseph (Joseph Qimḥi), and one each by Jacob, David HaQatan, Samuel, Levi bar Jacob, Simon Yeḥiel, Judah Itiel, and Dar'i (the Egyptian Karaite poet, Moses Dar'i?). There are approximately eighty poems by either Reuben b. Isaac or Simon b. Zemaḥ, and two poems with no acrostic signatures.

16. Both were popular subjects in Maghrebi communities. Ephraim Hazan, *HaShirah ha'Ivrit biTzefon Afriqa* (Jerusalem: Magnes, 1995), 65–66.

17. William C. Jordan, *The French Monarchy and the Jews* (Philadelphia: University of Pennsylvania Press, 1989); Elizabeth A. R. Brown, *Philip V, Charles IV and the Jews of France: The Alleged Expulsion of 1322* (Boston: Medieval Academy of America, 1991); Gerd Mentgen, *Studien zur Geschicht der Juden im mittelalterlichen Elsass* (Hannover: Hahnsche, 1995), 83.

18. William C. Jordan, "Home Again: The Jews in the Kingdom of France, 1315–1322," in F. R. P. Akehurst and Stephanie Cain Van D'Elden, eds., *The Stranger in Medieval Society*, Medieval Cultures, vol. 12 (Minneapolis: University of Minnesota Press, 1998), 34; idem, *The Great Famine* (Princeton, N.J.: Princeton University Press, 1996); Herbert H. Lamb, *Weather, Climate and Human Affairs* (London and New York: Routledge, 1988), 63–67; Emmanuel le Roy Ladurie, *Times of Feast, Times of Famine: A History of Climate Since the Year 1000* (Garden City, N.Y.: Doubleday, 1971); M. J. Larenaudie, "Les famines en Languedoc aux XIVe et XVe siècles," *Annales du midi* 64.1 (1952): 27–40; H. S. Lucas, "The Great European Famine of 1315, 1316, and 1317," *Speculum* 5.4 (1930): 343–78; Katherine Reyerson, *The Art of the Deal: Intermediaries of Trade in Medieval Montpellier* (Leiden: Brill, 2002), 73–75.

19. Notably, Montpellier's drought years—1313, 1323, and 1330—all fall outside of the period of Jewish residence. Reyerson, *The Art of the Deal*, 73.

20. See Jordan, *The French Monarchy*, 216–23, Jeanne Niquille, "Les prêteurs juifs de Morat," *Nouvelles Étrennes Fribourgeoises* 60 (1927): 89–101; Achille Nordmann, "Histoire des juifs à Genève de 1281–1780," *REJ* 80 (1925): 1–41.

21. See, e.g., Yom Tov Assis, "Juifs de France refugiés en Aragon (XIIIe–XIVe siècles," *REJ* 142 (1983): 285–322; Richard Emery, "Les juifs en Conflent et en Vallespir (1250–1415)," in *Conflent, Vallespir et montagnes catalanes: Actes du LIe congrès de la Fédération Historique du Languedoc Méditerranéen et du Roussillon, organizé à Prades et Villefranche-de-Conflent, les 10–11 juin 1978* (Montpellier: La Fédération, 1980), 85–91; A. Prudhomme, *Les juifs en Dauphiné* (Grenoble, 1883).

22. Jordan, *The French Monarchy*, 204–6; Isidore Loeb, "Les expulsions des juifs de France au XIVe siècle," in *Jubelschrift zum siebzigsten Geburtstage des Prof. Dr. H. Graetz* (Breslau: S. Schottlaender, 1887), 39–57; Gustave Saige, *Les juifs de Languedoc* (Paris: Alphonse Picard, 1881), 92 n. 2, and 101–2.

23. David Abulafia, *A Mediterranean Emporium: The Catalan Kingdom of Majorca* (Cambridge: Cambridge University Press, 1994), 183.

24. Ibid., 158.

25. "Adonai, rivah et yerivai," MS Hamburg 134; *Seder haTamid* 70b.

26. "Adonai, ro'ed ve-ḥared," v. 8 (MS Hamburg 134, fols. 4b–5a); "Adonai, ruḥi ḥuvalah," v. 9 (*Seder haTamid*, 83a).

27. *Seder haTamid*, "Adonai, ro'eh ne'eman," 72a.

28. "Adonai, ruḥi ḥuvalah," *Seder haTamid*, 83a; also in MS Hamburg 134, both under parashat Beha'alotekha.

29. The faithless sisters of Ezekiel 23, who represent the kingdoms of Israel and Judah.

30. *Seder haTamid*, 85a–b; MS Hamburg 134.

31. Also the year of a general expulsion of French Jews, who had been readmitted in 1315.

32. See Einbinder, "Hebrew Poems for the 'Day of Shutting In.'"

33. Ironically, the current had gone the other way only a century earlier, when Jews from Marseilles fled for Rome and Naples.

34. See Loeb, "Les juifs de Carpentras," 191.

35. Cincinnati, Hebrew Union College MS 396. The codex contains a blessing for Pope Nicholas V, whose pontificate covered that period. See fol. 131a, and Einbinder, "Hebrew Poems for the 'Day of Shutting In.'" I am not including the poem in Vatican Heb. 553 as definitively Reuben's. See above and, for more detail, my epilogue.

36. Einbinder, "Hebrew Poems for the 'Day of Shutting In.'"

37. Ibid.

38. Patrick Geary's description of a medieval "culture of memory" is apt, as it identifies a world "in which listening to texts is intended to key memory, not to provide the listeners with new information." Patrick Geary, "Oblivion: Between Orality and Textuality in the Tenth Century," in Gerd Althoff, Johannes Fried, and Patrick Geary, eds., *Medieval Concepts of the Past: Ritual, Memory, Historiography* (Washington, D.C.: German Historical Institute; Cambridge: Cambridge University Press, 2002), 115.

39. Isidore Epstein, *The Responsa of Rabbi Simon b. Zemaḥ Duran as a Source of the History of the Jews in North Africa* (London: Oxford University Press, 1930), 1–7.

40. Despite the universal assumption among later scholars that he was a physician, I am not sure about this. True, among Jewish practitioners, the professional distinction between physicians and surgeons was not as sharp as among Christian practitioners, but a Christian physician would not have practiced surgery. See Michael McVaugh, *Medicine before the Plague: Practitioners and Their Patients in the Crown of Aragon, 1285–1345* (Cambridge: Cambridge University Press, 1993). Simon's self-proclaimed difficulties with mathematics, geometry, and astronomy make it hard to believe he could have successfully followed the curriculum required for licensing as a physician. And finally, his inability to find work as a medical professional in Algiers suggests, too, that more may have been at stake than the anti-scientific "superstitions" of his new neighbors. Indeed,

Fez at least was noted as a medical center around this time, and in the increasingly anti-Muslim atmosphere of Reconquista Spain, North Africa was a magnet for "the able, the learned, and the ambitious" among Muslim physicians and surgeons; ibid., 54. See, e.g., the slightly earlier career of Muhammad al-Shafra (b. ca. 1280, emigrating to Fez in 1344); H. P. J. Renaud, "Un chirurgien musulman du royaume de Grenade: Muhammad al-Safra," *Hesperis* 20 (1935): 1–20. The great Andalusian physician Ibn al-Khatib, whom we will meet in Chapter 5, fled from Granada to Tlemcen in 1371 and was murdered in Fez in 1372. See Ann Campbell, *The Black Death and Men of Learning* (New York: Columbia University Press, 1931), 27 and chapter 5; and Ellen Jean Amster, "Medicine and Sainthood: Islamic Science, French Colonialism, and the Politics of Healing in Morocco, 1877–1935" (Ph.D. diss., University of Pennsylvania, 2003); chapter 2 of the dissertation contains some discussion of medieval physicians and sources.

    41. André Chouraqui, *Histoire des juifs en Afrique du Nord* (Paris: Hachette, 1985), 127.

    42. Ibid., 124.

    43. Ibid., 125 (re Tlemcen); Richard Lawless and Gerald Blake, *Tlemcen: Continuity and Change in an Algerian Islamic Town* (London: Bowker, 1976), 49.

    44. Lawless and Blake, *Tlemcen*, 28–59; Muhammad al-Tanassi, *Histoire des Beni Zeiyan: Rois de Tlemcen*, trans. J. J. L. Bargès (Paris: Benjamin Duprat, 1852); the Arabic edition has been edited by Mahmoud Bouayed, *Ta'arikh beny Ziyān: Mulūk Tlemcen* (Algiers: s.n., 1985).

    45. Renaud, "Un chirurgien musulman du royaume de Grenade," 74; Michel Abitbol, "Juifs d'Afrique du Nord et expulsés d'Espagne après 1492," *Revue de l'histoire des religions* 210.1 (1993): 49–90; idem, "Juifs maghrébins et commerce transsaharien au moyen âge," in Abitbol, ed., *Communautés juives des marges sahariennes du Maghreb* (Jerusalem: Ben Zvi Institute, 1982), 229–50; J. D. Latham, "Contribution à l'étude des immigrations Andalouses et leur place dans l'histoire de la Tunisie," 203–5.

    46. Thomas Glick, *Islamic and Christian Spain in the Early Middle Ages* (Princeton, N.J.: Princeton University Press, 1979), 286–88; and Brian Catlos, *The Victors and the Vanquished: Christians and Muslims of Catalonia and Aragon, 1050–1300* (Cambridge: Cambridge University Press, 2004). Maria Ferrer i Mallol has documented steady emigration from the end of the thirteenth century to the mid-fourteenth century; at that point, however, both Aragonese and Castilian policies attempted to restrict and even prohibit a Muslim exodus from their lands. These policies were in part a result of the plague years and the concentration of Muslim labor in agriculture. The nobility in both kingdoms protested permissive emigration policies in severely depopulated lands, and unsurprisingly, the outbreak of war between Aragon and Castile in 1364 halted such emigration altogether. Maria Teresa Ferrer i Mallol, *Els sarraïns de la corona Catalano-Aragonesa en el segle XIV* (Barcelona: Conseil superior d'investigacions cientifiques, 1987), 171.

    47. Ferrer i Mallol, *Els sarraïns de la corona Catalano-Aragonesa en el segle XIV*, 162–83.

48. Abitbol, "Juifs maghrébins et commerce transsahrien au moyen âge," 229–50; Jacob Oliel, *Les juifs au Sahara: Le touat au moyen âge* (Paris: CNRS, 1994), 68–69; Georges S. Colin, "Un juif marocain du XIVe siècle: Constructeur d'astrolabe," *Hesperis* 22 (1936): 83–84.

49. See, e.g., Haim Zeev Hirschberg, *A History of the Jews in North Africa* (Leiden: Brill, 1974–81), 2:9; Chouraqui, *Histoire des juifs en Afrique du Nord*, 126.

50. Hirschberg, *A History of the Jews in North Africa*, 1:386; Epstein, *The Responsa of Rabbi Simon b. Zemaḥ Duran*, 15–17, 36–37, 75–76; Abitbol, "Juifs maghrébins et commerce transsahrien au moyen âge," 244; Abitbol, "Juifs d'Afrique du Nord et expulsés d'Espagne après 1492," 83–86. Regarding similar responses to Muslim exiles of the late fifteenth to early seventeenth centuries, see Luce Lopez Baralt, "La angustia secreta del exilio: El testimonio de un morisco de Túnez," *Hispanic Review* 55 (1987): 47, 49–50. As for evidence of Muslim resentment of the Jewish immigrants, which also exists, Maya Shatzmiller has argued convincingly that in some sites, at least, notably Fez, local Muslim opposition to the Jews was politically motivated and related to the Fez intelligentsia's sense of the illegitimacy of their Merinid rulers. The Merinid reliance on Jews to fill administrative posts in the city was therefore a recipe for Jewish disaster. See Maya Shatzmiller, "An Ethnic Factor in a Medieval Social Revolution: The Role of Jewish Courtiers under the Marinids," in Milton Israel and N. K. Wagle, eds., *Islamic Society and Culture: Essays in Honour of Professor Aziz Ahmad* (New Delhi: Manohar, 1983), 149–61; and Nicole Serfaty, "Courtisans et diplomats juifs à la cour des sultans marocains (XIV–XVII)," in Nicole Serfaty and Joseph Tedghi, eds., *Présence juive au Maghreb: Homage à Haïm Zafrani* (Paris: Éditions Bouchène, 2004), 183–93.

51. This is especially evident in the relevant responsa of the Rashbatz and his Majorcan predecessor as chief rabbi of Algiers, Isaac bar Sheshet (the Ribish). See also Zafrani, *Juifs d'Andalousie et du Maghreb* (Paris: Maisonneuve et Larosse, 1996), 208–9; Epstein, *The Responsa of Rabbi Simon b. Zemaḥ Duran*, 26.

52. See the lengthy entry, written by Yedida Stillman, under "Libās" in the *Encyclopedia of Islam* (Leiden: Brill, 1986), 5:732–52, esp. 742, regarding the "distinctive" Berber style of dress, including the turban, and the failure of the turban to attract adherents in al-Andalus.

53. See below.

54. Joseph Chetrit, "Historical-Occasional Poems in Jewish Poetry from Morocco," 315–39, in Issachar Ben-Ami, ed., *Moreshet Yehude Sefarad vehaMizraḥ* (International Conference on Sephardi and Oriental Jewry) (Jerusalem: Magnes, 1982), 315–39.

55. The same predatory lions (and hawks) appear in Abu'l-Muṭarrif b. 'Amīra's lament for the fall of Valencia to the Aragonese army of James I. Whether the typology has its roots in an Arabic convention is worth considering. In addition, as Nicholas Howe has observed of the descriptions of landscape in Anglo-Saxon verse, such descriptions are capable of rendering "character" as much as landscape, i.e., the situation of a figure within a conventional landscape may be intended to reveal "much about characters that the poet cannot or will not say directly." Nicholas Howe, "The Landscape of Anglo-

Saxon England: Inherited, Invented, Imagined," in John Howe and Michael Wolfe, eds., *Inventing Medieval Landscape: Senses of Place in Western Europe* (Gainesville: University Press of Florida, 2002), 105.

56. "Adonai, lanu ashemim," vv. 6–7, parashat Vayera, fols. 5b–6b. The verse is capped with a citation of Ps. 130:7.

57. "Adonai, lanu ashemim," v. 16.

58. Ps. 5:13.

59. "Adonai, shafakhti siḥah," parashat Emor, vv. 5–6, fols. 32a–33a.

60. "Adonai, atah yadaʻta yitzri," parashat ḥaye-Sarah, v. 2.

61. Ibid., vv. 6–7.

62. Hazan, "Teḥinot haRashbatz for Mondays and Thursdays," 113–14. Hazan is missing the middle couplet.

63. The end of the verse is implied: "we looked for peace but no good came" (Jer. 8:15).

64. Ps. 1:4; Isa. 41:3.

65. Job 22:28; Num. 6:26.

66. "Adonai, ḥalti betzaratah," parashat Re'eh, v. 2, fols. 46a–b.

67. They may also have contributed to anti-Jewish prejudices that they brought with them from Andalusia and that had played a role there in the competitive claims of Jewish and Muslim minorities; see David Nirenberg, *Communities of Violence: The Persecution of Minorities in the Middle Ages* (Princeton, N.J.: Princeton University Press, 1996). Maya Shatzmiller relates the story of the Merinid sultan Abu al-Hassan (ruled 1331–48), who not only refused to employ Jews in his court but specifically refused the services of a Jewish physician brought to treat his leg. The story is recorded by Ibn Marzuk. See Shatzmiller, "An Ethnic Factor in a Medieval Social Revolution," 159–60. On the other hand, Hirschberg refers to a Malaga-born Jewish physician, Moses b. Samuel al-Ashqar, working in Tlemcen in 1438; see Hirschberg, *A History of the Jews in North Africa*, 1:388–92. Note that some of the Merinid rulers of the later fourteenth century were themselves returned exiles from Spain; see Maya Shatzmiller, *L'historiographie mérinide* (Leiden: Brill, 1982), 30–31. On Jewish physicians during this period, see also Chouraqui, *Histoire des juifs en Afrique du Nord*, 125; and Dr. Renaud, "Etat de nos connaissances sur la médecine ancienne du Maroc," *Hesperis* 20 (December 1920): 73 (it is advisable, given Renaud's reliance on Carmoly, to take some of his claims with a grain of salt).

68. Renaud, "Etat de nos connaissances," 71–84 ; Mohamed Benchekroun, *La vie intellectuelle marocaine sous les Mérinides et les Wattasides* (Rabat: s.n., 1974), 59–84, 477–84; Maya Shatzmiller, "Les premiers Mérinides et le milieu religieux de Fès: L'introduction des médersas," *Studia Islamica* 43 (1976): 109–18; Anwar G. Chejne, *Islam and the West: The Moriscos* (Albany: State University of New York Press, 1983), 116–17; Ahmed Khaneboubi, *Les premiers sultans mérinides 1269–1331: Histoire politique et sociale* (Paris: Éditions l'Harmattan, 1987), 188–91. See also Amster, "Medicine and Sainthood."

69. Abitbol, "Juifs d'Afrique du Nord et expulsés d'Espagne après 1492," 49–90; idem, "Juifs maghrébins et commerce transsaharien au moyen âge," 244.

70. Abitbol, "Juifs d'Afrique du Nord," 86–90. And see J. D. Latham, "Contribution à l'étude des immigrations Andalouses et leur place dans l'histoire de la Tunisie," 5:39; originally published as "Towards a Study of Andalusian Immigrations and Their Place in Tunisian History," *Les Cahiers de Tunisie* 5 (1957): 203–52, in idem, *From Muslim Spain to Barbary* (London: Variorum, 1986), essay 5: 42–43. For another type of evidence, see also Shalom Sabar, "Sephardi Elements in North African Manuscript Decoration," *Jewish Art* 18 (1992): 169–91.

71. Zafrani, *Juifs d'Andalousie et du Maghreb*, 138; Edwin Seroussi, "La musique andalouse-marocaine dans les manuscrits hébraïques," in Michel Abitbol, ed., *Relations judéo-musulmanes au Maroc: Perceptions et réalités* (Paris: Centre International de Recherche sur les Juifs du Maroc, 1997), 283–95. In the same volume, see also Avraham E.-Amzallag, "La ala andalouse chez les Juifs et les Arabes," 295–303, and Meir Attia, David Golan, and Jacques Azran, "Note sur les compositions musicales préservées dans la musique juive andalouse au Maroc," 303–7.

72. Stillman, "Libās." On the Andalusians' legendary love of bright color, particularly red, see Rachel Arié, "Quelques remarques sur le costume des Musulmans d'Espagne au temps des Naṣrides," *Arabica* 12 (1965): 249.

73. Yedida Stillman, "Spanish Influences on the Material Culture of Moroccan Jews" (in Hebrew), in Issachar Ben Ami, ed., *Moreshet Yehude Sefarad vehaMizraḥ* (International Conference on Sephardic and Oriental Jewry) (Jerusalem: Magnes, 1982), 359–66; Abitbol, "Juifs d'Afrique du Nord et expulsés d'Espagne après 1492," 70; Epstein, *The Responsa of Rabbi Simon b. Zemaḥ Duran*, 14; J. M. Haddey, *Le livre d'or des Israélites algériens* (Algiers: A. Bouyer, 1871), 3. The *Livre d'or* refers to "la robe et la coiffure espagnoles" of the exiles and their descendants, noting that special wedding regalia was reserved for the use of four families only. Latham observes that the Andalusian (Muslim) exiles in Tunis pointedly abandoned Spanish clothing to adopt "le costume des hautes classes socials," going to great extremes to differentiate between themselves and the locals. See Latham, "Contribution à l'étude des immigrations Andalouses et leur place dans l'histoire de la Tunisie," 5:42–43. Conversely, the description of the poverty of turbaned Jews in Tunis in the early modern period must refer to the miserable state of the *toshavim* at that time; their socioeconomic distress was ironically as much a consequence of the success of the Spanish exiles as it was of independent economic trends or social policies; see Chouraqui, *Histoire des juifs en Afrique du Nord*, 124–25.

74. There is no indication in the *Siete Partidas* that Muslim subjects were required to wear a distinguishing badge or garment. See also Arié, "Quelques remarques sur le costume"; and John Boswell, *The Royal Treasure: Muslim Communities under the Crown of Aragon in the Fourteenth Century* (New Haven, Conn.: Yale University Press, 1977), 331–32.

75. Note the rapid flip-flops of the 1390s, where we have already seen similar instability in emigration policies; Ferrer i Mallol, *Els sarraïns de la corona Catalano-Aragonesa en el segle XIV*, 54–59.

76. Ibid., 45–47. In Valencia in the 1370s, the haircut was in addition to a requisite cap for men and a veil for women. Ibid., 54. See also Allan Cutler, "Innocent III and the Distinctive Clothing of Jews and Muslims," *Studies in Medieval Culture* 3 (1970): 92–116.

77. See especially L. A. (Leo Ary) Mayer, *Mamluk Costume: A Survey* (Geneva: Albert Kundig, 1952).

78. Arié, "Quelques remarques sur le costume," 246, 253; Georges Marçais, *Le costume musulman d'Alger* (Paris: Librairie Plon, 1930), 82.

79. Marçais, *Le costume musulman d'Alger*, 85; Stillman, "Libās."

80. Mayer, *Mamluk Costume*, 70. The color coding is dated to the fourteenth century. For Muslim Spain, see Arié, "Quelques remarques sur le costume," 254–55.

81. Marçais, *Le costume musulman d'Alger*, 76.

82. J. D. Latham, "Towns and Cities of Barbary: The Andalusian Influence," in idem, *From Muslim Spain to Barbary* (London: Variorum, 1986), essay 6, 188–204, esp. 196–98.

83. Latham, "Towards a Study of Andalusian Immigrations and Their Place in Tunisian History," 234–37 (French trans., 1986, 50–53); Glick, *Islamic and Christian Spain*; and idem, "Tribal Landscapes of Islamic Spain: History and Archaeology," in Howe and Wolfe, *Inventing Medieval Landscape*, 113–36.

84. Latham, "Towards a Study of Andalusian Immigrations and Their Place in Tunisian History," 203–5 (French trans., 1986, 34–36).

85. Serfaty, "Courtisans et diplomats juifs"; and idem, *Les courtisans juifs des sultans marocains: XIIIe–XVIIIe siècles: Hommes politiques et hauts dignitaries* (Saint-Denis: Éditions Bouchène, 1999).

86. Certainly, this is a process replicated elsewhere, and not only by Jews. It describes the elevation of "German-ness" by Jewish refugees from Germany in the mid-twentieth century, or the internalization and transmission of American-ness (as lived by a white, racialized, middle class) by African American missionaries in nineteenth-century Liberia. See Josiah Ulysses Young III, *A Pan-African Theology: Providence and the Legacy of the Ancestors* (Trenton, N.J.: Africa World Press, 1992).

87. Duara, *Rescuing History from the Nation*. The notion of "soft" and "hard" borders is useful here; see, e.g., 65. Duara attempts to identify the ways in which bits of the past are embedded in and linked to events in the present in the formation of "totalizing" historical narratives; see, e.g., 80, 103, and passim.

88. I am aware of Joseph Chetrit's very appropriate distinction between "cyclic" and "historical" time in Maghrebi *piyyutim*, which is close to what I also attempt to describe. See Chetrit, *Shirah vePiyyut beYahadut Morocco* (Jerusalem: Hebrew University Press, 1999), 70–72. I think it is not necessary, however, to view these chronotypical markers in the poems as belonging to two different worldviews that are inherently contradictory. Rather, they coincide, in a form of historical seeing that lies beyond the secular and rational discursive preferences of Western historical narrative. See Duara, *Rescuing History from the Nation*; Dipesh Chakrabarti, *Provincializing Europe: Postcolonial Thought and*

Historical Difference (Princeton, N.J.: Princeton University Press, 2000); Shahid Amin, *Event, Metaphor, Memory: Chauri Chaura 1922–1992* (Berkeley: University of California Press with Oxford University Press, 1995).

89. Hirschberg, *A History of the Jews in North Africa*, 2:9. On the first of the two "Purims of Algiers" see the list of special Purims under the entry for "Purim" in the *Encyclopaedia Judaica* 13:1395. The Spanish defeat is celebrated on 4 Heshvan; a later local Purim, called Purim Tammuz and celebrated on the eleventh of that month, commemorates the defeat of the Spanish in 1774.

90. Although Hazan observes that there are surprisingly few laments or hymns that refer directly to the expulsion of 1492, there is a respectable list of poets and compositions that surfaces in his and Joseph Chetrit's work; see Ephraim Hazan, *HaShirah ha'Ivrit biTzefon Afriqa*; Chetrit, "Historical-Occasional Poems"; idem, *Shirah vePiyyut beYahadut Morocco*. A number were collected by one of the literary exiles himself, A. Gavison, and published under the title *'Omer haShikhehah* (Paris and Livorno: A. Meldola, 1748, repr. 1972). A number of poems by the poet Abraham the Spaniard (haSepharadi), who also signs himself "Abraham the Exile from His Country," are also scribbled in the margins of Cambridge, Massachusetts, MS Houghton 175 Heb. 38; thanks to Leon Jacobowitz Efron of Boston University for sharing these with me.

91. Chetrit, *Shirah vePiyyut beYahadut Morocco*, 11–13, 17, 26–27. As Joseph Chetrit has observed, an "obsessive" messianism characterizes even later Maghrebi Jewish verse, much of which recycles the motifs of exile and redemption dramatized by MS Hamburg 134. See ibid., 3–35 and 75–140; and Shalom Bar-Asher, "La poésie liturgique juive nord-africaine comme source historique," in Serfaty and Tedghi, *Présence juive au Maghreb*, 401–10.

92. For more on the *obros*, see Chapter 4 below.

93. For a description of the 1709 famine, written by someone with a clear eye for the price of grain staples, see New York, Columbia University, Butler Library MS X893 C-J55 v. 5, fols. 184a–186b. For more on this famine, see W. Gregory Monahan, *Year of Sorrows: The Great Famine of 1709 in Lyon* (Columbus, Ohio: Ohio State University, 1993). Cincinnati MS HUC 396 contains a blessing for Pope Nicholas V, and Columbia University MS X 893 C-J55 v. 15, a seventeenth-century liturgy, contains a generic prayer for the well-being of the pope and his *familia*. See also Roth, "The Liturgies of Avignon."

94. Schwarzfuchs, "On the Woes of Book Publishing"; Roth, "The Liturgies of Avignon."

95. Schwarzfuchs, "On the Woes of Book Publishing."

96. Ibid.; Roth, "The Liturgies of Avignon," 101–2.

97. Roth, "The Liturgies of Avignon," 102–3.

98. Roth, "Une mission des communautés du Comtat Venaissin à Rome," *REJ* 83–84 (1927): 1–14. Abraham Monteil was one of the two-member delegation sent to Rome to negotiate on Semé's behalf. The other was a Rabbi Jacob of Prague, at that time serving in Avignon. While the party did succeed in eliciting a bull deploring the forced

baptism of Jewish children, the fate of Semé was sealed. Remarkably, he ended his days as a cardinal in Rome.

99. The following summary draws on Jules Bauer, "Le chapeau jaune chez les juifs comtadins," *REJ* 36 (1898): 53–64. The story extends from the 1326 decree of the Council of Avignon requiring that Jewish residents of the Comtat wear a yellow badge to the late eighteenth-century Jewish appeal for relief from their yellow hats.

CHAPTER FOUR

1. London MS BL 19663, fol. 24b; Cincinnati MS HUC 396 fol. 22r; Columbia University X893 C-J55, vol. 31, fol. 76a.

2. The name Caslari, sometimes spelled Caylar, may refer to the town of Caylar (Latin, *Castlarium*), outside of Lodève in Provence. A small number of Crescas's contemporaries bear the same surname, most notably the physicians David b. Abraham Caslari and his son Abraham, who were in nearby Narbonne at the time of the 1306 expulsion of French Jews. Abraham Caslari made his way eventually to Besalú in Catalonia, where he managed to reestablish his medical career. Another Caslari, Astruc Bonafos, also of Narbonne and a wealthy spice merchant, was ruined in 1306. See H. Gross, *Gallia Judaica* (Paris: Léopold Cerf, 1897), 618–20; Jean Regné, "Étude sur la condition des juifs de Narbonne du Ve au XIVe siècle," *REJ* 59 (1910): 74, and 62 (1913): 27; Gustave Saige, *Les juifs de Languedoc* (Paris: Alphonse Picard, 1881), 118–19, 122, 289. Whether these Caslaris were related is unclear. The physicians, who shared a common circle of friends and interests, most likely knew each other; notably, Abraham b. Caslari was the recipient of a (now-lost) "Purim epistle" from another Jewish rationalist savant and poet, Abraham Bedersi in Perpignan.

3. I use the term "Judeo-Provençal" here. Colloquially, the term "Shuadit" is also found. Whether or not it is an actual dialect is irrelevant to this study. See George Jochnowitz, "Shuadit: La langue juive de Provence," *Archives Juives* 14.1 (1978): 63–67; Armand Lunel, "Quelques aspects du Parler Judeo-Comtadin," *L'Arche* 94 (November 1964): 43–45; and the introduction in Moshe Lazar, "*Lis Obros:* Chansons Hebraïco-Provençales," in *Romania et Occidentalia: Études dédiées à la mémoire de Hiram Peri (Pflaum)* (Jerusalem: Magnes, 1963), 290–345.

4. The Judeo-Provençal manuscript is in New York, Jewish Theological Seminary MS Adler 2039, fols. 23v–29r. A faulty transcription appeared in A. Neubauer and P. Meyer, "Le roman provençal d'Esther par Crescas du Caylar," *Romania* 21 (1892): 3–36 (= 194–227); the text was retranscribed by P. Pansier, "Le roman d'Esther," *Annales d'Avignon et du Comtat Venaissin* 11 (1925): 5–18, and again by Susan Milner Silberstein, "The Provençal Esther Poem Written in Hebrew Characters c. 1327 by Crescas de Caylar: Critical Edition" (Ph.D. diss., University of Pennsylvania, 1973). Unknown to these writers, a second fragment of the text, in very poor condition, has been tentatively identified; this is Casanatense, Biblioteca Casanatense MS Heb. 3140, fols. 190b–192a.

The 1402 Hebrew manuscript is Oxford Bodleian MS Heb. 2746, fols. 48a–58b; the Cincinnati copy is Hebrew Union College (HUC) MS 396. The first eighteenth-century copy is in London, British Library Addendum Heb. MS 19663, fols. 21a–34b. The copy owned by Columbia University is listed as Columbia University X893 C-J55, vol. 31, fols. 72a–85a. According to the library's records, the liturgy containing the text was acquired by Columbia in 1892, as a gift from Temple Emanu-El in New York; the congregation had acquired it from a dealer in Amsterdam in the 1840s. Only two of these sources—the Oxford Bodleian and British Library manuscripts—are listed in the IMHM database. Clearly, more copies await discovery. The printed edition of Crescas's Hebrew text is called the *Iggeret haPurim* (Purim epistle) of "Maestre Koskas" [*sic*] (Salonika, 1853).

5. In the next chapter, we will encounter yet another Avignon physician who wrote a narrative that is loosely based on the book of Job.

6. The term refers to a sequence of poetic compositions, fixed by theme and form, inserted into the section of the morning liturgy devoted to praise of God the "Creator" (= *yotzer*). Some of these sequences were quite elaborate. See Ezra Fleischer, *HaYotzrot* (Jerusalem: Magnes, 1984).

7. Ibid., 575–91. HaLevi's narrative poem also appears in HUC MS 396, fols. 6r–9r. See also Armand Lunel, "Pourim dans les letters comtadines," *La revue juive* 1.3 (1925): 316–30; the essay includes an excerpt from the eighteenth-century play of Mordecai Astruc, arguably a descendant of the tradition represented by Crescas's text. As Lunel observes, "[L]es Juifs du Comtat ne furent pas toujours aussi malheureux qu'on l'a laissé croire" (322)(!).

8. The southern region west of the Rhône, Languedoc, was incorporated into the French royal domain in 1229 by the Treaty of Paris. Its Jews were subject to the decree of expulsion issued by Philip IV in 1306. Many migrated to Provence, which, with the exception of Avignon, was under Angevin control (and technically in the empire). See William C. Jordan, *The French Monarchy and the Jews* (Philadelphia: University of Pennsylvania Press, 1989).

9. Crescas Caslari (or Caylar), *Sefer Iggeret haPurim* (The Book of the Purim Epistle), ed. Shlomo David (Salonika, 1853). Even the National Union Catalogue confuses the Hebrew and Ladino publications. The Ladino Purim texts, many titled *Sippur haNes* (A miraculous tale), are not derivations of Crescas's work. They describe themselves as popular redactions of midrashic and rabbinic traditions, particularly those found in the lengthy Aramaic commentary to Esther known as the Targum Sheni. The printed versions of *Sippur haNes*, worthy of a study in themselves, come from Salonika and Constantinople and date back at least to the Raphael Qal'ai and Mordecai Nahman edition of *Iggeret haPurim: Sippur haNes* (Salonika, 1766). I thank Dvora Bregman for her help in tracking the early editions. Isaac Jehun, the printer for Crescas's Hebrew text, also struck the Ladino *Sippur haNes* published in Salonika in 1853; he did so, curiously, at the printing house of Shlomo David, not his own. A quick survey of his career indicates that

Jehun began as an apprentice in one of the larger printing establishments in Salonika, and then proceeded to strike out on his own. Apparently, he could not survive without continuing to do some freelance work. What his role was in producing the Esther literature for public consumption is unclear, but it is a tantalizing question. See David Recanati, ed., *Zikkaron Salonika* (Tel Aviv: Ha-va'ad le-hotza'at sefer qehillat saloniqi, 1986), 2:240–42.

10. Joseph Nehama, *Histoire des juifs de Salonique*, vol. 6 (London: Communauté Israélite de Thessalonique, 1978), chapter 9, esp. 375–76; Gilles Veinstein, ed., *Salonique 1850–1918: La "ville des Juifs" et le réveil des Balkans* (Paris: Autrement, 1992), 91, 93, 101; Moses Attias, "The Purim 'Complas' in Ladino," *Sefunot* 2 (1978): 331–45; Jacob Hassan, "Una *Copla de Purim*: La endecha burlesca," *Estudios sefardíes* 1 (1978): 411–16.

11. As Luis García Ballester has noted of Castilian Jews (and the comment applies all the more to the Jews of Provence), "[T]he Jews were the only non-Christian socio-religious group. . . . that could count on a minority within their number who were interested in natural philosophy and in a form of medicine related to it, and who at the same time were actively practicing medicine." García Ballester, "A Marginal Learned World: Jewish, Muslim, and Christian Medical Practitioners and the Use of Arabic Medical Sources in Late Medieval Spain," in Jon Arrizabalaga et al., eds., *Practical Medicine from Salerno to the Black Death* (Cambridge: Cambridge University Press, 1994), 353–95, citing 369.

12. See Ernst Renan and Adolphe Neubauer, *Histoire littéraire de la France* (Paris: Imprimerie nationale, 1893), 31:647–50; Lunel, "Pourim"; Pansier, "Le roman d'Esther." Crescas's work is not mentioned in Barry Dov Walfish, *Esther in Medieval Garb: Jewish Interpretation of the Book of Esther in the Middle Ages* (Albany, N.Y.: State University of New York Press, 1993), or by Elliott Horowitz in his discussion of medieval Purim traditions, "The Rite to Be Reckless: On the Perpetration and Interpretation of Purim Violence," *Poetics Today* 15 (1994): 9–54.

13. A critical edition of the Latin text, one whose popularity is represented in abundant manuscript sources, appeared only recently. See Luis García Ballester, Michael McVaugh, and Juan Paniagua, eds., *Arnaldi de Villanova: Opera Medica Omnia* (hereafter cited as *AVOMO*) 10.1: *Regimen Sanitatis ad Regem Aragonum*, ed. Luis García Ballester and Michael McVaugh, introduction by Pedro Gil Sotres (Barcelona: Universitat Barcelona, 1996). For information on the Catalan and Hebrew manuscript sources and history, see below. See also Lola Ferre, "Hebrew Translations from Medical Treatises of Montpellier," *Korot* 13 (1998–99): 21–36, and Joseph Ziegler, "Steinschneider (1816–1907) Revised: On the Translation of Medical Writings from Latin into Hebrew," *Medieval Encounters* 3.1 (1997): 94–102.

14. Miguel Battlori, "La documentacio de Marsella sobre Arnau de Vilanova y Joan Blasi," *Analecta Sacra Tarraconensia: Revista de ciencias histórico ecclesiasticas* 21 (1948): 75–119; R. Manselli, "Arnaldo da Villanova e i papi del suo tempo: Tra religione e politica," *Studi Romani* 7.2 (1959): 146–62; Michael McVaugh, "Arnald of Villanova's *Regimen Almarie (Regimen Castra Sequentium)* and Medieval Military Medicine," *Viator*

23 (1992): 201–13, esp. 202–4, more fully discussed in the introduction to the critical edition of this regimen, *AVOMO* 10.2: *Regimen Almarie*, ed. Michael McVaugh (Barcelona: Universitat de Barcelona, 1998); Joseph Ziegler, *Medicine and Religion c. 1300: The Case of Arnau de Vilanova* (Oxford: Oxford University Press, 1998).

15. Michael McVaugh, *Medicine before the Plague: Practitioners and Their Patients in the Crown of Aragon 1285–1345* (Cambridge: Cambridge University Press, 1993); Luis García Ballester, Lola Ferre, and Eduard Feliu, "Jewish Appreciation of Fourteenth-Century Scholastic Medicine," *Osiris*, 2nd ser., 6 (1990): 85–117; Luis García Ballester, "Changes in the *Regimina Sanitatis*: The Role of Jewish Practitioners," in Sheila Campbell et al., eds., *Health, Disease and Healing in Medieval Culture* (New York: St. Martin's Press, 1992), 119–31; and García Ballester, "A Marginal Learned World"; Danièle Iancu-Agou, "Préoccupations intellectuelles des médecins juifs au moyen âge: Inventaires de bibliothèques," *Provence historique* 26 (1976): 21–44; Joseph Shatzmiller, "On Becoming a Jewish Doctor in the High Middle Ages," *Sefarad* 43 (1983): 239–50, and idem, *Jews, Medicine and Medieval Society* (Berkeley: University of California Press, 1994). Less reliable but useful treatments include Isaac Alteras, "Jewish Physicians in Southern France during the 13th and 14th Centuries," *JQR* 68.4 (1978): 209–23; Messaoud-Prosper Cohen, *Contribution à l'histoire des médecins juifs en Avignon (XIIe–XVe siècles)* (Paris: Amédée LeGrand, 1940); Jacques Pines, "Des médecins juifs au service de la papauté du XIIe au XVIIe siècle," *Revue d'histoire de la médecine hébraïque* (hereafter cited as *RHMH*) 69 (1965): 123–33; Isidore Simon, "Les médecins juifs en France, des origins jusqu'à la fin du XVIIIe siècle," *RHMH* 89 (October 1970): 89–92.

16. Shatzmiller, "On Becoming a Jewish Doctor"; and idem, "Livres médicaux et education médicale: À propos d'un contrat de Marseille en 1316," *Mediaeval Studies* 38 (1980): 463–70; García Ballester, "A Marginal Learned World," and idem, *La búsqueda de la salud: Sanadores y enfermos en la España medievale* (Barcelona: Ediciones Península, 2001), esp. chapter 4 ("La actividad intelectual médica de las minorías judía y mudéjar").

17. García Ballester et al., "Jewish Appreciation of Fourteenth-Century Scholastic Medicine"; McVaugh, *Medicine before the Plague*.

18. Nancy G. Siraisi, *Taddeo Alderotti and His Pupils* (Princeton, N.J.: Princeton University Press, 1981), and idem, *Medieval and Early Renaissance Medicine: An Introduction to Knowledge and Practice* (Chicago: University of Chicago Press, 1990); for northern France, see Danielle Jacquart, *La medicine médiévale dans le cadre parisien* (Paris: Fayard, 1998).

19. See the relevant discussion in Chapters 1 and 2. The literature on the controversy between the "philosophers and traditionalists" is more than abundant. See, e.g., Abraham Halkin, "Yedaiah Bedersi's 'Apology,'" in Alexander Altmann, ed., *Jewish Medieval and Renaissance Studies* (Cambridge, Mass.: Harvard University Press, 1967), 165–85; Marc Saperstein, "The Conflict over the Rashba's Herem on Philosophical Study: A Political Perspective," *Jewish History* 1 (1986): 27–38, and *Decoding the Rabbis: A Thirteenth-Century Commentary on the Aggadah* (Cambridge, Mass.: Harvard University Press, 1980); Joseph Sarachek, *Faith and Reason: Conflict over the Rationalism*

of Maimonides (Williamsport, Pa.: Bayard, 1935); Shatzmiller, "On Becoming a Jewish Doctor," and "Rationalisme et orthodoxie religieuse chez les juifs provençaux au commencement du XIVe siècle," *Provence historique* 22 (1972): 262–85. My impression is that the exemption of medicine from the 1305 ban on "Greek science" referred to the clinical, or empirical, practice of medicine and not to the study of theoretical medicine, which would have required mastery of precisely the philosophical and rhetorical disciplines attacked by the Jewish traditionalists.

20. Nakdimon Doniach, "Abraham Bedersi's Purim Letter to David Kaslari," *JQR*, n.s., 23 (1932–33): 63–69.

21. Haim Schirmann, completed by Ezra Fleischer, *Toldot haShirah ha'Ivrit bi-Sefarad haNotzrit uveDrom Tzarfat* (A history of Hebrew poetry in Christian Spain and southern France) (Jerusalem: Magnes, 1997), 524–27 (hereafter cited as Schirmann/Fleischer); Oxford, Oxford Bodleian Heb. MS 2746.

22. The second title puns on the name of the biblical prophet Habakkuk (חבקוק) and the Hebrew word *baqbuq* (בקבוק) for "bottle." Perhaps because of Qalonymos's and Gersonides' renown, their Purim works survived well into the modern period, in print and manuscript. They were occasionally printed together. As Schirmann/Fleischer indicates, the frivolity of the pieces, even of such distinguished authorship, also enraged more traditionalist Jews, and the works were periodically banned and burned as well. Of the earliest printed edition of Qalonymos's *Masekhet Purim* (Purim tractate) (Pisarro, 1513), only two copies are extant today; most of the copies, according to Steinschneider and Renan, were destroyed by the Jews themselves. Schirmann/Fleischer, 526–27 n. 53, and Renan, Les écrivains juifs, vol. 31 of J. Ernst Renan and Adolphe Neubauer, *Histoire littéraire de la France* (Paris: Imprimerie nationale, 1893), 600–602.

23. Schirmann/Fleischer, 614–16; Henry Ansgar Kelly, "Jews and Saracens in Chaucer's England," unpublished essay; M. Roest, "Brief van Salomo ha-Lewi aan Meir Alguadez," *Israelitische Letterbode* 10 (1884–85): 78–85.

24. Unlike the Jewish physicians of Provence, most of whom did not know Arabic, Ibn Ezra drew directly upon Arabic sources. Two of these, both major works, were written by Jews: Maimonides' regimen for the Egyptian sultan, *Al 'Afdal*, and the ninth-century physician Isaac Israeli's *Book of Foodstuffs*.

25. See Aurora Salvatierra, "Un poema médico de Abraham ibn Ezra," *Miscelánea de Estudios 'Arabes y Hebraicos* 40.2 (1991): 71–85; Shem Tov Falaquera, *Versos para la sana conducción del cuerpo: Traducción, edición crítica y commentario par M. A. Vorela Morena* (Granada: Universidad de Granada and Universidad Pontifica de Salamanca, 1986); Lola Ferre, "Los regimens [regímenes?] dietéticos medievales en prosa y en verso: Entre la medicina y la literatura," *Espacio, Tiempo y Forma*, 3rd ser., 7 (1994): 327–40.

26. ולא הנחתי דבר אלא או מפני שלא מצאתי לו שם בלשון הקדש יורה עליו או מפני שהוא זר ולא יבינוהו אלא היחידים ואין עליו בספרי הנבראים עדים. וכן קרה לי בשמות המאכלים. כי הייתי רוצה לזכר אל מה מזיקים ואל מה מועילים. ומפני שלא מצאתי שמות לכלם בלשון הקדש לא זכרתם מהם אלא מעטים ועל דרך כלל. ואני אביא מלות שהמעתיקים הרגלו לזכרם. כמו חלטים וחושים והדומה להם.

Moreno, 6 (Hebrew section), with a Spanish translation on 68 of the Spanish section (indicated in the original as 68*). I translate the passage as follows: "And I elided nothing unless I could not find a term in Hebrew to designate it, or unless it was a foreign [term] that only a few would understand and for which there was no corresponding designation in the books of the prophets. This is what happened to me with the terms for foods. For I wished to mention which were injurious and which beneficial, but because I could not find names for them in Hebrew, I mentioned only a few of them and in a generic fashion. I use words with which the copyists are familiar, such as *ḥalaṭim* [humors] or *ḥushim* [senses] and so on."

27. Lola Ferre, "La terminología médica en las versiones hebreas de textos latinos," *Miscelánea de Estudios 'Arabes y Hebraicos* 40.2 (1991): 87–107.

28. זאת שנית / האגרת הזאת מראש הואלתי באר / ללועזות בלעז טף ונשים נין ונכד ושאר / עברית לעברים ובמעשה ידי להתפאר / הסכת ושמע ישראל היום הזה

(I first explicated this epistle in romance for children and women, grandchildren and great-grandchildren, and the rest. This time I have made it in Hebrew for Hebraists and to take pride in my handiwork. Listen and hear, O Israel, this day.) The expression *nin venekhed* is found in Ben Sira 47,32. The nineteenth-century Salonika edition is damaged at this particular line, so that it is easy to confuse the *daled* and *resh*. I here correct my own misreading in the *Speculum* article.

29. Susan Einbinder, "The Troyes Elegies: Jewish Martyrology in Hebrew and Old French," *Viator* 30 (1999): 201–30, and idem, *Beautiful Death: Jewish Poetry and Martyrdom in Medieval France* (Princeton, N.J.: Princeton University Press, 2002), esp. chapter 5. Lola Ferre makes the same point about the use of vernacular botanical and food terms in Hebrew medical translations, namely, that one of their purposes is accessibility ("El traductor utilize un lenguaje asequible, más preocupado por ser claro que correcto. . . . El uso del provenzal o catalán en un texto hebreo suponía una 'concesión' a los miembros menos instruídos.") See Ferre, "La terminología médica," 105.

30. A slightly later and beautiful example is Leeds, University of Leeds Brotherton Library, Roth MS 32.

31. A. Grieco, "La dietética nel medio evo," in Giampiero Nigro, ed., *Et coquatur ponendo* (Prato: Francesco Datini Institute, 1996), 43–53; McVaugh, *Medicine before the Plague*, 145. For a comprehensive history and description of the genre, see Pedro Gil Sotres's introduction to the critical edition of Arnau au de Vilanova's *Regimen Sanitatis ad Regem Aragonem*, *AVOMO* 10.1, 481–568. Abridged versions appear in Pedro Gil Sotres, "Les régimes de santé," *Histoire de la pensée médicale en Occident* 1 (1995): 159–81; and idem, "El arte de la cocina y los médicos: Las recetas culinarias en los regimens de salud," in Lola Ferre, José Ramón Ayaso, and José Cano, eds., *La ciencia en la España medieval: Musulmanes, judíos y cristianos* (Granada: Universidad de Granada, Instituto de Ciencias de la Educación, 1992), 193–207. See also Danielle Jacquart, "Les régimes de santé au XIIIe siècle," in P. Guichard and D. Alexandre-Bidon, eds., *Comprendre le XIIIe siècle: Études offertes à Marie-Thérèse Lorcin* (Lyon: Presses Universitaires de Lyon, 1995), 201–14.

32. Louis Landouzy and Roger Pepin, *Le régime du corps de Maître Aldebrandin de Sienne* (Paris, 1911); Ariel Bar-Sela, "Moses Maimonides' Two Treatises on the Regimen of Health," *Transactions of the American Philosophical Society*, n.s., 54.4 (1964). Examples of universal regimens are those of Bernard de Gordon, written in 1308 (but not circulating for another two decades or so), and Maino de Maineri, written in 1330. See Gil Sotres, *AVOMO* 10.1, 535–43. Arnau's military regimen edited and described by Michael McVaugh is another form of general regimen, in this case designed for Jaime II's troops stalled at the siege of Almería. See n. 14 above.

33. This would become a factor in the willingness of municipal governments to commission tracts recommending procedures for coping with plague outbreaks. See Jon Arrizabalaga, "Facing the Black Death: Perceptions and Reactions of University Medical Practitioners," in Arrizabalaga et al., *Practical Medicine from Salerno to the Black Death*, 237–88. On the expansion of the *Regimina sanitatis* to wider segments of fourteenth-century society, see Gil Sotres, "Les régimes," 264–66; Jacquart, "Les régimes de santé au XIIIe siècle," 209.

34. García Ballester, "Changes in the *Regimina Sanitatis*," 121.

35. The six nonnaturals are discussed in many of the bibliographical references cited here; a thorough discussion appears also in Gil Sotres's introduction, *AVOMO* 10.1, 569/862.

36. Doniach, "Abraham Bedersi's Purim Letter to David Kaslari."

37. In 1322, twenty-one beguines (sixteen men and five women) were burned at the city gates. Inquisitorial activity was feverish in the region; at least four friars were burned in Marseilles in 1318, and forty-nine lay residents of Narbonne were brought before the Inquisition in 1328. Richard Emery, *Heresy and Inquisition in Narbonne* (New York: Columbia University Press, 1941), 132–34; David Burr, *The Spiritual Franciscans: From Protest to Persecution in the Century after Saint Francis* (University Park: Pennsylvania State University Press, 2001), 205/6.

38. The depiction of the king's amnesia, aggravated no doubt by alcohol, was considered a direct medical consequence of his melancholy. Arnau of Vilanova made the connection explicit (Gil Sotres trans.): "Porque constriñe el corazón y obscurece y engrose los espíritus, embota el entendimiento, impide la aprehensiva, ofusca el juicio y destruye la memoria." *AVOMO* 10.1, 822, citing Arnau.

39. Citations from the Romance text rely mainly on Silberstein, whose translation provides the basis for the translations here, unless otherwise indicated. All translations from the Hebrew are my own.

40. The Hebrew expression is curious: על לבו עלה שערוריה—following the medieval glosses to Hos. 6:10, the unique biblical use of שערוריה, it implies a mental disorder characterized by lascivious or impure thoughts. The modern meaning of the word is more neutral (like our "pandemonium").

41. OB fol. 49a; HUC fol. 20b; BL fol. 22a; Col. fol. 73a—ותתפעם; Salonika—ותפעם, 3a.

42. OB fol. 50a—תחת אשר עשה; HUC fol. 21a; BL fol. 22b; Col. fol. 74a; elided

from the Salonika edition. Memucan, following midrashic conventions, is identified with Haman in this text. The expression "more bitter than death" (*mar memavet*) comes from Eccles. 7:26, where it refers to "the woman whose heart is snares and nets," and so Crescas attributes to the dead queen some responsibility for her fate. At the same time, the expression cleverly evokes the very similar phrasing of 1 Sam. 15:32, where Agag (Haman's ancestor) stands captive before the prophet Samuel and hopes aloud that there is no need to execute him: "Agag said, surely the bitterness of death is past" (*sar mar hamavet*), an opinion that Samuel, alas, does not share. The printed version is slightly different (Salonika, 3a).

וחלו ממנו כי היה מלך טפש / ובסור יינו מעליו וינפש
דמה מידם יבקש להתעולל ולחפש / בא האיש הזה.

(They feared him for he was a foolish king, / and when his wine had left him / he would demand her blood from their hands. Seeking to act against them / this man would come.)

43. See, e.g., M. de Maulde, *Les juifs dans les états français du Saint Siège* (Paris: H. Champion, 1886), 54, citing the rhymed chronicle of Geoffrey of Paris; John Wrigley, "A Papal Secret Known to Petrarch," *Speculum* 39.4 (1964): 613–34; William C. Jordan, *Europe in the High Middle Ages* (London and New York: Penguin, 2001), 318.

44. Gil Sotres, *AVOMO* 10.1, 719 (citations are to the Spanish-language section of the volume, which follows the critical edition of Arnau's text and which is itself a translation of the Catalan version preceding the critical edition).

45. OB fol. 50b; BL fol. 23b; Col. fol. 74b; HUC fol. 21a: כפור אפר יפזר. Again, the tendency of the Salonika edition to glide over some of the racier allusions in the earlier version is evident. The quatrain form is obviously corrupt:

תלבש אסתר הנזר והעטרה / מאת ה' היתה זאת את הכבוד הזה

("Esther shall wear the crown and diadem. / This great honor was God's doing." [4b])

46. Specifically: just as a man who loses an article goes after it, and not the reverse, so a man goes after a woman, and so on. See B. Qiddushin 2b: בעל אבדה מחזר על אבדתו.

47. Indeed, the Hebrew text had already stated that Vashti's unwillingness to come before the king was partially based in sexual indiscretion that had erupted in the form of a skin disease ("boils" in the manuscripts and "leprosy" in the Salonika text, both descriptions concluding "and some say a horn sprouted from her forehead"). This motif appears in rabbinic literature as well.

48. Gil Sotres, *AVOMO* 10.1, 745–46 and 752; idem, "Les régimes," 272–73; this

symptom is also mentioned by Ibn Falaquera in the "Bate Hanhagat haGuf haBari'" (Verse Regimen for a Healthy Body), where the melancholic displays "bad temper, anger, and sighing / he does not sleep and has no calm or security, / and he contends and struggles in his dreams." Varela Moreno, 44* (my translation).

49. OB fol. 55b; HUC fol. 24b; BL fol. 28b; Col. fol. 80a; Salonika, 8b, all with slight variants. The allusion to 2 Sam. 19:43 ("Are you angry about this?") evokes a context of rivalry for the king's favor. My reading of the last verse relies on Rashi's gloss. The expression *nokhria 'avodato* in Isa. 28:21 is generally translated "strange [or alien] is his work!" However, Rashi writes:

לעבוד עבודתו: לעשות מלאכתו כמו עבודת האדמה לבורי"ר בלע"ז

i.e., "to do his work: to do his job, as in working the land, *laborer* in the vernacular." The midrash and Targum Sheni (one of the Aramaic paraphrases of the biblical text and a source for many of Crescas's elaborations) also describe a scene in which Haman is humiliated by having to shave and bathe his enemy. In the midrashic compilation known as Esther Rabba 10:4, Mordecai also refers to Haman's "twenty-two years" on Corinnus, which the commentators, drawing on a parallel reference in Midrash Leviticus Rabba 17:4, gloss as a Christian land (*eretz Edom*) neighboring the Land of Israel. I assume that Crescas's decision to eliminate the bathing motif and instead elaborate upon the beard-trimming reinforces an allusion to a specific historical figure we can no longer identify. We can say that this "Haman" was a "foreigner" (French?) who began his career as a barber and exploited that position to rise to great prominence and power, which he then abused. Such figures appear in the thirteenth century and are a mark of the social mobility that medical skill might confer. See, for instance, William C. Jordan's recent study of Pierre de la Broce, who rose (and fell) in the court of Philip III of France, "The Struggle for Influence at the Court of Philip III: Pierre de la Broce and the French Aristocracy," *French Historical Studies* 24.3 (2001): 439–68. In Narbonne, nearer to Crescas, another barber-turned-potentate acquired his first major financial and real estate holdings when he was officially overseeing the sale of Jewish property impounded during the 1306 expulsion. One of the Jews whose wealth, home, and vineyard he acquired was Astruc Bonafos Caylar (Caslari), who may have been a kinsman of our Crescas. This astounding bureaucrat, called Bernard, or Sanche, le Rasoir, also Sanche Barbier, was himself the son of a barber-merchant. See Saige, *Les juifs de Languedoc*, 289–90; and Léopold Delisle, ed., *Recueil des historiens des Gaules et de la France* (Paris: V. Palmé, 1904), 21: 517.

50. Horseback riding was quintessentially a nobleman's activity; it was also one of the forms of exercise (another nonnatural) recommended by Arnau of Vilanova for Jaime II. For the authors of medieval regimens, "exercise" referred to voluntary activity only; the physical exertion of labor was specifically excluded. For their royal or noble clients, equestrian activity was indeed a favorite recommendation of the physicians ("reservada para los sujetos que pertenecen a los estamentos sociales más elevados"); see Gil Sotres, *AVOMO* 10.1, 621–22.

51. Mordecai's garments of purple and blue silk are explicitly called physician's robes by Qalonymos b. Qalonymos in his satiric portrait of the profession in the *Even*

Boḥan (Touchstone): "and upon seeing the ring on his finger and his purple robe, the foolish masses will think he is an expert and reliable physician" (my translation, from the Hebrew text in Haim Schirmann, *HaShirah ha'Ivrit biSefarad uveProvans*, 4:510). A letter by Don Vidal Benveniste to the physician Meir Alguadez, still in manuscript, also refers to this costume:

> He who does these things I call a true physician. It is fitting for him to be praised among the multitude and among the mighty, in a sure place. For the man such as this deserves brocade inside and out, at the entrance to the gates, [raised] over all who wear crimson, blue and purple. Let us prepare him splendid garments and outer robes, so that his worth is recognized by our people and the Gentiles, so that all the peoples of the land shall know the power of his deeds and grant him fame, so his reputation be like the wine of Lebanon. Renew his name as he renewed my legs! (Cincinnati, Hebrew Union College MS 314, fol. 7, my translation)

52. This is calendrically difficult, as Passover does not precede Purim but follows it. Is Crescas claiming that the fourteenth of Adar marked for the destruction of the Jews came the following spring? I confess I am confused here. The Fast of Esther is observed on the thirteenth of Adar, the day preceding Purim.

53. In the Salonika edition: ולמשתה היין עם אסתר הביאו ("and he brought him to the wine feast with Esther").

54. OB fol. 53b; Salonika, 6b; HUC fol. 24b; and BL fol. 26b—וימהר את המן, he "hastened Haman"; BL fol. 26b—ויאכלו וישתכרו עמה—"they ate and got drunk with her"; HUC fol. 24b and Col. fol. 78a—ויאכלו וישכרו עמה, less grammatical but also "they ate and were drunk with her."

55. This is again a motif found in the Targum. Nonetheless, it cannot help but invoke the overreaching arrogance of a trusted minister gone bad.

56. OB fol. 56b; BL fol. 30a with minor variations; HUC fol. 25b and Col. fol. 81b—עבדי המן שמו הגן בתה ואסתר עם המן ברית כרותה / המערת פריצים הבית הזה? The Salonika edition tones down the trouble by bowdlerizing the second verse and ascribing the third to Esther: עבדי המן הגן בתה / ועוד מעט אסתר ענתה / המערת פריצים היתה הבית הזה? (Haman's servants stripped the garden/ and presently Esther said/ "Is this house a den of thieves?"—10b).

57. The following description is based on Gil Sotres, *AVOMO* 10.1, 821–23. "Los pasos siguentes en la producción de la tristeza afectan a la sangre. Por la falta de espiritus, el líquido hemático se engruesa, con lo cual se cierra el círculo que impide alimentarse a los miembres, pues su capacidad de penetratión en el miembro disminuye; por otro lado, la frialdad y la sequedad hacen que, en lo producción de los humores se aumente la proporción de la melancolía."

58. The standard formulation, which Gil Sotres illustrates from the work of Maino de Maineri, posits a dynamic of *tristitia* compounded by expectation and despair. Arnau's explanation turns on a loss of heat associated with *tristitia* compounded by an influx due

to anger: "In angustia quidem quia partim tristitia partim ira laborat animus." Ibid., *AVOMO* 10.1, 823 n. 56, citing the *Speculum medicine*, c. 80, p. 29rb.

59. OB fol. 48b; HUC fol. 20b; BL fol. 21b and Col. fol. 72b; Salonika, 2a.

60. I follow Pansier and Meyer/Neubauer here rather than Silberstein, who transcribes "a la noble maniera" for אלא נובאלא מאניירא.

61. I am indebted to Roy Harris for his investigation of the word "gratonia" (e-mail communication of March 7, 2006). Harris relates "gratonia" to the OFr. "cretonee," citing Godefroy, *Lexique de l'ancien français*, which describes a "sorte de mets; selon les uns purée de viande ou de legumes, assaisonnée de gingembre; selon d'autres, manière d'apprêter un mets en le faisant frire dans la poêle avec des morceaux de lard." The lard is not as problematic as Harris (or Silberstein, whose translation substitutes fat from a kid goat) supposes: the king and his guests are not obligated to observe Jewish dietary restrictions. Hebrew translations of Christian dietary regimens, including Crescas's translation of the *Regimen sanitatis*, retain all references to pork and pork products.

62. Immediately following this passage is a corrupt citation from Galen. Having badgered Romance scholars and medical historians in several countries and languages, I conclude that it is not traceable. As Samuel Rosenberg carefully observed, a critical couplet appears to have been dropped from the passage.

63. The Hebrew word for "swans" may here be intended to indicate just that, as it is a royal feast. However, the term recurs at the end of the Hebrew story, where the Jews in general are encouraged to enjoy this dish on Purim. It may refer generically to stuffed, non-domesticated, fowl.

64. OB fol. 48b—גם ושתי המלכה עשתה משתה לבנות; HUC fol. 20b; BL fol. 21b; Col. fol. 72b; Salonika, 2b.

65. Bruno Laurioux, "La cuisine des médecins à la fin du moyen âge," in *Maladies, médecines et sociétés* (Paris: L'Harmattan, 1990), 2:137; idem, "Cuisine et médecine au moyen âge: Allies ou ennemies?" in Bruno Laurioux, ed., *Cuisine et médecine au moyen âge*, special issue of the *Cahiers de Recherches Médiévales* in memory of Emmanuèle Baumgartner, no. 13 (2006): 223–39; Terence Scully, "The Opusculum de Saporibus of Magninus Mediolanensis," *Medium Aevum* 54 (1985): 178–207; Lynn Thorndike, "Three Tracts on Food in Basel Manuscripts," *Bulletin of the History of Medicine* 8 (1940): 355–69. According to Scully and Laurioux, the *Opusculum de Saporibus* was composed around 1330. See also the discussion by Paniagua and García Ballester in *AVOMO* 10.1, 87ff.

66. As García Ballester noted, one of the problems to which Crescas alludes in his translation of Arnau's work is precisely the custom-made nature of the regimen. How is it possible to prescribe a generic diet for a large, even unidentified, class of people? The new audience for the regimen made this problem seem acute even as it simultaneously encouraged a preference for pharmaceutical intervention over dietary regulation. See García Ballester, "Changes in the *Regimina Sanitatis*" and "Jewish Appreciation."

67. OB fol. 48b; HUC fol. 20b—לרוח; BL fol. 21b; Col. fol. 72b; Sal. 2a. I am translating חדת as "new" and not "sharp," as it operates in merismus to עתיק (old, ancient).

If Crescas meant it to be a feminine form of חד, i.e., "sharp," it should appear as חדה. חדת as "new" is found in the Targum to Num. 6:3 and Exod. 1:8. Also, I translate רוח, literally, "wind" or "spirit," as "temperament." Perhaps equally possible is "inclination" or "tendency," given Rashi's elaboration on the Ecclesiastes verse that Crescas is citing; the biblical verse refers to seeds: "In the morning sow your seed, and at evening withhold not your hand, for you do not know which will prosper, this or that" (RSV). Rashi comments that the sower cannot know דרך הרוח, the "path of the wind," a phrase that might have tickled Crescas's consciousness as "type of spirit."

68. Gil Sotres, "El arte de la cocina," 198; Jacquart, "Les régimes," 208; Mireille Ausecache, "Des aliments et des medicaments: Les plants dans la médecine médiévale," in Laurioux, *Cuisine et médecine au moyen âge*," 249–58, esp. 252, 255.

69. Scully, "The Opusculum," 189.

70. Laurioux, "La cuisine des médecins à la fin du moyen âge," 138; Scully, "The Opusculum."

71. Laurioux, "La cuisine des médecins à la fin du moyen âge," 138 and n. 26; Scully, "The Opusculum," 187; Jacqueline Brunet and Odile Redon, "Vins, jus et verjus: Du bon usage culinaire des jus de raisins en Italie à la fin du moyen âge" (Vin des historiens: Actes du 1er symposium, vin et histoire, 19, 20 et 21 mai 1989, Suze-la-Rouss, 1990), 109–17; and see 112. Arnau tempers the pepper sauce with ginger, saffron, and vinegar—to much the same effect.

72. Gil Sotres, "El arte," 204; Laurioux, "La cuisine des médicins à la fin du moyen âge," 145 n. 26; Scully, "The Opusculum," 190 and 197.

73. Scully, "The Opusculum," 183–84 and 187; Landouzy and Pepin, *Le régime du corps*, 164, 170; *AVOMO* 10.1, 30b, 34a, 35a. The cinnamon sauce is recommended specifically for winter.

74. Landouzy on Aldebrandin, 131; Scully on Maino, 191; Gil Sotres, "El arte," 201.

75. Laurioux cites Maino's recipe for galantine with the author's prefatory comment: "Si l'on veut le conserver pendant plusieurs jours, que l'on fasse une gelée (*gelatina*)." Similarly, the Latin cookbook known as the *Liber de coquina* recommends the galantine for the same reason: "Et quand cette gelée est refroidie, mets dedans les morceaux de poisson et laisse reposer pendant un jour ou une nuit ou plus encore jusqu'à ce que tout soi pris. Et ainsi on peut longtemps preserver le poisson." Laurioux, *Cuisine et médecine au moyen âge*, 236–37.

76. Pansier, "Le roman d'Esther," 7.

77. Allen Grieco, "Savoir de poésie ou savoir de botaniste?: Les fruits dans la poésie italienne du XVe siècle," *Médiévales* 16–17 (1989): 146; Thorndike, "Three Tracts on Food in Basel Manuscripts," 363 and 365; Laurioux *Cuisine et médecine au moyen âge*, 234.

78. Cited by García Ballester, "Changes in the *Regimina Sanitatis*," 124 (I use his translation).

79. Landouzy on Aldebrandin, 123–24 (beef), 126–27 (venison), 129 (geese).

80. The end of the quatrain is missing. It appears in BL fol. 31b, HUC fol. 26b, and Col. 83b:

ואעידה לי עדים נאמנים / היה לבבם זה

The relevant passage in the Salonika edition is on 12b, where the lead-in couplet has been altered, but the conclusion remains the same as in BL and Col:

מציעין מצועות ובגדי שש לבוש שנים / וכולם נשכרים מיין הרקח ועסיס רמונים
ואעידה לי עדים נאמנים / והיה לבבם זה.

(They shall lay out cloths and garments of silk and scarlet, / and all shall get drunk on new wine and pomegranate nectar. / I shall make faithful witnesses testify for me / and they shall wish to.)

The final phrase of the quatrain comes from Deut. 5:26, where its sense is "[if only] they were of a mind to. . . ."

81. Filling in the elided verses from the other sources, as listed in the preceding note.

82. OB fols. 58a–b; HUC fols. 26b–27a; BL fols. 31b–32a; Col. fol. 83b; Salonika, 12b–13a, some with minor variants. The pointing of the BL and HUC manuscript preserves a reading of *sum tasim 'alav* ("you shall surely put on it") instead of *shum tasim 'alav* ("put garlic on it").

83. Jer. 16:7—לא יפרסו לחם על אבל, "they shall not break bread with the mourner."

84. Scully, "The Opusculum."

85. E.g., Grieco, "Savoir de poèsie ou savoir de botaniste?," 144; here the little poem on the pomegranate notes, "Che lo malato de sede fo stare zoioxo / e tute ore son bon con lo rosto," which Grieco translates as "Je réjouis qui est malade et assoifé / A toute heure j'accompange bien le rôti." On the pear, mentioned above, the fifteenth-century poet has written, "Eyo son pera, prexa per ragione / Chi dò conforto alla disgestione" (Je suis la poire, mangée modérèment / J'aide à la digestion), 146.

86. The addition of pheasants may reflect another version that had them in the first Hebrew-language feast as well. My sense of the discrepancies in the two Hebrew texts is that the Salonika edition is based on a variant manuscript source, which it may further corrupt with intentional and unintentional emendations. The frontispiece tells us that the editor, Nathan Amram, relied on a manuscript that he found among his father's papers.

87. *Bulletin of Judaeo-Greek Studies* 11 (winter 1992): inside back cover. See illustration ("Esdras Esdra dressed as King Ahasuerus, Larissa, 1935").

88. According to Ferre and Gil Sotres, Crescas was in all likelihood translating from the Catalan text and not the original Latin. The Catalan version, produced by Berenguer ça Riera for Jaime II's wife, Blanca, was completed in 1309–10, just shortly after the Latin original and testifying to the work's instant success. See Ferre, "La terminología médica," 89, and idem, "Los regímenes de salud de Maimónides y Arnau

de Vilanova en sus versiones hebreas," in Ferre et al., *La ciencia en la España medieval*, 117–24; and Paniagua and García Ballester, *AVOMO* 10.1, 863 and 877–80. For the Catalan edition, see *Arnau de Vilanova: Obres Catalanes II (Escrits Medics)*, ed. P. Miguel Batllori (Barcelona: Editorial Barcino, 1947), 139–40.

89. In fact, this must have been the accepted usage for chickpeas. It appears also in Estori HaParhi's translation of the *Tabula Antidotarii* of Armengaud of Blaise (Arnau's nephew). See Michael McVaugh and Lola Ferre, eds., *The Tabula Antidotarii of Armengaud Blaise and Its Hebrew Translation* (Philadelphia: American Philosophical Society, 2000), 92–93 and 120–21.

90. For the plebeian status of the chickpea, see Gil Sotres, "Les régimes," 273; Grieco, "La dietética nel medio evo," 51. On the relative pricing, see *AVOMO* 10.1, 217/680; Louis Stouff, *Ravitaillement et alimentation en Provence aux XIVe et XVe siècles* (Paris: Mouton, 1970), 105.

91. Gil Sotres, "El arte," 202–3, citing Arnau de Vilanova and Maino de Mainerus; Amador Diaz Garcia, "Un Tratado nazari solore alimentos: 'Al-Kalām 'alā l-agoiya de Al-Arbūlī. Edicion, Traduccion y estudio, con glosarios (I)," *Cuadernos de Estudios Medievales* (Granada) 6–7 (1978–79): 5–91 (citing Abu Bakr al-Arbūlī's regimen); Landouzy citing Aldebrandin, 140–43; E. Wickersheimer, "Le régime de santé de Jean Chanczelperger, bachelier en médecine de l'université de Bologne (XVe siècle)," *Janus* 25 (1925): 245–50, citing the Provençal regimen. For Arnau's recipes, see the *Regimen Sanitatis*, *AVOMO* 10.1, chapter 9 (De leguminibus), 440, cited also in Gil Sotres, "El arte," 202–3. Ibn Falaquera also repeats Maino's warning against chickpeas and cauliflower, 15* of the Hebrew.

92. *AVOMO* 10.1, 440: "Et inter cetera legumina minus nociva sunt sanis corporibus pisa rotunda et cicera et fabe; et istorum eciam trium minus nociva sunt pisa rotunda et alba."

93. Ibid., 217/681.

94. Battlori, "La documentacio de Marsella," 139–40.

95. St. Petersburg, Institute of Oriental Studies MS B290, fols. 26a–b. Munich Heb. MS 288, fol. 7a, adds fish to the list of customary Lenten foods.

96. Stouff, *Ravitaillement et alimentation*, 324ff.

97. De Maulde, *Les juifs*, 34.

98. A very similar illustration is Cincinnati, MS HUC 339.

99. García Ballester, "Changes in the *Regimina Sanitatis*." As is true today, diets are risky gambles from the physician's perspective: patients may not follow them, and even if they do, the results are rarely swift or permanent. The interest of early fourteenth-century physicians in this region in pharmaceutical over dietary recommendations thus held immediate financial promise for the prescribing physician.

100. P. Pansier, "Les médecins juifs à Avignon aux XIIIe, XIVe et XVe siècles," *Janus* 15 (July 1910): 430–31; in 1357, the patient is treated by Crescas and a Christian physician, Paul de Viterbe.

101. MS Parma 1953 (= De Rossi 1053), fols. 22r–25r.

102. So does Haman as the physician and royal adviser who turns against the Jews echo the charges of Arnau himself. Arnau was hardly a barber and quack. Still, one wonders if Crescas's critique is in some way also leveled at high-ranking physicians whose counsel to their powerful patients includes anti-Jewish statements.

103. OB fol. 51b; HUC fol. 22a; BL fols. 24a–b; Col. fol. 75b; Sal. 4b—ואם אדוני המלך באצבע קטנה יגענו.

104. OB fol. 52b; HUC fol. 22b; BL fol. 25b ; Col. fol. 77a; Sal. 5a–b. All versions except HUC MS 396 point עברים as ʿivrim (i.e., Hebrews, which I have translated as "Jews"); HUC writes עוברים (lit., "pass over," or indicating continuous action), i.e., with "Jews" as the antecedent in the preceding verse, the Jews "continue to flee from this side and that." The Salonika edition is unpointed.

105. The legal terminology and motifs of the two stories are also striking. The vernacular text includes descriptions of the king's councillors and court and notaries. Both texts clearly allude to specific legal and historical issues—the use of French versus Spanish (why not Occitan?) among would-be husbands, the claim of the councillors that expulsion and exile have undermined their knowledge of "ancient law," the implication that the plot against the king's life involved poisoning (a motif found also in the Targum Sheni), the low-class origins of Haman—to list just a few.

106. Allatini funded the first Alliance Israélite schools in Salonika; in addition, he promoted a number of Jewish religious and educational endeavors, and his hand can be seen behind much of the revival of learning and culture of the period. See Nehama, *Histoire des juifs de Salonique*, vol. 6, chapters 6–7.

107. David Kaufmann, "Tranquillo vita corcos: Bienfaiteur de la communauté de Carpentras," *REJ* 26 (1893): 268–73; Cecil Roth, "Une mission des communautés du Comtat Venaissin à Rome," *REJ* 83–84 (1927): 1–14; Simon Schwarzfuchs, "On the Woes of Book Publishing: The Maḥzor Carpentras" (in Hebrew), *ʿAle-Sefer* 6–7 (1979): 145–56.

CHAPTER FIVE

1. For descriptions of the manuscript, see *Catalogues des manuscrits hébreu et Samaritans de la bibliothèque impériale* (Paris: Imprimerie Impériale, 1866), 119; Malachi Beit-Arié and Colette Sirat, eds., *Manuscrits médiévaux en caractères hébraïques* (Jerusalem: Israel Academy of Science and Letters; Paris: Centre National de la Recherche Scientifique, 1979), vol. 2, entry 1395. As Beit-Arié and Sirat indicate, the manuscript is no longer considered an autograph.

2. Oxford Bodl. Opp. Add. Hebrew 2583 (Neubauer), now listed as 40, 174. The manuscript is a miscellany dated to the mid-fifteenth century and written in "Ashkenazi or Italian" cursive and semi-cursive scripts. Jacob's treatise runs from fol. 26 to fol. 31 and is sandwiched between Hippocrates' aphorisms (arranged according to Moses ibn Tibbon's translation of Ibn Jazzar's *Viaticum*, with marginal notes by Judah b. Solomon

Nathan) and Juan de San Amand's commentary on the *Antidotarium Nicolai*. On the Wolf Haggadah, see below.

3. The only article on the philosophical writings seems to be Judah (Georges) Vajda, "On the History of the Polemic between Philosophy and Religion" (in Hebrew), *Tarbiz* 24.3 (1955): 307–22.

4. David Kaufmann, "Le 'grand-deuil' de Jacob b. Salomon Sarfati d'Avignon," *REJ* 30 (1895): 52–64; Ron Barkai, "On Child Mortality during the Black Death" (in Hebrew), in Miri Eliav Feldon and Yitzhaq Hen, eds., *Nashim, Zeqenim veTaf: Qovetz Ma'amarim Likhvodah shel Shulamith Shaḥar* (Jerusalem: Zalman Shazar, 2001), 67–84.

5. Kaufmann's article begins with the flat declaration: "La littérature juive du moyen âge manque absolument de subjectivité, on met une sorte de pudeur à cacher ses propres sentiments," 52.

6. Barkai, "On Child Mortality." For Barkai's recent work on the plague, see his "Jewish Treatises on the Black Death (1350–1500): A Preliminary Study," in R. French et al., eds., *Medicine from the Black Death to the French Disease* (Aldershot: Ashgate, 1998), 6–25; or the Spanish version, "Los médicos judeo-españoles y la peste negra," in *Luces y sombras de la Judería europea (siglos XI–XVII): Primeros encuentros Judaicos de Tudela* (Pamplona: Gobierno de Navarra, 1996), 121–32. David Herlihy argued that affective parent-child ties grew stronger from the twelfth century onward in Europe; see, e.g., "Medieval Children," in Bede Karl Lackner and Kenneth Roy Philip, eds., *Essays on Medieval Civilization* (Austin: University of Texas Press, 1978), 109–41; idem, "Family," in Samuel Cohn, Jr. and Steven A. Epstein, eds., *Portraits of Medieval and Renaissance Living: Essays in Honor of David Herlihy* (Ann Arbor: University of Michigan Press, 1996), 7–28; the article is a revised version of the piece by the same name in *AHR* 96 (1991): 1–16.

7. Elliott Horowitz, "The Jews of Europe and the Moment of Death in Medieval and Modern Times," *Judaism* 55 (1995): 271–81. I thank the author for alerting me to this article, as well as for his insightful comments following a seminar discussion of this text at Johns Hopkins University in April 2007.

8. Ann Carmichael, "The Last Past Plague: The Uses of Memory in Renaissance Epidemics," *Journal of the History of Medicine and Allied Sciences* 53.2 (1998): 141–42.

9. As Barkai has noted, of sixteen extant plague tractates translated or composed by Jewish physicians from 1350 to 1500, fourteen are still in manuscript and have never been studied. The two published tractates are by Isaac b. Todros and Abraham Caslari; see David Ginzburg, "*Be'er Lehi*: The Plague Tractate of R. Isaac b. Todros," in *Tiferet Seivah: Articles in Honor of Yom Tov Lippman Zunz on His Ninetieth Birthday* (in Hebrew) (Berlin, 1884), 91–126; and H. Pinkhoff, *Abraham Kashlari over pestachtige Koorsten* (Amsterdam: n.p., 1891); my thanks to Dr. Samuel Kottek of the Hebrew University Medical School for generously forwarding a copy of Caslari's work. The unavailability of a larger selection of Hebrew texts means also that the anthologies and analyses of the known Christian and Muslim tractates have little, if any, knowledge that these works

exist. See, e.g., Karl Sudhoff's collection of more than 300 tractates, "Pestschriften aus den ersten 150 Jahren nach der Epidemie des Schwarzen Todes," *Archiv für Geschichte der Medizin*, vols. 1–17 (1909–25); Dorothy Waley Singer, "Some Plague Tractates (Fourteenth and Fifteenth Centuries), *Proceedings of the Royal Society of Medicine* 9 (1915–16): 159–212, or the more recent work of John Aberth, *The Black Death: The Great Mortality of 1348–1350—A Brief History with Documents* (New York: St. Martin's Press, 2005). Indispensable was the article by Jon Arrizabalaga, "Facing the Black Death: Perceptions and Reactions of University Medical Practitioners," in Arrizabalaga et al., eds., *Practical Medicine from Salerno to the Black Death* (Cambridge: Cambridge University Press, 1994), 237–88. As Lawrence Conrad has noted, the plague tractate in Arabic constitutes the emergence of a new literary genre and is abundantly attested as well; see Lawrence Conrad, "Arabic Plague Chronologies and Treatises: Social and Historical Factors in the Formation of a Literary Genre," *Studia Islamica* 54 (1981): 51–93.

10. Even when Jacob declares that "in days to come, all who see my words . . . will know that I did not change a word of the language or rhyme," we must find this a peculiar statement at best. The daily language of his household was not Hebrew, and it is unlikely that the family communicated in rhymed biblical prose. See Barkai, "Jewish Treatises on the Black Death," 83: וידעו כל הרואים מאמרי זה וכל החוזים. לימים הבאים כי אני לא שניתי מלת הלשון והחרוזים.

11. See the preceding chapter, or Susan Einbinder, "A Proper Diet: Medicine and History in Crescas Caylar's *Esther*," *Speculum* 80.2 (2005): 437–63. Abraham Bedersi in Perpignan wrote a Purim text, which he sent to David Caslari, the father of Abraham Caslari (whose plague tractate I mention in this chapter). See N. S. Doniach, "Abraham Bedersi's Purim Letter to David Kaslari," *JQR* 23 (1932–33): 63–69; and Barry Walfish, *Esther in Medieval Garb* (Albany: State University of New York Press, 1993).

12. As Joseph Ziegler has noted, physicians' testimony played an increasingly important role in canonization processes from the late thirteenth century on, and, in a sense, Jean de Tournemire's testimony also represents a generic innovation on the simpler, less "scientific" miracle collections of the twelfth and thirteenth centuries. Joseph Ziegler, "Practitioners and Saints: Medical Men in Canonization Processes in the Thirteenth to Fifteenth Centuries," *Social History of Medicine* 12.2 (1999): 191–225. Peter of Luxembourg is treated in this article. See also Ernst Wickersheimer, "Les guérisons miraculeuses du Cardinal Pierre de Luxembourg (1387–1390), in *Comptes rendus du 2e Congrès International d'Histoire de la Médecine* (Évreux: Imprimerie Ch. Hérissey, 1922), 371–89.

13. See Ziegler, "Practitioners and Saints"; Wickersheimer, "Les guérisons miraculeuses." Jean's tractate on the plague, *Preservatio contra pestilenciam*, was written in 1370 and translated twice into Hebrew, the first time by an anonymous author and the second time by Leon Joseph of Carcassonne in 1394. See Barkai, "Jewish Treatises on the Black Death," 7 n. 10; and Moritz Steinschneider, *Die hebraeischen Uebersetzungen des Mittelalters* (Berlin: Kommissionsverlag des Bibliographischen Bureaus, 1893), no. 516, p. 833, "Ein Consilium über die Pest."

14. Wickersheimer, "Les guérisons miraculeuses"; J. Ziegler, "Practitioners and Saints"; *Acta sanctorum julii* (1718), 1:598–99. My thanks to Thomas Boeve of Princeton University for his translation of the Latin text of the deposition.

15. P. Pansier, "Les médecins juifs à Avignon aux XIIIe, XIVe et XVe siècles," *Janus* 15 (July 1910): 430–31. Much of Pansier's article, including this information, is recapitulated in Messaoud-Prosper Cohen, *Contribution à l'histoire des médecins juifs en Avignon (XIIe–XVe siècles)* (Paris: Amédée LeGrand, 1940), esp. 25.

16. Renate Blumenfeld-Kosinski, *Poets, Saints, and Visionaries of the Great Schism, 1378–1417* (University Park: Pennsylvania State University Press, 2006), 75.

17. See n. 82 below.

18. Oxford Bodleian Opp. Add. Heb. 2583, fol. 26r.:

כי החולי והסיבה בלתי נודעה אל הרופא אם שלא באמצעות ספורי החולה או מקריו שהם ראיות אל הרופא.

19. In Moses Narboni's words, penned in 1350, the pestilence "already roams about in all parts of human settlement," leaving "not one in a thousand . . . saved." His numerical estimate was exaggerated but not his sense of devastation. Gerrit Bos, "R. Moshe Narboni: Philosopher and Physician, A Critical Analysis of *Sefer Oraḥ Ḥayyim*," *Medieval Encounters* 1.2 (1995): 242.

20. *Evel Rabbati*, 83. All translations from Hebrew, unless otherwise indicated, are mine.

21. Many writings from the era of the Black Death ponder the fragility of collective and personal memory.

22. This is also a historiographical problem when treating this period. Simon Bernfeld's anthology of Hebrew laments, a classic exemplar of "lachrymose" history, contains sixty-seven pages of poetry described as poetry of the Black Death. Without exception, the examples commemorate incidents of persecution and have nothing to do with the devastation wrought by the disease itself. Simon Bernfeld, *Sefer haDema'ot* (Berlin: Eshkol, 1924), 2:87–154. For a more modern example, see Joseph Shatzmiller, "Les juifs de Provence pendant la peste noire," *REJ* 133 (1974): 457–80.

23. Clement VI's position is repeated (perhaps strategically) by Conrad of Megenberg in his 1350 plague tractate; see Dagmar Gottschall, "Conrad of Megenberg and the Causes of the Plague: A Latin Treatise on the Black Death Composed ca. 1350 for the Papal Court in Avignon," in Jacqueline Hamesse, ed., *La vie culturelle, intellectuelle et scientifique à la cour des papes d'Avignon* (Turnhout: Brepols, 2006), 319–32 and the excerpt cited on 324. For a scattering of sources on the persecutions and papal reactions, see Aberth, *The Black Death*; Camille Arnaud, *Essai sur la condition des juifs en Provence au moyen âge* (Forcalquier: Librairie d'Auguste Masson, 1879), 55–64; L. Bardinet, "Condition civile des juifs du Comtat Venaissin (1309–1376)," *Revue historique* 12.1 (1880): esp. 18ff.; J. M. W. Bean, "The Black Death: The Crisis and Its Social and Economic Consequences," in Daniel Williman, ed., *The Black Death: The Impact of the Fourteenth-Century Plague* (Binghamton, N.Y.: Medieval and Renaissance Texts and Studies, 1982), 23–38 and esp. 26; Jules Bauer, "La peste chez les juifs d'Avignon," *REJ* 34 (1897):

251–62; Adolphe Crémieux, "Les juifs de Toulon au moyen âge et le massacre du 13 avril 1348," *REJ* 89 (1930): 33–72 and 90 (1931): 43–64; Séraphine Guerchberg, "La controverse sur les prétendus semeurs de la 'peste noire' d'après les traités de peste de l'époque," *REJ* 108 (1948): 3–40; Shatzmiller, "Les juifs de Provence pendant la peste noire," *REJ* 133 (1974): 457–80; *Histoire littéraire de la France*, ed. Ch.-Victor Langlois et al. (Paris: Imprimerie Nationale, 1936), 37:220–21 and treating the plague literature on 325–90.

24. From the *Sicut Judeis* of Clement VI issued on October 1, 1348: "And although we would wish that the Jews be suitably and severely punished should perchance they be guilty of or accessories to . . . crime. . . nevertheless it does not seem credible that the Jews on this occasion are responsible for the crime nor that they caused it, because this nearly universal pestilence, in accordance with God's hidden judgment, has afflicted and continues to afflict the Jews themselves, as well as many other races who had never been known to live alongside them, throughout the various regions of the world." In Shlomo Simonsohn, ed., *The Apostolic See and the Jews* (Toronto: Pontifical Institute of Medieval Studies, 1988–91), 1:396–99, reprinted in John Aberth, *The Black Death: The Great Mortality of 1348–1350, A Brief History with Documents*, 158–59.

25. Bernfeld, *Sefer haDema'ot*, 2:87–154. Joseph Shatzmiller's 1974 article on Provençal Jewry during the Black Death begins, aptly enough, with the statement that "the history of the calamities that struck the Jews of Provence during the Black Death of 1348 is not known to us either in its entirety nor its details." The article turns promptly to a consideration of anti-Jewish persecutions related to the plague. Shatzmiller, "Les juifs de Provence pendant la peste noire."

26. For Avignon, Biraben lists plague outbreaks in 1348, 1361, 1372–73, and 1382. See Jean-Noël Biraben, *Les hommes et la peste en France et dans les pays européens et méditerranéens* (Paris: Mouton and École des Hautes Études en Sciences Sociales, 1975), vol. 1, appendix 4, p. 377. See also Jules Bauer, "La peste chez les juifs d'Avignon"; Ann Campbell, *The Black Death*, 154–55.

27. For an exception to the emphasis on 1348, see Melissa P. Chase, "Fevers, Poisons, and Apostemes: Authority and Experience in Montpellier Plague Treatises," in Pamela O. Long, ed., *Science and Technology in Medieval Society* (New York: New York Academy of Sciences, 1985), 153–69. Carmichael has also concentrated on the Italian plague cycles of the fifteenth century. As she notes in the article cited above, "the children and grandchildren of one plague suffered another with consciously used memory of the previous epidemic"; Carmichael, "The Last Past Plague," 133.

28. While scholars have routinely observed that Jacob must have come south as a small child with his parents or been born in the Comtat to French parents, they have not made this connection. It is, of course, possible that his French ancestry was older, but I think it is unlikely, given the determined attachment he shows to northern custom and liturgy. His presence in Paris as a medical practitioner does not demonstrate that he began his life there and migrated south by the early 1380s; his script is indisputably a product of southern upbringing.

29. My deep thanks to Colum Hourihane of the Index for Christian Art and

Katrin Kogman-Appel of Ben-Gurion University for their examination of the text and drawings in July 2006; it is their opinion that the drawings represent a later—probably, Italian—hand.

30. Michel Garel, "The Rediscovery of the Wolf Haggadah," *Journal of Jewish Art* 2.2 (1975): 22–26; Shlomo Zucker, "The Twists of Fate of the Wolf Haggadah and Its Research" (in Hebrew), *'Al sefarim ve-anashim* (English title: *Books and People*, the Jewish National and University Library, Jerusalem), no. 11 (May 1997): 4–13.

31. Kaufmann, "Le 'grand-deuil' de Jacob b. Salomon Sarfati d'Avignon." See also Katrin Kogman, *Illuminated Sephardic Haggadot* (Cambridge: Cambridge University Press, 2006), chap. 1.

32. Zucker, "The Twists of Fate," 8, cites Jacob's description of a royal knight treated for vertigo by "the great physician and sage, Master Gilbert, physician to the king of France, long may he live!" Jacob must be referring to Guibert de Celsoy (d. 1390), physician to Jean II and Charles V and on the medical faculty of the University of Paris.

33. Ibid., 7.

34. On the positive side, so is Ruth, which is cited heavily, as well as Esther. There are also a number of citations relating to other biblical women—Sarah, Rachel, Lot's daughters, Jephtha's daughter, Samson's first wife, the bride of Canticles, the ideal wife of Proverbs 31, and the prostitute of Proverbs 7. Some of these are more problematic for the psychological resonance they create and for the context in which they are reused. For more on this point, see below.

35. Kaufmann reads Israel's Romance name as "Maurilet."

36. Sirat cites fol. 34v of the *Yeshu'ot Ya'akov*, where Jacob has written, "this is completely explicated by my son in his book." According to Sirat, the book and its author are today unknown. Sirat, in Beit-Arié and Sirat, *Manuscrits médiévaux en caractères hébraïques*, vol. 2, 40, for entry 1395 (the date of BN Heb. 733's colophon).

37. *Evel Rabbati*, 79. I have elided the first use of רגליה, which I think the copyist must have added in anticipation of its appearance at the end of the sentence.

38. Or, imposed by society: Herlihy describes the family as *multitude ordinate*, a moral unit and "organized and stable community . . . within another organized community, the state itself." One of his examples of the articulation of this ordering is Peter Lombard, whose sentences include a chapter on the "order of loving" whereby "above all we love God, ourselves in second place, in third our parents, then our children and siblings, and finally domestics, finally enemies." Spouses are notably absent from the lineup. Herlihy, *Portraits of Medieval and Renaissance Living*, 14, 20.

39. On Peter (Pierre), see Andre Vauchez, *Sainthood in the Later Middle Ages* (Cambridge: Cambridge University Press, 1997), throughout, but note esp. 233, 307–10, 503, 508–9; Wickersheimer, "Les guérisons miraculeuses"; Ziegler, "Practitioners and Saints."

40. Blumenfeld-Kosinski, *Poets, Saints, and Visionaries*, 75–79.

41. *Acta sanctorum julii* (1719): 1:598–99, section 232. As Joseph Ziegler notes,

there are problems with the redaction of the canonization hearings, and the texts suffered for them. I thus rely gingerly upon the version to hand.

42. Cf. Jacob's "the wife who gave birth to such a daughter."

43. *Acta sanctorum julii*, 1:599, from para. 234.

44. Laura Smoller, "Miracle, Memory, and Meaning in the Canonization of Vincent Ferrer, 1453–54," *Speculum* 73 (1998): 429–54.

45. Here, as Elliott Horowitz notes, we have our only information on the use of tapers at the deathbed of medieval Jews. Oral communication, April 25, 2007.

46. Specifically, he prohibits "salted meat, cheese, the substance of legumes, hard fruit, chestnuts, pears"—"carnes salsas, caseum, substantiam leguminum, fructus durae substatiae, castaneas, pira" A.S., par. 233.

47. Bos, "R. Moshe Narboni," 235–37 and nn. 120–21; Michael McVaugh, "Treatment of Hernia in the Later Middle Ages: Surgical Correction and Social Construction," in Roger French et al., eds., *Medicine from the Black Death to the French Disease* (Aldershot: Ashgate, 1998), 133, 135, 140–41. Valesco was also the author of a plague tractate translated into Hebrew by an anonymous Jew; the sole surviving manuscript copy is in the Jewish Theological Seminary library, JTS MS 2669/1, fols. 1r–17v. See Barkai, "Jewish Treatises on the Black Death," 9.

48. "Car si la corrupció ho putreffacció de l'aèr és venguda per nostres peccats ho per nostres merits poch valen en aquest cas los remeys de la art de medecina, car aquell qui ligue ha a desligar," in Joan Veny i Clar, ed., *"Regiment de preservació de pestilència" de Jacme d'Agramont (s. XIV)* (Tarragona: Sugrañes, 1971), 78. Jacme's regimen was translated by M. L. Duran-Reynals and C.-E. A. Winslow, "Regiment de preservacio a epidimia o pestilencia e mortaldats," *Bulletin of the History of Medicine* 23 (1949): 57–89; this passage appears on 78. See also Arrizabalaga, "Facing the Black Death," 272.

49. His Haggadah, too, refers several times to his teacher, R. Nathan, who has instructed him to honor the French Passover customs and rites. See Kaufmann, "Le 'grand-deuil' de Jacob b. Salomon Sarfati d'Avignon."

50. See, e.g., Michael McVaugh, *Medicine before the Plague* (Cambridge: Cambridge University Press, 1993), 136, 148.

51. Similarly, in the previous chapter, I have argued that Crescas Caslari's Esther romance dramatized Arnau of Vilanova's theories of therapeutic diet. It may be that other texts perform this function and, in a sense, constitute an interdisciplinary genre of their own.

52. The phrasing draws on Gen. 19:19, "lest disaster overtake me and I die" (RSV) (פן תדבקני הרעה ומתי). The use of the root *d-b-q* is unsettling because of its modern connotations of infection or contagion, but medieval physicians did not use this root to convey transmissibility of disease. See the discussion of contagion below.

53. Who is the antecedent of "his"? Nathan's siblings have already died. Is Esther bidding farewell to her father's relatives and then to her mother's?

54. Vajda remarks that Jacob's exegetical and theological writings also display a

"tendency to aggrandize miracles." Vajda, "On the History of the Polemic," 311. Thus, for example, Jacob argues that most of the occurrences in Egypt and at the Red Sea were miracles, but not all—a few followed natural law, "in order to distinguish the supernatural from the natural and emphasize it; for if everything had happened unnaturally [lit., "outside the natural"], it would give an opening to the apostate to claim that all that had happened was witchcraft or 'necromancia.'" Ibid.

55. Presumably, if its origins are divine, the chief effect of the plague is to inspire the survivors to repent and live piously. Conrad of Megenberg offers an unusual argument against the theory that the plague comes to punish humanity for its moral dereliction: the onslaught of epidemics has, he noted, brought about no improvement in morality, so this could not have been its aim. See Gottschall, "Conrad of Megenberg," 323. It is Jacme d'Agramont, of course, who creates a category of pestilence called "moral," which directly links social behavior to disease and catastrophe. As any number of modern scholars have observed, there are obvious parallels in the twentieth-century responses to AIDS.

56. Duran-Reynals and Winslow, "Regiment de preservació," 78–79. In the original: "E a açò a confermar se pot enduyr .i. test de la Sancta Escriptura, lo qual és estat allegat dessús en lo segon article lo qual és escrit *Deuteronomii, XXVIII capitulo,* hon se diu axí: *Percuciat te Dominus ulcere Egipti et partem corporis, per quam stercora egeruntur, scabie quoque prurrigine, ita ut curare nequeas.* Diu-se encara vulgarment que can Déus no vol, sants no poden, car no és degú que a la mà ni al poder de Déu pugue contrastar. Emperò lo major remey que en aquest cas podem aver, sí és que regonegam nostres pecats e nostres deffalliments avén cordial contricció. . . . Lo qual regiment nos fo figurat Regum .III., capítulo octavo, hon se diu axí: *ffames si aborta fuerit in terra aut pestilencia aut corruptus àer,*" Veny i Clar, *"Regiment de preservació de pestilència,"* 79. The two editions do not seem to be relying on the same manuscript.

57. Duran-Reynals and Winslow, "Regiment de preservació," 65; Veny i Clar, *"Regiment de preservació de pestilència,"* 55.

58. The exclusion of Deuteronomy 28 is curious. It may be that Jacob did not wish to suggest such an apocalyptic level of punishment for sin.

59. The biographical material is taken from Luis García Ballester, *La búsqueda de la salud: Sanadores y enfermos en la España medieval* (Barcelona: Ediciones Peninsula, 2001), 435–38; McVaugh, *Medicine before the Plague,* 440–43.

60. Of the latter, his translation of Bernard de Gordon's *Lilium medicine,* completed in Seville in 1362, survives. Oxf. Bodl. Heb. 2127/2; García Ballester, *La búsqueda de la salud,* 301–2.

61. García Ballester, *La búsqueda de la salud,* 303: "en el sentido de un ambiente físico, pero humanizado, de urbe bajomedieval conneto."

62. Juan de Aviñon, *Sevillana medicina,* ed. José Mondéjar (Madrid: Arco, 2000), 511–13.

63. On its originality, see ibid., 21: "La obra tiene muy poco de original; me at-

revería a decir que las dos únicas cosas verdaderamente tales son los 6 capítulos especialmente dedicados al studio del aire de Sevilla (II–VII) y los párrafos dedicados a la diamagna, fármaco de propiedades curatives insospechadas." On its religious character, see 10, "Sus conocimientos teológicos católicos, en un punto por lo menos, es, creo, poco ajustado."

64. Lawrence Conrad, "Epidemic Disease in Formal and Popular Thought in Early Islamic Society," in Terence Ranger and Paul Slack, eds., *Epidemics and Ideas: Essays on the Historical Perception of Pestilence* (Cambridge: Cambridge University Press, 1992), 91; Dols, "Plague in Early Islamic History," *JAOS* 94.3 (1974): 373.

65. Ann Carmichael, "Contagion Theory and Contagion Practice in Fifteenth-Century Milan," *Renaissance Quarterly* 44 (1991): 213.

66. Ibid.

67. As Arrizabalaga notes, modern scholars have also attempted to differentiate the varieties of medieval plague by their season of appearance. According to this theory, bubonic plague—that form of the plague transmitted by fleas and characterized by the swellings in neck, groin, or armpit known as buboes—would have thrived in the late spring to fall. Pneumonic plague, in contrast, would have thrived when pneumonia did (and fleas did not), namely, the winter months. This differentiation is appealing but problematic in the case of Jacob's family. Jacob and his son fell ill in Tishri (November–December), but it is highly unlikely that the father would have survived pneumonic plague. His daughters Esther and Sarah fell ill in Adar (March). Of Sarah's symptoms we can say little, not even how long she was sick before she died. Jacob is also curiously silent about any identifying symptoms accompanying Esther's illness, other than her parched throat and shortness of breath, both listed by Abraham Caslari as characteristic of pestilential fever. However, Caslari also refers repeatedly to mental confusion, delirium, and continuous fever, and the first two are notably absent in Jacob's representation of Esther's self-possession and clarity. Once again, we have to ask if Jacob has deliberately elided medical—in this case, diagnostic—information from the text. See Arrizabalaga, "Facing the Black Death."

68. See, especially, the work of Michael W. Dols, e.g., "The Comparative Communal Responses to the Black Death in Muslim and Christian Societies," *Viator* 5 (1974): 269–87; idem, "Al-Manbiji's 'Report on the Plague': A Treatise on the Plague of 764–65/1362–64 in the Middle East," in Daniel Williman, ed., *The Black Death: The Impact of the Fourteenth-Century Plague* (Binghamton, N.Y.: Medieval and Renaissance Texts and Studies, 1982), 65–75; idem, *The Black Death in the Middle East* (Princeton, N.J.: Princeton University Press, 1971). See also Lawrence I. Conrad, "The Social Structure of Medicine in Medieval Islam," *Society for the Social History of Medicine* 37 (1985): 11–15.

69. See, e.g., Dols, "Al-Manbiji's 'Report on the Plague'"; Conrad, "Epidemic Disease," 77–100.

70. I draw here on a number of sources, but see, e.g., Dols, "Al-Manbiji's 'Report on the Plague'"; Conrad, "Epidemic Disease," (n. 52); Manfred Ullmann, *Islamic*

Medicine, trans. Jean Watt (Edinburgh: Edinburgh University Press, 1978). See also Jacqueline Sublet, "La peste prise aux rêts de la jurisprudence," *Studia Islamica* 33 (1971): 141–51. These notions find a wonderful parallel in later Christian imagery, which likewise depicts the arrows of pestilence and explaining the association of Saint Sebastian with the plague. (The other great plague saint is Saint Roch, often depicted with an abscess on his leg.)

71. Ibn Khatima's treatise, written in February 1349, states: "It is clear and obvious that it is the nature of the disease to spread and contaminate the surroundings. Both experience and observation confirm this. . . . It is a law which God imposed in this matter. . . . We [thus] . . . reject 'infection,' which Arabs believe in their ignorance of Islam." Cited in Aberth, *The Black Death*, 56.

72. The entire passage from which I have drawn this excerpt is found in Aberth, *The Black Death*, 114–16. A fuller rendition offers a better sense of the author's boldness: "[T]he existence of contagion has been proved by experience, deduction, the senses, observation, and by unanimous reports. . . . [W]hoever has looked into this matter [knows] . . . that those who come into contact with [plague] patients mostly die, while those who do not come into contact survive. Moreover, disease occurs in a household or neighborhood because of the mere presence of a contagious dress or utensil." In the same passage, Ibn al-Khatib denounces those religious scholars who issued fatwas against fleeing plague-ridden cities, concluding: "[T]he discussion about whether the divine law agrees or disagrees with the contagion theory is not the business of the medical art, but is incidental to it. And in conclusion, to ignore the proofs for plague contagion is an indecency and an affront to God and holds cheap the lives of Muslims." Ibn al-Khatib paid a high price for his willingness to challenge religious authority. Forced to flee Granada in 1371, he spent time in Tlemcen before ending up in house arrest in Fez, in part for his beliefs. He was assassinated in prison in 1374; see Campbell, *The Black Death*, 19–20, 26–28; Aberth, *The Black Death*, 114.

73. Dols, "Al-Manbijī's 'Report on the Plague,'" 65–75.

74. Ibid., 65–67.

75. Sublet, "La peste prise aux rêts de la jurisprudence," 142. From the other side of the parent-child narrative, the famed historian Ibn Khaldun apparently lost both his parents and some beloved teachers during the epidemic of 1348; as he notes in the *Muqaddimah*, ed. Franz Rosenthal (Princeton, N.J.: Princeton University Press, 1967), 1:64, "The entire inhabited world changed." But he did not write to commemorate his personal loss. I emphasize this because I think it is also more true to the characteristics of the Jewish genres and their authors' sensibilities—and this matters because it underlines how little this was likely to have been Jacob's primary impulse. See Dols, "The Comparative Communal Responses," 270.

76. See, e.g., Carmichael, "The Last Past Plague," 137, re "pestis manufacta."

77. See, for instance, some of the studies in Neithard Bulst and Robert Delort, eds., *Maladies et société (XIIe–XVIIe siècles): Actes du colloque de Bielefeld* (Paris: Centre National de la Recherche Scientifique, 1986).

78. Pinkhoff, *Abraham Kashlari*, 42. Thanks to my former professor Leonard Kravitz for improving my translation.

79. Aberth, *The Black Death*, 116.

80. From our perspective, of course, the corpse example comes close to a notion of contagion. But from the medieval perspective, it more significantly links social disorder and specifically war with cosmological disruptions.

81. Paris BN Heb. 733, fol. 33a.

82. *Acta sanctorum julii* 1 (1719), 161 (597, ¶231); Wickersheimer, "Les guérisons miraculeuses," 379.

83. Pansier, "Les médecins juifs à Avignon aux XIIIᵉ, XIVᵉ at XVᵉ siècles," *Janus* 15 (1910): 433, 435.

84. The same sentiment shapes Ben Jonson's small poem on his first son, written after his son's death during the plague of 1603:

> Farewell, thou child of my right hand, and joy;
>   My sin was too much hope of thee, lov'd boy.
> Seven years thou wert lent to me, and I thee pay,
>   Exacted by thy fate, on the just day.
> Oh, could I lose all father now! For why
>   Will man lament the state he should envy?
> To have so soon 'scaped world's and flesh's rage,
>   And if no other misery, yet age!
> Rest in soft peace, and asked, say, Here doth lie
>   Ben Jonson his best piece of poetry.
> For whose sake henceforth all his vows be such
>   As what he loves may never like too much.

Ben Jonson, "On My First Son," http://www.luminarium.org/sevenlit/jonson/son.htm.

CHAPTER SIX

1. Roger Kohn, *Les juifs de la France du nord dans la seconde moitié du XIVe siècle* (Louvain and Paris: Peeters, 1988), 5, 270ff. A recent volume of essays edited by Gilbert Dahan contains a number of relevant studies; for general background, see Dahan's introduction and Roger Kohn, "Les juifs en France du nord dans la seconde moitié du XIVe siècle: Un état de la question," in Gilbert Dahan, ed., *L'expulsion des juifs de France: 1394* (Paris: Cerf, 2004), 13–29.

2. On the so-called APAM liturgy (an acronym for the communities of Asti, Fossano, and Moncalvo), see Dario Disegni, "Il rito di Asti-Fossano-Moncalvo (APAM)," *Sefer Zikkaron le-Shelomo S. Mayer* (Milan: Sally Mayer Foundation, 1956), 78–81; Daniel Goldschmidt, "A Forgotten Anthology and Remnants from the APAM Festival Liturgy"

(in Hebrew), in Goldschmidt, ed., *Meḥqere Tefillah uFiyyut* (Jerusalem: Magnes, 1979), 80–121; Aaron Rau, "The *Qerovah 'Aggan haSahar*'" (in Hebrew), *Sefer haYuval Likhvod haRav Ya'aqov Freimann* (Berlin: Buchdruckerei "Viktoria" GmbH, 1937), 128–48.

3. Joseph Green, "The Trabot Family" (in Hebrew), *Sinai* 79 (1976): 147–63. Green identified sixty-four Italian Jews using the surname טרבוט, sometimes read "Trévoux," sometimes "Trabot." His list, which has been enormously helpful to me, spans the late fourteenth to the eighteenth centuries; it does not include Gabriel Trabot, whose poems I discuss below, and its chronology for Peretz Yeḥiel cannot be entirely correct. See also Henri Gross, *Gallia Judaica* (Paris: Léopold Cerf, 1897), 219–23; Ernst Renan, *Les écrivains français du XIVe siècle* (vol. 31 of *L'histoire littéraire de la France*) (Paris: Imprimerie Nationale, 1893), 713–16; A. Berliner, "Recensions," *Magazin für jüdischer Geschichte und Literatur* 2 (1875): 16.

4. Simon Schwarzfuchs, "Yohanan Trèves et le dernier refuge de l'école talmudique française après l'expulsion de 1394," in Gilbert Dahan, ed., *Rashi et la culture juive* (Paris: E. Peeters, 1997), 83–94; Kohn, *Les juifs de la France du nord*, 215, 235ff. On the general history of the medieval community, see Costa de Beauregard, "Notes et documents sur la condition des juifs en Savoie," *Mémoires de l'Académie des sciences, belles-lettres et arts de Savoie*, 2nd ser., 2 (1854): 81–126; Ferdinando Gabotto, "Per una storia degli Israeliti in Piemonte nel medio evo," *Il vessillo israelitico* 65.19–20 (1917): 433–37, and 66.15–16 (1918): 288–92; M. Gerson, "Notes sur les juifs des états de la Savoie," *REJ* 8 (1884): 235–42; Jean-Daniel Morerod, "La maison de Savoie et les juifs en Suisse Romande à la fin du moyen âge," *Equinoxe* 13 (1995): 65–79; Renata Segre, *The Jews in Piedmont* (Jerusalem: Israel Academy of Sciences and Humanities; Tel Aviv: Tel Aviv University, 1988), vol. 1.

5. The poem מי גם בכם appears also in the collection of Spanish Hebrew laments dated by Joseph Yahalom to 1438; the Firkovitch manuscript that he describes includes a number of laments that respond specifically to the persecutions of 1391. See Joseph Yahalom, "Poetic Unity as an Expression of Spiritual Reality" (in Hebrew), in *Galut Aḥar Golah* (Jerusalem: Ben Zvi Institute, 1988), 337–46; the poem is no. 87 on his appended list. The Firkovitch manuscript testifies to a tradition of reciting laments during the "three weeks" preceding the Ninth of Av.

6. The earlier Peretz Yeḥiel composed several poems preserved in MS Parma Biblioteca Palatina Heb. 2306. See Benjamin Richler, *Hebrew Manuscripts in the Biblioteca Palatina in Parma* (Jerusalem: JNUL, 2001), 408, entry 1420.

7. Fols. 27v–29r.

8. Fols. 20v–22r. The hymns begin on fol. 17r and conclude on fol. 27v.

9. This combination—Ashkenazi script, Sephardic poetic form—is one indication of the hybridity of Jewish culture in the Savoy, Dauphiné, and Piedmont.

10. Dan Pagis, "Laments for the Persecutions of 1391 in Spain" (in Hebrew), *Tarbiz* 37 (1968): 355–73; Yahalom, "Poetic Unity," 337.

11. Pagis, "Laments for the Persecutions," 357–58.

12. This may be the place to note that, while studies of the Hebrew literature produced in medieval and early modern Italy have grown apace in recent years, the case of medieval northern Italy is entirely unrepresented by those studies. The center of literary production during the fourteenth century is in the south, where the dominance of Sephardi and vernacular Italian influence is evident. See the various studies by Dvora Bregman and Alessandro Guetta, as well as Dan Pagis, "The Invention of the Hebrew Iamb and Contributions to Hebrew Metrics in Italy" (in Hebrew), in Ezra Fleischer, ed., *HaShir Dibbur 'al Ofnav* (Jerusalem: Magnes, 1993), 166–256, and, of course, the classic work by Haim Schirmann, *Mivhar haShirah ha'Ivrit be'Italia* (Berlin: Schocken, 1934). For a forgotten but charming essay, see Isaiah Sonne, *HaYahadut ha'Italqit* (Jerusalem: Ben Zvi Institute, 1961).

13. Renan, *Les écrivains français*, 713.

14. Segre, *The Jews in Piedmont*, xii.

15. Often this metaphor describes the subjugation of the Jews in Islamic lands (Ishmael, the progenitor of Islam, is the son of Abraham's maidservant, Hagar). Here, I suspect that it constitutes a conscious riposte to the Christian legal definition of the Jews as "children of the maidservant," condemned to eternal servitude. See Shlomo Simonsohn, *The Apostolic See and the Jews: History* (Toronto: Pontifical Institute of Medieval Studies, 1991), 7:94–102, for a discussion of the legal concept and its specific application in this period.

16. As Renan observed, the use of the third-person plural here does not distinguish Peretz from the refugees. On the contrary, it permits him to exploit terms for this expulsion used by other Provençal and Catalonian writers. From Profiat Duran, he borrowed the gematria for כלה (= 55), referring to the Hebrew year (5055 = 1395), and the verse גרש יגרש comes from the Efodi.

17. The sense of the last line is, I think, "they were forced to give up their bread but would not sin for a loaf." *Maqré Dardaqé* (Naples, 1488), 1.

18. Ibid.

19. Mary Allies, *Three Catholic Reformers* (1878; Freeport, N.Y.: Books for Libraries Press, 1972), 51, 54; Thomas Bardelle, *Juden in einem Transit- und Brückenland* (Hannover: Hahnsche, 1998), 86–89, 108–10; H. Fages, *Histoire de Saint Vincent Ferrier* (Louvain: A. Uystpruyst; Paris: Alph. Picard, 1901), 1:137–43, 144–48; José de Darganta and Vicente Forcada, *Biografía y escritos de San Vicente Ferrer* (Madrid: Biblioteca de Autores Cristianos, 1956), 154–62, 227–31; Gerson, "Notes sur les juifs des états de la Savoie," 236; Bernard Hodel, "Sermons de Saint Vincent Ferrier à Estavayer-le-lac en mars 1404," *Mémoire dominicaine* 2 (1993): 149–93; Isidore Loeb, "Un episode de l'histoire des Juifs de Savoie," *REJ* 10 (1884): 33; Morerod, "La maison de Savoie," 76.

20. On Capistran, see Allies, *Three Catholic Reformers*; Vittore Colorni, "Shemuel (Simone) da Spira contro fra Giovanni da Capestrano," *La Rassegna Mensile di Israel* 38.7–8 (1972): 69–86; Ramón Lourido Díaz, "San Juan de Capistrano y su pretendido Antisemitismo," *Miscelánea de Estudios Arabes y Hebraicos* 12–13 (1963–64): 99–129;

Johannes Hofer, *Johannes von Capestrano: Ein Leben im Kampf um die Reform der Kirche* (Innsbruck: Tyrolia, 1936); Leon de Kerval, *Saint Jean de Capistran: Son siècle et son influence* (Bordeaux and Paris, 1887); Christopher Ocker, "Contempt for Friars and Contempt for Jews in Late Medieval Germany," in Steven J. McMichael and Susan E. Myers, eds., *Friars and Jews in the Middle Ages and Renaissance* (Leiden: Brill, 2004), 119–46; Simonsohn, *The Apostolic See and the Jews*, 7:71–74; idem, *A History of the Jews in the Duchy of Mantua* (Jerusalem: Qiryat Sefer, 1977), 6; Joshua Starr, "Johanna II and the Jews," *JQR* 31 (1940–41): 67–78.

21. Thomas Bardelle and Jean-Daniel Morerod, "La lutte contre l'usure au début du XVe siècle et l'installation d'une communauté juive à Lausanne," *Études de Lettres* 4 (1992): 3–21; Hodel, "Sermons de Saint Vincent Ferrier," 149–51; Segre, *The Jews in Piedmont*, xxxv.

22. In this sense, it is important to reassess Jeremy Cohen's now-classic case for the rising star of mendicant preaching, propaganda, and anti-Jewish designs with an eye to the specific realities that characterized the northern Italian communities. There is trouble in the Piedmont, but the infrastructure of the Jewish community remains resilient. Despite the trend toward greater segregation of the Jews, both popes and kings (or, as the case may be, dukes) resist the utter debilitation of these communities and the revenues they promised. See Jeremy Cohen, *The Friars and the Jews* (Ithaca, N.Y.: Cornell University Press, 1986), and the essays revisiting Cohen's thesis in McMichael and Myers, *Friars and Jews in the Middle Ages and Renaissance.*

23. Jurisdictional strife sometimes worked in the Jews' favor. This is visible in the cyclic, sometimes flip-flopping, charters of privileges issued by the counts and later dukes of Savoy, or, for instance, in the papal protections issued in 1422 by Martin V and revoked one year later, apparently under the influence of John of Capistran. In the period of our concern, this means primarily the statutes issued by Amadeus VIII in 1402–4, 1418, and 1430; see Laurent Chevalier, "Une source inédite du droit savoyard: Les 'Antiqua Sabaudiae Statuta' d'Amédée VIII de 1402–1404," *Bulletin philologique et historique (jusqu'à 1610) du comité des travaux historiques et scientifiques* 1 (1960): 361–91. See also Simonsohn, *The Apostolic See and the Jews*, 7:70.

24. Schwarzfuchs, "Yohanan Trèves," 87, 90; Kohn, *Les juifs de la France du nord*, 235–39; Segre, *The Jews in Piedmont*, xiv and doc. 100; H. Merhavia, "A Spanish-Latin Manuscript on the Struggle over the Talmud in the Early Fifteenth Century" (in Hebrew), *Qiryat Sefer* 45.2 (1969–70): 271–87; and 45.4: 590–609; Bardelle, "L'integration des juifs exilés dans une ville savoyarde—l'exemple de Chambéry," in Gilbert Dahon, ed., *L'expulsion des juifs de France, 1394* (Paris: Éditions du Cerf, 2004), 210, 217; Loeb, "Un épisode de l'histoire des juifs," 48–49.

25. Max Bruchet, *Le château de ripaille* (Paris: Librairie Ch. Delagrave, 1907), 382; Schwarzfuchs, "Yohanan Trèves," 87, 90.

26. See the discussion below. On Sanson (Samson, Sampson) de Louent (Louhans), see Kohn, *Les juifs de la France du nord*, 230ff.; Segre, *The Jews in Piedmont*, doc.

80, and the section titled "Sampson's Confession" in Merhavia, "A Spanish-Latin Manuscript," 592–93.

27. See, e.g., Adolfo Robles, "Sant Vicent Ferrer en el context de diàleg: Les minories religioses," in *Paradigmes de la Història* I: Actes del Congrès 'Sant Vicent Ferrer i el seu temps'" (Valencia: Biblioteca Josep Giner, 1997), 15–45; David J. Viera, "Sant Vicent Ferrer: Francesc Eixemenis i el pogrom de 1391," *Col·loqui d'Estudis Catalans a Nord-Amèrica* (6th: 1990, Vancouver, B.C.) (Barcelona: Publicacions de l'Abadia de Montserrat), 243–54. For a somewhat different perspective, see Mark Meyerson, "Samuel of Granada and the Dominican Inquisitor: Jewish Magic and Jewish Heresy in Post-1391 Valencia," in McMichael and Myers, *Friars and Jews in the Middle Ages and Renaissance*, 181; Meyerson, *A Jewish Renaissance in Fifteenth-Century Spain* (Princeton, N.J.: Princeton University Press, 2004), 59–61; and Giacomo Todeschini, "Franciscan Economics and Jews in the Middle Ages," 99–117, also in McMichael and Myers. Yahalom claims a *piyyut* refers specifically to Saint Vincent, אללי לי ברוב אבלי (Woe is me in my great mourning); Yahalom, "Poetic Unity," 339. The full text, reproduced in Pagis, does not name the friar explicitly but refers (in a censored verse) to "the prayers of the oppressor and the voice of the priest" (בתפלת צר וקול כומר), 361, v. 14.

28. The Christian team was led by the convert to Christianity, Joshua Lorki—baptized Jerónimo de Santa Fé.

29. Merhavia, "A Spanish-Latin Manuscript."

30. Daniel Cohen, "An Autograph Letter of the Maharil on the Persecutions in the Savoy and on the Collection of the *Bullengeld* in 1418" (in Hebrew), *Zion* 44 (1979): 173–87; Gabotto, "Per una storia degli Israeliti in Piemonte nel medio evo," 290; Schwarzfuchs, "Yohanan Trèves," 90; Segre, *The Jews in Piedmont*, xiv.

31. See below.

32. Segre, *The Jews in Piedmont*, xix and docs. 23, 126 (March 15, 1426); 148 (February 18, 1429)—in both cases recording the payment of Jewish fees in exchange for acquittal of charges against their books and for an extension of ducal privileges, 55–57 and 67–68. Simonsohn, *The Apostolic See and the Jews*, 7:362–64, describes Pons's commission to include "Christians and Jews who were reportedly inventing new sects and prohibited rites . . . magicians, sorcerers, fortune-tellers and the like. To this list the pope [Alexander V, in 1409] added Jews who were seducing converts to revert to Judaism, were publicly demonstrating the Talmud and other books and errors, and were acting against the Christian faith and even against Mosaic law. The inquisitor was also to take action against Christians and Jews who were asserting that usury was no sin. . . . This was one of the most comprehensive tasks ever entrusted to an inquisitor." See also Bardelle and Morerod, "La lutte contre l'usure," 7; Gabotto, "Per una storia degli Israeliti in Piemonte nel medio evo," 291; I. Loeb, "Un épisode de l'histoire des juifs," 50–51. For a reminder that the Inquisitors did not limit their activities to Jews, see M. Esposito, "Un auto-da-fé a Chièri en 1412," *Revue d'histoire ecclésiastique* 42 (1947): 422–32.

33. See Pagis, "The Invention of the Hebrew Iamb."

34. According to Bar-Tikva, it is the first lament in the Carpentras rite. Benjamin Bar-Tikva, *Piyyute: R. Yitzhaq HaSeniri* (Ramat-Gan: Bar-Ilan University, 1996), 63–64; Aaron Mirsky, *HaPiyyut* (Jerusalem: Magnes, 1990), 522–30. Mirsky demonstrates that the *piyyut* is a poetic reworking of an ancient midrashic *piyyut* by Yannai.

35. Eva Frojmovic, "Messianic Politics in Re-Christianized Spain: Images of the Sanctuary in Hebrew Bible Manuscripts," in Eva Frojmovic, ed., *Imagining the Self, Imagining the Other: Visual Representation and Jewish-Christian Dynamics in the Middle Ages and Early Modern Period* (Leiden: Brill, 2002), 91–128.

36. איילותי בגלותי לך נשאתי את עיני. Note also that the practice of running autonomous texts around the margins is considered Ashkenazi. For a luxury illustration, see *The Rothschild Miscellany* (also north Italian), facsimile edition, 2 vols. (London: Facsimile Editions; Jerusalem: Israel Museum, 1989). Israel Ta-Shema treats the phenomenon in an essay in the companion volume to the facsimile edition, "The Literary Content of the MS," in *The Rothschild Miscellany: A Scholarly Commentary* (Jerusalem: Israel Museum; London: Facsimile Editions, 1989), 49. As he notes, the texts are autonomous but not unrelated in terms of a larger ideological design.

37. MS Parma 1883, fol. 18v.

38. Cited in Yahalom, "Poetic Unity," 340. The expression appears also in one of the hymns cited in the Spanish collection he treats.

39. Kohn, "Les juifs en France du nord," 24.

40. "Les morts ont dû être expulsés peu après les vivants!" Kohn, *Les juifs de la France du nord*, 204. No Jewish cemetery is documented in the Savoy until 1409, and I have found no record of its early destruction. See Bardelle, "L'integration des juifs exilés," 7 (with a date of 1413) and Kohn, *Les juifs de la France du nord*, 203. But note Segre, *The Jews in Piedmont*, doc. 160, dated 1430, with an order to Christians not to disturb the cemetery of the Jews.

41. How little this approach was valued by medieval Jewish poets is reflected in the corresponding indifference of modern historians to reading them for historical purposes. Nor do I see *my* purpose as limited to tethering poems to events: the refraction of historical occurrences, as well as their affective display in a theological frame, has literary and historical meaning now, as it did then. The quest is to retrace some of the process and how it worked.

42. MS Parma 1883, fols. 19r–v.

43. Indicating that he is counting the new year from Nisan and not Tishri (Rosh Hashanah).

44. MS Parma 1883, fol. 19v.

45. Hanoch Albeck, ed., *Shishah Sidre Mishnah* (Jerusalem: Mossad Bialik; Tel Aviv: Dvir, 1973), Seder Mo'ed, Tractate Ta'anit 4:6 (343–44). The passage is also cited in Haim Nahman Bialik and I. L. Ravnitzky, *Sefer haAggadah* (Tel Aviv: Dvir, 1973), 391, col. 2.

46. For this and the following chronology, see Schwarzfuchs, "Yohanan Trèves,"

89–90, where the citation is found on 90; Loeb, "Un épisode de l'histoire des juifs," 48; Gerson, "Notes sur les juifs des états de la Savoie," 238–95; Merhavia, "A Spanish-Latin Manuscript," 590–93.

47. Yohanan Trèves, the would-be chief rabbi of the transalpine communities, was over the border in Trévoux in 1417, but in 1426 he was arrested in Chambéry and held throughout the period during which Jewish books were on trial again. Bardelle, "L'integration des juifs exilés," 211–12. In 1429, the Jewish books in Trévoux, the hometown of our writers, were confiscated, and an order for their burning was issued later that year. Loeb, "Un épisode de l'histoire des juifs," 33–34, 54. It is not obvious that the order was executed. That the Inquisitors were not 100 percent successful in their endeavors is revealed in an extant letter that Yohanan sent from prison, ordering his students to make copies of hidden books. As several scholars have noted, it is surely no accident that the one complete manuscript copy of the Talmud to survive the Middle Ages, now known as MS Munich 95, belonged to the son of Yohanan Trèves. See Kohn, *Les juifs de la France du nord*, 227; Gerard Nahon, " 'Tam in Gallica quam in Occitania . . .': Livres et savoir des juifs de France," in Gilbert Dahon, ed., *L'expulsion des juifs de France, 1394* (Paris: Cerf, 2004), 33.

48. Loeb, "Un épisode de l'histoire des juifs," 33–34, 54. It is not clear if the order was executed.

49. Green, "The Trabot Family," 155, no. 28.

50. שלח יד על ציד, in MS Parma 2306 (De Rossi 1050), fol. 11v.

51. *Even mi-qir tiz'aq* (Can a stone cry out from the wall), MS Parma 1883, fols. 19r–v.

52. MS Parma 1883, fol. 23r, v. 1.

53. See, e.g., Simonsohn, *The Apostolic See and the Jews*, vol. 2, docs. 658, 748, 771, 786, spanning the years 1429–51.

54. MS Parma 1883, fol. 23r, vv. 4–5.

55. Pagis, "Laments for the Persecutions," 360, 362.

56. MS Parma 1883, fol. 23r.

57. Ibid. See Hab. 3:1, נתן תהום קולו רום ידיהו נשא for a good example of the clever linguistic games the Trabots could play. Here the biblically literate auditor (or reader) would expect to hear God send forth His voice (*qolo*) and instead hears that God sends forth "calamity" (*qalon*).

58. *Gever darko yarum malko*, MS Parma 1883, fol. 24v.

59. Ibid.

60. *Im omri eshkekhah siḥi*, MS Parma 1883, fol. 23v.

61. Gabriel, we know, was not always preoccupied with such grim meditations on history; a handful of epigrams dedicated to friends survive in MS Parma 2306, where their stilted wit and prosody testify to an interest in the mannerist, allegorical, and ethical literature that constitutes much of this miscellany. MS Parma 2306 (De Rossi 1050), fol. 14r. The folio begins with a riddle by Abraham Ibn Ezra.

62. Exodus 28—Aaron's breastplate.

63. Exod. 27:3; Num. 7:13–84, referring to the basin that collects the blood of the sacrificial offerings (see Rashi to Exod. 27:3). Note that in Numbers 7, each tribe makes its own offering that includes something for the *mizraq*. In this sense, the "ruby and topaz" of the preceding verse are also a merismus (priesthood and tribes).

64. Gen. 27:29. Isaac's blessing to Jacob (disguised as Esau) that "you will be a lord to your brother." I translate to fill the gap.

65. Job 28:8 (again mining imagery)—לא עדה עליו שחל. Job 28 is an extended description of mining for ore. Ada and Zillah are Lamech's wives, Gen. 4:23–24, and Tubal-cain, the son of Tzilah, is "the forger of all instruments of bronze and iron" (Gen. 4:22). Netanel has a specific incident in mind here, but for now it is lost to us.

66. Literally, casts menstrual blood into the basin that should hold the blood of the sacrificial offerings.

67. To illustrate what I am calling the "pointillist" style of the authors, let me retranslate the second of the two stanzas more literally:

> Seir will make burn / a youth oppresses them / the eastern mountains / ruby and topaz.
> In the basin / he surely spit / he will throw on it / menstrual blood.
> The brother did not redeem / the nobleman's servant / sits mighty / strong, *selah*.
> The revered one / his hand repulsed / the lion crossed over / Ada and Zillah.

68. Pagis, "Laments for the Persecutions," 338.

69. Rinaldo Comba, "Les *Decreta Sabaudiae* d'Amédée VIII: Un projet de so-ciéte?," in B. Andenmatten and A. Paravicini Bagliani, eds., *Amédée VIII—Félix V* (Lausanne: Fondation Humbert II et Marie José de Savoie, Bibliothèque historique vaudoise, 1992), 179–90. Comba claims that Vincent Ferrer's influence on the 1403 statutes is observable.

70. Curiously, contemporary Christian art and literature documents the same process but with antithetical readings. As Cathleen Fleck has shown, the lavishly illuminated Bible owned by Clement VII in Avignon tapped a common reservoir of imagery according to which the Avignon of the antipopes was "Babylon" and Rome the longed-for "Jerusalem." See Cathleen Fleck, "The Cultural Politics of the Papal Library at Avignon: The Meaning and Movement of the Bible of Antipope Clement VII," in Jacqueline Hamesse, ed., *La vie culturelle, intellectuelle et scientifique à la cour des papes d'Avignon* (Turnhout: Fédération Internationale des Instituts d'Études Médiévales and Brepols, 2006), 65–87.

71. Pagis, "Laments for the Persecutions," 355.

72. Green, "The Trabot Family," 162; the manuscript is NY JTS 157 D, dated 1499.

73. Green, "The Trabot Family," 150.

74. E.g., in Michel Garel, *D'une main forte: Manuscrits hébreux des collections fran-çaises* (Paris: Seuil/ Bibliothèque Nationale, 1991), no. 128 on 170, a folio from MS BN

Heb. 114, a Psalter with Targum and commentary by David Qimḥi dated c. 1470–80, double colophon by Levi Ḥalfan and Netanel Trevot.

75. Louis Feldman, "A Responsum of Rabbenu Yoḥanan ben Rabbenu Mattatya Trèves in MS Oxford 875" (in Hebrew), *Sinai* 67 (1970): 18.

76. Renan, *Les écrivains français*, 713; he cites MS Oxf. Bodl. 1137.

1. I refer to the unpublished catalog description produced by Dr. Israel O. Lehmann, who wrote, "Fol. 43, the section dealing with בדיקת חמץ, is wrongly bound in, followed by the Pesach liturgy. After שפוך חמתך follows a curse pointing to a period of severe persecution."

2. סדר הפסח לכל גאוני צרפת וגם לרב עמרם ז"ל.

3. Thanks to Benjamin Richler for providing, prepublication, the full description from his forthcoming new catalog of Hebrew manuscripts in the Vatican.

4. In Qalonymos's case, I intend the famous passage in the *Even Boḥan*, which I cite in Hebrew and in English translation in my article "Recall from Exile: Literature, Memory and Medieval French Jews," ed. Peter Schäfer, *Jewish Studies Quarterly*, forthcoming. Estori HaParḥi refers twice to his expulsion past, first in his introduction to the halakhic work *Kaftor vaFerah* (see, e.g., the Salonika 1540 edition, 2b) and again in his introduction to his translation of a pharmaceutical guide by Armengaud Blaise, the *Tabula Antidotarii* (recently edited by Michael McVaugh and Lola Ferre).

5. The self-identification of Iberian Jews with "Sepharad" (or "al-Andalus") is another important story, which intersected with the story of French and Provençal exiles in North Africa treated in Chapter 3. For a study entirely devoted to this topic, see the forthcoming work of Ross Brann cited in the introduction.

BIBLIOGRAPHY

ABBREVIATIONS

AHR	*American Historical Review*
AJ	*Archives Juives*
AVOMO	*Arnaldi de Villanova: Opera Medica Omnia* (see Arnau of Vilanova, below)
HPSP	*Hebrew Poetry from Spain and Provence* (see Schirmann, *HaShirah ha'Ivrit biSefarad uveProvans*, below)
IMHM	*Institute for Microfilmed Hebrew Manuscripts*
JAOS	*Journal of the American Oriental Society*
JNUL	*Jewish National and University Library*
JQR	*Jewish Quarterly Review*
MGWJ	*Monatsschrift für Geschichte und Wissenschaft Judentums*
PAAJR	*Proceedings of the American Academy for Jewish Research*
PMLA	*Proceedings of the Modern Language Association*
REJ	*Revue des Études Juives*
RHMH	*Revue d'histoire de la médecine hébraïque*

MANUSCRIPTS

In parentheses, following each manuscript's shelf number, is the manuscript's microfilm number in the Institute for Microfilmed Hebrew Manuscripts at the Jewish National and University Library in Jerusalem.

Berlin

Staatsbibliothek (Preussischer Kulturbesitz) 825 Qu.Or. (F 10055)

Cambridge

Cambridge Add. Heb. 1499.2 (F 17116)
Cambridge Add. Heb. 1499.3 (F 17116)
Cambridge Add. Heb. 1512.1 (F 17129)

Cincinnati

Hebrew Union College MS 314 (F 18265)
Hebrew Union College MS 396 (F 18678)
Hebrew Union College MS 2000 (F 41666)
Hebrew Union College MS Acq. 2007–12 (no microfilm)

Hamburg

Staats- und Universitätsbibliothek Cod. Heb. 134 (F 965)

Jerusalem

JNUL MS Heb. 38°7246 (F 10116)

London

British Library Add. Heb. MS 27168 (= 930/1) (F 05833)
British Library Add. Heb. MS 19663 (F 4997)

Madrid

Biblioteca de San Lorenzo de El Escorial G-III-20 (F 8846)
Biblioteca de San Lorenzo de El Escorial G-IV-5 (F 10074)

Munich

Bayerische Staatsbibliothek Cod. Heb. MS 128 (F 1613)

New York

Columbia University MS X893 C-J55, vols. 5, 15, 31 (no microfilm listings)
Jewish Theological Seminary MS 3740 (F 29545)
Jewish Theological Seminary MS 4067 (F 24969)
Jewish Theological Seminary MS Adler 2039 (F 29545)

Oxford

Oxford Bodleian Can. Or. MS 104 (F 22427)
Oxf. Bodl. MS Heb. 2746/4 (F 22713)
Oxf. MS Mich. 146 (old no. 846) = Neubauer 1180 (F 16639)
Oxf. Bodl. Opp. Add. Heb. 2583, now cataloged 4°, 174 (F 22286)

Paris

Bibliothèque Nationale MS Heb. 733 (F 11620)
Bibliothèque Nationale MS Heb. 970 (F 30340)

Parma

Biblioteca Palatina Cod. Parma MS Heb. 1883 (= De Rossi 485) (F 13048)
Biblioteca Palatina Cod. Parma MS Heb. 2306 (= De Rossi 1050) (F 13214)
Biblioteca Palatina Cod. Parma MS Heb. 1953 (F 13108)

Rome

Biblioteca Casanatensa MS Heb. 3140 (F 100)

Saint Petersburg

Institute of Oriental Studies B290 (F 53430)

Vatican City

Vaticana Biblioteca Apostolica Heb. 366/2 (F 447)
Vaticana Biblioteca Apostolica Heb. 553 (F 557)

PUBLISHED WORKS

N.a. 1619. *Histoire ters* [*sic*] *pitoyable de deux Peres Capucins, qui ont esté cruellement mar-tyrisez, par une famille de juifs de Carrieu en Piedmont*. Paris: Jean Villiet.

Aberth, John. 2005. *The Black Death: The Great Mortality of 1348–1350—A Brief History with Documents*. New York: St. Martin's Press.

Abitbol, Michel. 1993. "Juifs d'Afrique du Nord et expulsés d'Espagne après 1492." *Revue de l'histoire des religions* 210.1: 49–90.

———. 1982. "Juifs maghrébins et commerce trans-saharien au moyen âge." In Michel Abitbol, ed., *Communauté juives des marges sahariennes du Maghreb*. Jerusalem: Ben Zvi Institute and Hebrew University, 229–50.

Abulafia, David. 1994. *A Mediterranean Emporium: The Catalan Kingdom of Majorca*. Cambridge: Cambridge University Press.

Al-Aḥdav, Yitzhaq. 1988. *Shire Yitzḥaq ben Shlomo al-Aḥdav*. Ed. Ora Ra'anan. Lod: Makhon Habermann.

Alcantara, Dom Pedro II d', ed. and trans. 1891. *Poésies hébraïco-provençales du ritual Israélite Comtadin*. Avignon: Seguin frères.

Allies, Mary. 1972 repr. of 1878 ed. *Three Catholic Reformers*. Freeport, N.Y.: Books for Libraries Press.

Alteras, Isaac. 1978. "Jewish Physicians in Southern France during the 13th and 14th Centuries." *JQR* 68.4: 209–23.

Amster, Ellen Jean. 2003. "Medicine and Sainthood: Islamic Science, French Colonial-ism, and the Politics of Healing in Morocco, 1877–1935." Ph.D. diss., University of Pennsylvania.

Amundsen, Darrel W. 1977. "Medical Deontology and Pestilential Disease in the Late Middle Ages." *Journal of the History of Medicine and Allied Sciences* 32.4: 403–21.

Amzallag, Avraham E. 1997. "La ala andalouse chez les juifs et les arabes." In Michel Abitbol, ed., *Relations judéo-musulmanes au Maroc: Perceptions et réalités*. Paris: Centre International de Recherche sur les Juifs du Maroc, 295–303.

Anderson, Benedict. 1983. *Imagined Communities*. London and New York: Verso.

Arié, Rachel. 1965. "Quelques remarques sur le costume des Musulmans d'Espagne au temps des Naṣrides." *Arabica* 12: 244–61.

Arnau of Vilanova. 1998. *Regimen Almarie*. In *Arnaldi de Villanova: Opera Medica Omnia* (*AVOMO*) 10.2, ed. Michael McVaugh. Barcelona: Universitat de Barcelona.

———. 1996. *Regimen Sanitatis ad regem Aragonum*. In *AVOMO* 10.1, ed. Luis García Ballester, Michael McVaugh, and Juan Paniagua. Barcelona: Universitat de Barcelona.

Arnaud, Camille. 1879. *Essai sur la condition des juifs en Provence au moyen âge*. For-calquier: Librairie d'Auguste Masson.

Arrizabalaga, Jon. 1994. "Facing the Black Death: Perceptions and Reactions of Uni-versity Medical Practitioners." In Luis García Ballester, Jon Arrizabalaga, Roger

French, and Andrew Cunningham, eds., *Practical Medicine from Salerno to the Black Death*. Cambridge: Cambridge University Press, 237–88.

Assis, Yom Tov. 1989. "Les juifs de Montpellier sous la domination aragonaise." *REJ* 148: 5–16.

———. 1987. "Social Unrest and Class Struggle among the Jewish Communities in Spain before the Expulsion" (in Hebrew). In Yosef Dan, ed., *Tarbut veHistoria: LeZikhro shel Professor Ino Saki*. Jerusalem: Misgav Yerushalayim, Institute for Research in the Heritage of Spanish and Oriental Jewry, 121–45.

———. 1983. "Juifs de France réfugiés en Aragon (XIIIe–XIVe siècles)." *REJ* 142: 285–322.

Assmann, Jan. 2002. *The Mind of Egypt: History and Meaning in the Time of the Pharaohs*. Trans. Andrew Jenkins. New York: Metropolitan.

Attias, Moses. 1978. "The Purim 'Complas' in Ladino." *Sefunot* 2: 331–45.

Aviñon, Juan de. 2000. *Sevillana medicina*. Ed. José Mondéjar. Madrid: Arco.

Ausecache, Mireille. 2006. "Des aliments et des médicaments: Les plants dans la médecine médiévale." In Bruno Laurioux, ed., *Cuisine et médecine au moyen âge*, special issue of the *Cahiers Recherches Médiévales in memory of Emmanuèle Baumgartner*, no. 13: 249–58.

Azran, Jacques. 1997. "Note sur les compositions musicales préservées dans la musique juive andalouse au Maroc." In Michel Abitbol, ed., *Relations judéo-musulmanes au Maroc: Perceptions et réalités*. Paris: Centre International de Recherche sur les Juifs du Maroc, 303–7.

Baer, Isaac. 1991 repr. of 1961 ed. *A History of the Jews in Christian Spain*. Vol. 1. Philadelphia: Jewish Publication Society.

Baralt, Luce Lopez. 1987. "La angustia secreta del exilio: El testimonio de un morisco de Túnez." *Hispanic Review* 55: 41–57.

Bar-Asher, Shalom. 2004. "La poésie liturgique juive nord-africaine comme source historique." In Nicole Serfaty and J. Tedghi, eds., *Présence juive au Maghreb: Homage à Haïm Zafrani*. Paris: Éditions Bouchène, 401–10.

Bardelle, Thomas. 2004. "L'integration des juifs exilés dans une ville savoyarde-l'exemple de Chambéry." In Gilbert Dahan, ed., *L'expulsion des Juifs de France, 1394*. Paris: Éditions du Cerf.

———. 2004. *Juden in einem Transit- und Bruckenland*. Hannover: Hahnsche.

Bardelle, Thomas, and Jean-Daniel Morerod. 1992. "La lutte contre l'usure au début du XVe siècle et l'installation d'une communauté juive à Lausanne." *Études de Lettres* 4: 3–21.

Bardinet, L. 1880. "Condition civile des juifs du Comtat Venaissin (1309–1376)." *Revue historique* 12.1: 1–47.

Barkai, Ron. 2001. "On Child Mortality during the Black Death" (in Hebrew). In Miri Eliav Feldon and Yitzhaq Hen, eds., *Nashim, Zeqenim ve-Taf: Qovetz Ma'amarim liKhvodah shel Shulamit Shahar*. Jerusalem: Zalman Shazar, 67–84.

———. 1998. "Jewish Treatises on the Black Death (1350–1500): A Preliminary Study."

In Roger French et al., eds., *Medicine from the Black Death to the French Disease.*
Aldershot: Ashgate, 6–25.

————. 1996. "Los médicos judeo-españoles y la peste negra." In *Luces y sombras de la
Judería europea (siglas XI–XVII): Primeros encuentros judaicos de Tudela.* Pamplona:
Gobierno de Navarra, 121–32.

————. 1987. "L'astrologie juive médiévale: Aspects théoriques et pratiques." *Le Moyen
Âge* 93.3–4: 323–48.

Bar-Sela, Ariel. 1964. "Moses Maimonides' Two Treatises on the Regimen of Health."
Transactions of the American Philosophical Society, n.s., 54.4: 3–50.

Bar-Shalom, Rami. 1996. "Communication and Propaganda between Provence and
Spain: The Controversy over Extreme Allegorization." In Sophia Menache, ed.,
Communication in the Jewish Diaspora. Leiden: Brill, 171–226.

Bar-Tikva, Benjamin. 1993. "Reciprocity between the Provençal School of Piyyutim
and the Schools of Catalonia and Ashkenazi France." In G. Sed-Rajna, ed., *Rashi:
1040–1990: Hommage à Ephraim Urbach.* Paris: Éditions du Cerf, 375–83.

————. 2002. "Two *Qedushta'ot* for the Special Lections by R. Isaac b. Zerachia" (in
Hebrew). *Qovetz 'al Yad,* n.s., 16: 143–85.

————. 1996. *Piyyute R. Yitzḥaq HaSeniri.* Ramat-Gan: Bar-Ilan University.

Bataillon, Louis-Jacques. 1982. "Intermédiares entre les traités de morale pratique et les
sermons: Les *Distinctiones* bibliques alphabétiques." In *Les genres littéraires dans les
sources théologiques et philosophiques médiévales.* Actes du Colloque International
de Louvain-la-Neuve (1981). Louvain-la-Neuve: Université Catholique de Louvain,
213–26.

Bato, Jomtov Ludovico. 1956. "L'immigrazione degli ebrei tedeschi in Italia dal trecento
al cinquecento." In *Scritti in memoria di Sally Mayer (1875–1953): Saggi sull'Ebraismo
italiano.* Jerusalem: Fondazione Sally Mayer, 19–34.

Battlori, P. Miguel. 1948. "La documentacio de Marsella sobre Arnau de Vilanova y
Joan Blasi." *Analecta Sacra Tarraconsensia: Revista de ciencias histórico ecclesiasticas*
21: 75–119.

————. 1947. *Arnau de Vilanova: Obres Catalanes II (Escrits Medics).* Barcelona: Editorial Barcino.

Bauer, Jules. 1898. "Le chapeau jaune chez les juifs comtadins." *REJ* 36: 53–64.

————. 1897. "La peste chez les juifs d'Avignon." *REJ* 34: 251–62.

Bean, J. M. W. 1982. "The Black Death: The Crisis and Its Social and Economic Consequences." In Daniel Williman, ed., *The Black Death: The Impact of the Fourteenth-
Century Plague.* Binghamton, N.Y.: Medieval and Renaissance Texts and Studies,
23–38.

Beattie, Blake. 1996. "The Preaching of the Cardinals at Papal Avignon." *Medieval
Sermon Studies* 38: 17–37.

Beauregard, Costa de. 1854. "Notes et documents sur la conditions des juifs en
Savoie." *Mémoires de l'Académie des sciences, belles-lettres et arts de Savoie,* 2nd ser.,
2: 81–126.

Bedersi, Yedaiah (Penini). 1890. *Sefer haPardes*. In Y. Luzzato and A. Lass, eds., "Orot mi'Ofel." *Otzar haSifrut* 3.1: 1–18.

Beit-Arié, Malachi. 1992. "Hebrew Script in Spain: Development, Offshoots and Vicissitudes." In Haim Beinart, ed., *Moreshet Sepharad*. Jerusalem: Magnes Press and the Hebrew University, 1: 282–317.

Beit-Arié, Malachi, and Colette Sirat, eds. 1979. *Manuscrits médiévaux en caractères hébraïques*. Jerusalem: Israel Academy of Science and Letters; Paris: Centre National de la Recherche Scientifique.

Benchekroun, Mohamed. 1974. *La vie intellectuelle marocaine sous les Mérinides et les Wattasides*. Rabat: s.n.

Ben-Menahem, Naftali. 1967. "The Book *Ho'il Moshe Be'er* of Moses Carmi/Crémieu" (in Hebrew). In *BeSha'are Sefer*. Jerusalem: Mossad Harav Kook, 164–72.

Berbrugger, Adrien. 1846. "Voyages dans le sud de l'Algérie et des états barbaresques de l'ouest et de l'est par El-'Aïchi et Moula-Ah'med." In *Exploration scientifique de l'Algérie pendant les années 1840, 1841, 1842*. Paris: Imprimerie Royale, 127–34.

Berliner, A. 1875. "Recensions." *Magazin für jüdischer Geschichte und Literatur* 2: 16.

Bernard, J. 1949. "Le népotisme de Clément V et ses complaisances pour la Gascogne." *Annales du Midi* 61.7–8: 369–411.

Bernfeld, Simon. 1924. *Sefer haDema'ot*. Vol. 2. Berlin: Eshkol.

Bernstein, Simon. 1938–39. "New *Piyyutim* from Spain and France" (in Hebrew). *Tarbiz* 10: 1–29.

Biraben, Jean-Noël. 1975. *Les hommes et la peste en France et dans les pays européens et méditerranéens*. 2 vols. Paris: Mouton and École des Hautes Études en Sciences Sociales.

Blumenfeld-Kosinski, Renate. 2006. *Poets, Saints, and Visionaries of the Great Schism, 1378–1417*. University Park: Pennsylvania State University Press.

Blumenkranz, Bernard. 1962. "En 1306: Chemins d'un exil." *Évidences* 13: 17–23.

Bonafed, Solomon. 1895. "The *Dīwān* of R. Solomon Bonafed [Bonfed]" (in Hebrew). In Aaron (Armand) Kaminka, ed., *Meshorere Sefarad ha-Aḥronim*, part 1, *Mi-Mizraḥ umiMa'arav* 2: 107–27.

Bos, Gerrit. 1995. "R. Moshe Narboni: Philosopher and Physician, A Critical Analysis of *Sefer Oraḥ Ḥayyim*." *Medieval Encounters* 1.2: 219–51.

Boswell, John. 1977. *The Royal Treasure: Muslim Communities under the Crown of Aragon in the Fourteenth Century*. New Haven, Conn.: Yale University Press.

Boyer, Raymond. 1956. "Un payout judéo-comtadin inédit." *Évidences* 8.59: 27–29.

Brann, Ross, and Adam Sutcliffe. 2003. *Renewing the Past, Reconfiguring Jewish Culture: From al-Andalus to the Haskalah*. Philadelphia: University of Pennsylvania Press.

Brener, Ann. 2001. "Isaac haGorni and the Troubadour Persona." *Zutot* 1: 84–91.

Bridel, Philippe. 1831. "Procès des juifs à Chinon (1348)." *Conservateur Suisse, ou Étrennes helvétiennes* 13: 313–37.

Bruchet, Max. 1907. *Le château de ripaille*. Paris: Librairie Ch. Delagrave.

Brun, Robert. 1928. *Avignon au temps des papes*. Paris: Librairie Armand Colin.

Brunet, Jacqueline, and Odile Redon. 1990. "Vins, jus et verjus: Du bon usage culinaire des jus de raisins en Italie à la fin du moyen âge." Vin des historiens: Actes du 1er symposim, vin et histoire. May 19–21, 1989, Suze-la-Rouss, 109–17.

Brunner, Fernand. 1997. *Métaphysique d'Ibn Gabirol et de la tradition platonicienne.* Burlington, Vt.: Ashgate Variorum.

Bruzzone, P. L. 1889. "Les juifs au Piémont." *REJ* 19: 141–46.

Buchner, Zeev Wolf. 1808. *Sefer Shire Tehillah.* Berlin: Jüdischer Freischule.

Burr, David. 2001. *The Spiritual Franciscans: From Protest to Persecution in the Century after Saint Francis.* University Park: Pennsylvania State University Press.

Campbell, Ann. 1931. *The Black Death and Men of Learning.* New York: Columbia University Press.

Cardoner Planas, Antonio. 1962. "El 'hospital para judíos pobres' de Barcelona." *Sefarad* 22: 373–75.

———. 1949. "Seis mujeres hebreas practicando la medicina en el reino de Aragon." *Sefarad* 9: 441–45.

Cardoner Planas, Antonio, and Francisca Vendrell Gallostra. 1947. "Aportaciones al studio de la familia Abenardut, médicos reales." *Sefarad* 7: 303–48.

Carmichael, Ann G. 1998. "The Last Past Plague: The Uses of Memory in Renaissance Epidemics." *Journal of the History of Medicine and Allied Sciences* 53.2: 132–60.

———. 1991. "Contagion Theory and Contagion Practice in Fifteenth-Century Milan." *Renaissance Quarterly* 44: 213–56.

Carmoly, E. 1866. "Zikkaron leRishonim vegam le-Aḥronim." *HaKarmel* 6.11: 85.

Caslari, Crescas. 1853. *Sefer Iggeret haPurim.* Ed. Shlomo David. Salonika: Isaac Jehun.

Cassard, Jean-Christophe. 1978. "Vins et marchands de vins Gascons au début du XIVe siècle." *Annales du Midi* 90: 121–42.

Catlos, Brian. 2004. *The Victors and the Vanquished: Christians and Muslims of Catalonia and Aragon, 1050–1300.* Cambridge: Cambridge University Press.

Chabás, José. 1991. "The Astronomical Tables of Jacob ben David Bonjorn." *Archive for History of Exact Sciences* 42: 279–314.

———. 1988. "Une période de recurrence de syzygies au XIVe siècle: Le cycle de Jacob ben David Bonjorn." *Archives internationales d'histoire des sciences* 38.120–21: 242–51.

Chakrabarti, Dipesh. 2000. *Provincializing Europe: Postcolonial Thought and Historical Difference.* Princeton, N.J.: Princeton University Press.

Chase, Melissa P. 1985. "Fevers, Poisons, and Apostemes: Authority and Experience in Montpellier Plague Treatises." In Pamela O. Long, ed., *Science and Technology in Medieval Society.* New York: New York Academy of Sciences, 153–69.

Chejne, Anwar G. 1983. *Islam and the West: The Moriscos.* Albany: State University of New York Press.

Chetrit, Joseph. 1999. *Shirah vePiyyut beYahadut Morocco.* Jerusalem: Mossad Bialik; Ashkelon: HaMikhlalah haEzorit.

———. 1982. "Historical-Occasional Poems in Jewish Poetry from Morocco" (in Hebrew). In Issachar Ben-Ami, ed., *Moreshet Yehude Sefarad vehaMizrah.* International conference on Sephardi and Oriental Jewry. Jerusalem: Magnes and Hebrew University Press, 315–39.

Chevalier, Laurent. 1960. "Une source inédit du droit Savoyard: Les 'Antiqua Sabaudiae Statuta' d'Amédée VIII de 1402–1404." *Bulletin philologique et historique (jusqu'à 1610) du comité des travaux historiques et scientifiques* 1: 361–91.

Chism, Christine. 2002. *Alliterative Revivals*. Philadelphia: University of Pennsylvania Press.

Chouraqui, André. 1985. *Histoire des juifs en Afrique du Nord*. Paris: Hachette.

Cifuentes, Lluís. 2004. "Université et vernacularisation au bas moyen âge: Montpellier et les traductions catalanes médiévales de traités de médecine." In *Université de médecine de Montpellier et son rayonnement (XIIIe–XVe siècles): Actes du colloque international de Montpellier organisé par le Centre historique de recherches et d'études médiévales sur la méditerranée occidentale, Université Paul Valéry*. Turnhout: Brepols, 273–90.

———. 1999. "Vernacularization as an Intellectual and Social Bridge: The Catalan Translations of Teodorico's *Chirurgia* and of Arnau de Vilanova's *Regimen Sanitatis*." *Early Science and Medicine* 4: 127–48.

Cohen, Daniel. 1979. "An Autograph Letter of the Maharil on the Persecutions in the Savoy and on Collection of the *Bullengeld* in 1418" (in Hebrew). *Zion*, n.s., 44: 173–87.

Cohen, Esther. 1981. "Jewish Criminals in France during the Fourteenth Century" (in Hebrew). *Zion*, n.s., 46: 146–64.

Cohen, Jeremy. 1986. *The Friars and the Jews*. Ithaca, N.Y.: Cornell University Press.

Cohen, Messaoud-Prosper. 1940. *Contribution à l'histoire des médecins juifs en Avignon (XIIe–XVe siècles)*. Paris: Amédée LeGrand.

Colahan, Clark. 1979. "Santob's Debate: Parody and Political Allegory." *Sefarad* 29.1: 87–107, and 39.2: 265–308.

Colin, Georges S. 1936. "Un juif marocain du XIVe siècle: Constructeur d'astrolabe." *Hesperis* 22: 83–84.

Colorni, Vittore. 1972. "Shemuel (Simone) da Spira contra fra Giovanni da Capestrano." *La Rassegna Mensile di Israel* 38.7–8: 69–86.

Comba, Rinaldo. 1992. "Les *Decreta Sabaudiae* d'Amédée VIII: Un projet de société?" In B. Andenmatten and A. Paravicini Bagliani, eds., *Amédée VIII–Félix V.* Lausanne: Fondation Humbert II et Marie José de Savoie, Bibliothèque historique vaudoise, 179–90.

Conrad, Lawrence. 1992. "Epidemic Disease in Formal and Popular Thought in Early Islamic Society." In Terence Ranger and Paul Slack, eds., *Epidemics and Ideas: Essays on the Historical Perception of Pestilence*. Cambridge: Cambridge University Press, 77–100.

———. 1985. "The Social Structure of Medicine in Medieval Islam." *Society for the Social History of Medicine* 37: 11–15.

———. 1981. "Arabic Plague Chronologies and Treatises: Social and Historical Factors in the Formation of a Literary Genre." *Studia Islamica* 54: 51–93.

Coulet, Noël. 1990. "L'expulsion des juifs de France." *L'histoire* 139: 9–16.

Crémieu, Moses. 1830. *Ho'il Moshe Be'er*. Part 1, vol. 2 (*Al seder arba' parshiyot vetzom Esther*). Aix: Pontier fils ainé.

Crémieux, Adolphe. 1930, 1931. "Les juifs de Toulon au moyen âge et le massacre du 13 avril 1348." *REJ* 89: 33–72, and 90: 43–64.

Crémieux, Jules Salomon, and Mardochée Crémieux. 188–?. *Chants hébraïques suivant le rite des communautés Israélites de l'ancien Comtat Venaissin*. Aix-en-Provence.

Cribiore, Raffaella. 2001. *Gymnastics of the Mind: Greek Education in Hellenistic and Roman Egypt*. Princeton, N.J.: Princeton University Press.

———. 1996. *Writing, Teachers and Students in Graeco-Roman Egypt*. Atlanta: Scholars Press.

Crisciani, Chiara, and Michela Pereira. 1998. "Black Death and Golden Remedies: Some Remarks on Alchemy and the Plague." In Agostino Paravicini Bagliani and Francesco Santi, eds., *The Regulation of Evil: Social and Cultural Attitudes to Epidemics in the Late Middle Ages*. Florence: SISMEL, 7–39.

Cutler, Allan. 1970. "Innocent III and the Distinctive Clothing of Jews and Muslims." In John R. Sommerfeldt, ed., *Studies in Medieval Culture*. Vol. 3. Kalamazoo, Mich.: Medieval Institute, Western Michigan University, 92–116.

Dahan, Gilbert. 2004. *L'expulsion des juifs de France: 1394*. Paris: Cerf.

Daly, Lloyd. 1967. *Contributions to a History of Alphabetization in Antiquity and the Middle Ages*. Brussels: Latomus.

Darganta, José de, and Vicente Forcada. 1956. *Biografía y escritos de San Vicente Ferrer*. Madrid: Biblioteca de Autores Cristianos.

Davidson, Israel. 1918. "Frivolities of Hebrew Poetry" (in Hebrew). In Simon Ginzburg, ed., *Luaḥ Aḥi'ever*. New York: Histadrut Aḥi'ever, 90–109.

De la Volta, Samuel. 1836. "Notes." *Kerem Ḥemed* 2: 115–17.

Delisle, Léopold, ed. 1904. *Recueil des historiens des Gaules et de la France*. Paris: V. Palmé, vol. 21.

De Maulde, M. 1886. *Les juifs dans les états français du Saint Siège*. Paris: H. Champion.

Diago Hernando, Máximo. 2003. "La movilidad de los judíos a ambos lados de la frontera entra las coronas de Castilla y Aragón durante el siglo XV." *Sefarad* 63.2: 237–82.

Diaz Garcìa, Amador. 1978–79. "Un Tratado nazari sobre alimentos: *Al-Kalam 'alā-l-Agdiya* de al-Arbūlī. Edicion, traduccion y estudio, conglosarios (I)." Cuadernos de Estudios Medievales (Granada), vols. 6–7: 5–91.

Disegni, Dario. 1956. "Il rito di Asti-Fossano-Moncalvo (APAM)." *Sefer Zikkaron le-Shelomo S. Mayer*. Milan: Sally Mayer Foundation, 78–81.

Dols, Michael. 1987. "The Origins of the Islamic Hospital: Myth and Reality." *Bulletin of the History of Medicine* 62: 367–90.

———. 1982. "Al-Manbijī's 'Report on the Plague': A Treatise on the Plague of 764–65/1362–64 in the Middle East." In Daniel Williman, ed., *The Black Death:*

The Impact of the Fourteenth-Century Plague. Binghamton, N.Y.: Medieval and Renaissance Texts and Studies, 65–75.

———. 1974a. "The Comparative Communal Responses to the Black Death in Muslim and Christian Societies." *Viator* 5: 269–87.

———. 1974b. "Plague in Early Islamic History." *JAOS* 94.3: 371–83.

———. 1971. *The Black Death in the Middle East.* Princeton, N.J.: Princeton University Press.

Doniach, Nakdimon. 1932–33. "Abraham Bedersi's Purim Letter to David Kaslari." *JQR*, n.s., 23: 63–69.

Dorveaux, P., ed. 1896. *L'antidotaire Nicolai.* Paris: H. Welter.

Duara, Prasenjit. 1995. *Rescuing History from the Nation.* Chicago: University of Chicago Press.

Dubuis, Pierre. 1988. "Documents sur le clergé: Les fidèles et la vie religieuse dans le Valais occidental et les vallées d'Aoste et de Suse aux XIVe et SVe siècles." *Vallesia* 43: 163–204.

Dufour, A., and F. Rabut. 1875. "Louis de Nice: Juif converti, filleul et médecin du Duc Louis." In *Mémoires et documents publiés par la société savoisienne d'histoire et d'archéologie.* Chambéry: Albert Bottero, 15: 5–51.

Dukes, Leopold. 1851. "Gedichte über die בקשת הממין des Jedaiah Penini." *Der Orient* 12.21: 368–71.

Duran-Reynals, M. L., and C.-E. A. Winslow. 1949. "Regiment de preservaio a epidimia o pestilencia e mortaldats." *Bulletin of the History of Medicine* 23: 57–89.

———. 1948. "Jacme d'Agramont and the First of the Plague Tractates." *Bulletin of the History of Medicine* 22: 747–65.

Egan, Margarita. 1984. *The Vidas of the Troubadours.* New York: Garland.

Einbinder, Susan L. Forthcoming. "Recall from Exile: Literature, Memory and French Jews." *Jewish Studies Quarterly.*

———. 2007. "Yedaiah Bedersi's *Elef Alafin.*" In Jonathan Decter and Michael Rand, eds., *Studies in Arabic and Hebrew Letters in Honor of Raymond P. Scheindlin.* Piscataway, N.J.: Gorgias Press, 37–46.

———. 2005. "A Proper Diet: Medicine and History in Crescas Caslar's *Esther.*" *Speculum* 80.2: 437–63.

———. 2005. "On the Borders of Exile: The Poetry of Solomon Simḥah of Troyes." In T. Barolini, ed., *Medieval Constructions in Gender and Identity: Essays in Honor of Joan M. Ferrante.* Tempe: Arizona State University, 69–87.

———. 2004. "Hebrew Poems for the 'Day of Shutting In': Problems and Methods." *REJ* 163.1–2: 111–35.

———. 2002. *Beautiful Death: Jewish Poetry and Martyrdom from Medieval France.* Princeton, N.J.: Princeton University Press.

———. 1999. "The Troyes Elegies: Jewish Martyrology in Hebrew and Old French." *Viator* 30: 201–30.

———. 1994. "Pen and Scissors: A Medieval Debate." *Hebrew Union College Annual* 65: 261–76.

Emery, Richard W. 1991. "Jewish Physicians in Medieval Perpignan." *Michael* 12: 113–34.

———. 1980. "Les juifs en Conflent et en Vallespir (1250–1415)." In *Conflent, Vallespir et montagnes catalanes: Actes du LIe Congrès de la Fédération Historique du Langue-doc Méditerranéen et du Roussillon, organize à Prades et Villefranche-de-Conflent, les 10–11 juin 1978*. Montpellier, 85–91.

———. 1967. "The Black Death of 1348 in Perpignan." *Speculum* 42.4: 611–21.

———. 1941. *Heresy and Inquisition in Narbonne*. New York: Columbia University Press.

Epstein, Isidore. 1930. *The Responsa of Rabbi Simon b. Zemaḥ Duran as a Source of the History of the Jews in North Africa*. London: Oxford University Press.

Esposito, M. 1947. "Un auto-da-fé à Chièri en 1412." *Revue d'histoire ecclésiastique* 42: 422–32.

———. 1938. "Un process contre les juifs de la Savoie en 1329." *Revue d'histoire ecclésiastique* 34: 785–801.

Evans, Richard J. 1982. "Epidemics and Revolutions: Cholera in Nineteenth-Century Europe." In Daniel Williman, ed., *The Black Death: The Impact of the Fourteenth-Century Plague*. Binghamton, N.Y.: Medieval and Renaissance Texts and Studies, 149–74.

Fages, H. 1901. *Histoire de Saint Vincent Ferrier*. 2 vols. Louvain: A. Uystpruyst; Paris: Alphonse Picard.

Falaquera, Shem Tov. 1986. *Versos para la sana conducción del cuerpo: Traducción, edición critica y commentario par M. A. Vorela Morena*. Granada: Universidad de Granada and Universidad Pontifica de Salamanca.

Faraj, Abdalmalik. 1935. *Relations médicales hispano-maghrébines au XIIe siècle*. Paris: Éditions Véga.

Feldman, Louis. 1970. "A Responsum of Rabbenu Yoḥanan ben Rabbenu Mattatya Trèves in MS Oxford 875" (in Hebrew). *Sinai* 67: 18.

Fenster, Thelma, and D. L. Smail, eds. 2003. *Fama: The Politics of Talk and Reputation in Medieval Europe*. Ithaca, N.Y.: Cornell University Press.

Ferre, Lola. 1998–99. "Hebrew Translations from Medical Treatises of Montpellier." *Korot* 13: 21–36.

———. 1994. "Los regímenes dietéticos medievales en prosa y en verso: Entre la medicina y la literatura." *Espacio, Tiempo y Forma*, 3rd ser., 7: 327–40.

———. 1992. "Los regímenes de salud de Maimónides y Arnau de Vilanova en sus versiones hebreas." In Lola Ferre et al., *La ciencia en la España medieval*. Granada: Universidad de Granada, Instituto de Ciencias de la Educación, 117–24.

———. 1991. "La terminología médica en las versiones hebreas de textos latinos." *Miscelánea de Estudios Árabes y Hebraicos* 40.2: 87–101.

Ferrer i Mallol, Maria Teresa. 1987. *Els sarraïns de la corona Catalano-Aragonesa en el segle XIV*. Barcelona: Conseil Superior d'Investigacions Científiques.

Fine, Rashi. 1861. "By Yedaiah haPenini" (in Hebrew). *HaKarmel* 1: 337.

Finucane, Ronald C. 1977. *Miracles and Pilgrims: Popular Beliefs in Medieval England.* London: J. M. Dent.

Fleischer, Ezra. 1984. *HaYotzrot.* Jerusalem: Magnes.

———. 1975. *Shirat HaQodesh ha'Ivrit biyeme haBeinayim.* Jerusalem: Keter.

Fleck, Cathleen. 2006. "The Cultural Politics of the Papal Library at Avignon: The Meaning and Movement of the Bible of Antipope Clement VII." In Jacqueline Hamesse, ed., *La vie culturelle, intellectuelle et scientifique à la cour des papes d'Avignon.* Turnhout: Fédération Internationale des Instituts d'Études Médiévales and Brepols, 65–87.

Fleming, John. 1981. "The Centuple Structure of the *Pearl.*" In Bernard Levy and Paul Szarmach, eds., *The Alliterative Tradition in the Fourteenth Century.* Kent, Ohio: Kent State University Press, 81–98.

Foa, Anna. 2000. *The Jews of Europe after the Black Death.* Trans. Andrea Grover. Berkeley: University of California Press.

Foa, Salvatore. 1953. "Ebrei medici in Piemonte nei secoli XVI e XVII." *Rassegna mensile di Israel* 19: 542–51.

Fontaine, Resianne. 2000. "Judah ben Solomon ha-Cohen's Midrash ha-Hokhmah: Its Sources and Use of Sources." In Steven Harvey, ed., *The Medieval Hebrew Encyclopedias of Science and Philosophy.* Dordrecht: Kluwer Academic Publishers, 191–211.

Francés, Antoni Ferrando. 1997. "Vicent Ferrer (1350–1419): Predicador políglota de l'Europa occidental." *Paradigmes de la Història, I: Actes del Congrès "San Vicent Ferrer i el seu temps,"* Valencia, May 13–16, 1996. Valencia: Editorial SAÓ, 71–95.

Friedberg, Haim. 1956. *Toldot haDefus ha'Ivri be'Italia, Aspamia, Portugalia ve-Tugremah.* Tel Aviv: Bar-Yuda.

Frojmovic, Eva. 2002. "Messianic Politics in Re-Christianized Spain: Images of the Sanctuary in Hebrew Bible Manuscripts." In Eva Frojmovic, ed., *Imagining the Self, Imagining the Other: Visual Representation and Jewish-Christian Dynamics in the Middle Ages and Early Modern Period.* Leiden: Brill, 91–128.

Gabotto, Ferdinando. 1917, 1918. "Per una storia degli Israeliti in Piemonte nel medio evo." *Il vessillo israelitico* 65.19–20: 433–37, and 66.15–16: 288–92.

Galinsky, Judah. 2005. "Jewish Charitable Bequests and the Hekdesh Trust in Thirteenth-Century Spain." *Journal of Interdisciplinary History* 35.3: 423–40.

García Ballester, Luis. 2001. *La búsqueda de la salud: Sanadores y enfermos en la España medievale.* Barcelona: Ediciones Peninsula.

———. 1994. "A Marginal Learned World: Jewish, Muslim, and Christian Medical Practitioners and the Use of Arabic Medical Sources in Late Medieval Spain." In Jon Arrizabalaga, Luis García Ballester, Roger French, and Andrew Cunningham, eds., *Practical Medicine from Salerno to the Black Death.* Cambridge: Cambridge University Press, 353–95.

———. 1992. "Changes in the *Regimina Santitatis*: The Role of Jewish Practitioners." In Sheila Campbell et al., *Health, Disease and Healing in Medieval Culture.* New York: St. Martin's Press, 119–31.

García Ballester, Luis, Lola Ferre, and Eduard Feliu. 1990. "Jewish Appreciation of Fourteenth-Century Scholastic Medicine." *Osiris*, 2nd ser., 6: 85–117.

Garel, Michel. 1991. *D'une main forte: Manuscrits hébreux des collections françaises.* Paris: Seuil/Bibliothèque Nationale.

———. 1975. "The Rediscovery of the Wolf Haggadah." *Journal of Jewish Art* 2.2: 22–26.

Garganta, Fr. José M. de, and Vicente Forcada. 1956. *Biografía y escritos de San Vicente Ferrer.* Madrid: Biblioteca de autores cristianos.

Garivini, Fausta. 1972 repr. of 1904 ed. "Je suis Gascon, et si . . ." In Joseph Michelet, ed., *Poètes gascons du Gers depuis le XVIe siècle à nos jours.* Repr. Geneva: Th. Bouquet, 141–51.

Gavison, Abraham. 1972 repr. of 1748 ed. *'Omer HaShikhehah.* Repr. (of Livorno). Paris: A. Meldola.

Geary, Patrick. 2002. "Oblivion: Between Orality and Textuality in the Tenth Century." In Gerd Althoff, Johannes Fried, and Patrick Geary, eds., *Medieval Concepts of the Past: Ritual, Memory, Historiography.* Washington, D.C.: German Historical Institute; Cambridge: Cambridge University Press, 111–22.

Gerson, M. 1884. "Notes sur les juifs des états de la Savoie." *REJ* 8: 235–42.

Ghéon, Henri. 1939. *Saint Vincent Ferrier.* Paris: E. Flammarion.

Ginzburg, David. 1884. *"Be'er Lehi:* The Plague Tractate of R. Isaac b. Todros." In *Tiferet Seivah: Articles in Honor of Yom Tov Lippman Zunz on His Ninetieth Birthday* (in Hebrew). Berlin, 91–124.

Glick, Thomas. 2002. "Tribal Landscapes of Islamic Spain: History and Archeology." In John Howe and Michael Wolfe, eds., *Inventing Medieval Landscape: Senses of Place in Western Europe.* Gainesville: University Press of Florida, 113–36.

———. 1979. *Islamic and Christian Spain in the Early Middle Ages.* Princeton, N.J.: Princeton University Press.

Goldschmidt, Daniel. 1979. "A Forgotten Anthology and Remnants from the APAM Festival Liturgy" (in Hebrew). In Daniel Goldschmidt, ed., *Mehqere Tefillah uFiyyut.* Jerusalem: Magnes, 80–121.

———, ed. 1970. *Mahzor leYamim haNora'im (lefi minhage bene-Ashkenaz).* Vol. 1. Jerusalem: Koren.

Goldstein, Bernard. 1992. "Levi ben Gerson's Contributions to Astronomy." In Gad Freudenthal, ed., *Studies on Gersonides.* Leiden: Brill, 3–20.

———. 1985. "The Role of Science in the Jewish Community in Fourteenth-Century France." In Bernard Goldstein, ed., *Theory and Observation in Ancient and Medieval Astronomy.* London: Variorum, chapter 20.

———. 1981. "The Hebrew Astronomical Tradition: New Sources." *Isis* 72: 237–51.

———. 1974. *The Astronomical Tables of Levi ben Gerson.* Hamden, Conn.: Archon.

Goldstein, Bernard, ed. 1967. *Ibn al-Muthannā's Commentary on the Astronomical Tables of al-Khwārizmī: Two Hebrew Versions.* New Haven, Conn.: Yale University Press.

Goldstein, Bernard, and José Chabás. 2000. *Astronomy in the Iberian Peninsula: Abraham Zacut and the Transition from Manuscript to Print*. Philadelphia: American Philosophical Society.

Goodman, Lenn E., ed. 1992. *Neoplatonism and Jewish Thought*. Albany: State University of New York Press.

Gottschall, Dagmar. 2006. "Conrad of Megenberg and the Causes of the Plague: A Latin Treatise on the Black Death Composed ca. 1350 for the Papal Court in Avignon." In Jacqueline Hamesse, ed., *La vie culturelle, intellectuelle et scientifique à la cour des papes d'Avignon*. Turnhout: Brepols, 319–32.

Granara, William. 2002. "*Extensio Animae*: The Artful Ways of Remembering 'Al-Andalus.' " *Journal of Social Affairs* 19.75: 45–72.

Green, Joseph. 1976. "The Trabot Family" (in Hebrew). *Sinai* 79: 147–63.

Greenblatt, Stephen, ed., with Catherine Gallagher. 2000. *Practicing New Historicism*. Chicago: University of Chicago Press.

Grieco, Allen. 1996. "La dietética nel medio evo." In Giampiero Nigro, ed., *Et coquatur ponendo*. Prato: Francesco Datini Institute, 43–55.

———. 1989. "Savoir de poésie ou savoir de botaniste?: Les fruits dans la poésie italienne du XVe siècle." *Médiévales* 16–17: 131–46.

Gross, Henri. 1897. *Gallia Judaica*. Paris: Léopold Cerf.

———. 1882. "Zur Geschichte der Juden in Artes." *MGWJ* 31: 510–23.

Gruss, Noé. 1966. "L'imprimerie hébraïque en France (XVIe–XIXe siècles)." *REJ* 125: 77–91.

Guerchberg, Séraphine. 1948. "La controverse sur les prétendus semeurs de la 'peste noire' d'après les traités de peste de l'époque." *REJ* 108: 3–40.

Habermann, Abraham. 1935–36. "The Hebrew Printer Abraham Conat and His Letter Types" (in Hebrew). *'Alim* 2: 81–88.

Haddey, J. M. 1871. *Le livre d'or des israélites algériens*. Algiers: A. Bouyer.

Halkin, Abraham S. 1967. "Yedaiah Bedersi's 'Apology.' " In Alexander Altmann, ed., *Jewish Medieval and Renaissance Studies*. Cambridge, Mass.: Harvard University Press, 165–85.

———. 1966. "Why Was Levi ben Hayyim Hounded?" *PAAJR* 34: 65–76.

Harkavy, Tzvi. 1959. "Abraham = Eliyahu Harkavy." In Samuel Mirsky, ed., *Ishim uDemuyot beHokhmat Yisrael beEuropa haMizrahit*. New York: Ogen, 116–37.

Hassan, Jacob. 1978. "Una *Copla* de Purim: La endecha burlesca." *Estudios sefardies* 1: 411–16.

Haverkamp, Alfred, and Gerd Mentgen, eds. *Judenvertreibungen in Mittelalter und früher Neuzeit*. Hannover: Hahn, 119–33.

Hazan, Ephraim. 2000. "*Tehinot* haRashbatz for Mondays and Thursdays" (in Hebrew). *Masoret haPiyyut* 2: 111–17.

———. 1995. *HaShirah ha'Ivrit biTzefon Afriqa*. Jerusalem: Magnes.

———. 1987. "The Scriptural Lection in Liturgical and Secular Poetry" (in Hebrew). In Hazan, ed., *Mehqere Misgav Yerushalayim veSifruiyot 'Am Yisrael* (International

Congress on Sephardi and Oriental Jewry). Jerusalem: Institute for Research in the Heritage of Spanish and Oriental Jewry.

————. 1980. *Shiru Lo Zamru Lo: Piyyutim haMusharim befi Yehude Tzefon Afriqa.* Jerusalem: Ministry of Education and Culture, Religious Education branch; and Center for Integrating the Heritage of Oriental Jews.

————. 1979. *Piyyutim veQit'e Tefillah min haSiddur.* HaSifriyah laMoreh haDati. Jerusalem: Ministry of Education and Culture, 33–37.

Henderson, John. 1992. "The Black Death in Florence: Medical and Communal Responses." In Steven Bassett, ed., *Death in Towns: Urban Responses to the Dying and the Dead, 100–1600.* Leicester: Leicester University Press, 136–50.

————. 1989. "Epidemics in Renaissance Florence: Medical Theory and Government Response." In Neithard Bulst and Robert Delort, eds., *Maladies et société (XIIe–XVIIe siècles): Actes du colloque de Bielefeld.* November 1986. Paris: Centre National de la Recherche Scientifique, 165–86.

Herlihy, David. 1996. "Family." In Samuel Cohn, Jr., and Steven A. Epstein, eds., *Portraits of Medieval and Renaissance Living: Essays in Honor of David Herlihy.* Ann Arbor: University of Michigan Press, 7–28. A revised version of the piece by the same title is in *AHR* 96 (1991): 1–16.

————. 1978. "Medieval Children." In Bede Karl Lackner and Kenneth Roy Philip, eds., *Essays on Medieval Civilization.* Austin: University of Texas Press, 109–41.

Hirsch, Marianne. 2001. "Surviving Images: Holocaust Photographs in Work of Post-memory." *Yale Journal of Criticism* 14.1: 5–37.

Hirschberg, Haim Zeev. 1974–81. *A History of the Jews in North Africa.* Leiden: Brill.

Hodel, Bernard. 1993. "Sermons de Saint Vincent Ferrier à Estavayer-le-lac en mars 1404." *Mémoire dominicaine* 2: 149–93.

Hofer, Johannes. 1936. *Johannes von Capestrano: Ein Leben im Kampf un die Reform der Kirche.* Innsbruck: Tyrolia.

Horowitz, Elliott. 1995. "The Jews of Europe and the Moment of Death in Medieval and Modern Times." *Judaism* 44: 271–81.

————. 1994. "The Rite to Be Reckless: On the Perpetration and Interpretation of Purim Violence." *Poetics Today* 15: 9–54.

Howe, Nicholas. 2002. "The Landscape of Anglo-Saxon England: Inherited, Invented, Imagined." In John Howe and Michael Wolfe, eds., *Inventing Medieval Landscape: Senses of Place in Western Europe.* Gainesville: University Press of Florida, 91–112.

Hue, Dennis. 2002. *La poésie palinodique à Rouen.* Paris: Champion.

Hyams, Paul. 2003. *Rancor and Reconciliation.* Ithaca, N.Y.: Cornell University Press.

Iancu, Danièle. 2003. "Les parentés juives comtadines de quelques néophytes aixois (1490–1525). In G. Audisio et al., eds., *Identités juives et chrétiennes: France méridionale XIVe–XIXe siècle.* Aix-en-Provence: Publications de l'Université de Provence, 72–85.

————. 2001. *Juifs et néophytes en Provence (1469–1525).* Paris and Leuven: Peeters.

————. 1999. "Les juifs exilés de Provence (1486–1525)." In Friedhelm Burgard,

A. Haverkamp, and Gerd Mentgen, eds., *Judenvertreibungen in Mittelalter und früher Neuzeit.* Hannover: Hahnsche, 119–33.

———. 1988. "Médecins juifs et néophytes en Provence (1460–1525)." *Vesalius: Acta Internationalia Historiae Medicinae* 4 (special number): 28–36.

———. 1983. "Astronomie et astronomes juifs dans le midi de la France au moyen âge." In *Sénéfiance no. 13: Le soleil, la lune, et les étoiles au moyen âge.* Aix-en-Provence: Université de Provence; Marseille: Laffitte, 197–213.

———. 1981. "La communauté juive aixoise à l'extrême fin du XVe siècle: Dissensions internes et clivage social." Proceedings of the Seventh World Congress of Jewish Studies. Jerusalem: World Congress of Jewish Studies, 9–27.

———. 1976. "Préoccupations intellectuelles des médecins juifs au moyen âge: Inventaires de bibliothèques." *Provence historique* 26: 21–44.

———. 1975. "L'inventaire de la bibliothèque et du mobilier d'un médecin juif d'Aix-en-Provence au milieu du XVe siècle." *REJ* 134.1–2: 47–80.

Ibn Ezra, Abraham. 1939. *The Beginning of Wisdom (Reshit Ḥokhmah),* ed. Raphael Levy and Francisco Cantera. Baltimore: Johns Hopkins University Press.

Isaac ben Todros. 1884. *Be'er Lehi: A Plague Tractate,* ed. David Ginzburg. In *Tiferet Seivah: Jubelschrift zum neunzigsten Geburstag des L. [= Yom Tov Lipman] Zunz.* Berlin: Louis Gerschel, 91–126.

Jacme d'Agramont. 1998. *Regiment de preservació de pestilència (Lleida, 1348).* Intro. Jon Arrizabalaga, Luis García Ballester, and Joan Veny, ed. Joan Veny. Barcelona: Enciclopèdia Catalana.

Jacquart, Danielle. 1998. *La médecine médiévale dans le cadre parisien.* Paris: Fayard.

———. 1995. "Les régimes de santé au XIIIe siècle." In P. Guichard and D. Alexandre-Bidon, eds., *Comprendre le XIIIe siècle: Études offertes à Marie-Thérèse Lorcin.* Lyon: Presses Universitaires de Lyon, 201–14.

———. 1990. "Theory, Everyday Practice, and Three Fifteenth-Century Physicians." *Osiris,* 2nd ser., 6: 140–60.

———. 1980. "Le regard d'un médecin sur son temps: Jacques Despars (1380?–1458)." *Bibliothèque de l'École des Chartres* 138: 35–86.

James, Margery Kirkbride. 1971. "The Fluctuations of the Anglo-Gascon Wine Trade during the Fourteenth Century." In *Studies in the Medieval Wine Trade.* Oxford: Clarendon, 1–38.

Jochnowitz, George. 1981. ". . .Who Made Me a Woman." *Commentary* 71.4: 63–64.

———. 1978. "Shuadit: La langue juive de Provence." *AJ* 14.1: 63–67.

Jones, Colin. 1983. "Plague and Its Metaphors in Early Modern France." *Representations* 53: 97–127.

Jordan, William C. Forthcoming. "Administering Expulsion in 1306." *Jewish Studies Quarterly.*

———. 2001a. *Europe in the High Middle Ages.* London and New York: Penguin.

———. 2001b. "The Struggle for Influence at the Court of Philip III: Pierre de la Broce and the French Aristocracy." *French Historical Studies* 24.3: 439–68.

———. 1998. "Home Again: The Jews in the Kingdom of France, 1315–1322." In F. R. P. Akehurst and Stephanie Cain van D'Elden, eds., *The Stranger in Medieval Society*. Medieval Cultures, vol. 12. Minneapolis: University of Minnesota Press.

———. 1996. *The Great Famine*. Princeton, N.J.: Princeton University Press.

———. 1989. *The French Monarchy and the Jews*. Philadelphia: University of Pennsylvania Press.

Juan de Aviñón. 2000. *Sevillana medicina*. Intro. and ed. José Mondéjar. Madrid: Arco.

Justice, Steven. 1994. *Writing and Rebellion: England in 1381*. Berkeley: University of California Press.

Kahane, Abraham. 1896. "R. Abraham HaBedersi and the Nature of His Books" (in Hebrew). *'Otzar haSifrut* 5: 219–21.

Kahn, Leon. 1889. *Les juifs à Paris depuis le VIe siècle*. L'histoire de la communauté israélite de Paris, vol. 5, 1884–94. Paris: M. Lipschutz.

Kaminka, Aaron. 1926. "Poetry and Belle Lettres of R. Solomon b. Reuven Bonafed" (in Hebrew). *HaTzofeh LeHokhmat Yisrael = HaTzofeh meEretz Hagar* 10: 288–95; and 1928, 12: 33–42.

Kanarfogel, Ephraim. 2000. *Peering through the Lattices: Mystical, Magical, and Pietistic Dimensions in the Tosafist Period*. Detroit: Wayne State University Press.

———. 1993. *Jewish Education and Society in the High Middle Ages*. Detroit: Wayne State University Press.

Kaufmann, David. 1895. "Le 'grand-deuil' de Jacob b. Salomon Sarfati d'Avignon." *REJ* 30: 52–64.

———. 1893. "Tranquillo Vita Corcos: Bienfaiteur de la communauté de Carpentras." *REJ* 26: 268–73.

———. 1892. "Une haggada de la France septentrionale ayant appartenu à Jacob ben Salomon." *REJ* 25: 65–77.

Kellner, Menahem. 2001. *Perush leShir haShirim leRabbi Levi ben Gershon*. Ramat-Gan: Bar-Ilan University.

Kelley, Henry Ansgar. 2006. " 'The Prioress's Tale' in Context: Good and Bad Reports of Non-Christians in Fourteenth-Century England." In Philip Soergel, ed., *Nation, Ethnicity and Identity in Medieval and Renaissance Europe*. Studies in Medieval and Renaissance History, 3rd ser., vol. 3. Tempe, Ariz.: AMS, 71–131.

Kennedy, E. S. 1966. "Late Medieval Planetary Theory." *Isis* 57.3: 365–78.

Kerval, Leon de. 1887. *Saint Jean de Capistran: Son siècle et son influence*. Bordeaux and Paris: Les Soeurs Franciscaines and Chez Haton.

Khaneboubi, Ahmed. 1987. *Les premiers sultans mérinides 1269–1331: Histoire politique et sociale*. Paris: Éditions l'Harmattan.

Kogman-Appel, Katrin. 2006. *Illuminated Sephardic Haggadot*. Cambridge: Cambridge University Press.

Kohn, Roger. 2004. "Les juifs en France du nord dans la seconde moitié du XIVe siècle: Un état de la question." In Gilbert Dahan, ed., *L'expulsion des juifs de France: 1394*. Paris: Cerf, 13–29.

———. 1988. *Les juifs de la France du nord dans la seconde moitié du XIVe siècle*. Leuven and Paris: E. Peeters.

Labarge, Margaret Wade. 1980. *Gascony: England's First Colony 1204–1453*. London: Hamish Hamilton.

Ladurie, Emmanuel le Roy. 1971. *Times of Feast, Times of Famine: A History of Climate Since the Year 1000*. Garden City, N.Y.: Doubleday.

Lamb, Herbert H. 1988. *Weather, Climate and Human Affairs*. London and New York: Routledge.

Landouzy, Louis, and Roger Pepin. 1911. *Le régime du corps de maître Aldebrandin de Sienne*. Paris: H. Champion.

Langermann, Tzvi. 2000. "Some Remarks on Judah ben Solomon ha-Cohen and His Encyclopedia, *Midrash haHokhmah*." In Steven Harvey, ed., *The Medieval Hebrew Encyclopedias of Science and Philosophy*. Dordrecht: Kluwer Academic Publishers, 371–90.

Larenaudie, M. J. 1952. "Les famines en Languedoc aux XIVe et XVe siècles." *Annales du Midi* 64.1: 27–40.

Latham, J. D. (John Derek). 1986. "Contribution à l'étude des immigrations Andalouses et leur place dans l'histoire de la Tunisie." In J. D. Latham, ed., *From Muslim Spain to Barbary*. London: Variorum, essay 5: 21–63; originally published as "Towards a Study of Andalusian Immigrations and Their Place in Tunisian History," *Les Cahiers de Tunisie* 5 (1957): 203–52.

———. 1986. "Towns and Cities of Barbary: The Andalusian Influence." In J. D. Latham, ed., *From Muslim Spain to Barbary*. London: Variorum, essay 6, 188–204.

Lattes, M. 1882. "Documents et notices sur l'histoire politique et littéraire des juifs en Italie." *REJ* 5: 223–37.

Laurioux, Bruno. 2006. "Cuisine et médecins au moyen âge: Allies ou ennemies?" In Bruno Laurioux, ed., *Cuisine et médecine au moyen âge*. Special issue of the *Cahiers Recherches Médiévales in memory of Emmanuèle Baumgartner* no. 13 (Paris): 223–39.

———. 1993. "La cuisine des médecins à la fin du moyen âge." In *Maladies, Médecines et Sociétés* (Paris: L'Harmattan), 2: 136–48.

LaVoie, Rodrigue. 1987. "La délinquance sexuelle à Manosque (1240–1430): Schéma général et singularités juives." *Provence historique* 37: 571–87.

Lawless, Richard, and Gerald Blake. 1976. *Tlemcen: Continuity and Change in an Algerian Islamic Town*. London and New York: Bowker.

Lazar, Moshe. 1963. "Lis obros: Chansons hébraïco-provençales." *Romania et Occidentalia: Études dédiées à la mémoire de Hiram Peri (Pflaum)*. Jerusalem: Magnes.

Lebegue, R. 1958. "Rabelais et les grands rhétoriqueurs." *Lettres romanes* 12: 5–18.

Leibowitz, O. 1968. "A. Cashlari's (14th Century) Hebrew Manuscript of His Acolytes 'Pestilential Fevers' Edited by H. Pinkhoff." *Korot* 4.8–10: 517–21.

Leiser, Gary. 1983. "Medical Education in Islamic Lands from the Seventh to the Fourteenth Century." *Journal of the History of Medicine and Allied Sciences* 38: 48–75.

Lerner, Robert E. 1982. "The Black Death and Western European Eschatological Mental-
ities." In Daniel Williman, ed., *The Black Death: The Impact of the Fourteenth-Century Plague.* Binghamton, N.Y.: Medieval and Renaissance Texts and Studies, 77–105.

Leroy, Béatrice. 1998. *Les édits d'expulsion des juifs.* Biarritz: Atlantica.

———. 1984. "Entre deux mondes politiques: Les juifs du Royaume de Navarre." *AJ*
20: 35–39.

Levi Della Vida, Giorgio Levi. 1939. *Richerche sulla formazione del più antico fondo dei
manoscritti orientali della Biblioteca Vaticana.* Vatican City: Biblioteca apostolica
vaticana.

Loeb, Isidore. 1887. "Les expulsions des juifs de France au XIVe siècle." In *Jubelschrift
zum siebzigsten Geburtstag des Prof. Dr. H. Graetz.* Breslau: S. Schottlaender, 39–57.

———. 1886. "Les juifs de Carpentras sous le government pontifical." *REJ* 12: 34–64
and 161–235.

———. 1884. "Un épisode de l'histoire des juifs de Savoie." *REJ* 10: 32–59.

López-Baralt, Luce. 1987 (winter). "La angustia secreta del exilio: El testimonio de un
morisco de Tunez." *Hispanic Review* 55.1: 41–57.

Lourido Díaz, Ramón. 1963–64. "San Juan de Capistrano y su pretendido Antisemitismo." *Miscelánea de Estudios Arabes y Hebraicos* 12–13: 99–129.

Lucas, H. S. 1930. "The Great European Famine of 1315, 1316, and 1317." *Speculum* 5.4:
343–78.

Lunel, Armand. 1964 (November). "Quelques aspects du parler Judeo-Comtadin."
L'arche 94: 43–45.

———. November 14, 1958. "Lost Jewish Music of Provence." *Reconstructionist* 224.14:
25–28.

———. 1925. "Pourim dans les lettres comtadines." *La Revue Juive* 1.3: 316–30.

MacKinney, L. C. 1928. "Medieval Medical Dictionaries and Glossaries." In *Medieval
and Historiographical Essays in Honor of James Westfall Thompson.* Chicago: University of Chicago Press, 240–68.

Maimonides, Moses. 1990. *Moses Maimonides' Three Treatises on Health*, trans. and an-
not. Fred Rosner. Haifa: Maimonides Research Institute.

———. 1963. *Hanhagat ha-Beri'ut, be-Tirgumo shel Moshe Ibn-Tibbon.* Ed. Zisman
Muntner. Jerusalem: Mossad Harav Kook.

Malvezin, Théophile. 1875. *Histoire des juifs à Bordeaux.* Bordeaux: Ch. Lefebvre.

Mancha, José Luis. 1998. "The Provençal Version of Levi ben Gerson's Tables for
Eclipses." *Archives internationales d'histoire des sciences* 48: 269–352.

Manselli, R. 1959. "Arnaldo da Villanova e i papi del suo temp: Tra religione e politica."
Studi Romani 7.2: 146–62.

Margolin, Claude. 1981. "Bonet de Lattes, médecin, astrologue et astonome du pape."
In G. T. Tarugi, ed., *L'umanesimo e l'ecumenismo della cultura—Atti del XIVe Convegno internazionale del Centro di Studi Umanistici.* Florence: L. S. Olschki, 107–48.

Marilier, Jean. 1957. "Les établissements juifs à Dijon au début du XIVe siècle." *Mémoires de la Commission des antiquités du département de la Côte d'Or* 24: 171–78.

Maurin, Mario. 1959. "La poétique de Chastellain et la "Grande Rhétorique." *PMLA* 74.4: 482–84.

Marx, Alexander. 1928. "The Darmstadt Haggadah with Notes on Illuminated Haggadah MSS." *JQR*, n.s., 19: 1–16.

Mayer, L. A. (Leo Ary). 1952. *Mamluk Costume: A Survey.* Geneva: A. Kundig.

McMichael, Steven J., and Susan E. Myers, eds. 2004. *Friars and Jews in the Middle Ages and Renaissance.* Leiden: Brill.

McNeil, David. 1998. "Plague and Social Attitudes in Renaissance Florence." In Agostino Paravicini Bagliani and Francesco Santi, eds., *The Regulation of Evil: Social and Cultural Attitudes to Epidemics in the Late Middle Ages.* Florence: Sismel, 137–44.

McVaugh, Michael. 1998. "Treatment of Hernia in the Later Middle Ages: Surgical Correction and Social Construction." In Roger French et al., eds., *Medicine from the Black Death to the French Disease.* Aldershot: Ashgate, 131–55.

———. 1994. "Royal Surgeons and the Value of Medical Learning: The Crown of Aragon, 1300–1350." In Jon Arrizabalaga, Andrew Cunningham, Roger French, and Luis García Ballester, eds., *Practical Medicine from Salerno to the Black Death.* Cambridge: Cambridge University Press, 211–36.

———. 1993. *Medicine before the Plague: Practitioners and Their Patients in the Crown of Aragon, 1285–1345.* Cambridge: Cambridge University Press.

———. 1992. "Arnald of Villanova's *Regimen Almarie (Regimen Castra Sequentium)* and Medieval Military Medicine." *Viator* 23: 201–13.

McVaugh, Michael, and Luis García Ballester. 1990. "Jewish Appreciation of Fourteenth-Century Scholastic Medicine." *Osiris*, 2nd ser., 6: 85–118.

———. 1989. "The Medical Faculty at Early Fourteenth-Century Lerida." *History of Universities* 8: 1–25.

McVaugh, Michael, and Lola Ferre, eds. 2000. *The Tabula Antidotarii of Armengaud Blaise and Its Hebrew Translation.* Philadelphia: American Philosophical Society.

Meir bar Simon haMe'ili (of Narbonne). 1964. *Sefer haMe'orot.* Ed. Moses Yehuda Cohen Blau. New York, n.p.

Menache, Sophia. 1987. "The King, the Church and the Jews: Some Considerations on the Expulsions from England and France." *Journal of Medieval History* 13.3: 223–36.

———. 1985. "Faith, Myth and Politics: The Stereotype of the Jews and Their Expulsion from England and France." *JQR* 75.4: 351–74.

Mentgen, Gerd. 1995. *Studien zur Geschichte der Juden im mittelalterlichen Elsass.* Hannover: Hahnsche.

Merhavia, H. 1969–70. "A Spanish-Latin Manuscript on the Struggle over the Talmud in the Early Fifteenth Century" (in Hebrew). *Qiryat Sefer* 45.2: 271–87, and 45.4: 590–609.

Metzger, Mendel. 1976. "Un maḥzor italien enluminé du XVe siècle." In *Mitteilungen des Kunsthistorischen Institutes in Florenz* 20: 158–96.

Meyerson, Mark. 2004a. *A Jewish Renaissance in Fifteenth-Century Spain.* Princeton, N.J.: Princeton University Press.

———. 2004b. "Samuel of Granada and the Dominican Inquisitor: Jewish Magic and Jewish Heresy in Post-1391 Valencia." In Steven J. McMichael and Susan E. Myers, eds., *Friars and Jews in the Middle Ages and Renaissance*. Leiden: Brill, 161–89.

Miret y Sans, Ioachim. 1909. "Médecins juifs de Pierre, roi d'Aragon." *REJ* 57: 268–78.

Mirsky, Aaron. 1990. *HaPiyyut*. Jerusalem: Magnes.

Moraly, Isaac. 1896–97."*Tzafenat Fa'aneakh*: Remnants of the Poetry of the Ribish and the Rashbatz" (in Hebrew). *Qovetz 'al Yad* 7: 5–47.

Morerod, Jean-Daniel. 1995. "La maison de Savoie et les juifs en Suisse Romande à la fin du moyen âge." *Equinoxe* 13: 65–79.

Moulinas, René. 1970–71. "Documents sur des livres en Hebreu imprimés à Avignon ou à l'usage des juifs d'Avignon et du Comtat au XVIIIe siècle." *Archives juives* 7.2: 23–25.

Mousnier, Mireille. 1997. *La Gascogne toulousaine aux XIIe–XIIIe siècles*. Toulouse: Presses Universitaires du Mirail.

Mundill, Robin. 1990. *England's Jewish Solution: Experiment and Expulsion 1262–90*. Cambridge: Cambridge University Press.

Mussons, Ana. 1993. "Estudio del *Recull de Exemples y Miracles per Alfabeto*." *Literatura Medieval* 2: 105–9.

Mutgé Vives, Josefa. 1992. *L'aljama sarraïna de Lleida a l'edat mitjana: Aproximació a la seva història*. Barcelona: Conseil Superior d'Investigacions Cientifiques, Institució Milà i Fontanals.

Myers, David. 1995. *Reinventing the Jewish Past: European Jewish Intellectuals and the Zionist Return to History*. New York: Oxford University Press.

Nahon, Gérard. 1966. "Les juifs dans les domains d'Alfonse de Poitiers, 1241–71." *REJ* 125: 167–211.

Nehama, Joseph. 1978. *Histoire des israélites de Salonique*. Vol. 6. London: Communauté Israélite de Thessalonique.

Neubauer, Adolphe, and P. Meyer. 1892. "Le roman provençal d'Esther par Crescas du Caylar." *Romania* 21: 3–36 (= 194–227).

Neubauer, Adolphe. 1885. "Documents inédits: Documents sur Avignon." *REJ* 10: 79–97.

Niquille, Jeanne. 1927. "Les prêteurs juifs de Morat." *Nouvelles Etrennes Fribourgeoises* 60: 89–101.

Nirenberg, David. 1996. *Communities of Violence: The Persecution of Minorities in the Middle Ages*. Princeton, N.J.: Princeton University Press.

Nordmann, Achille. 1925. "Histoire des juifs à Genève de 1281–1780." *REJ* 80: 1–41.

Ocker, Christopher. 2004. "Contempt for Friars and Contempt for Jews in Late Medieval Germany." In Stephen McMichael and Susan E. Myers, eds., *Friars and Jews in the Middle Ages and Renaissance*. Leiden: Brill, 110–46.

Oliel, Jacob. 1994. *Les juifs au Sahara: Le touat au moyen âge*. Paris: CNRS.

Otis, Leah. 1985. "Prostitution and Repentance in Late Medieval Perpignan." In Julius Kirshner and S. Wemple, eds., *Women of the Medieval World: Essays in Honor of John H. Mundy*. London: Basil Blackwell, 137–60.

Pagis, Dan. 1993. "The Invention of the Hebrew Iamb and Contributions to Hebrew Metrics in Italy" (in Hebrew). In D. Pagis, *HaShir Dibbur 'al Ofnav*, ed. Ezra Fleischer. Jerusalem: Magnes, 166–256.

———. 1968. "Laments for the Persecutions of 1391 in Spain" (in Hebrew). *Tarbiz* 37: 355–73.

Palmer, Richard. 1982. "The Church, Leprosy and Plague in Medieval and Early Modern Europe." In W. J. Sheils, ed., *The Church and Healing*. Oxford: Basil Blackwell, 79–99.

Pansier, P. 1925. "Le Roman d'Esther." *Annales d'Avignon et du Comtat Venaissin* 11: 5–18.

———. 1910 (July). "Les médecins juifs à Avignon aux XIIIe, XIVe et XVe siècles." *Janus* 15: 421–51.

Passerat, Georges. 1979. "Les juifs en Tarn-et-Garonne au moyen âge." *Bulletin de la Société Archéologique de Tarn-et-Garonne*, 85–96.

Pearsall, Derek. 1981. "The Origins of the Alliterative Revival." In Bernard Levy and Paul Szarmach, eds., *The Alliterative Tradition in the Fourteenth Century*. Kent, Ohio: Kent State University Press, 1–25.

Pines, Jacques. 1965. "Des médecins juifs au service de la papauté du XIIe au XVIIe siècle." *RHMH* 69: 123–33.

Pinkhof, H. 1891. *Abraham Kashlari over pestachtige Koorsten*. Amsterdam, n.p.

Provençali, Jacob. 1969 repr. of 1849 ed. "Responsum on the Matter of Studying the Sciences" (in Hebrew). In Eleazar Ashkenazi, ed., *Sefer Divre Hakhamim*. Metz: Imprimerie J. Mayer Samuel; repr. Jerusalem: n.p., 63–70.

Prudhomme, A. 1883. *Les juifs en Dauphiné*. Grenoble.

Pullan, Brian. 1992. "Plague and Perceptions of the Poor in Early Modern Italy." In Terence Ranger and Paul Slack, eds., *Epidemics and Ideas: Essays on the Historical Perception of Pestilence*. Cambridge: Cambridge University Press, 101–23.

Qal'ai, Raphel, and Mordecai Nahman, eds. 1766. *Iggeret haPurim: Sippur haNes*. Salonika.

Rau, Aaron. 1937. "The *Qerovah 'Aggan haSahar*'" (in Hebrew). *Sefer haYuval Likhvod haRav Ya'aqov Freimann*. Berlin: Buchdruckerei 'Viktoria' GmbH, 128–48.

Rav-Shalom, Ram. 1991. "The Disputation of Tortosa, Vicente Ferrer, and the Problem of the Conversos according to the Testimony of Isaac Nathan" (in Hebrew). *Zion* 56: 21–43.

Recanati, David, ed. 1986. *Zikkaron Salonika* 2. Tel Aviv: Ha-va'ad le-hotza'at sefer qehillat saloniqi.

Regalado, Nancy. 1998. "Chronique Métrique and the Moral Design of BN fr. 146: Feasts of Good and Evil." In Margaret Bent and A. Wahey, eds., *Fauvel Studies: Allegory, Chronicle, Music and Image in Paris, Bibliothèque nationale, MS français 146*. Oxford: Clarendon, 467–94.

———. 1970. *Poetic Patterns in Rutebeuf: A Study in Noncourtly Poetic Modes of the Thirteenth Century*. New Haven, Conn.: Yale University Press.

Regné, Jean. 1981 repr. of 1912 ed. *Études sur la condition des juifs de Narbonne*. Narbonne: F. Caillard; repr. Marseille: Laffitte.

————. 1908–13. "Étude sur la condition des juifs de Narbonne du Ve au XIVe siècle." *REJ* 55: 1–36, 221–43; 58: 75–105, 200–26; 59: 59–89; 61: 228–54; and 62: 248–66.

Renan, J. Ernst. 1877. *Histoire littéraire de la France*, vol. 27 (*Les rabbins français*). Paris: Imprimerie nationale, 431–776.

Renan, J. Ernst, and Adolphe Neubauer. 1893. *Histoire littéraire de la France*, vol. 31 (*Les écrivains juifs français du XIVe siècle*). Paris: Imprimerie nationale.

Renaud, H. P. J. December 1920. "État de nos connaissances sur la médecine ancienne du Maroc." *Hesperis* 20: 71–83.

————. 1920. "Un chirurgien musulman du royaume de Grenade: Muhammad al-Safra." *Hesperis* 20: 1–20.

Reyerson, Katherine. 2002. *The Art of the Deal: Intermediaries of Trade in Medieval Montpellier*. Leiden: Brill.

Richler, Benjamin. 1994. *Guide to Hebrew Manuscript Collections*. Jerusalem: Israel Academy of Sciences and Humanities.

Richler, Benjamin, and Malachi Beit-Arié, eds. 2001. *Hebrew Manuscripts in the Biblioteca Palatina in Parma*. Jerusalem: JNUL.

Robles, Adolfo. 1997. "Sant Vicent Ferrer en el context de diàleg: Les minories religioses." In *Paradigmes de la Història I: Actes del Congrès Sant Vicent Ferrer I el seu temps*. Valencia: Biblioteca Josep Giner, 15–45.

Roest, M. 1884–85. "Brief van Salomo ha-Lewi aan Meir Alguadez." *Israelitische Letterbode* 10: 78–85.

Rosenwein, Barbara, ed. 1998. *Anger's Past: The Social Uses of an Emotion*. Ithaca, N.Y.: Cornell University Press.

Roth, Cecil. 1939. "The Liturgies of Avignon and the Comtat Venaissin." *Journal of Jewish Bibliography* 1–2: 99–105.

————. 1927. "Une mission des communautés du Comtat Venaissin à Rome." *REJ* 83–84: 1–14.

Rothschild, Jean-Pierre. 1998. "La part des livres dans la succession du médecin juif Bendic de Noves (Avignon, 1507)." In J-Fr. Genest and D. Nebbiai-dalla Guarda, eds., *Du copiste au collectionneur: Mélanges d'histoire des textes et des bibliothèques en l'honneur d'André Vernet*. Turnhout: Bibliologia, 405–19.

Rouse, Mary, and Richard Rouse. 1991. "*Statim Invenire*: Schools, Preachers, and New Attitudes to the Page." In Rouse and Rouse, *Authentic Witnesses: Approaches to Medieval Texts and Manuscripts*. Notre Dame, Ind.: University of Notre Dame Press, 191–220.

————. 1990. "Concordances et index." In Henri-Jean Martin and Jean Vezin, eds., *Mise en page et mise en texte du livre manuscrit*. Paris: Promodis, 219–28.

————. 1982. "La naissance des index." In *Histoire de l'édition français*, vol. 1 (*Le livre conquérant*), 77–86.

————. 1974. "Biblical Distinctions in the Thirteenth Century." *Archives d'histoire doctrinale et littéraire du moyen âge* 41: 27–37.

Rouse, Richard. 1977. "La diffusion en occident au XIIIe siècle des outils de travail facilitant l'accès aux texts autoritatifs." In George Makdisi et al., eds., *Enseignement en Islam et en Occident au moyen âge*. Paris: Librairie orientaliste P. Geuthner, 115–47.

Roussiaud, Jacques. 1976. "Prostitution, jeunesse et société dans les villes du sud-est au XVe siècle." *Annales ESC* 31.1: 289–325.

Ruiz, Teofilo. 2004. *From Heaven to Earth: The Reordering of Castilian Society, 1150–1350*. Princeton, N.J.: Princeton University Press.

Sabar, Shalom. 1992. "Sephardi Elements in North African Manuscript Decoration." *Jewish Art* 18: 169–91.

Sabatier, E., ed. and trans. 1927. *Chansons hébraïco-provençales des juifs Comtadins*. Paris: Librairie Lipschutz.

Saige, Gustave. 1881. *Les juifs de Languedoc*. Paris: Alphonse Picard.

Salvatierra, Aurora. 1991. "Un poema médico de Abraham ibn Ezra." *Miscelánea de Estudios Árabes y Hebraicos* 40.2: 71–85.

Saperstein, Marc. 1986. "The Conflict over the Rashba's Herem on Philosophical Study: A Political Perspective." *Jewish History* 1: 27–38.

———. 1980. *Decoding the Rabbis: A Thirteenth-Century Commentary on the Aggadah*. Cambridge, Mass.: Harvard University Press.

Sarachek, Joseph. 1935. *Faith and Reason: Conflict over the Rationalism of Maimonides*. Williamsport, Pa.: Bayard.

Satz, Yitzhaq. 1979. "A Letter and Responsum by Rabbenu Yoḥanan of Troyes from Paris" (in Hebrew). *Moriah* 8.10–12 (issues 94–96): 5–9.

Schirmann, Haim (Jefim). 1961. "Observations on the Collected Poems and Rhetorical Exercises of Abraham Bedersi" (in Hebrew). In Salo W. Baron, S. Ettinger, B. Dinur, I. Heilprin, eds., *Sefer Yuval leYitzḥaq Baer*. Jerusalem: Jewish Historical Association, 154–74. Reprinted in *LeToldot haShirah vehaDrama ha'Ivrit* (1979). Jerusalem: Mossad Bialik, 1: 397–438.

———. 1960. *HaShirah ha'Ivrit biSefarad uveProvans* (Hebrew poetry from Spain and Provence, cited as *HPSP*). 4 vols. Jerusalem: Mossad Bialik; Tel Aviv: Dvir.

———. 1949. "Isaac Gorni: Poète hébreu de Provence." *Lettres romanes* 3.3: 175–200.

———. 1934. *Mivḥar haShirah ha'Ivrit be'Italia*. Berlin: Schocken.

Schirmann, Haim (Jefim), ed. and completed by Ezra Fleischer. 1997. *Toldot haShirah ha'Ivrit biSefarad haNotzrit uveDrom Tzarfat*. Jerusalem: Magnes.

Schwartz, Dov. 1999. *Astrologia uMagia beHagut haYehudit*. Ramat-Gan: Bar-Ilan University.

Schwarzfuchs, Simon. 1998. "Rabbi Isaac Joshua ben Immanuel of Lattes and the Jews of the Apostolic States." *Italia Judaica: Gli ebrei nello stato pontificio fina al ghetto (1555)*. Atti del VI Convegno internazionale, Tel Aviv, June 18–22, 1995, 66–79.

———. 1997. "Yohanan Trèves et le dernier refuge de l'école talmudique française après l'expulsion de 1394." In Gilbert Dahan, ed., *Rashi et la culture juive*. Paris: E. Peeters, 83–94.

———. 1988. "La communauté juive de Montpellier au XIIIe et au début du XIVe siècle dans les sources hébraïques." In Carol Iancu, ed., *Les juifs à Montpellier et dans le Languedoc*. Montpellier: Université Paul Valéry, Centre de recherches et d'études juives et hébraïques, 99–112.

———. 1979. "On the Woes of Book Publishing: The Carpentras *Maḥzor*" (in Hebrew). '*Ale-Sefer* 6–7: 145–56.

Scully, Terence. 1985. "The Opusculum de Saporibus of Magninus Mediolanensis." *Medium Aevum* 54: 178–207.

Segre, Renate. 1988. *The Jews in Piedmont*. Jerusalem: Israel Academy of Sciences; Tel Aviv: Tel Aviv University.

———. 1967–68. "Familles judéo-françaises au Italie du nord." *AJ* 4: 38–39.

Serfaty, Nicole. 2004. "Courtisans et diplomats juifs à la cour des sultans marocains (XIV–XVII)." In Nicole Serfaty and Joseph Tedghi, eds., *Présence juive au Maghreb: Homage à Haïm Zafrani*. Paris: Éditions Bouchène, 183–93.

———. 1999. *Les courtisans juifs des sultans marocains: XIIIe–XVIIIe siècles: Hommes politiques et hauts dignitaires*. Paris: Éditions Bouchène.

Seroussi, Edwin. 1997. "La musique andalouse-marocaine dans les manuscrits hébraïques." In Michel Abitbol, ed., *Relations judéo-musulmanes au Maroc: Perceptions et réalités*. Paris: Centre International de Recherche sur les Juifs du Maroc, 283–95.

Shatzmiller, Joseph. 1999. *Justice et injustice au début du XIVe siècle: L'enquête sur l'archevêque d'Aix et sa renunciation en 1318*. Paris: École française de Rome.

———. 1994. *Jews, Medicine, and Medieval Society*. Berkeley: University of California Press.

———. 1989. *Médecine et justice en Provence médiévale: Documents de Manosque 1262–1348*. Aix-en-Provence: L'Université de Provence.

———. 1983. "On Becoming a Jewish Doctor in the High Middle Ages." *Sefarad* 43: 239–50.

———. 1980. "Livres médicaux et education médicale: À propos d'un contrat de Marseille en 1316." *Mediaeval Studies* 38: 463–70.

———. 1974. "Les juifs de Provence pendant la peste noire." *REJ* 133: 457–80.

———. 1973. *Recherches sur la communauté juive de Manosque au moyen âge*. Paris: Mouton.

———. 1972. "Rationalism et orthodoxie religieuse chez les juifs provençaux au commencement du XIVe siècle." *Provence historique* 22: 262–85.

Shatzmiller, Maya. 1983. "An Ethnic Factor in a Medieval Social Revolution: The Role of Jewish Courtiers under the Marinids." In Milton Israel and N. K. Wagle, eds., *Islamic Society and Culture: Essays in Honour of Professor Aziz Ahmad*. New Delhi: Manohar, 149–61.

———. 1982. *L'historiographie mérinide: Ibn Khaldūn et ses contemporains*. Leiden: Brill.

———. 1976. "Les premiers Mérinides et le milieu religieux de Fès: L'introduction des médersas." *Studia Islamica* 43: 109–18.

Shepard, Sanford. 1978. *Shem Tov: His World and His Words*. Miami: Ediciones Universal.

Silberstein, Susan Milner. 1973. "The Provençal Esther Poem Written in Hebrew Char-

acters c. 1327 by Crescas de Caylar: Critical Edition." Ph.D. diss., University of
Pennsylvania.

Simon, Isidore. October 1970. "Les médecins juifs en France, des origins jusqu'à la fin
du XVIIIe siècle." *RHMH* 89: 89–92.

Simonsohn, Shlomo. 1991. *The Apostolic See and the Jews: History*, vol. 7. Toronto: Pontifical Institute of Medieval Studies.

———. 1976. "Procura Hester Fq. Natan Creyssenti." *Michael* 4: 446–49.

———. 1964, English trans. 1977. *Toldot haYehudim beDikusat Mantova* (History of the
Jews in the duchy of Mantua). Jerusalem: Qiryat Sefer.

Singer, Dorothy Waley. 1915–16. "Some Plague Tractates (Fourteenth and Fifteenth
Centuries)." *Proceedings of the Royal Society of Medicine* 9: 159–212.

Siraisi, Nancy. 1990. *Medieval and Early Renaissance Medicine: An Introduction to
Knowledge and Practice*. Chicago: University of Chicago Press.

———. 1981. *Taddeo Alderotti and His Pupils: Two Generations of Italian Medical Learning*. Princeton, N.J.: Princeton University Press.

Sirat, Colette, et al., eds. 2003. *Les méthodes de travail de Gersonide et le maniement du
savoir chez les scholastiques*. Paris: Librairie Philosophique J. Vrin.

———. 2002. *Hebrew Manuscripts of the Middle Ages*. Trans. Nicholas de Lange. Cambridge: Cambridge University Press.

———. 1988. "La composition et l'édition des texts philosophiques juifs au moyen âge:
Quelques examples." *Bulletin de Philosophie Médiévale* 30: 224–32.

———. 1985. *A History of Jewish Philosophy in the Middle Ages*. Cambridge: Cambridge
University Press; Paris: Éditions de la Maison des Sciences de l'Homme.

———. 1980. "La qabbale d'après Judah b. Salomon ha-Cohen." In Gérard Nahon and
Charles Touati, eds., *Hommage à Georges Vajda*. Leuven: Peeters.

Smail, Daniel Lord. 2003. *The Consumption of Justice: Emotions, Publicity, and Legal
Culture in Marseille 1264–1463*. Ithaca, N.Y.: Cornell University Press.

———. 1996. "Accommodating Plague in Medieval Marseille." *Continuity and Change*
2.1: 11–41.

Smoller, Laura. 1998. "Miracle, Memory, and Meaning in the Canonization of Vincent
Ferrer, 1453–54." *Speculum* 73: 429–54.

Snir, Reuven. 2006. *'Araviyut, Yahadut, Tziyonut: Ma'avaq Zehuiyot Beyetziratam shel
Yehude 'Iraq* (Arabism, Jewishness, Zionism: Clashing identities in the writings of
Iraqi Jews). Jerusalem: Ben Zvi Institute.

Solon, Peter. 1970. "The *Six Wings* of Immanuel Bonfils and Michael Chrysokokkes."
Centaurus 15: 1–20.

Sonne, Isaiah. 1961 repr. of 1924 ed. *HaYahadut ha'Italqit*. Jerusalem: Ben Zvi Institute.

———. 1949. "Excerpts from a Tract on Expulsions" (in Hebrew). *Hebrew Union
College Annual* 22: 23–43 (Hebrew section).

Sotres, Pedro Gil. 1996. Introduction to Arnau of Villanova's *Regimen Sanitatis ad
Regem Aragonem*. In Luis García Ballester and Michael McVaugh, eds., *Arnaldi de
Villanova: Opera Medica Omnia* 10.1. Barcelona: Universitat Barcelona, 481–568.

————. 1995. "Les régimes de santé." *Histoire de la pensée médicale en Occident* 1: 159–81.

Spiegel, Gabrielle. 1993. *Romancing the Past: The Rise of Vernacular Prose Historiography in Thirteenth-Century France*. Berkeley: University of California Press.

Starr, Joshua. 1940–41. "Johanna II and the Jews." *JQR* 31: 67–78.

Steinschneider, Moritz. 1965. *Hartza'ot 'al Kitve-Yad 'Ivri'im*. Jerusalem: Mossad Harav Kook.

————. 1893. *Die hebraeischen Uebersetzungen des Mittelalters*. Berlin: Kommissionsverlag des Bibliographischen Bureaus.

Stillman, Yedida. 1986. "Libās." *Encyclopedia of Islam*. Leiden: Brill, 5: 732–52.

————. 1982. "Spanish Influences on the Material Culture of Moroccan Jews" (in Hebrew). In Issachar Ben Ami, ed., *Betokh Moreshet shel Yehude-Morocco* (cotitled: International Conference on Sephardic and Oriental Jewry). Jerusalem: Magnes, 359–66.

Stock, Brian. 1990. *Listening for the Text: On the Uses of the Past*. Philadelphia: University of Pennsylvania Press.

Stern, Samuel Miklos. 1983 repr. of 1961. "Ibn Ḥasdāy's Neoplatonist: A Neoplatonic Treatise and Its Influence on Isaac Israeli and the Longer Version of the Theology of Aristotle." Reprinted from *Oriens* 13–14: 58–120 as essay no. 7 in idem., ed. F. W. Zimmerman, *Medieval Arabic and Hebrew Thought*. London: Variorum reprints.

Stouff, Louis. 1970. *Ravitaillement et alimentation en Provence aux XIVe et XVe siècles*. Paris: Mouton.

Straus, Raphael. 1942. "The 'Jewish Hat' as an Aspect of Social History." *Jewish Social Studies* 4: 59–72.

Striedl, Hans. 1957. "Geschichte der Hebraica-Sammlung der bayerischen Staatsbibliothek." In *Orientalisches aus Münchener Bibliotheken und Sammlungen*. Wiesbaden: F. Steiner, 1–37.

Sublet, Jacqueline. 1971. "La peste prise aux rêts de la jurisprudence." *Studia Islamica* 33: 141–51.

Sudhoff, Karl. 1909–25. "Pestschriften aus den ersten 150 Jahren nach der Epidemie des Schwarzen Todes." In *Archiv für Geschichte der Medizin*, vols. 1–17.

Al-Tanassi, Muhammad. 1852. *Histoire des Beni Zeiyan: Rois de Tlemcen*, trans. J. J. L. Bargès. Paris: Benjamin Duprat.

Tanenbaum, Adena. 2002. *The Contemplative Soul: Hebrew Poetry and Philosophical Theory in Medieval Spain*. Leiden: Brill.

Ta-Shema, Israel. 1989. "The Literary Content of the MS." Companion volume to the facsimile edition of the Rothschild Miscellany, *The Rothschild Miscellany: A Scholarly Commentary*. Jerusalem: Israel Museum and Facsimile Editions.

Taylor, Andrew. 2002. *Textual Situations: Three Medieval Manuscripts and Their Readers*. Philadelphia: University of Pennsylvania Press.

Thorndike, Lynn. 1940. "Three Tracts on Food in Basel Manuscripts." *Bulletin of the History of Medicine* 8: 355–69.

Toaff, Ariel. 1996. *Love, Work and Death: Jewish Life in Medieval Umbria*. Trans. Judith Landry. London and Portland, Ore.: Littman Library of Jewish Civilization.

———. 1988. "Conversioni al cristianesimo in Italia nel quattrocento. Movimenti e tendenze: Il caso dell'Umbria." In Michele Luzzati, M. Olivari, and A. Veronese, eds., *Ebrei e cristiani nell'italia medievale e moderna: Conversioni, scambi, contrasti*. Rome: Carucci. 105–12.

———. 1979. *The Jews in Medieval Assisi, 1305–1487*. Florence: L. S. Olschki.

Todeschini, Giacomo. 2004. "Franciscan Economics and Jews in the Middle Ages." In Steven J. McMichael and Susan E. Myers, eds., *Friars and Jews in the Middle Ages and Renaissance*. Leiden: Brill, 99–117.

Touati, Charles. 1968. "La controverse de 1303–1306 autour des études philosophiques et scientifiques." *REJ* 127: 21–37.

Trabut-Cussac, J. P. 1972. *L'administration anglaise en gascogne sous Henry III et Edouard I*. Geneva: Librairie Droz.

Ullman, Manfred. 1978. *Islamic Medicine*. Trans. Jean Watt. Edinburgh: Edinburgh University Press.

Vajda, Judah (Georges). 1955a. "On the History of the Polemic between Philosophy and Religion" (in Hebrew). *Tarbiz* 24.3: 307–22.

———. 1955b. "On the History of the Controversy between Philosophy and Religion (the Methods and Ideas of R. Jacob b. Solomon)" (in Hebrew). *Tarbiz* 24: 307–22.

Van Koningsveld, P. Sj. 1992. "Andalusian-Arabic Manuscripts from Christian Spain: A Comparative Intercultural Approach." *Israel Oriental Studies* 12: 75–110.

Vauchez, André. 1997. *Sainthood in the Later Middle Ages*. Cambridge: Cambridge University Press.

Veinstein, Gilles, ed. 1992. *Salonique 1850–1918: La 'Ville des juifs' et le réveil des Balkans*. Paris: Autrement.

Vendrell, Francisca. 1953. "La actividad proselitista de San Vicente Ferrer durante el reinado de Fernando I de Aragon." *Sefarad* 13: 87–104.

Veny i Clar, Joan, ed. 1971. *"Regiment de preservació de pestilència" de Jacme d'Agramont (s. XIV)*. Tarragona: Sugrañes.

Vidal, Pierre. 1992. *Les juifs des anciens comtés de Roussillon et de Cerdagne*. Perpignan: Mare nostrum.

Viera, David J. 1990. "Sant Vicent Ferrer, Francesc Eixemenis I el pogrom de 1391." Col.loqui *d'Estudis Catalans a Nord-Amèrica*. Vancouver, B.C.: Publicacions de l'Aadia de Montserrat, 243–54.

Viguier, M. C. 1988. "Un troubadour juif à Narbonne au XIIIe siècle." In *Juifs et source juive en Occitanie*. Valdarias: Ven Terral, 81–92.

Walfish, Barry Dov. 1993. *Esther in Medieval Garb: Jewish Interpretation of the Book of Esther in the Middle Ages*. Albany: State University of New York Press.

Weijers, Olga. 1996. *Le maniement de savoir*. Turnhout: Brepols.

Weil, Gérard. 1983. "Astrugon Massip Péager et Gabelier du Gapençais et Helyet fils de

Jacob Péager de Montfleury, fermiers du fisc et financiers juifs du Dauphin Humbert II." *108e Congrès national des Sociétés savants, Section de philologie et d'histoire jusqu'à 1610*, 211–30.

White, Hayden. 1978. *Tropics of Discourse*. Baltimore: Johns Hopkins University Press.

Wickersheimer, E. 1925. "La régime de santé de Jean Chanczelperger, bachelier en médecine de l'Université de Bologne (XVe siècle)." *Janus* 25: 245–50.

————. 1922. "Les guérisons miraculeuses du Cardinal Pierre de Luxembourg (1387–1390)." *Comptes rendus du 2e Congrès International d'Histoire de la Médecine*. Évreux: Ch. Hérissy, 371–89.

Wolff, Hans. 1914. "Dichtungen von Matthäus dem Juden und Matthäus von Gent." Berlin: Königlichen Universität, Greifswald.

Wolfson, Elliot. 2000. *Abraham Abulafia: Kabbalist and Prophet*. Los Angeles: Cherub.

Woolf, Jeffrey. 2001. "New Light on the Life and Times of R. Joseph Colon Trabotto (Maharik)." *Italia* 13–15 (special issue in memory of Giuseppe Sermoneta, ed. Robert Bonfil). Jerusalem: Magnes, 151–80.

Wray, Shona Kelly. 2004. "Boccaccio and the Doctors: Medicine and Compassion in the Face of Plague." *Journal of Medieval History* 30: 301–22.

Wrigley, John. 1964. "A Papal Secret Known to Petrarch." *Speculum* 39.4: 613–34.

Yahalom, Joseph. 1988. "Poetic Unity as an Expression of Spiritual Reality" (in Hebrew). In *Galut Aḥar Golah*. Jerusalem: Ben Zvi Institute, 337–46.

Yarden, Dov. 1984. "The *Qinot* of R. Joseph ben Sheshet ibn Latimi" (in Hebrew). In Meir Benyahu, ed., *Sefer Zikkaron lehaRav Yitzḥaq Nissim*. Vol. 5. Jerusalem: Yad haRav Nissim, 185–236.

Young, Josiah Ulysses, III. 1992. *A Pan-African Theology: Providence and the Legacy of the Ancestors*. Trenton, N.J.: Africa World Press.

Zafran, Eric. 1979. "Saturn and the Jews." *Journal of the Warburg and Courtauld Institutes* 42: 16–27.

Zafrani, Haim. 1996. *Juifs d'Andalousie et du Maghreb*. Paris: Maisonneuve et Larosse.

Zerubavel, Yael. 1995. *Recovered Roots: Collective Memory and the Making of Israeli National Tradition*. Chicago: University of Chicago Press.

Ziegler, Joseph. 1999. "Practitioners and Saints: Medical Men in Canonization Processes in the Thirteenth to Fifteenth Centuries." *Social History of Medicine* 12.2: 191–225.

————. 1998. *Medicine and Religion c. 1300: The Case of Arnau of Villanova*. Oxford: Oxford University Press.

————. 1997. "Steinschneider (1816–1907) Revised: On the Translation of Medical Writings from Latin into Hebrew." *Medieval Encounters* 3.1: 94–102.

Ziegler, Philip. 1969. *The Black Death*. London: Harper Collins.

Zucker, Shlomo. 1997 (May). "The Twists of Fate of the Wolf Haggadah and Its Investigation" (in Hebrew). *'Al Sefarim veAnashim* (English title: Books and People). Jerusalem: JNUL, no. 11: 4–13. (Summary in English version appears as "Rare 14th Century Haggadah from Provence Presented to the JNUL by the Prime Minister

of Poland" [!], Books and People no. 11, May 1997, 5–7.) A correction was issued
later to the Hebrew version regarding the autograph status of the manuscript.

Zumthor, Paul. Winter 1979. "From Hi(story) to Poem, or the Paths of Pun: The *Grands
Rhétoriqueurs* of Fifteenth-Century France." *New Literary History* 10.2: 231–63.

———. 1978a. *Le masque et la lumière: La poétique des grands rhétoriqueurs.* Paris: Éditions du Seuil.

———. 1978b. *Anthologie des grands rhétoriqueurs.* Paris: Union générale d'éditions.

———. 1976. "Le carrefour des rhétoriqueurs: Intertextualité et rhétorique." *Poétique:
Revue de théorie et d'analyse littéraires* 27: 317–37

———. 1974. "Les grands rhétoriqueurs et le vers." *Langue française* 23: 88–98.

———. 1963. "Note sur le style poétique de langue vulgaire au XIIe siècle." In Moshe
Lazar, *Romania et Occidentalia: Études dédiées à la mémoire de Hiram Peri (Pflaum).*
Jerusalem: Magnes, 194–205.

INDEX

ACKNOWLEDGMENTS

Most of the material in this book has never appeared in print. The exception is Chapter 4, which largely replicates my article "A Proper Diet: Medicine and History in Crescas Caslari's *Esther*," *Speculum* 80 (2005): 437–63. Additions, including two new manuscript sources (and a few corrections), bring it into the framework of expulsion and memory that shapes this book. Approximately nine pages of Chapter 3 are adapted from a talk at the Shelby Collum Davis Center that marked the origins of this project. That talk, on literary commemorations of the 1306 expulsion, was given in February 2003 and in revised form at the New York Medieval Club in April 2003. It is now forthcoming in Bar-Ilan University's *Pirqe-Shirah* series. I thank Mary-Jo Arn at *Speculum*, and Ephraim Hazan and Benjamin Bar-Tikva at *Pirqe-Shirah*, for permission to recycle passages here.

The remaining chapters were all tested in oral form in a variety of public venues, where audience feedback was warmly constructive. I presented a microversion of Chapter 1 at the University of Pennsylvania's "Material Texts" workshop and the Institute for Advanced Study in the fall of 2004 and at the 2005 International Medieval Congress in Kalamazoo. An early version of Chapter 2 was delivered at the meeting of the Medieval Hebrew Poetry Colloquium in July 2004 at the University of Aix-en-Provence. An abridged version of Chapter 3 served as my contribution to the small conference honoring María Rosa Menocal at the University of Toronto in March 2007. Chapter 4 was sampled in Heidelberg at the Hochschule für Judische Studien in July 2006 and again at the International Medieval Congress in Kalamazoo in May 2007. Finally, a portion of Chapter 6 was presented at Northwestern University on March 2, 2006, and again at Princeton University in April at a small conference in honor of John Fleming.

Those friends who read, criticized, and discussed along the way have been greatly appreciated as well. They include David Aaron, Renate Blumenfeld-Kosinski, Caroline Bynum, Indrani Chatterjee, Paulla Ebron, Julia Einbinder, Joan Ferrante, Judah Galinsky, Monica Green, Roy Harris, William C. Jordan, Stephen Kaufmann, Joel Kaye, Marnia Lazreg, Michael McVaugh, Samuel N. Rosenberg, Roy Rosenstein, and Haym Soloveitchik. Benjamin Richler of the Institute for Microfilmed Hebrew Manuscripts at the Jewish National Library in Jerusalem was indispensable; my thanks also to the current director, Avraham David, and to acting head Yael Okun. I am indebted to many libraries and librarians, especially Arnona Rudavsky and Marilyn Krider at the Hebrew Union College Library in Cincinnati; I owe more than I can say to Herbert Zafren, ל"ז, for teaching me to read manuscripts and to love them. Don Skemer at Princeton University's Firestone Library, the librarians of the Institute for Advanced Study, and the curators of Hebrew manuscripts at Columbia University, the Jewish Theological Seminary, and the Brotherton Library at the University of Leeds were all most helpful. Jerry Singerman at the University of Pennsylvania Press has steadily encouraged this work, and me, during our annual dinners at Kalamazoo and throughout the months between them. To Bill Farmer, who is, quite simply, always there, my deepest thanks.

The generosity of the Guggenheim Foundation, the American Philosophical Society, and the Institute for Advanced Study made possible what surely would have been impossible without relief from teaching; the Institute also provided a year-long haven over which three of these chapters took shape.

All translations, unless otherwise attributed, are my own—and certainly all errors as well.